This volume is dedicated to the memory of
WILLIAM SAMUEL GADD *(13.6.1902 to 9.4.1983),*
whose Odyssey took him from the coal faces of South Wales to the luxury of five star hotels.

A hint of the man to come. "Will" or "Bill" Gadd, as he was known, is the small boy with both hands holding his waistcoat on the left of this pre-1914 photo. He came from a Non-Conformist family and it was always believed that the photo was taken at a religious occasion at Newbridge, Gwent, where other relations lived.

Born at 31, Wood Street, Cwmcarn, Wales, lived at 12, Gelli Unig Terrace, Pontywain, Wales; 2, Farrier Street, Deal, Kent....and hotels from the Tollard Royal, Bournemouth, to the Regency Hotel, Ramsgate.

Merry of smile, mild of manner and soft spoken, yet a renowned fighter on the cobbles who they wanted to turn professional, until he discovered The Cause. Born into a Salvation Army family where his father, literally, carried the banner, yet himself became an atheist.

Whose passion for knowledge was greater than all else but who, through the issue of "Labour Certificate, No. 1 (a) for total exemption after 13 years of age", was removed from school at that age and put to hard physical labour in a quarry.

Then a coal miner (there was then little else in South Wales) who was buried in a fall and whose hands and back carried the tell-tale blue scars, yet spent most of his life as Head Chef of well known hotels.

A member of the I.L.P. and the Communist Party, eventually black-listed in South Wales coal mines for trade union activities, who started scrubbing hotel floors and rose to live by "Le Repertoire de la Cuisine".

The only man I ever met who really had read Karl Marx's "Das Kapital" from first word to last but whose affection was reserved for Edward Fitzgerald's translation of "Omar Khayyám" and the works of Jack London and Robert Tressell.

Who spoke on platforms with Nye Bevan, sent reports to the "Daily Worker" and shared the comradeship that bound the Welsh miners, yet was forced by unemployment to leave his community and become part of the Welsh Diaspora.

Who left the Communist Party in 1945 but who never left Socialism.

Whose intellectual powers were greater than mine; who loved debate and the triumph of logic. Who, faced with an agnostic son, proclaimed the scientific inevitability of atheism and won every argument about the existence of God but always admitted the one question he could not answer: Why are we here? "Does there have to be a reason?" he would always ask. "Yes", I would always say.

But who, despite his atheism, never passed a Salvation Army band without asking for "The Old Rugged Cross" and donating a shilling.

Who smilingly promised me that when they took power I'd be the first behind the barbed wire but, after 80, could still sing for me all the verses of "Beulah land, Sweet Beulah Land!" From whom I would have liked to have learned more and with whom I wished I had shared a great deal more if it had not been for a World War, his life as a Head Chef and mine as a footloose Hack.

From a coal miner working with pick and shovel, Will Gadd transformed himself into a Head Chef, starting his hotel career by scrubbing kitchen floors. Here he is shown in a photo of c.1937-38 on the seafront at Deal, Kent, walking with his small son. Behind them is the Royal Hotel where Will Gadd was Head Chef both before and after the Second World War.

At the end he had been blind for some 20 years and was poor. His immaculate trilby was about the grandest thing he owned. I asked him how he could justify his life when, with his mind and character, he could have enriched himself if he had but been prepared to abandon his politics. "Look around you", he said, "look now at the condition of the working man. That is my justification. When the World was against you, you had to be a man to be a Communist."

My mother, brought up to the Primitive Methodists and herself a lifelong Church member, insisted on a Methodist funeral and I expected three mourners outside the family but the Church was full with those who had enjoyed his conversation, a number of them friends with white sticks and guide dogs.

Will Gadd shown in the years of his blindness at his home, 2, Farrier Street, Deal, Kent. The photo was taken about 1978 and the smile was typical.

The British Art Piano and Piano Design

Volume 1

A conversation with a reader with many digressions

by G.S.Gadd

And, always, the assistance and technical advice of

Hilda Colquhoun Gadd

"The only qualities essential for real success in journalism are rat-like cunning, a plausible manner, and a little literary ability".

Nicholas Tomalin, killed by rocket fire while covering the Yom Kippur War, 1973.

Volume One

The handiness of an African elephant

The author has not the slightest knowledge of pianos but, naturally, has not allowed such a small matter to inhibit him. Nor can he now read a note of music, having given up the banjo-mandolin at the age of 12 for more worldly pursuits. His knowledge of 18th Century furniture is decidedly sketchy. He makes no claims that he is other than a mildly interested layman who has whiled away the odd half-hour reading a few dusty tomes. He declares that his own taste is for the furniture designs of Charles Francis Annesley Voysey and Charles Rennie Mackintosh and that this book should be evaluated in the light of such preferences.

Contents

List of Illustrations

Chapter One: The Changing Shape of the Piano

Chapter Two: The Rise and Slow Decline of The British Piano

Chapter Three: Attitudes to Piano Design

Chapter Four: Style, Fashion and the Early Piano

Chapter Five: 1800-1850: Three Major Changes

Chapter Six: The Emergence of the Designers

Chapter Seven: Early British Artist Painted Pianos

Chapter Eight: Zumpe: Form follows Function

Page 240: Plate 342, Meinke and Peter Meyer square piano, c.1795. Photo by courtesy of The Haags Gemeentemuseum, Den Haag, The Netherlands.
Page 242: Plate 343, Frederick Schoene and Co. square piano, c.1788, appeared as Lot 1375, Sotheby's of Amsterdam, Dec 17th., 2003. Photo by courtesy of Sotheby's of Amsterdam.
Page 242: Plate 344, Buntebart and Sievers square piano, 1787. Photo by courtesy of The Period Piano Co.
Page 242: Plate 345, Buntebart and Sievers square piano, 1788. Photo by courtesy of The Haags Gemeentemuseum, Den Haag, The Netherlands.
Page 242: Plate 346, Buntebart and Sievers square piano, 1792, auctioned by Sotheby's, as Lot 178, Nov 17th., 1994. Photo by courtesy of Sotheby's of New Bond Street, London.
Page 242: Plate 347, Schrader and Hartz square piano, Late 18th Century, auctioned as Lot 174, Sotheby's, Nov 20th 1980. Photo by courtesy of Sotheby's of New Bond Street, London.
Page 244: Plate 348, Square piano stated to be Zumpe and Buntebart, 1770, which appeared as Lot 100, Sotheby's, Nov 17th., 1977. Photo by courtesy of Sotheby's of New Bond Street, London.
Page 245: Plate 349, Square piano stated to be Zumpe and Buntebart, 1770. Photo by courtesy of The Smithsonian Institution (N.M.A.H.).
Page 246: Plate 350, Zumpe and Buntebart square piano, 1774. Photo by Mr Laurence Libin, courtesy of The Palace of Pavlovsk, Russia.
Page 246: Plate 351, Decoration over legs of Zumpe and Buntebart square piano, 1774. Photo by Mr Laurence Libin, courtesy of The Palace of Pavlovsk, Russia.
Page 246: Plate 352, Female profile on Zumpe and Buntebart square piano, 1774. Photo by Mr Laurence Libin, courtesy of The Palace of Pavlovsk, Russia.

Photo by courtesy of The Victoria and Albert Museum

This is The Ionides Grand, the piano that captured the most public interest in the furniture section of The First Exhibition of the newly formed Arts and Crafts Exhibition Society, in 1888, one of the seminal moments in the history of British design. Now recognised as a significant British Art Piano, particularly because of the light it throws on the Morris circle, it was shown at a height of popularity for the instrument, when you could expect to find a grand in a Mayfair drawing room or an upright in a working man's cottage. Credit for The Ionides, now among the treasures of the Victoria and Albert Museum, was mistakenly given to Sir Edward Burne-Jones but I believe the principal honours should go to the artist who decorated the case, Kate Faulkner, an associate of William Morris. Kate Faulkner was a leading proponent of the gesso revival and the case was decorated with spring flowers "in raised and silvered gesso....varying tints of coloured silver upon a groundwork of Celadon Green". Plate No. 1.

The Changing Shape of the Piano

Chapter One

The piano was, perhaps surprisingly, the vehicle for occasionally radical design experiments in the Victorian era but The Ionides Grand, the most publicised piece of furniture at the opening Arts and Crafts Exhibition of 1888, was not one of them, at least so far as form was concerned. The shape was avowedly meant to be an adaptation of the traditional, angular harpsichord, incorporating a "golden" curve.[1]

Essentially, the shape of the Ionides was dictated by a conservative impulse to a safe past, not a devil-may-care dive into a dangerous future. "The Athenaeum" observed: "The design of the instrument is somewhat affectedly commonplace, not to say void of grace, but its decorations are superb". [2]

The claimed influence of Sir Edward Burne-Jones over the shape of The Ionides Grand is a tangled question but the makers of that instrument, Broadwood and Sons, later declared that: "Repeatedly has it been advanced that the outline of the precursor of the pianoforte—namely the harpsichord—are more to be recommended….long before this question was generally discussed, Sir Edward Burne-Jones, Bart., R.A., had in various ways adapted to the Broadwood horizontal pianoforte the admired harpsichord shape".[3]

If you had wanted to see the real revolution at work at the 1888 Arts and Crafts Exhibition, you would have been better advised to turn your attention to exhibit no.128 where the genius of A.H. Mackmurdo was expressed in his "Century Guild Cottage Piano"[4], a humble upright piano, but that is a matter we shall come to later.

The shape of the piano, reflected in the concerns of Burne-Jones and Broadwood, was to become an obsession with those who contemplated its design or decoration. And, in the case of Messrs B-J. and B. in 1888, the reality was so frightening that they had to take refuge in the antique.

The history of the piano from its introduction in Britain is one of constant turmoil and splendid ingenuity through entrepreneurial attempts to re-invent and refine its mechanics leading, inevitably, to repercussions for the design of the case. To say that the piano was literally stood on its head is but the truth.

But the Designers were never in the same happy state of grace as the Inventors. No matter what variations were produced, it was the shape of the instrument that continued to baffle, enrage and defeat so many of them.

The piano, a descendant of the harpsichord, had been invented before 1700 by Bartolomeo Cristofori, custodian of musical instruments to Prince Ferdinand of Florence, one of the fearsome but artistic Medici family. Since Cristofori was a builder of harpsichords it was almost inevitable that his pianos should resemble that instrument.[5]

In the past Cristofori's invention has been dated to 1709 but one modern piano historian suggests it was as early as 1698 and even a date of 1694 has been put forward. Academics now believe it was "before 1700". One authority suggests that "30 or more fortepianos"[6] were built by Cristofori but there are other estimates and only three of them are now known to survive.[7]

For a while the piano's future must have seemed uncertain and it was not until 1732 that the first sonatas were published for the new instrument.[8]

From this small beginning the piano was to become the most pivotal of all musical instruments, a one-man band in the home and the most prominent instrument of the concert orchestra. One academic[9] has called it "the most popular musical instrument of all time" and I have no doubt it established itself as the most important item of furniture in thousands of 19th Century British homes.

For the case designer it was to develop, eventually, in three basic forms: The harp-shape, albeit horizontal, grand piano; the small "square" piano (which wasn't square at all but oblong) and the upright. But from these basic themes mechanical necessity, and the unfaithful mistress of fashion, were to create many weird options.

The exact development of the piano in Britain in the 18th Century is complex and how much we are to believe in the legend of an English monk, Father Wood, making a copy of a Cristofori piano while in Rome,[10] possibly in the late 1730s, which was later brought to England, I leave to the readers of teacups and more erudite scholars. Respectable voices give it some credence[11] though I confess that such ancient tales always start with raised eyebrows on my part.

According to the piano historian David Rowland[12] this "Father Wood" mystery piano may have been copied by one Roger Plenius, who came to London from Amsterdam by 1741 and, poor fellow, receiving little encouragement for his ambitions and failing to rescue his finances by running a raffle, was bankrupt by 1756.

A mysterious advert appeared in the "Universal Director" of 1763 in which the harpsichord maker Frederick Neubauer listed "Piano Fortes" amongst his offerings[13] but no example is known and it is proven that the main developments in Britain occurred a little later in the mid-1760s.

Effectively, we can date the British piano from the introduction of the first squares, the most popular form of the early piano. Previous accounts of this episode,

Photo by courtesy of The Metropolitan Museum of Art, New York

It seems the unanimous conclusion of piano historians that the piano was invented by Bartolomeo Cristofori of Padua, although there has long been controversy about the date—anywhere between 1694 and 1709 has been put forward although, traditionally, it has been "c.1700". Experts like Dr Eszter Fontana, director of the famous Leipzig museum, now believe it was "before 1700". It must have been completely logical for Cristofori, a harpsichord maker, to construct his new piano in the traditional harpsichord shape. Just three surviving Cristofori pianos are known and this one, made in 1720, is stated to be the oldest. Now in The Metropolitan Museum of Art in New York it is inscribed in ink "MDCCXX". The Museum's Inventory record says the instrument has been "much altered and restored" and suggests the existing case may itself have been "possibly once enclosed in a decorated outer case". Plate No. 2.

Illustration by courtesy of Musiksinstrumenten-Museum der Universität, Leipzig

Bombs no more respect pianos than they do humanity. In London a bomb on the fashionable furniture store, Maple's, destroyed one of the greatest pianos of the 19th Century, Alma Tadema's remarkable "Byzantine" grand. In Leipzig they lost many of their historic pianos and among the instruments damaged was one of the three surviving pianos by the inventor of the instrument, Bartolomeo Cristofori and also a Cristofori harpsichord of the same year. This drawing, from the old catalogue by Georg Kinsky, shows their 1726 Cristofori piano as it was known before the War, the case having a traditional Italian look. Plate No. 3.

Under the tender care of the staff of the Musikinstrumenten-Museum, Leipzig, where the splendid Dr Eszter Fontana reigns supreme as Director, their 1726 Cristofori piano has been given a new stand, as shown in this photo. Cristofori described his new instrument as a "gravicembalo col piano e forte", a harpsichord which played soft and loud. Dr Fontana has in her custody the finest surviving collection of Cristofori instruments - the 1726 piano, an oval spinet of 1693 from the Medici Collection, a Spinettone dal Theatro, c.1720, a clavichord, c.1722 and two harpsichords of 1722 and 1726. Plate No. 4.

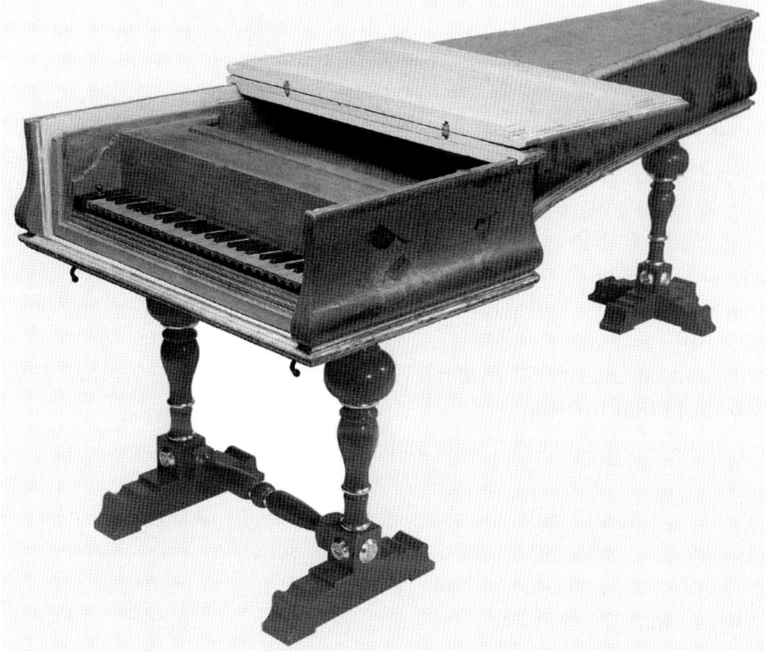

By courtesy of Musiksinstrumenten-Museum der Universität, Leipzig. Photo by Janos Stekovics.

apparently set in scholastic concrete, have now been convincingly demolished by Michael Cole, a seeker after truth with determination and logic.[14]

A romantic tale of a cohesive group of "Twelve Apostles" fleeing the Continent *en masse* to Britain to escape the Seven Years War (1755-62) and then founding a piano industry now looks more like exaggerated romantic myth than hard fact.

What does seem evident, if from nothing else than the many foreign names on British-made pianos, is that Continental craftsmen must have played a crucial role.

Trying to investigate the subsequent history of the British piano, as with the wider furniture field at this time, is a tricky business. As the expert Mr C.F. Colt pointed out, "One can never be sure 'What's in a name'."[15]

In other words: Don't believe every name you see on a piano.

Mr Colt said that the making of a piano by one firm and its sale under the name of another was common practice. And this is quite apart from the activities of retail shop owners who would often put their own name on an instrument (a practice known as "Stencilling"), or that perennial pack of rogues bent on outright deceit, the fakers.

Michael Cole, also one of our leading restorers, told me[16] that "Clementi's workmen, under the Collard brothers from shortly after 1800, supplied ready-made pianos for two or three other firms, notably John Longman of Cheapside. In fact, I once had a Clementi and a Longman square in succession through my workshop, made in the same year from the same batch of timber, with the same inlays, and identical sprays of flowers painted on the front.

"Also, I have investigated a Mexican square piano, thinking that I could trace the Spanish influence either from Seville or Madrid in this apparent colonial work. Nothing of the sort! It was in reality a Clementi square, with the blue-painted oval cartouche over-written by the Mexicans."

Confusing as such examples are, this is the trail we must try and trace from the 1760s.

Prominent among 18th Century British makers we find the names of immigrants such as Johann Christoph Zumpe (born near Nuremberg),[17] renowned for his development, from around 1766, of the so-called English "square" piano and Americus Backers[18] (often suggested to be Dutch born) who was particularly associated with the grand piano about 1767-1772.

It was inventive craftsmen like these who brought their knowledge and skills to bear in London some 60 to 70 years after Cristofori's original invention.

This, of course, encouraged native talent and the growth of the most dominant of the British piano firms, John Broadwood and Sons who, in the second half of the 19th Century, were to play the most important role in the creation of artist-designer pianos despite an earlier disdain for such matters.

The firm grew at a prodigious rate after a Scotsman, John Broadwood (1732-1812), described variously as a cabinet maker or joiner,[19] wisely married the daughter of his boss, a London maker of harpsichords who came from Switzerland, Burkat Shudi.[20] During Shudi's time they had made about 20 harpsichords a year but, according to the Broadwood record books, the firm made square piano No. 1266 in 1790 and by 1796 had produced grand piano No. 1000.[21]

Other men might have been in the field first with both the square and the grand but John Broadwood saw the potential of each and, more importantly, proved to have the stamina for the commercial fray.

Early models of both the grand and the square followed harpsichord practice by being made to rest upon a separate stand.

The term "grand" piano is believed to have been first used[22] in 1777 by Robert Stodart who was Broadwood's foreman but set up on his own and made outstanding pianos from the late 1770s.[23]

I have referred to "the English square", as it became known and Mr Cole puts forward[24] facts which suggest that Zumpe not only introduced the instrument to Britain but could have invented the square piano itself. Unless and until better evidence comes forward I find the suggestion a plausible one.

By courtesy of The Colonial Williamsburg Foundation, Virginia, U.S.A.

The very essence of a plain man's Puritanism, this simple, modest piano is the instrument which played a giant's part in the foundation of the powerful British piano industry. Known as "the English square" it was, in fact, almost always in this oblong shape and this rare example, which I am told still has its original strings, textiles and stand, is one of the most important instruments in the noted Collection of The Colonial Williamsburg Foundation of Virginia. It was made by Johannes Zumpe in London in 1766, the first year from which any have survived. The expert on the Collection and a lecturer on Zumpe, the Conservator of Instruments, Mr John R. Watson, told me that "it appears that Zumpe did have an orientation to the clavichord in terms of the shape and overall dimensions of the case. Ours is plain, solid walnut without any veneer." Plate No. 5.

There are many who think that "the English square" piano took its shape and case design from the clavichord, the instrument which it displaced with cuckoo-like ruthlessness. The clavichord had been invented in the Middle Ages, the 14th Century it has been suggested, and the strings were struck with small metal wedges. The clavichord continued to be made until about the 1840s and was revived by Arnold Dolmetsch in the Late Victorian period. Today, enthusiasts have banded together in societies and about 400 modern recordings have been made on the instrument. This engraving, from the "English Illustrated Magazine" of 1884, shows a famous example in the South Kensington Museum, the 18th Century "Green Clavichord" by Barthold Fritz of Brunswick which, inside the lid, has a painting of a stag hunt. Plate No. 6.

A Square that was Oblong

The first austere Zumpe squares, I presume modelled on the clavichord, were just over 4 feet long, some 1ft 6in in width and over 6in in depth and the case was essentially a box enclosing the works.[25] The instrument could be sat upon a stand or a table and thus was easily transported.

A musical instrument catalogue of 1789 is thought likely to have been referring to these new-fangled square pianos when it talked of "portable clavecins....Their tones are remarkably sweet and delicate, and their structure renders them agreeable for travelling with, as they may be conveyed and even performed upon in a coach."[26]

It seems to me that the simplicity of Zumpe's early squares must have resulted from his determination to keep the price down and this enabled him to sell his basic model for 16 guineas, thus undercutting the market and, conversely, making his fortune.[27]

Until the end of the 18th Century, of course, the square and the grand still had to compete with the harpsichord.

In the 1780s music publishers were still selling scores "for harpsichord or pianoforte" but "In the 90s the description 'for the pianoforte' became more common".[28]

The expert William Dale investigated the demise of the harpsichord and wrote that, in 1794, "That most conservative institution, the King's band, retained it as long as possible but this year it had to go. A harpsichord was used for the rehearsal but a grand piano for the performance".[29]

The last Broadwood harpsichord, No. 1155, is stated to have been made in 1793 and the last Kirkman harpsichord is reported to have been made in 1809.[30]

The grand piano had thus established itself, and remains to this day, as the aristocrat of the piano world, the chosen instrument for the concert platform and the ornament of the wealthy.

As that intense watcher of the British, Hermann Muthesius, was to explain to his German audience (without the slightest sign

Photo by courtesy of Her Majesty Queen Elizabeth II
© The Royal Collection

The familiar harpsichord shape adapted by Bartolomeo Cristofori was common throughout Europe as in this British Royal harpsichord of 1740, made for Frederick, Prince of Wales by Burkat Shudi, effectively the founder of what became the firm of Broadwood and Sons. The shape was common but instrument makers of the time would have seen immediately that the decoration of the main case was peculiarly British, a series of inlaid veneer panels along the side in which the burr walnut of the main case was cross-banded with plain walnut. Plate No. 7.

Photo by courtesy of The Neumeyer-Junghanns-Tracey Collection, Bad Krozingen, Germany

The specialist harpsichord maker's shop established in London by Burkat Shudi grew to eventually become one of the most powerful piano making factories in the World after a Scot named John Broadwood married Burkat's daughter and inherited the business. As can be seen from this typical Broadwood grand piano of 1798, there was a continuation of shape from the harpsichord to the grand, so close to the original that the layman does not immediately spot the differences. Likewise, the British style of decoration of the main case of the harpsichord continued as the preferred fashion for the grand piano even to the end of the 18th Century and beyond. In this Broadwood, now in the Bad Krozingen Collection in Germany, the familiar cross-banded veneer panels dominate the sides of the mahogany main case. Plate No. 8.

of humour): "Last of all the necessities in the drawing-room is the piano. But a grand is considered the only piano of good quality in England....In view of the fact that the English are probably the most unmusical race in the world, the presence of a grand piano in every house is slightly surprising. Dilettantism is in its element in England and even among the educated there is a lack of critical judgement of quality in music that would be impossible in any other country. But despite the absence of discrimination in musical matters, love of music is deep and general among the British."[31]

No-one was more prolific in producing examples of the 18th Century "British Style" grand, immediately recognizable by its distinctive veneered panels, than John Broadwood.

According to the Broadwood records[32] the firm were only up to grand piano No. 40 in 1786 but, when they reached No. 1000 well before the end of the Century, all must have known that the grand had overcome the harpsichord.

The squares and the horizontal grands were not the only two shapes on offer to the public.

Upright harpsichords or spinets[33] had been known for many a year, to be followed on the Continent, from 1735, by upright pianos, which might seem innovative but were, in reality, winged grand pianos stood "vertically on a stand, or table".[34] A British version of a similar upright piano was patented[35] by John Landreth in 1787.

Photo by courtesy of
The Bowes Museum, Barnard Castle, Co. Durham

To build a piano upwards instead of sideways was not a new idea. Tall Continental upright pianos of 1735 and 1745, with the strings starting above the keyboard, were mentioned by the piano historian Rosamond Harding but, even in Britain, a vertical piano had been patented in 1787 by John Landreth of Tabernacle Walk, London. What was different about William Stodart's patent of January 12th., 1795, was that it was intended specifically to be "an upright piano in the form of a bookcase". This fine example of 1806 in The Bowes Museum, 220cm tall, demonstrates precisely what Stodart had in mind, a piano that, when the lid was closed, might pass as another piece of handsome mahogany drawing room furniture. One of many disguises that the piano was to adopt. Plate No. 9.

Upright pianos of the Stodart type presumably had their origin in the clavicytherium or upright spinet. This example with its profusely decorated interior, once in the Donaldson Collection, was illustrated by an early pioneer of piano history, A. J. Hipkins, in his 1888 publication "Musical Instruments". Mr Hipkins suggested that this upright spinet was of North Italian or South German origin and could hardly be "of later date than the first years of the sixteenth century". The spinet itself is 4ft 10½in high and stands on a table which is 2ft high. Plate No. 10.

▸

One of the most original of all piano makers, William Southwell of Dublin, also had a go at a vertical piano by turning the small English "square" piano on its side to become an "upright square". Southwell was responsible for a number of inventions and he patented his upright square on November 8th., 1798 but it had a comparatively short life before being left behind by new developments. This example in The National Museum of Ireland is 150cm in height. Plate No. 11.

Photo by courtesy of
The National Museum of Ireland, Dublin

A Piano Disguised as a Bookcase

Then, in 1795, William Stodart registered[36] a more popular "Upright Grand….an upright piano in the form of a bookcase"—as implied, a grand again turned upwards but the top half now appearing to be a bookcase sat upon four legs. In fact, when you opened the glazed top doors (which were usually draped with handsome fabrics) you found most of the space taken up by the strings and only a few real bookshelves fitted over the shortest strings.[37] Presumably these were meant to hold music scores.

Upright grands were designed, it has been claimed, "so that the instrument might stand up against the wall and economize space"[38] but one expert describes this as a common misconception and points out that the upright grands were "much louder" than the ordinary horizontal grands. He tells me that "there is no doubt in my mind that upright grands were chiefly desired for their extra sound".[39]

What is certain is that such instruments, built on legs which ensured the strings could only start upwards from the keyboard level, immediately took on Brobdingnagian qualities, growing to dizzying heights. They may have covered less floor space but this skyscraper tendency was just as practical a disqualification.

According to one piano historian: "The problem with these instruments lay chiefly in their height—in excess of eight feet".[40] In fact, one is known of 9ft 1in, which came complete with two heavy, mirrored doors.[41] They were threateningly precarious and came to be described as "wall-climbers".[42]

An alternative solution was offered in 1798 when a Dubliner, William Southwell[43] (although suggested not to be the first to do so) received recognition when he reduced the height by copying the idea but, instead, standing the smaller "square" piano upright on a stand. This model, however, had only a brief life.

Reducing the Height - the Cabinet Piano

The inventive Mr Southwell then offered a more practical alternative to the Upright Grand, which he called the Cabinet Piano. Basically, he reduced the height by starting the strings from floor level and thus abolishing the need for four legs.

Southwell patented[44] his cabinet piano in 1807 and this, again, looked rather like a bookcase. It was to have a vogue for much of the half-century and I suspect it was this design that finished off the old Upright Grand. The latter, Lord knows how, somehow remained "in good demand"[45] until about 1830, despite its evident handicaps.

Photo by courtesy of The Royal College of Music, London

From its introduction to Britain there was a recurring idea of trying to miniaturise the piano. The upright grands made by Stodart and other firms were often in excess of 8ft high and an alternative was offered by the inventive William Southwell who, in 1807, patented a smaller "cabinet piano", where he started the strings from floor level. Even here, however, the height typically varied from 6ft to 7ft 2in. This good example in mahogany by John Broadwood and Sons, 1,737cm high, now in the collection of The Royal College of Music, was made c.1821 and has one of the trade mark features of the cabinet type: A silk panel in the top section which became known as the "Sunburst" or "Cloudburst" design. Astoundingly, the College example still has its original silk panel in a sandy-yellow colour. Plate No. 12.

Inevitably, someone tried to miniaturise the cabinet piano. I am not sure who was responsible or when it first appeared but early in the Victorian period, possibly in the 1840s, D'Almaine & Co. were offering a piano they called the "Cottage or Semi-Cabinet". From such phraseology it is unclear whether this well known firm had in mind a slightly taller version of what we now recognise as the modern upright piano or a smaller version of the cabinet but the height of this "Semi-Cabinet", shown in a D'Almaine catalogue in the author's possession, was declared to be 4ft 8½in, so a considerable reduction from the normal cabinet height. Plate No. 13.

Writing many years later, James Shudi Broadwood was to claim that: "The Vertical or Cabinet Piano was first produced by William Southwell, from a sketch given him by James Broadwood about 1804; so little was it then appreciated, that the first manufactory in the line refused to purchase the patent he took out".[46] This reflected great credit on Broadwood and Sons but I am unclear where there is a jot of evidence to support this suggestion of Broadwood authorship.

A quite different version[47] was given in 1867 by A.N. Wornum who stated that "in 1807 William Southwell adopted Loud's suggestion of carrying the sound board to the floor and introduced an Upright which he called a 'Cabinet Pianoforte'.

"At that time George Wilkinson....was desirous of entering into Pianoforte making. He engaged with Southwell for the supply of the 'New Cabinet Pianoforte'. This instrument, however, when it got into the hands of the dealers, turned out unsuccessful, and brought Wilkinson into trouble."

Since other piano makers, notably Broadwoods, later went on to produce large numbers of cabinet pianos, one presumes they did so under licence from William Southwell.

With the cabinet, Southwell solved the question of how to reduce the height but, according to an account of 1812, the cabinet still varied "from six to seven feet two inches" in height.[48]

A later writer confirmed that the upright grand had been "superseded" by the cabinet but complained that the latter was still "a monstrosity taller than a full-grown man".[49]

So, even though it saved height by doing away with the legs, the cabinet was still a tall instrument and one that others later strove to "miniaturise".[50]

After Queen Victoria came to the throne, D'Almaine and Co. had managed to reduce the height of their cabinet pianos to 5ft 8in high, with a width of 4ft 3in. They also offered the "Cottage or Semi-Cabinet" piano at 4ft 8½in a name so ambiguous it is hard to know whether they were making a taller upright or a mini-version of the Cabinet.[51]

Upright Grands and Cabinets were disliked by some performers. Singer-pianists complained that the audience could see only their backs and that their voices were muffled by the textiles often used in panels in the top section ("at least half the delight we should feel from those 'dulcet sounds' is lost in the silk which faces the singer").[52]

One also wonders to what degree such lofty items were compatible with the growing demands for more modest, mass housing.

As smaller pianos appeared, Southwell's cabinet style also began to decline in popular appeal, although they went on being made even into the 1850s and Broadwood, for example, who started making cabinets in 1812, only ceased production with No 8963 in 1856.[53]

A Giraffe, a Pyramid and a Lyre

On the Continent there were three tall, highly decorative competitors (always, one suspects, too exotic for British taste) in the "Pyramid" (Pyramidenflügel),[54] the "Giraffe" (Giraffenflügel)[55] and the "Lyre" (Lyrenflügel).[56]

The first two of these, particularly, made an immediate impression by virtue of their metamorphic qualities. The "Pyramid",

Photo by courtesy of The Haags Gemeentemuseum, Den Haag, The Netherlands

Too intoxicating, too lavish and altogether too dangerous for Britons of Puritan taste, three new types of exotic piano, up to 8ft in height, emerged on the Continent, all of strangely metamorphic shape. One of these was the Pyramidenflügel in the form, in case you hadn't guessed, of a Pyramid and this must be the best known example in the World, the much illustrated instrument made by Conrad Graf of Vienna, c.1829. It is now in the Haags Gemeentemuseum where you can be astonished by its black and gilt figures holding the candelabra, the sunburst decoration in the bottom, the double-headed eagle peering from the top panel and a vase surmounting all. Plate No. 14.

Photo by courtesy of Sotheby's of New York

The Giraffenflügel was, of course, reminiscent of a giraffe and few came more laden with gilt, sculpture and decoration than this French example, c.1830, which appeared as Lot 24 at Sotheby's of New York on October 29th., 1976. The figure perched on top is Orpheus, summoning devotees with his own instrument, while around him the gilt-bronze decorations spread their tentacles across the ebonised case. In the front panel is a portrait medallion of Napoleon and Josephine, while carved heads support the keyboard. Plate No. 15.

Photo by courtesy of Sotheby's of New Bond Street, London

The Lyrenflügel took its shape from one of the oldest of all musical instruments, the lyre and in this c.1830 example, by Johann Schleip of Berlin, the form begins to dissolve into hypnotic curves and sweeps that threaten to embrace and enclose the pianist. Auctioned by Messrs Sotheby's as Lot 171 on October 9th., 1981, the instrument was in a mahogany case, had gilt metal mounts, with the front panel backed with green pleated silk and stood on outcurved lion's paw feet. Plate No. 16.

which appeared in 1745, had the outline of an Egyptian pyramid. The "Giraffe" gave an almost comical reminder of Africa's tallest animal. The "Lyre", as you might guess, somewhat resembled in shape that ancient instrument.

All three, growing in some instances to 8ft, came to be enriched and garlanded as though they were instruments of the Gods which, presumably, some thought they were.

A British variation on such themes, much decorated with fretwork but still subdued compared to its Continental cousins, was an upright harp-shaped piano called a "Euphonicon", in which the upper part had the works exposed, showing a metal frame and the strings.

This was the invention, in 1842, of Dr John Steward[57] but similar forms had certainly been known on the Continent for many years, one

At The Great Exhibition of 1851, held in London, William Akerman exhibited a "Lyric Grand...its back being formed like a lyre" and Frederick Hund showed his "Lyra", said to stand on "a peculiar constructed platform" and "formed like a lyre with openings covered with silk" but, unfortunately, I can trace no illustration of either. One further attempt was made to revive such fashions late in the Victorian era and shown in "The Queen" magazine on August 22nd., 1896, after Percy Macquoid designed this "elaborately decorated upright of Harp shape", built by Broadwood. Somehow you feel that Macquoid's design lacks conviction and the unashamed exhibitionism of the Continentals, even if there is a tinge of Art Nouveau round the edges. It may well have been a one-off "special" since I know of no other such examples by the firm. Plate No. 18.

Photo by courtesy of The Victoria and Albert Museum, South Kensington, London

As you might expect, the British riposte to the Continental challenge of the Pyramidenflügel, the Giraffenflügel and the Lyrenflügel was more restrained in temper and more utilitarian in approach. The best known example was Dr John Steward's "Euphonicon", patented in 1841, in which the upper part had the works exposed, showing the metal frame and strings, the decoration being mainly in the form of fretwork. A later British critic said the ornament reflected "the degraded taste of the period...but the instrument has this saving merit, at any rate, that it does not attempt to disguise or falsify its construction". Plate No. 17.

of like shape having been made by the Swiss instrument maker, Maussard of Lausanne,[58] in 1819. There is also a piano "with high 'harp' back", stated to be by Mardon and Co., in the Museum of London and for which I have been given the date "1840-1850".[59]

A later critic said the ornament of Steward's "Euphonicon" reflected "the degraded taste of the period....but the instrument has this saving merit, at any rate, that it does not attempt to disguise or falsify its construction".[60]

I presume that two British pianos shown at the Great Exhibition of 1851 may have had some point of identity with the Continental "Lyre" but I have so far been unable to trace an illustration of either.

The first was the "Lyric Grand", with "its back being formed like a lyre", shown by William Akerman of Bridgwater.[61] The second was the "Lyra" by Frederick Hund and Son of Pimlico, London, which had a "peculiar constructed platform" and was said to be "formed like a lyre, with openings covered with silk".[62] Somehow, Hund managed to constrain the height of his "Lyra" to 3ft 5in.

One British attempt to revive the style was made in 1896 with an "elaborately decorated upright of Harp shape"[63] designed by Percy Macquoid and built by Broadwood but it did not spark any wholesale comeback.

All of these were merely false notes in the evolution of the piano. From their ranks only the horizontal grand piano was to become a long term survivor and it too was to be far outsold, after a hesitant start, by a new type introduced at the turn of the century: What we now recognise as the modern upright.

The Modern Upright appears in 1800

In 1800 the English engineer John Isaac Hawkins, the man who gave us the ever-pointed pencil, patented a small upright piano,[64] one of the first examples being only 3ft 7in tall,[65] where the strings descended below the keyboard and the stand on legs was banished.

One piano historian has described Hawkins' invention as "The True Upright" and that seems to me to be accurate.[66]

Hawkins, one-time medical student, civil engineer, poet, preacher and phrenologist, invented this instrument while living for a period in the United States and his father, Isaac Hawkins, took out the British patent.[67]

It is only right to acknowledge that his claim is challenged in Austria where a Viennese man is said, quite independently, to have revealed the same invention in the same year.[68]

Hawkins's upright did not immediately become popular but others saw the potential and in the mid 19th Century it was said that "by far the largest number of instruments constructed are of a small size and low price".[69]

What really finished the bulky giants was a double pressure: the demands for cheap instruments and economy of space, forcing makers to look in quite the opposite direction, towards what eventually became the "mini-upright" and, for the more affluent middle class, the "Baby Grand".

The poor might long for a piano but they could hardly offer a spacious Belgravia reception room.

When the piano penetrated the Turkish harems, it was placed on stumpy legs so that it might be played from a sitting position on cushions.[70] Before the century ended they had to be squeezed into new British dwelling places with tight constraints: the bungalow and the flat. By the early 1890s there were public complaints about the difficulty of fitting pianos into "the corners of modern flats".[71]

This trend must have begun much earlier than is commonly thought since in 1826 a cabinet piano was recommended in the "Repository of Arts" as "admirably calculated for a small apartment, in which a horizontal piano would be heavy and inconvenient; it has also a very pleasing appearance when placed in a recess, such as that formed by the projection of the chimney".[72]

The Grand is "So Awkward"

In the early 1830s the architect Edward Buckton Lamb wrote that: "The horizontal grand pianoforte which is the most perfect instrument now in use, is of such an awkward shape, that it is almost impossible to give any expression of style to it; and, in a moderate-sized house, it occupies so large a portion of the room in which it is placed, that now the upright grand pianoforte is generally substituted for it."[73]

The True Upright, what we would now recognise as the modern upright piano, was invented in 1800 by an English civil engineer, preacher and phrenologist, John Isaac Hawkins, who was responsible for the ever-pointed pencil and various advances in sugar refining. Through technical innovations Hawkins, himself a skilled musician, was able to produce an instrument just 3ft 7in high and which he intended to be portable. Although he was living at the time in a country dedicated to free enterprise, the United States of America, Hawkins was never able fully to exploit his invention and very few were produced. This example, which is marked No. 6 and was made in 1801, is a great rarity, now to be found in one of the most impressive collections of musical instruments, housed in The Smithsonian. Plate No. 19.

Photo by courtesy of The Smithsonian Institution (N.M.A.H), Washington, U.S.A.

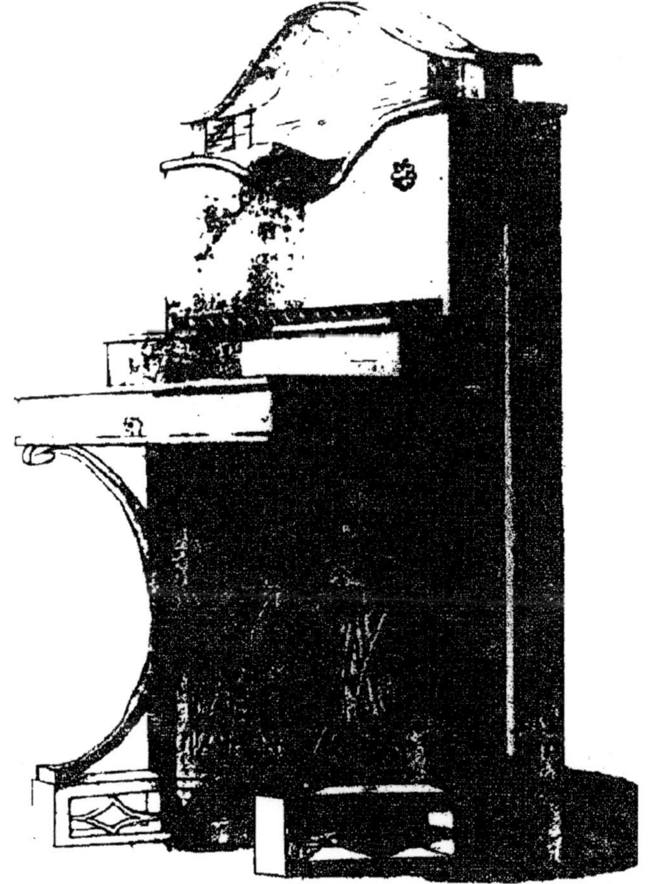

It appears that, quite independently, another inventor was also working in 1800 on his own version of an upright piano, which he called The Ditanaklasis. This was the idea of Mathias Muller, a piano maker in Vienna, Austria, who tried harder for stylishness but was less utilitarian in approach, producing an instrument with an arched top, which was bound to increase the height. This illustration of Muller's Ditanaklasis, which was stated to be 1.54m high and thus, apparently, taller than the Hawkins version, appeared in "Allgemeine Musikalische Zeitung" in September, 1803. Plate No. 20.

Illustration by courtesy of The British Library

A catalogue produced by D'Almaine and Co, in the earlier part of Queen Victoria's reign, offered upright pianos of 3ft 11in in height and claimed "their smallness of size renders them admirably adapted for Rooms of limited space, wherein they can be moved about at pleasure, without the risk of sustaining the slightest injury, while the elegance of their appearance makes them a most attractive Ornament to any Apartment".[74]

The introduction of Hawkins' upright also lead to the slow death of the "square" piano, although this could not have been guessed at when "Around 1825 the square was undoubtedly the favourite type".[75]

Technical experts say that one of the reasons for the demise of the square was that the limited space available for the strings presented mechanical problems but, paradoxically, the square itself grew in size.[76]

A new iron frame,[77] introduced in 1825, improved the range of the square but was another reason why "wider still and wider shall thy bounds be set". An increase from 59 to 85 keys inevitably led to what became known as the "grand square".[78]

Instead of occupying a special niche for a tiny, portable piano, the square was asking to compete with the big boys. By mid-century it had also become vastly inflated in physical size, to such a degree it must have been astonishing for those who had seen a Zumpe.

But at the top end of the market it was the grand that won the day and at the bottom the upright proved more appealing.

By mid-century most squares then still being manufactured were intended for the Colonies, especially India, where taste had the inevitable time delay. Squares were, I think, decidedly in the minority at the 1851 Exhibition.

Henry Fowler Broadwood issued an order in July, 1860, to "Discontinue all squares which are not made solid for the tropics...Turn over any really good men to other jobs and reduce the Indian instrument men". [79]

The second of the "Big Two" British makers, Collard and Collard, still felt it important to show a square in mahogany at the 1862 Exhibition but this was "manufactured... expressly for the East Indies and tropical climates".[80]

Broadwood are recorded[81] to have made their last square in 1866, number 64,161 but by then the square had, effectively, had its day in Britain. The decision of Robert Wornum and Sons to show a square at the Paris Universal Exhibition of 1867 might almost have been for historical reasons, the firm explaining how they had taken out a patent for it in 1842.[82] A Japanese firm showed another square at the 1878 Paris Exhibition[83] but this was a rare misjudgement of the market.

As the square expired in Europe, British musical instrument dealers did not go to quite the same lengths as their American counterparts.

The square remained popular in the States long after its vogue was over in Europe but, inevitably, in the late 1880s it declined there also[84] as fashion turned its back on a faithful old friend. One of the American market leaders, Steinway, made their last square in 1888, though others struggled on into the 1890s and a tiny few even later.

On May 24th., 1904, this rejection led to a cathartic happening, reminiscent of a Pagan exorcism, at the convention of the National Association of Piano Dealers of America in Atlantic City. An American journalist named Harry Freund organised a ceremonial burning of, allegedly, some 1,000 old square pianos, to take them out of circulation; "prove" that they were now out of date; and encourage the public to embrace the new. [85]

Thus were the old squares torched on the pyre with a salesman's fervour but, nevertheless, their legend lives on with modern enthusiasts all over the world who still cherish the remaining antique survivors and curse Mr Freund's name.

Many years after the square had disappeared from the British scene one eccentric attempt was made to revive the form but it resulted in a square quite unlike any other.

Around 1900 one of the famed figures of the design movement, the architect C.R. Ashbee, founder of The Guild of Handicraft, created a huge grand piano (now in the Cheltenham Museum and Art Gallery) but using the square form instead of the traditional harp shape—"5 feet wide and 7 feet long, supported on a forest of legs....like nothing so much as an over-sized cigar-box". For his pains Ashbee was attacked for designing "an immense square mass....really about as ugly and unwieldy an object, and as little suggesting a musical instrument, as could well be".[86]

The collapse in the market for the square yet proved a boon for some. Alongside the routine pirating of designs went a thriving trade in forged and bogus pianos and the rogues simply bought up old squares by reputable firms and transferred the nameplate or nameboard to an inferior instrument in a more acceptable current style. Many a square also magically transformed itself into a desk or a dressing table (and even cocktail cabinets in the post-1920s) in the hands of "restorers".[87]

Appearance of the "Cottage Upright"

The market forces that must have driven the development of the upright can be seen, above all, in the work of Robert Wornum who, by 1811, was offering a practical, well designed upright of 3ft 5in in height.[88] Hawkins, for all his brilliance, was unable to exploit his invention commercially but Wornum was the 19th Century entrepreneur personified.

According to the piano historian Rosamond Harding, in 1811 there were three attempts to overcome various technical problems and make a small upright piano that would meet the market's needs.

In one instance the idea was to try and help singers who did not wish to perform with their back to the audience but with the other two inventions, by Robert Wornum and Frederick William Collard, they became part of a series of efforts by British piano makers "to obtain a good small upright Instrument suitable to the size of the small room that most of Londoners have to be contented with".[89]

So successful was Wornum's venture of 1811 that "as many as a hundred and odd hands were employed in the factory. From this time the London manufacture of Upright Pianofortes takes its rise".[90]

It was through the work of Wornum that the description "Cottage Piano" is said to have emerged and this stuck to the upright for much of the century. An eminent writer on keyboards history, Howard Schott, states that: "The term 'cottage piano', introduced by Wornum, has also gained currency for small uprights".[91]

Wornum had called his upright of 1811 the "Unique" and his upright of 1813 the "Harmonic" When Wornum first used the term "Cottage Piano" I do not know but the description occurs, for certain, in his 1838 price list.[92]

According to A.N. Wornum, writing in the Victorian era, it was after his father introduced the "Harmonic" that "shortly afterwards (*it was*) made by other manufacturers and known under the name of the Cottage Pianoforte".[93]

Part of this can readily be confirmed by studying a price list issued by John Broadwood and Sons in 1828 who were by then producing three models they termed simply "Cottage" pianos.[94]

Was it the salesmen who dreamed up the term "Cottage Piano" to suggest an instrument small enough to fit into a tiny home? By the middle Victorian period, when most buyers would already have been "townies", it may also have provided a sentimental reminder of a Rural idyll already disappearing into the industrial smoke.

To match the "Cottage" uprights there were "Cottage Wall Pictures" by Sampson Low but even these modest Woodbury process photos were thought, at 18 pence each, to be "perhaps too great for them to find their way, except as gifts, into the homes of the very poor".[95] And if you did not fancy the "Cottage Piano" why, there was always the tiny "Cottage Harmonium", sold for seven guineas by Boosey & Co.[96]

That the "Cottage" description struck some deep chord we can see because the influential home art-work movement first started as the Cottage Arts Association.[97]

With successive technical innovations in 1826 and 1828, Wornum produced yet another improved, small upright he called the "Piccolo",[98] and this achieved such repute it was treated as though it was a completely new invention. It was copied by other makers in Britain and on the Continent under a variety of fancy names.[99]

"The original invention and introduction of the Square and the Grand Pianoforte is certainly due to foreigners but we claim the 'Upright' as the work of Englishmen", boasted A.N. Wornum.[100]

Whatever the humble associations of the upright piano, its progress was unstoppable.

Up to 1842 Broadwoods had produced "eighty or ninety thousand pianofortes" and the firm's analysis of those figures showed that, historically, the square had been the top seller. For every 100 squares they had made there had been 28 grands, 16 cabinets, 9 cottage and 5 upright grands and semi-grands. In other words squares had been over three times more popular than the grand piano.[101]

Yet, seven years later, by the time of the 1851 Exhibition, there was a recognition, simply from the number of uprights shown (various Continentals displaying a particular interest in this form) that the square was on the way out and the upright was heir apparent.

According to the piano historian David Grover: "In 1851 only 5-10 per cent of English output was accounted for by grands compared with 80-90 per cent by uprights".[102]

The success of the piano at this point must have been akin to the later arrival of moving films and the cinema.

A House of Commons Select Committee on Coal was told by a Yorkshire miner in 1873 that "we have got more pianos and perambulators in recent years" but that the piano was "a cut above the perambulator".[103]

In the poorest part of the East End of London, where none came poorer and more despairing, a wall advertisement asked: "What is a home without a piano?"[104]

Fortunes were made in the five big piano manufacturing countries, Britain, France, the United States, Austria and Germany, while hundreds of thousands of children were forced to piano studies, often taught by "reduced ladies"[105] and sometimes with the threat of a ruler across the knuckles.

As "Punch" put it:

"Little females and tiny males
All of them thumping out their scales
Little Halles in socks and shorts
Beating their Broadwood's pianofortes". [106]

Of the many hundreds of world firms making pianos, the British view was that one was pre-eminently the world leader: Broadwood.[107]

In the transformation from craft workshops to mass manufacturing, Broadwood seized the initiative and grew into a giant.[108]

Piano making was an obvious candidate for division of labour and such efficiencies resulted in the price of the instrument actually going down[109] between the 1780s and 1815. It is said that by 1815 the London piano makers were already using circular saws and planing machines.[110]

By mid-19th century, Broadwood alone had made 103,750 pianos and, of these, 60,382 had been produced between 1824 and 1850, an average of 2,236 a year during that time.[111]

As the world's largest maker, Broadwood were, by the latter date, employing 573 people at their factory but this was far from the total because there were "numerous persons working at home".[112]

Two other firms were seen at this time as leading competitors of Broadwood: Erards (who had a London factory[113] for a great many years, until 1890, but whose main base was in Paris) and Collard & Collard.

An insight into what they perceived to be the pecking order comes from the main report[114] of the Jury (containing such eminent men as the Austrian Professor of Music and renowned pianist, Sigismund Thalberg) on the Music Section of the 1851 Exhibition.

This talked, in detail, of "the three great European makers, Messrs Broadwood, Collard and Erard". Although nine pages were given to discussion of pianos and the Jury mentioned that "Several other makers of the pianoforte have contributed to the success of the musical department", not another firm was mentioned by name, even though others were awarded medals.

But in this expanding market the 18th Century survivors and scores of brash 19th Century newcomers fought for the trade. Among them were: Clementi (later to evolve into Collard and Collard), Isaac Mott, Thomas Tomkison, William Stodart, Robert Wornum, Joseph Kirkman and Son, Pohlmann and Sons, J. Brinsmead and Sons, J. and J. Hopkinson, Chappell and Co., Cramer and Co., Arthur Allison and Co., Challen (who made what was claimed, at the time, to be the world's largest grand, 11ft 8in long, specially built for the Silver Jubilee of George V in 1935[115]), Eavestaff and Sons, Monington and Weston, Samuel Barnett and Son, B. Squire and Sons, Barratt and Robinson, Rogers and Sons, and Strohmenger's, among them.

The appeal of the piano was summed up in a resonating phrase by "The Times", which called it "the orchestra of the drawing-room".[116]

As Professor Thalberg[117] commented: "The social importance of the piano is beyond all question far greater than that of any other instrument.

"Formerly....amusements were away from home and in public; now, with the more educated portion of society, the greater part is at home and within the family circle, music on the piano contributing the principal portion of it".[118]

In the 1890s a writer could say: "The pianoforte is to music what the pen is to the historian, printing to poetry, food to the body....The education of the average girl is based on a knowledge of the pianoforte... (*it has*) made this generation the most musical of any we have knowledge of."[119]

Will someone one day see the television set as a similar unifying family deity?

The piano also played a role in society that could never have been foreseen.

A prominent clergyman contended that "the piano makes a girl sit upright and pay attention to details" and, further, that "a good play on the piano has not infrequently taken the place of a good cry upstairs".[120]

This delicately skirted around the other vital role the piano played for young ladies—as an aid to courtship. Skill on the piano was seen as a social asset and Mary Gladstone, daughter of the Prime Minister, was not the first young girl to lose her heart to her piano teacher.[121]

No wonder that by the time of the Great Exhibition, 23,000 pianos a year were made in Britain, involving 40 separate branches of the trade.[122] Like cowboys fearing unmusical natives, three quarters of the firms were eventually to set up business in a tight little community centred on Camden Town.[123]

According to Edgar Brinsmead,[124] by 1860 the number of British pianos made had risen to 35,000 a year. The census of 1861 revealed there were 5,079 musical instrument makers and dealers in Britain. By 1901 there were 13,747.

Most of this commercial empire was built on the success of the small, upright piano, which proved that, to fit in to flats and working class homes, size mattered. This had inevitable repercussions for other piano types.

Even the grand piano, the very name of which spelt out its pretensions, was forced to compete in this area. The "Pocket Grand" and the "Bijou Grand" appeared (later to be joined by the "Baby Grand" and even the "Large Baby") and Wornums followed their "Piccolo" upright with a pocket grand which had been reduced to a length of 5ft 4¾in.[125]

Such developments posed their own problems for 19th Century furniture designers. The demand for the ever-smaller upright set new challenges for them and the length of strings in the grand piano imprisoned them in a different kind of straight-jacket. The increased number of strings, to meet the demands of music enthusiasts,[126] compounded this by introducing a weight element that demanded sturdy construction—thin, elegant legs would hardly do from that point.

Designers not only had to cope with such restrictions but try and reconcile other, very different, tendencies.

The Piano takes on Many Disguises

One of these, presumably influenced by the need to economise on space and the wish to "disguise" the piano, was the recurring customer demand[127] for "combination" furniture, sometimes known as "Harlequin" furniture.

For example, in the 18th Century one harpsichord[128] was produced with a row of drawers hanging beneath and, from a date suggested to be around 1785, the Dublin maker William Southwell produced some half-dozen pianos of superb craftsmanship which appeared to be half-round tables.[129]

As the scholarly work of Ian Woodfield has revealed, in 1786 a merchant ship, the "Earl of Oxford", transported to India "A new invented Ladies Commode, Solid Mahogany furnished in high stile, *(sic)* and containing a curious Piana *(sic)* Forte to draw out".

A catalogue issued by the dealers Longman and Broderip in March, 1790, advertised: "Piano Fortes in Commodes, Side Boards and Dressing Tables for convenience of small rooms".[130] An advertisement placed in a Madrid newspaper in 1795 offered two English pianos "of the latest fashion....Each is in the shape of a writing desk". Another Spanish announcement by a dealer in 1796 was for the sale of two London pianos, the first "in the shape of a chest of drawers" and the second as "a beautiful bookcase". In 1797 a Madrid dealer said that he had received from London a piano "of a new

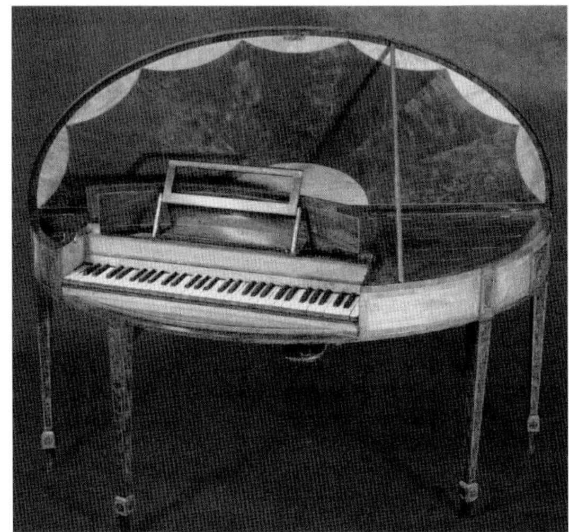

Photo by courtesy of Sotheby's of New Bond Street, London

From the earliest days of the piano in Britain there were attempts to transform the instrument, whose bulk was an eternal problem, into a piece of multi-purpose, combination furniture that would make the most of the space it occupied and, often, disguise its true purpose. Some of these efforts were risible but others produced cabinet making of superlative, breath-taking quality. This was never seen better than in the work of William Southwell who, it is suggested between c.1785 and c.1798, was responsible for a series of demi-lune, or half moon, Georgian table pianos of Neo-Classical style. These are unmistakably the work of master craftsmen and this is generally attributed (on exactly what basis I am unclear) to a Royal cabinet maker, William Moore of Dublin. This example, in satinwood banded with yew wood and given a date of c.1785, appeared as Lot 284 at Sotheby's, on March 20th., 1980. Plate No. 21.

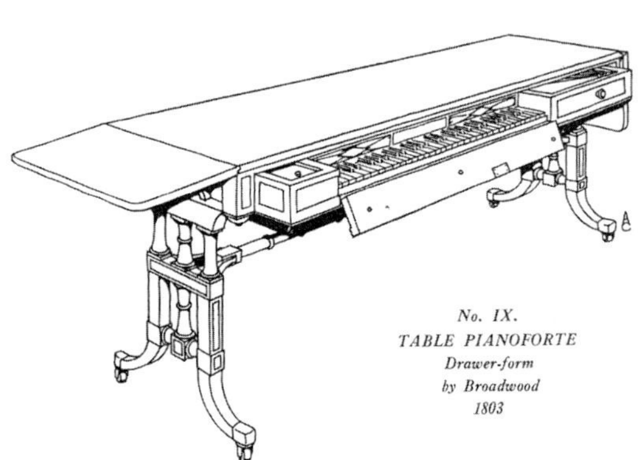

A
No. IX.
TABLE PIANOFORTE
Drawer-form
by Broadwood
1803

Broadwood's main output was of fine quality and, from a case point of view, safe predictability. Rarely did they take a walk on the wild side. One of the exceptions, shown here in a Broadwood & Sons publication, was this splendid design of 1803 that, to most people, would have looked like a conventional sofa table but which did, in fact, enclose a piano which could "be removed entirely from the table, like a drawer". An example appeared as Lot 296 in a Sotheby's auction on March 20th., 1980, when it was described as being mahogany with ebony stringing. Plate No. 22.

and special type, perpendicular, with stops, in the shape of a desk".[131]

Stodart's Upright Grand of 1795 introduced the idea of a very tall upright piano that might be a bookcase (albeit one with little space for books) and, much later than you might think, around 1815-1820, George Wilkinson produced a design for the square piano that seems an obvious notion: A delightful square with a cupboard below on either side.[132]

This was just the beginning.

A more complex alternative was a "Combination Piano, Desk and Toilet Table".[133]

In 1833 a piano by Robert Wornum "could hardly be distinguished from a library table"[134] and before 1850 inventors patented triangular, hexagonal, oval, semi-circular, circular and corner[135] instruments; plus one that really was mathematically square[136] and not just "square" in name. The undulating curves of another were "symmetrically concave".[137] Southwell offered the public a "piano sloping backwards"[138] and, while in London during 1815, Camille Pleyell wrote to his parents that "As for the oval pianos, Dettmer is practically the only one who makes them".[139]

One firm, Lyon and Duncan of Wells Street, London, declared themselves, in about 1820, to be "Circular & Square Piano Forte Builders".[140]

After establishing himself in London the Parisian maker Jean-Henri Pape advertised in a British music magazine in 1836 his new hexagon shaped piano that served also as a table and was "particularly adapted to cabins of ships and cottages where room is an object".[141]

Piano-secretaires were designed for ladies' boudoirs[142] and, supplying a different need, there was a piano which served as a "flat writing table....well adapted for the composer's study".[143] Broadwood produced at least one elegant sofa table from which the piano could be pulled out as you would a drawer.[144]

Another piano design appeared with a full-scale china cabinet tacked on the back[145] and, of course, there was the sideboard-piano.[146]

Feminists will be appalled to learn that someone, evidently a man, invented a "Sewing-Table Piano"[147] and "work-box pianos" with diminutive keys on which "The young lady could amuse herself between threading her needles or console herself, when she pricked her finger, with a little tune".[148]

A Collard and Collard instrument appeared to be nothing but a desk with many drawers.[149] A Glasgow maker, James Semple, produced a piano "in the form of a student's desk".[150] Another piano had the appearance of a chiffonier[151] with a keyboard supported by four console legs. A fourth was a dining table by Richard Hunt[152] that opened on springs to reveal a secret piano. A fifth, a pianoforte for the bedroom, doubled up as a chest of drawers.[153]

A bookcase-piano must have seemed quite tame after these.

The ultimate example of the piano as combination furniture came with a design registered[154] with the British Patent Office by one John Millward of Birmingham (who possibly was acting as an agent) in 1866.

This was an instrument of which a magician would have been proud: Inside a hollow base was a couch mounted on rollers, to emerge when the piano was not in use; on one side was a closet to contain the bed clothes; on the other a bureau with drawers; yet another closet contained a wash-hand basin, jug, towels and other articles of toilet. The bureau and second closet were made to open at the ends, the front being fitted with false drawers.

Nor was this all. A matching music stool, need one explain, contained yet a further work-box, looking glass, writing table and "a small set of drawers".

Odd to relate, a piano keyboard was to be found somewhere in the middle of this muddle.

Some pianos emerged in curious guise for quite other reasons.

A Broadwood upright, now in a leading Belgium museum,[155] was made with a strange dip in the middle of the top—to aid a singer, it has been suggested. One piano historian goes so far as to suggest there was "a further family of instrumental shapes in which the centre was cut away for the voice to penetrate through the gap, the height to left and right retained so that the bass strings lengths were unaffected and symmetry upheld".[156]

The perpendicular piano,[157] patented in 1878, allowed the musician to stand to one side and play a vertical keyboard, so that he could face the audience and sing to them.

Another bizarre example must, surely, have been a candidate for the tallest upright in the world, if it was ever built.[158] The design showed an impossibly elongated case and the pianist had to mount a flight of stairs so that she could be seen by the audience.

Presumably motivated by the same reasoning, another hopeful inventor patented an upright that was to be "in height equal to the length of a grand"[159] and also came complete with steps in the base.

Of curious contraptions for the piano there was no end. Weighted gloves were devised for playing so that the pianist might strengthen the fingers.[160] Heated pianos were thought by some a good thing. A Heath Robinson contraption allowed a pianist to study her own lips while singing.[161]

I retreated baffled when faced with the 1894 patent of the gentleman who devised a piano with its legs resting on iron stands "containing telephone transmitters".[162] Perhaps a visionary who anticipated broadcasting, or just a compulsive talker who wished to play a concerto and chat to a friend at the same time. Not exactly a mobile phone but....

What is one to say in the face of such remarkable ingenuity?

But no matter how many such alternative shapes the piano industry produced in their drive for technical advance it did nothing to increase the happiness of the case designers who, above all, were expected to adapt the piano to every swirl and eddy of current fashion.

Many hopeful inventors have made the trek to the British Patent Office apparently convinced that they had solved one of the persistent problems facing human kind: What to do about the awkward shape of the piano. When confronted with their actual solutions, one can only look with wonder at the ingenuity of which they were capable, while sighing for the undoubted disappointments that must have followed. I will pass over such brave souls as the gentleman who devised a piano with its legs resting on iron stands "containing telephone transmitters" and present you here with this High Rise answer to theatrical performances, Patent Number 1376, registered in Britain on May 9th., 1867, by A. Herce. Sadly, I do not know of any actual piano made according to his tall notions. Plate No. 23.

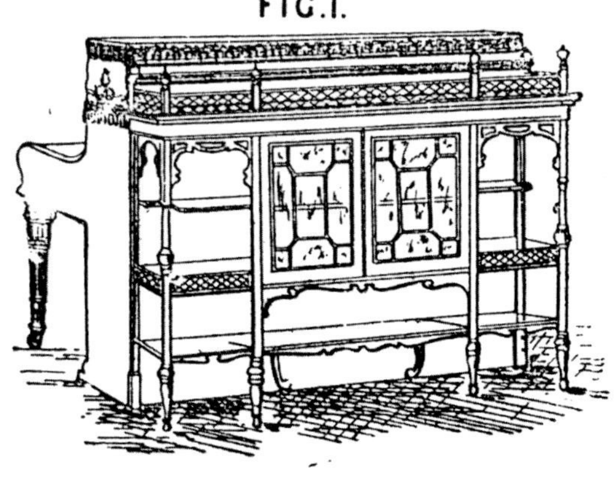

The eternal dissatisfaction felt by designers with the shape of the piano led to many, many attempts to solve household problems by marrying the poor instrument to any fashionable suitor who was currently in favour. When the china cabinet became a passion at the end of the Victorian era, S.G.L. Giles registered Patent Number 19,248 on October 14th., 1895—his answer to how to tie the knot for the piano and a (detachable) china cabinet. I have not seen any surviving examples of this type although I know of a number of other designs which attempted to use the front of the piano for display shelves built on to the top or sides. Plate No. 24.

The invective unleashed in 1894 in the "Art Journal" by John F. Runciman[163] was the cry of a man who could hardly bear to look upon the current article.

"Like the patent medicines, you should always have it in the house....where shall you place it? If your drawing-room be sufficiently spacious, say not less than sixty by forty-five to fifty feet, it is a question easily answered....you will realise what an intractable leviathan it is. It stands there in the most helpless and ponderous manner... without a beautiful line about it....so long as it is in view you are painfully conscious that it rests heavily on its ugly legs....Was ever such a hotch-potch devised since Adam delved and Eve span! Of all forms of furniture invented by man it takes the palm for obtrusive lack of adaptability."

At this stage Mr Runciman was just getting into his stride with his analysis of the grand. The piano was, he declared, "a masterpiece of ugliness". As for the cottage piano, "there seems no more possibility of making it elegant than there is of making a household pet of an elephant."

What Mr Runciman advocated was "first, a smaller piano".

Size, size, size....when some designers looked at a piano then, like the tormented Mr Runciman, they kept seeing an elephant.

Main Sources

Serious scholars may scoff and mutter about "Coffee Table books" but, for amateurs like myself who are interested in the Design aspect, I consider by far the best introduction to the subject is David Crombie's "Piano", published by Balafon in 1995. It is, by a country mile, the best illustrated book of any kind I have seen on the subject and thus one may study the forms of these instruments. You also get from Mr Crombie a popular, potted version of the facts, the author being either a master of the brief resume or having (as most of us did) a good sub behind him. So far as I can tell he has a grasp of both the facts and the big picture.

As far as the decorative aspects of the piano case are concerned no study of British design in this area should begin without reading the various articles of a handful of pioneers. Chief among these is a contemporary, Michael I. Wilson of the Victoria and Albert Museum but articles were published in 1901 by both Aymer Vallance and Hugh B. Philpott; in 1907 by William Dale; and in 1911 by Kathleen Purcell.

For those who wish to look at piano history there are acknowledged classics in the field, such as Rosamond E.M. Harding's "The Pianoforte: Its History Traced to the Great Exhibition of 1851", published by Cambridge University Press, in 1933 (2nd revised ed. 1978) but, inevitably, outdistanced by later research.

In my layman's judgement, so far as published books are concerned, the best of the fact finders and probably the best modern piano historian, is Michael Cole, author of "The Pianoforte in the Classical Era", published Clarendon Press, 1998, although it concentrates on the early piano. And Mr Cole has just written another book that will become a standard, "Broadwood Square Pianos" pub Tatchley Books, 2005. Original research in ancient documents, combined with intense study of the actual instruments, is Mr Cole's forte.

Although it centres mainly on his own collection, C.F. Colt's book "The Early Piano", published by Stainer and Bell in 1981, is superbly illustrated; wise and knowledgeable; and redolent of a deep learning and love of the instrument.

However, of books on the piano there is no end and there are other serious general histories: Cyril Ehrlich, "The Piano", published by J.M. Dent, 1976; Edwin M. Good, "Giraffes, Black Dragons and other Pianos", published Stanford University Press, 1982; and many others.

"The Cambridge Companion to the Piano", Edited by David Rowland, published Cambridge University Press, 1998, comes at it from a slightly different angle. So does the "Encyclopedia of the Piano", Edited by Robert Palmieri, published Garland, 1996, which has known scholars among the contributors.

A more popular but very readable version is "The Piano: Its Story from Zither to Grand", published in 1976 by Robert Hale. It was written by David S. Grover, a gentleman who has given me kind help as I blundered my way onwards.

A book which particularly appeals to me, not least because of its quirky, opinionated style and unconventional path, is Arthur Loesser's "Men, Women and Pianos: A Social History", re-published by Dover in 1990.

Casting a wider net but well illustrated is Franz Josef Hirt's "Stringed Keyboard Instruments", first published in Switzerland in 1955 as "Masterwerke Des Klavierbaus" but subsequently reprinted.

Another author who made an immense contribution is David Wainwright, whose history of one firm, "Broadwood by Appointment", published Quiller, 1982, is now fervently sought, rarely found and offered at sums many, many times its original cover price. It casts light on much outside of the Broadwood firm. Mr Wainwright also wrote a pioneering work, "The Piano Makers", published by Hutchinson in 1975.

If you wish to delve in detail then there is a work of head-shaking ambition, Martha Novak Clinkscale's two volumes on "Makers of the Piano", published Oxford University Press, 1995 and 1999, in which she sets out to try and record every surviving piano up to 1860 and give potted biographies of many of the makers.

Drawings reproduced by courtesy of Sir John Soane's Museum, London.

These two drawings of square pianos, made by the architect Robert Adam in 1774, are the earliest British piano designs the author has been able to trace. Plate No.25.

The Rise and Slow Decline of The British Piano

Chapter Two

After a number of years spent at the Library and Museum coal faces, braving the dangers of fierce custodians, clouds of dust mites, vending machine coffee (don't even ask about the sandwiches) and haunted figures searching for the Secret of the Universe, I must report that the earliest piano design I have been able to trace is by Robert Adam in 1774.

I do not say that this was the first—merely that this is the earliest I can prove. Since Zumpe had virtually invented the British piano industry in the mid-1760s, it leaves but a small time frame for other Designers to have beaten Adam to the drawing board.

Of course, it depends what you mean by a design. Does one consider that Zumpe, who I think must have been responsible for the look of his square piano cases, was a Designer? If so, I have been unable to find any cabinet maker's drawings by him, or the merest sketch.

No, if proof is the measure, and it is certainly what I demand, then Adam is your man and you will find his original piano designs still among the vast treasure trove of his work in Sir John Soane's Museum in Lincoln's Inn Fields, London, where they hold almost 9,000 of his drawings.

In fact Adam produced two alternative ideas for square pianos for Catherine the Great, Empress of Russia and these were evidently made around the same time as his much-reproduced harpsichord design for the Empress.

That it should be Adam who is the first known British piano designer might almost be expected. Robert Adam was unquestionably one of the greatest of our 18th Century architects, a potent force whose influence spread far beyond architecture into other areas of design, especially furniture.

As is immediately evident, Adam's two piano designs mirror the known ideas of the man who invented his own Neo-Classical style of decoration, a light and elegant amalgamation of all the influences he had absorbed on The Grand Tour. Though it was not without its critics, being dismissed by Horace Walpole in a famous putdown as "Gingerbread and sippets of embroidery".

Where the form of these pianos is concerned I am reminded of the side tables that you might see in the aristocratic houses that Adam furnished and the decoration is typical Adam—Classical female figures set in ovals, two of them with musical allusions, and the usual motifs that were part of the Adam lexicon.

What the designs also demonstrate is the gulf between the utilitarian Puritanism of Early Zumpe and the work of the professional Designer. No-one could ever confuse the two.

As the Late 18th Century drew towards its close the emphasis in the design of square pianos (far more than with the grand piano) turned more and more emphatically towards the sort of Neo-Classicism pioneered by Robert Adam.

What I have been quite unable to discover is the degree to which Robert Adam himself influenced the makers of other piano cases at this time. Did they see, or know of, his Neo-Classical designs for the Empress of Russia? I can offer no opinion.

What we can say is that Robert Adam signalled the entry of professional designers into the making of piano cases. It took many years but, as the 19th Century progressed, these professionals became more and more a force within the industry.

The English Square on the Continent

"The Gore family with George, 3rd Earl Cowper", by Zoffany.
Plate No.26.

Photo by courtesy of The Yale Center for British Art (Paul Mellon Collection)

Ignore the magic of the Master's brush. Take your eyes off this compelling cast of characters. Do not be side-tracked by the style of the day, their evident enjoyment in each other's company or this freeze-frame of the cultured life of a distant age. Especially do not, as I did, strive foolishly to work out what book she must have been reading.

Instead, treat this as you would a piece of modern forensic evidence. In that case the conclusion is inescapable: From a more or less standing start, c.1766, the humble square piano had, by c.1775, already inserted itself into the highest echelons of society.

Here, before your very eyes, is incontestable evidence of the rise and rise of the piano. Before the 18th century's end it had, proof positive of Darwinism, brutally dispatched the harpsichord and the clavichord, pushing them to the marginal care of amusing eccentrics and elitists.

From London to the far reaches of Empire the piano was to become the people's choice. How it could happen with such speed at a time when there was no television, radio or mass circulation papers, and advertising was in its infancy, is baffling. Madison Avenue would give (someone else's) blood for the secret.

This sumptuous conversation piece was the work of a man, the German-born Baron Johann Joseph Zoffany (1733-1810), who rose in British estimation but, you feel, never quite as highly as he should have done. The natives granted him naturalisation but revealed parochialism in placing him below Gainsborough, Reynolds and Romney.

You could say that it is hard to recall any other painter to whom the early British Theatre owed more, with his series of (themselves theatrical) canvases of David Garrick and his rivals strutting their stuff across the Georgian stage. Then there was the picture that created a sensation, "Life Class at the Royal Academy", in reality a group portrait of the founder members (of whom he himself was one, being personally nominated by the King). Or his acknowledged masterpiece "The Tribuna of the Uffizi", demonstrating the artistic treasures to be found there.

For more earthy tastes there is "Colonel Mordaunt's Cock Match", one of a revelatory group of life in India. Or, a personal favourite of mine, "Charles Townley's Library in Park Street". In idle moments you may wonder what other treasures might not have been brought back if the well-travelled Zoffany had, as at first planned, gone with Captain Cook round the World.

But Zoffany's strength, I feel, was the conversation pieces, of which the work illustrated here, "The Gore Family with George, 3rd Earl Cowper", is an example supreme. What Zoffany brought to the conversation piece was a new intimacy and informality. You have the slightly uncomfortable feeling that you should have apologised for entering the room uninvited.

Earl Cowper (1738-1789) was one of those English gentlemen who went on the grand tour....and stayed away for 30 years. He was able to defy his family and home-grown responsibilities by inheriting a bountiful British fortune which he spent on an Italian life style that centred round music, science, art and the good life. His hours were taken up by such endeavours as finding suitable singers for the Italian Opera in London.

When he did show his face in London eventually he fell under the merciless pen of Horace Walpole who wrote "I was curious to see an English Earl....who is more proud of a Pinchbeck Principality and a paltry order from Wirtemberg than he was of being a peer of Great Britain when Britain was something....He answered very well to my idea, for I should have taken his Highness for a Doge of Genoa; he has the awkward dignity of a temporary representative of temporal power".

This was a sideswipe at Cowper having finagled himself the titles "Prince of the Holy Roman Empire" and "Knight of the Order of St Hubert of Bavaria".

Ouch, as they say. If he suffered the Walpole put-down then, at least, Zoffany granted Earl Cowper a slice of immortality. This great painting, now in the care of an institution to which Britain owes much, The Yale Center for British Art, is given a date of c.1775, during Zoffany's stay in Italy to carry out the Uffizi commission for Queen Caroline.

It is always said that the Yale painting of Earl Cowper was "probably commissioned by the Gore family" to celebrate the marriage of one of their daughters to the Earl, a wedding which took place in 1775. The painting on the wall, behind the bride, is suggested to be a humorous allusion to the quashing of old love affairs, showing Hercules beating and expelling the figure of

Calumny from an allegorical wedding ceremony.

But of central interest for the purposes of this book is the piano, without question an English square. It is being played by another of the Gore daughters, Emilie, and a leading authority suggests that the piano shown was "most likely" by Zumpe but whether it was indeed by him, or by one of his imitators, it could not have made its way to Italy without Zumpe's pioneering work.

From Zumpe alone came the impetus which propelled this modest piano into a society setting. And the style of the case is determinedly Early Zumpe: plain, Puritan and uncompromising in its utilitarian approach.

Zumpe had laid the foundations c.1766 and the piano was about to take over the musical world.

The English Square in India

"Col. Blair with his Family", credited to Zoffany. Plate No.27. *Courtesy of Sotheby's of New Bond Street, London*

Where Empire reached, so did the Square Piano.

The highly portable square must have looked particularly appealing when Kipling, who trudged so many Indian mountains, complained in verse: "You couldn't pack a Broadwood half a mile; You mustn't leave a fiddle in the damp".

Harpsichords were shipped to India, certainly by the 1760s and, at the same time, an Harmonic Society was formed in Calcutta, to be followed closely by The Catch Club. In this latter gathering of 25 members, with a permanent waiting list of never less than 50, they heard formal concerts, followed by the singing of catches, glees and solos.

This was the transplanted, exotic society that the artist Johann Joseph Zoffany entered when he landed at Calcutta on September 15th., 1783. Depending on which version you accept, his journey was necessary because the Royal family were highly displeased that he had (for private payment) chosen to introduce various Englishmen into their commission intended to show the glories of "The Tribuna of the Uffizi"; or he had grossly offended by portraying the Queen in too close a proximity to a supposed lover; or he was simply out of fashion after years absent from London and took William Hodges' advice that there were lakhs of rupees to be made from Indian Rajas and Nawabs.

At any rate, it was in Asia that Zoffany made his fortune, being introduced as "without dispute the greatest Painter that ever visited India". This painting of 1786, "Col. Blair with his family and an Ayah in an interior" provides us with a glimpse of the Blairs' domestic life and a record of the inexorable march of the square piano, here being played by their elder daughter. A number of authorities state that Zoffany was the artist, the painting being in a loan exhibition at the Royal Academy in 1885; reproduced in a standard reference work; and "by descent" in the Blair family.

Col. Blair was in the Bengal Army from 1768 to 1788 and was appointed Governor of Chunar Fort c.1780. The painting is said to have been made in Cawnpore, so the square had indeed travelled far since its introduction by Zumpe. Expert opinion is that it was either a Pohlmann or a Zumpe.

In a splendid article by Raymond Head in "Early Music", he showed that a lady named Margaret Fowke had written from Calcutta in August, 1783, mentioning that a friend had a fine piano and she herself also had a piano: "Its tone is very pleasing, but soft".

At a sale in the city in July, 1784, "Pianofortes with Organs underneath" were advertised and later the same year a Mr Bondfield was offering "Forte-Pianos" and other instruments.

In May, 1786, Calcutta saw the first performance of "Messiah" and by 1785-90 enough musicians, repairers and tuners had arrived to form The Calcutta Band. An important impetus to the spread of the piano in India must have been the establishment in 1786 of a branch of the famous London firm of Longman and Broderip, who sent out Mr Mann and Mr Russell to open a music shop in Loll Bazaar.

Zoffany's conversation piece proves that the piano had already established itself in other parts of India even by 1786.

....and Piano makers join the Raj

The importance eventually to be attached to the Indian market by British piano makers can be readily gauged by this highly fanciful depiction of an Indian dignity shown in his imaginary home, complete with upright piano by the advertisers, Wood & Co....plus dangerously exotic tiger skin rug.

WOOD & CO.

HIGH-CLASS PIANOS FOR INDIA, HOME, AND COLONIES.
3, RATHBONE PLACE, LONDON, W.
CORRESPONDENCE INVITED.

Plate No.28.

What associations such rugs had for Edwardians one hardly dare ask when they produced couplets like "How would you like to sin, With Elinor Glyn, On a tiger skin".

But note that, proof of the power of money at a time when racism had replaced the relaxed attitudes of the early Raj, it is the Indian *lady* who is shown at the piano. The advert was published in "The Piano, Organ and Music Trades Journal", Nov 1st., 1890.

It should not be imagined that the policy of Wood & Co. was an isolated example. Cramer & Co., to mention but one, marketed another upright, "The Indian Pianette", in mahogany for 35 guineas, which they claimed as "The most portable Pianoforte yet made...May be sent to any climate with perfect safety".

The Most Important 18th Century Art Grand

Photo by courtesy of The Museum of Fine Arts, Boston

The Don Godoy grand piano designed by Thomas Sheraton and now in the well known Collection of the Boston Museum of Fine Arts. Plate No.29.

Looked at purely in terms of the Art Piano, I have no doubt that the most important British grand piano of the 18th Century was the Don Godoy "Wedgwood" grand made by Broadwood in 1796 for Don Manuel de Godoy.

At a time when most British grand pianos were decorated with restraint, usually just panels of mahogany outlined with inlay, the Don Godoy grand was exuberant—a case of satinwood, ornamented with different woods and water gilt mouldings, garnished overall with a medley of Wedgwood cameos and Tassie medallions.

Thanks to the scholarly work of Mr John Koster, we know that there were a total of 99 small pieces of Wedgwood on the exterior "like jewels in a crown" and, additionally, large medallions of white-on-blue jasperware in the centre of each panel.

One of these is of particular interest being the well known abolitionist piece designed by Josiah Wedgwood himself and modelled by William Hackwood.

Above the keyboard were 11 coin casts by the sculptor James Tassie, the white casts matching the ivory colouring of the keys.

This scheme was further embellished with the coat of arms and an oil portrait by Taylor of Don Godoy himself (known as "The Prince of Peace" but still remembered in England a century later as "that undesirable Spanish political scoundrel Godoy").

Around the sides were a number of lozenge-style decorative panels with concave sides, the contrasting veneers under a band of purpleheart wood. The top was decorated with circular panels.

As is evident, money was little concern in this exercise. The eventual cost was £257 4s 6d which now sounds derisory but, £ for £, was one of the most expensive instruments ever made by Broadwood, it has been suggested.

Over and above its decorative appeal, however, the Don Godoy grand, now in

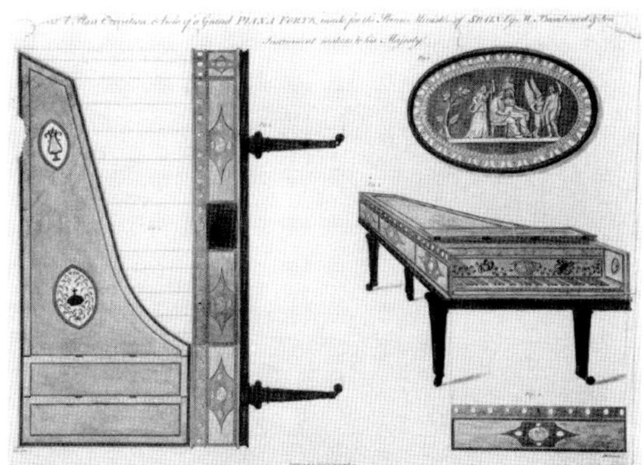

Thomas Sheraton's only provable furniture commission—his design for the 1796 Don Godoy grand, shown here by courtesey of The Museum of Fine Arts, Boston. Plate No.30.

The Museum of Fine Arts, Boston, has a still greater historical importance. It is the only provable commission of Thomas Sheraton, author of those historical works the "Cabinet-Makers' and Upholsterers' Drawing-Book", published in parts between 1791 and 1794; the "Cabinet Dictionary" of 1803; and, in 1805, a year before his death, the single volume of his projected "Cabinet-Maker, Upholsterer, and General Artists' Encyclopaedia".

There must have been many other Sheraton commissions ("makes designs for Cabinet-makers" said his trade card) but these have never been identified. By odd coincidence it was always folk history within Broadwood, the firm that made the Don Godoy grand, that Sheraton had provided various pieces of furniture for their London headquarters.

Evidently inspired by the Godoy instrument there were at least two further grands made by Broadwood which employed Wedgwood pottery decoration but neither was as ambitious as the Godoy piano.

Launch of "Piano-Forte Magazine", 1797

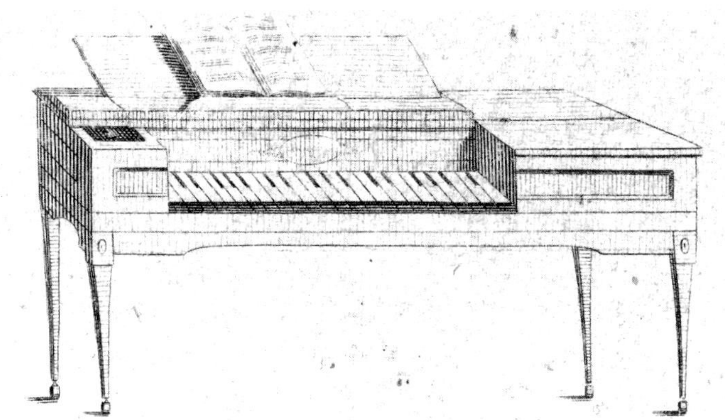

Illustration from The "Piano-Forte Magazine". Plate No.31.

Nothing could have bespoken more evidently the rise of the piano and the forthcoming demise of the harpsichord than the launch, in 1797, of the "Piano-Forte Magazine".

In May of that year an advertising flyer announced that "On Saturday next, May 6th., 1797, will be published, (price two shillings and six-pence) number 1. (To be continued weekly till completed) of the Piano-Forte Magazine…."

To give it the full title it was "The Piano-forte magazine; or, compleat and elegant library of ancient and modern musick". As the title suggests, each volume consists of a compilation of music for piano, and voice and piano, as I was told by Ms Amelie Roper, Curator of The Music Collections of The British Library, who kindly gave me the bibliographical background.

For those of us interested in the design of the case the most interesting part of this journal was the illustration they chose for the title page which depicts a square piano and one obviously designed in the new Neo-Classical manner with tapered legs and, presumably, "French frame" for the stand.

Ms Roper told me: "It seems that regular subscribers could collect tokens included with the periodical in order to receive a free 'specimen instrument'. I believe that the illustration (which is also on the advertising flyer) is a depiction of the instrument that would be on offer. One of the tokens is included with the flyer in volume 1, and is signed in ink 'Harrison and Co'."

A Satirical Genius adopts the Piano

"Ars-musica", by Gillray. Plate No.32 *Illustration by courtesy of The National Portrait Gallery*

The piano has always been fortunate in its painters....Zoffany, Renoir, Holman Hunt, Whistler, Lavery, even Salvador Dali. The list would be a very long one.

But the Early British Piano attracted a man like no other. He was described by a German literary and arts review "London und Paris" as "the foremost living artist in his genre" but I suspect that if I sat you down with all the many volumes of Bryan's, the Benezit and Thieme-Becker you would still have a hard job deciding who they meant.

He was James Gillray, the etcher with the acid who, despite a respectful nod to Hogarth, is rightly considered the founder of a school of British caricaturists and satirists who gave us, in modern times, such as David Low, Philip Zec, Vicky, Ralph Steadman and, even more true to the blood, Gerald Scarfe and Steve Bell.

Gillray (1757-1815) was born at Chelsea into that most evangelical, austere and good body of folk The Moravians, who believed in literacy (to read The Bible), noble and upright conduct, and the suppression of sin in all its forms.

I found one old account that claimed: "In the Brethren's Church there were no dice makers, no actors, no painters, no professional musicians, no wizards or seers, no alchemists, no astrologers, no courtesans or panderers."

How true this was I know not but Gillray, educated in The Moravian Academy at Bedford, still managed to become an artist, a hard drinker and a man interested in music. In mitigation one may say that he at least managed to give the sinners a foretaste of hell.

Exactly where Gillray developed his musical interest, or whether he simply saw musicians as pictorial fodder, is a matter for guesswork but the evidence is to be seen in many of his prints, such as "Ancient Music" of 1787 in which he ridicules George III's passion for Handel and olden music.

Gillray includes in the orchestra a pig whose tail has been tweaked; two unhappy schoolboys who are being used as kettledrums; a gang of fishwives; two howling cats hung up by their tails; and William Pitt piping up on a whistle!

The earliest depiction I can find of a piano in Gillray's work is in "A County

Concert—or an evening's entertainment in Sussex", published in September, 1798, in which the pianist is said to have been the singer Mrs Billington who, in the absence of her husband, had entered into a notorious affair with the Duke of Sussex.

The print shown here, "Ars-musica", published on February 16th., 1800, places a square piano in centre stage, the instrument sitting on a Zumpe-style stand, though an expert tells me it is incorrect to show the pianist in this position as it would make it a "left-handed" piano. It appears, very unusually, to have a broad band of inlay round the back of the case, which would be a sign of a quality maker.

One cannot say that this print is as notable as later musical satires in which he features a piano, such as "The Pic-nic Orchestra", "Matrimonial Harmonics", or "Farmer Giles" but it is not without its charm.

"Ars-musica", a hand-coloured etching and aquatint to be found in the National Portrait Gallery, appears to be a straight-forward social parody and if there are any political overtones I must confess they are lost on me.

It depicts a grinning, wildly enthusiastic woman pianist pounding away solo while two furious old fellows, one a violinist and the other a cellist, sit helplessly on either side, apparently waiting to see if they will ever get a chance to join in. The lady's feet rest against the bottom bar but an unhappy dog (there was usually an unappreciative dog in musical caricatures), evidently unconvinced, threatens to nip her ankles.

I have seen it suggested that "Ars-musica" was, in fact, based on the design of an amateur who also supplied sporting subjects for Gillray. As supporting evidence we are directed to study a hieroglyph in the corner of the plate.

However that may be, Gillray went on to use "Ars-musica" as the basis for a far more ambitious print which he called "Playing in Parts". Published in 1801 this showed a much expanded group of amateur players, seven in total but with the lady pianist still the dominating figure. She now seems distinctly threatening and the others try anxiously to keep up with her furious attack.

During his career, Gillray produced over 1,000 prints (one source suggests over 1,500) and left us an alternative, illustrated history of his times. That included a recognition of the growing importance of the piano to music making.

"Playing in Parts", 1801, by Gillray. Plate No.33.

The Countess pianist of the Pic-nic Orchestra

"The Pic-nic Orchestra" by Gillray. Plate No.34. *Illustration by courtesy of Princeton University Library*

Good Lord! I don't like the impudent look of that small fellow! And what on earth is he about to do with that sharp looking bow? Tut, tut, this must be the musical entertainment of some rather low and coarse tavern.

But, as you might expect when James Gillray was having his fun, it was quite the reverse. The victims of Gillray's wicked sally were the very highest in the land, the titled dilettanti of The Pic-nic Society, who all fancied themselves as either musicians, stage performers, or the like.

What we have here is "The Pic-nic Orchestra", shown in all their amateur and satirical glory on April 23rd., 1802. How well any of them could really play an instrument I know not but it was an age in which musical accomplishments were a desirable asset for the well educated.

The Pic-nic Society had been founded in the Spring of 1802 and was unapologetically elitist and exclusive. It existed to perform "farces and burlettas….relieved with feasts and ridottos and a variety of other entertainments"—in the early years at an establishment called The Tottenham Rooms off Tottenham Court Road, London.

According to the "Reminiscences" of Henry Angelo the fencing master: "Here, some descendant from the great and mighty baron of old, instead of being cased in armour, drew forth the fiddle-case….a giant lord warbled on the tiny flute, and a tiny lordling thundered on the double-bass."

If I have worked it out correctly the cheeky chappie with the bow in Gillray's caricature was meant to be no less a one than Richard Edgcumbe, 2nd Earl of Mount Edgcumbe, writer of an opera, "Zenobia", that lasted for all of one night and a rather more successful book, "Musical Reminiscences of an Old Amateur". The Earl, well known for his gift for mimicry, was an enthusiastic layman of both music and stage.

The fellow with the flute and the superior air (facial grimace, rather than musical form) is probably George James Cholmondeley, 1st Marquess Cholmondeley and you might wear a look just like that if you had had the good fortune to inherit a piece of property heaven—the flamboyant Palladian mansion Houghton Hall, home of the Walpoles.

The Marquess was a close friend of the Prince of Wales and kept as mistress the notorious courtesan Grace Dalrymple Elliott. Leading to some confusion when, a daughter subsequently appearing, the Prince claimed that it was HE who was the father.

The violinist is thought to be one of the co-founders of The Pic-nic Society, Colonel Henry Francis Greville of The Guards and the gallant Enniskillens who, if I have it right, was the son of the Fulke Greville who wrote the well-received "Maxims and Characters" in 1756, rather than Fulke Greville the diarist.

From the Colonel's pocket dangles a paper "Pic Nic Concert—Imitations—Nightingale by Lord C.—Tom Tit Lord ME.—Jack daw Genl G.—Screech Owl Lady B.—Poll Parrot…."

When the Society came under attack the Colonel, who was also its Secretary, hurriedly launched his own newspaper, "The Pic Nic"— a wise military stratagem with enemies like Richard Brinsley Sheridan and James Gillray.

But the ladies, ah the ladies. I say, with much confidence, that they don't make 'em like that any more.

The tally-ho matron with the horn is Mary Amelia, the Marchioness of Salisbury (shown in somewhat less glamorous profile than her elegant Reynolds portrait of 1787) and the pose is a double-edged joke.

The Marchioness was not only a political hostess and dabbler in the arts ("pretty, witty, intelligent and outspoken") she was also a renowned sportswoman, excelling as an archer but, above all, fearless on the hunting field.

She took over the mastership of the Hertfordshire hounds from her husband in 1793 and habitually led the field in her sky-blue habit with black collar and hunting cap. Slight in build she could still, in her 70s, yet exhaust people half her age and, at 78 and with her eyesight failing, she made them tie her to a horse.

You get some glimpse of her energy and vitality from the account of her, in old age, driving her own phaeton 20 miles, drawn by four tasselled horses. Or mounting her own steed "like an arrow from the hand of her groom, the horse being an uncommonly high one, milk white".

But Gillray allows only one person to dominate this picture: A lady of, how does one put it, broad appeal. This is the pianist, the well blessed Albinia, Countess of Buckinghamshire, and Gillray puts her forward with relish.

A man evidently entranced as by the sight of a mighty, rotund monument; a somnambulant; or perhaps simply in love: Gillray returned to Albinia time after time in his cartoons. Just like another great artist, Edward Burne-Jones (not the wraith-like sylphs of his publicly exhibited paintings but the jolly, bulging femmes of his private caricatures) Gillray, a lifelong bachelor, seems to have had a thing about pneumatic and callipygous ladies.

By my count Albinia appears in at least 14 Gillray satires, a number of them concerning The Pic-nic Society. But, most wittily, she features in a geometric joke, "A sphere projecting against a plane", in which she is drawn as perfectly spherical, overwhelming a stick-like William Pitt; and as a plum-duff shaped milk maid in "Enter Cowslip with a bowl of cream", an allusion to her best known role as Cowslip in O'Keefe's "The Agreeable Surprise" .

Gillray was not the only caricaturist intoxicated by Albinia's charms. Dr George notes that there were 52 references to her in satires between 1784 and 1804.

And the lady's largesse appealed to a surprising number of men. Another evident admirer Angelo, a fellow Pic-nicker, describes how "The gorgeous Lady Albina's dimpled fingers pressed the ivory keys of the grand piano".

As Angelo delicately put it: "Lady Albina…. 'mighty mover' of festive fame, was the nucleus of such a circle as the annals of fashion cannot match. The love of society grew with her growth, which fructified in the rich soil of fêtes and banqueting, until she was the model of carnation to another Rubens; her ladyship indubitably shining the greatest star in the hemisphere of fashion."

In reality, Albinia must have been a trifle rotund (a contemporary likened her as to a beefsteak) but then, all her appetites were large.

She was, infamously, a female gamester and one of the principals of the Faro scandal of 1797 when, with Lady Elizabeth Luttrell and others, she was fined £50 for boosting her fortunes by promoting illicit gambling. Gillray, naturally, had her as the central figure in "Exaltation of Faro's daughters" and again in "The loss of the faro bank; or—the rook's pigeon'd".

It was said that in London there were six ladies' gambling houses.

Matters reached such a point that the Chief Justice, Lord Kenyon, threatened to put such feminine aristos in the stocks, a punishment usually reserved for the common class of women who were whores or brothel keepers. So Gillray followed up with yet another portrayal of Albinia, this time stripped to the waist and tied to a cart, being whipped by an altogether too enthusiastic Lord Keynon, such punishment being an alternative open under the Act.

Long before these events Albinia had already become known to the public prints when, in 1784, she entered the political cockpit. She took to the hustings as a supporter of one of the candidates in the no-holds-barred Westminster election, pitting herself against a prominent backer of the other side, that most beautiful and accident-prone of women Georgiana, Duchess of Devonshire (another female gamester who accumulated debts of £62,000 as a result of her reckless gambling).

If hard words were then exchanged it did not prevent social amities, since after Albinia became one of the co-founders of The Pic-nic Society, Georgiana became a Patron.

Albinia had for many years had a long-standing contact with the Arts since her husband George, the 3rd Earl, was, prior to his elevation, manager of an opera house, the King's Theatre, bringing the castrato Gaetano Guadagni to London and the French dancer Anne-Frédérique Heinel.

The Buckinghamshires home at Ham was named "Sans-Souci", in reflection of and homage to that other intoxicated music lover, Frederick the Great and it was in Surrey (and at their country home, Nocton Hall in Lincolnshire) that Albinia and her daughters staged amateur entertainments of their own in which, naturally, they were the stars.

A magical insight into an evening with Albinia comes in the account of a Persian traveller who, in 1810, noticed "groups of sunny-faced girls and houri-like ladies chatting together, their beauty illuminated by candlelight".

Mirza Abul Hasan Ilchi talked to a "rare beauty", "another fairy creature" and a young "girl of noble birth" who reminded him of an ancient quatrain:

"Like a rosebud your ruby lips but when did a rosebud talk?"

But Albinia's am-drams sound like mild stuff—aristos trying to pretend they could tread the boards.

Unfortunately for them, it provoked the vituperation of a true professional and a dangerous one at that, Richard Brinsley Sheridan, author of "The School for Scandal" and regarded as the wittiest man of the age.

For some bizarre reason Sheridan, who had himself run The Drury Lane Theatre from 1776, seemed to see The Pic-nic Society as a threat, one which might lure away the wealthy or the socially ambitious.

An M.P. (courtesy of votes bought at five guineas a time) and as much a politician as dramatist, Sheridan launched the most poisonous attacks on the Society, resulting in another Gillray satire, "The Manager in Despair", with Sheridan shown holding a dagger and declaiming "Say am I doomed to see Pic-Nic succeed, and my Paragraphs prove vain?"

The playwright went so far as to accuse the Pic-nickers of "licentious and immoral behaviour" and this proved a rallying point for widespread political and Press attacks, particularly in the Post, Chronicle, Herald and Evening Courier. The charge against the Pick-nickers was upper-class decadence. There was talk of "orgies" involving "unblushing matrons of fashion" (guess who!) and condemnation of extravagant productions. I have also seen a suggestion that such theatrics or musical concerts were often, in reality, a cover for illicit gambling.

Into this maelstrom charged Gillray, a man with no need of a bayonet so long as he had his crayon or etching tool. "Blowing up the Pic-Nic's" (showing Albinia and friends assailed by Sheridan, in the role of Harlequin) in April, 1802, was followed by "The Pic-Nic orchestra" in the same month and "Dilettanti-theatricals" in February, 1803 (in which The Prince of Wales is portrayed with two of his mistresses).

Despite the furore, The Pic-nic Society survived the critics and played on, I have been told, until the final curtain came down, around the 1850s.

The Piano's part in Marriage

"Matrimonial Harmonics" by Gillray. Plate No.35 *Illustration by courtesy of New York Public Library*

Just how, you muse, did James Gillray find out about music? After all, a lad born into The Moravians was hardly going to be off to "The Dancin'" on a Saturday night.

It is difficult to guess the answer when his father belonged to a sect that forbade "boys and girls to roam the daisied fields together", or the poor to wear silk, and warned against "staying out at night and frequenting the card-room and the liquor-saloon".

Their reward was to be in "the better land" where "their troubles would vanish like dew before the rising sun". In Gillray's case he would have had need of such a philosophy for he was the only one of five children to survive past the age of ten.

Perhaps it is not surprising that a number of accounts suggest that the greatest and most original caricaturist this nation has produced was shy and melancholic. One of his earliest admirers was forced to write that Gillray was "a stranger to the feelings of friendship....a careless sort of cynic, one who neither loved nor hated society".

A devoted follower and a man better acquainted with Gillray than most, his fellow caricaturist George Cruikshank, said that he was "never admitted to personal familiarity with him".

The 1,000-plus (or 1,500) plates tell their own story of a perpetually industrious artist and we are informed that when etching "he worked furiously". Undoubtedly a life of toil.

So how then to explain his apparent familiarity with musical subjects? I think we may put forward two possible hypotheses.

Perhaps arising from a repressed childhood, there was a startling instance of rebellion on young Gillray's part. The secret came out, in a contemporary account of 1798, because the Germans took a surprisingly intense interest in his work.

A report in "London und Paris" of that year revealed that Gillray had been apprenticed at a very early age to a lettering engraver in Holborn but the work proved tiresome and he "left to join a company of strolling players". This episode seems to have been short-lived and he was back in London by 1775 but it had to be a revelatory shock for a boy brought up in a Moravian household. Surely he must have been exposed to music during this episode.

"Harmony Before Matrimony" by Gillray. Plate No.36. *Illustration by courtesy of New York Public Library*

The second matter provides even harder evidence of a musical connection.

In his early career Gillray worked for quite a number of different publishers and I have found at least two accounts that state, as hard fact, that he was employed for a time in the shop of one William Napier "musician and music publisher".

Napier was a figure of some account in late 18th Century music.

A Scotsman who played the violin in an Edinburgh theatre, he had moved to London by 1765 and became professionally successful. He joined George III's private band; played in the concerts of the Academy of Ancient Music; and was principal viola at Handel commemoration concerts, according to his biography in the "D.N.B."

More importantly, he launched himself as a music publisher by 1772, selling a variety of material from ballad operas (such as "The Maid of the Mill") to dance collections and works for amateurs. In 1784 he established a circulating music library.

Napier is best known, however, for his connection with his friend the composer Joseph Haydn. When Haydn made his first London visit in 1791 he rescued Napier's financial fortunes through the publication of arrangements of popular "Scots Songs" made by the composer. Eventually three such volumes were published by Napier.

It would be fascinating to know precisely what work Gillray carried out for Napier but since one, at least, of the Scot's other volumes had a Bartolozzi frontis, it seems possible Gillray would have been employed in the production of illustrated or decorative title pages.

How could Gillray not have learned something of music while employed by Napier?

Gillray's interest in music, to my eye never resulting in anything as savage as his usual treatment of Kings and politicians, was to be seen again in a pair of prints issued on October 25th., 1805, though some would argue that they demonstrate more a bachelor's jaundiced views on marriage.

The two plates were titled "Harmony before Matrimony" and "Matrimonial Harmonics".

In the first *(see Page 36)* a handsome, love-struck young pair are shown in a duet, the maiden playing a harp while he opens a music book at "Duets de l'Amour". Above the lovers, Cupid fires a blunderbuss at two cooing doves, while on the table is an open copy of "Ovid". In a bowl, two goldfish swim towards each other; on the mat two cats play amorously; a butterfly floats towards its own reflection in the mirror; carvings alongside Cupid show his bow and arrows and the crossed torches of Hymen. All is watched by a grinning satyr on cloven hoof.

"Matrimonial Harmonics" *(see Page 35)* tells us the sad outcome and Dr George gives us an understanding of the graphic details.

Now the married woman has acquired a handsome piano (note the panelled sides) at which she pounds and screeches, but the music is open at "Torture Fiery Rage; Despair I cannot, can not bear". Lying on the piano is another piece of music, "Separation, a Finale for Two Voices with Accompaniment". The music on the floor is "The Wedding Ring—a Dirge".

The wife's features are contorted and the tough-looking nurse enters holding the squalling baby and swinging a watchman's rattle. On the sofa the cat hisses and arches its back, while the dog barks a protest.

The book resting on the chair is "The Art of Tormenting", showing a picture of a cat playing with a mouse. The urn on the table is about to boil over and a bottle of Holland's gin is set by the woman's place.

The thermometer on the wall has the temperature fast falling to freezing; and the bust of Hymen near the door has a broken nose. Cupid is by now fast asleep on the mantel under a weeping willow, the arrows falling from his quiver. The two vases alongside having twisted snakes as handles. Two birds are caged together but angrily turn their backs while their offspring, above, are ignored.

In the middle of all this the husband sits in painful isolation, his hand jammed to his ear to keep out the sound. No longer a slim, debonair figure but with fat, frowning features, he tries to ignore all and concentrate on his copy of the "Sporting Calendar".

Surely there can never have been a marital scene such as this?

Since he was a life-long bachelor it might be assumed that Gillray had as fleeting a knowledge of domestic felicities as he did of music but, again, there is a surprise.

The credit lines on both the "Matrimonial" plates disclose that his publisher was a lady named Hannah Humphrey of St. James's Street, London and behind this fact there is another story.

Gillray lived much of his adult life as a lodger with Hannah Humphrey and there are stories that they once planned to wed but that he called it off at the very Church door. Whether there is a word of truth in this I know not but others maintain it was a chaste arrangement ("a liaison did not exist") though she was devoted to his care.

What we know is that Gillray went to lodge with Hannah by at least 1793 when she had a print-seller's shop in Old Bond Street and moved with her to New Bond Street and then to St. James's Street. She was said to be 15 to 20 years his senior and there is a portrait of her and her maid in Gillray's "Two-Penny Whist".

One question remains in my mind: Did they have a piano in the house?

A Necessary aid for Social Climbing

"Farmer Giles and his wife shewing off their daughter Betty" by Gillray. Plate No.37.

I have little doubt that when James Gillray drew the square piano shown in this satire he was copying from the real article. It is far too detailed to simply be the creature of his imagination. So specific, in fact, that one historian, David S. Grover, states unhesitatingly "The square piano is by Longman & Broderip".

The odd thing is that the piano Gillray illustrates was already out of date.

This print, "Farmer Giles & his wife shewing *(sic)* off their daughter Betty to their Neighbours on her return from School", was published on January 1st., 1809 and by then fashion had taken a marked swing.

The square drawn by Gillray is instantly recognizable as in the Neo-Classic style which had been at its height in the 1790s. The most obvious characteristic is that it sits on straight legs.

But around 1805-1807 the Regency exerted its overwhelming personality. The most noticeable change was that the legs became turned and, within a short span, the number of legs on the square often increased to six.

One might add that Longman & Broderip went bankrupt in 1798, when the firm was rescued by the eminent pianist Muzio Clementi, the firm continuing to make some superb instruments.

My suspicion is that Gillray was drawing a piano that he knew well, an old friend owned by someone with whom he was closely acquainted. According to Dr George, who studied the original drawing for the plate, Gillray corrected his work and altered the piano's date from "1770" to "18..."

Why does he show the piano in this print?

What Gillray was about was ridiculing the social pretensions of the newly prosperous farming class who were trying to ape the gentry and an essential accompaniment to their new status was, of course, their very own piano. Complete with musically educated daughter.

As usual with Gillray, you must study the detail for the hidden barbs. Betty's alleged sampler, hanging on the wall, bears the quotation "Evil communications Corrupt good Manners" and declares them to live at "Cheese Hall".

One last point must be made.

Gillray's last years were the stuff of horror. His eyesight declined, he suffered a breakdown around 1807, attempted suicide in 1811 and died insane in 1815 despite the devoted care of Hannah Humphrey, his print-seller landlady.

It has been written that after his 1807 collapse "his production continued to decline until in the summer of 1810 he slowly lapsed into insanity".

I think that "Farmer Giles", of 1809, is as fine a social satire as he produced and demonstrates the triumph of a mighty talent over the worst of physical and mental handicaps..

Disguised as a Bookcase

"The Triumph of Music" by Burney. Plate No.38. *Courtesy of The Yale Center for British Art (Paul Mellon Collection)*

One could cover a great many pages considering why "The Glee Club or, The Triumph of Music" is such a very intriguing picture: Where the artist, Edward Francesco Burney, fits into English caricature; what it tells us about Regency society and manners; its lessons for fashion historians; how, and why, Burney chose to show a black man as, presumably, the butler; the triumph of Burney's composition and the hypnotic rhythm he has introduced into the figures, as though two opposing, but equally matched, waves were flowing into the room.

Not just pages but books could (and a number have) been written about the much-blessed Burney family, incandescent with talent.

None of these are our concern. Our eye should go instantly to the central group of figures clustered around what appears at first glance to the layman to be a bookcase. In fact it is an Upright Grand piano and here, as though we were able to look in a mirror of c.1815, we have indisputable proof of what the instrument meant to them and the way in which it was used.

Of particular interest are the meagre shelves, pushed into a cramped space in the top right hand corner, next to the strings. With the aid of a magnifying glass we see that the labels Burney has written for the shelves say "Catches", "Canons", "Glees and Rounds" and we now know for certain that these shelves were always intended for the music sheets the musicians needed.

"Catches" were part-songs for singers to follow each other (a society called The Noblemen's and Gentlemen's Catch Club had been formed in 1761 for similar social gatherings); "Canons" were a musical form in which a single voice introduced the melody, to be then repeated by another voice; and "Glees" were part-songs for male voices (one particularly well known Glee Club was formed in London in 1783 and lasted until 1857).

As to the accuracy or musical insights of "The Glee Club" picture, have no doubts. Burney (1760-1848) was brought up in Worcester and his father was in charge of a school of dancing and music. The family included their uncle, the musicologist Charles

Burney; their cousin, novelist Fanny Burney; Edward's brother Thomas, a "genius for pen-and-ink drawing" who died at 20; and their elder brother Charles Rousseau, a well known harpsichordist.

When this picture *(see Page 39)* was exhibited in the "London, World City, 1800-1840" exhibition at Essen, Germany, in 1992, the catalogue commented that: "By the late 18th Century there were numerous Glee Clubs in London, where gentlemen met to eat, drink and sing English 'glees' or part songs. The degrees of bawdiness in the punning lyrics depended on whether ladies were admitted, though their presence in this watercolour does not entirely exclude risqué material."

The Upright Grand shown here is faithful to the bookcase form introduced by William Stodart on January 12th., 1795 but, since the type was made by other firms such as Broadwood and the Royal maker, Jones, it is difficult to say who was responsible for the example shown by Burney.

According to Arthur Loesser the Upright Grands "remained in good demand until about 1830" and cost 10 to 15 per cent more than the normal horizontal grand. Showing his purist approach to piano design, Mr Loesser observed that such Upright Grands "gave decorators another chance for playing their expensive games".

In Burney's picture (one more jewel in The Yale Collection, to which we British owe so much) we see the two large doors in the upper part that were common in this type. They opened to give immediate access to the strings and book shelves, but the glazed doors were commonly backed by textiles to disguise the interior.

We have no evidence as to whether it was common to place decorative objects on top of such Uprights Grands but Burney here places a bust of "Glorious Apollo", which was, says the catalogue, also the title of a famous glee.

Some similar jest must be intended by the four birds perched alongside but I fear it is lost on me. Again, with the aid of a magnifying glass, we see that the two plinths are inscribed with a verse which holds that the owl (seen on the right) is the fairest.

Oil drips down on the music being played. It is "Life's a Bum per", "a pun on the shape revealed by the pianist's parted tailcoat".

Upright Grands have been criticised, above all, for their height (reaching 9ft 1in); for being top heavy; and for the fact that, if the pianist was also a singer, he or she could not see the audience. But the piano historian Michael Cole says that "there is no doubt in my mind that upright grands were chiefly designed for their extra sound".

An Invitation to the Dance

"Taking Lessons", Richard Dagley. Plate No.39.

Getting inside the mind of the Georgians often seems impossible but occasionally something comes along and you feel: Ah, yes, that is how it must have been. Perhaps more accurately: That is how I would have liked it to have been. This gently humorous print of 1821 by the painter Richard Dagley, who exhibited at the Royal Academy between 1785 and 1833, gives us a glimpse inside the top half of a society of grace and formal manners….and how accepted it had become to have a piano for dancing. Called "Taking Lessons" it reminds us of the age of the Chaine Anglaise, the Ladies Chain, Le Pantalon, the Quadrille and the rest and a time when etiquette was becoming ever more formalised. It was expected that a gentleman would know the way you asked a partner to dance, the correct conversation for dancing, the issuing of calling cards, the latest ballroom fashions. Dagley's plate was one of 26 he did for a book called "Takings; or the life of a collegian" and was published at the very height of the square piano's popularity. But was it meant to show a form of upright square?

Living it up with Corinthian Kate

Illustration by courtesy of Birmingham Central Library

"Gay moments of Logic, Jerry, Tom and Corinthian Kate" by I.R. and G. Cruikshank. Plate No.40.

Wouldn't you just love to have met someone called Corinthian Kate? I did, in my day, know a lady called Shaky Sheila, another with the soubriquet The Duchess (as in Duke Ellington, Count Basie and Sir Charles Thompson) and others picaresquely named but, tragically, never a Corinthian Kate.

Those dull fellows who are prepared to take their eyes off the spirited cavorting of Corinthian Kate will note, as I have been forced to in the search for scholastic truth, that the instrument of choice for the dance was an upright grand: proved by the fact that the pianist has his leg far under the keyboard, so the strings can only start above that point. The doors in the top have been draped with silk in the characteristic, and I suspect French-inspired, manner. The legs are reeded, turned and tapered; the side is embellished; two candles burn in side sconces; and the whole is topped with what I judge to be a scroll pediment.

Around 1821 the upright grand was, we thus learn, a socially acceptable choice for the well-to-do.

The scene demonstrates the style of a Regency man about town, one of The Flash, The Swells, or The Corps of Bucks if you prefer. Few played harder and, if they were in the Beckford mould, were able to "bag a fox in Greek, find a hare in Latin, inspect his kennels in Italian, and direct the economy of his stables in exquisite French". In between, of course, racing a coach in hand to Brighton, or settling a gentleman's differences through "The Noble Science".

The above Plate is from a book by the man who invented that phrase, Pierce Egan the Elder, known to one and all as "Glorious Pierce", the first great sports journalist and thus one who should be venerated by all who practice The Old Black Art. The Victorians had "The Origin of Species" and "Das Kapital" but for the Georgians there was rather more fun with Egan's "Life in London; or, The Day and Night Scenes of Jerry Hawthorn, Esq., and his elegant friend Corinthian Tom, accompanied by Bob Logic, The Oxonian, in their Rambles and Sprees through the Metropolis".

Egan spent his life, with no known regrets, reporting horse racing, prize fights (for which he had a passion and a knowledgeable eye), cock-fights, cricket matches, trials and executions. He satirized the Prince Regent in The Lives of Florizel and Perdita (which didn't prevent "Prinny" insisting that the author was presented at Court) and published a sporting classic, "Boxiana, or Sketches of Modern Pugilism". But his best work and best known was "Life in London", a series of sketches of Regency amusements and life.

I am aware, of course, that the Regency formally ended with George IV's accession on Jan 29th., 1820 but design historians class the Regency period as from c.1805 to 1830 and I do not think anyone could question the Regency flavour of this drawing of Tom and Jerry at play *(shown in the plate on page 41)* .

The "gay" (yes, a word that was the unfortunate victim of a hit-and-run accident) dancing takes place at Corinthian House which the trio visit because Kate wishes Tom to hear "a new song she has recently acquired". Kate, we learn, is excessively fond of music and Logic is welcome because he has "an excellent touch on the pianoforte". Jerry is enlisted for his "merry song".

Kate is a lady who "could sing well—dance elegantly—was a proficient in music—an adept at drawing—a delightful scholar, and the *tout ensemble* completed with the manners of a lady". After tea it is requested that Corinthian Kate and Tom "would have the kindness to perform a waltz….LOGIC struck up a favourite air, when the lascivious dance took place." The Oxonian was anxious to witness the elegant pair and turned round from the pianoforte, "presenting his comical mug to their notice, crying out 'Bravo'."

The fact they are shown dancing a waltz does, of course, convey its own message. The waltz did not reach Britain until 1812-13 and, as Cecil Sharp has pointed out, "the position in which partners were required to engage in the new dance shocked the national sense of propriety and was deemed grossly indecorous".

Or as another writer put it: "The Anti-waltzing party took the alarm, cried it down, mothers forbade it, and every ballroom became a scene of feud and contention….sarcastic remarks flew about, and pasquinades were written to deter young ladies from such a recreation."

Which is not exactly how I remember the waltz at those Old Time Dancing evenings at Deal Drill Hall. Stately as a galleon, was rather more like it.

Egan "wrote nothing so popular as this *(book)*…Indeed, the taste for it amounted to a craze", we are told. Today "Tom and Jerry" is a synonym for engaging in riotous behaviour (should we blame Egan for Lager Louts and The Happy Hour?). It became an alternative name for a low beer hall; the illustrious Transport and General Workers Union (the initials, you understand, for they are renowned for their gentle habits); a modern cocktail; the title of the original Van Beuren cartoons and the later Metro Goldwyn Mayer series (Tom as the cat and Jerry the street-wise mouse); not to mention the original pop name of Simon and Garfunkel.

The artists could not colour the plates fast enough to keep up with the demand for Egan's book. No less than ten theatre productions were based on "Life in London", one of them boasting that it was "Replete with Prime Chaunts, Rum Glees and Kiddy Catches". It was translated into French and, by repute, there were 65 books in imitation. It provided endless material for a Dictionary of Slang. Today it is used by social historians, set designers and Fashion Editors.

I was delighted to find a modern academic who enlightens us that the book "rejoices in the role-playing nature of modern urban existence….is more interested in viewing class society as a repertoire of possibilities….*(and)* can be seen as a truly 'Cockney' text, because of the way in which it re-interprets the insecurity and isolation of the lower middle-class Londoner".

Now why didn't I guess that from the very beginning?

Sadly, not all are admirers.

The respectable Cambridge History says there is not a word of true sport in the book and the remainder "is mainly drinking, gambling, rioting, cock-fighting and other branches of debauchery, either practised or contemplated".

This critic says that the author may have praised Corinthian Tom for his elegance and accomplishment but "he remains the type of polished blackguard, unworthy to associate with his country cousin, Jerry Hawthorn, the cheery fool, to whom he shows 'the pleasures of the town' and only a shade more intolerable than the bestial creature, Bob Logic, who is intended for a model of good-humour and wit".

Those of us who have jived to Ted Heath at the Hammersmith Palais, smooched all night at The Flamingo and haunted various illegal "drinkers" in Soho, Bayswater, Notting Hill and The Bush, must hang our head in shame along with Corinthian Tom. And as for the journalists of The Press Club, the Wig and Pen and The Stab in the Back (and like haunts in Manchester, Liverpool and Glasgow) their doings are too terrible to contemplate.

Still, as W.T. Moncrieff said when he defended Egan, "Any age is better than the age of cant".

For every distinguished academic of the Cambridge History who mounts the pulpit I do not doubt you will find many a hundred who take a different view. For myself, I think that one of the book's greatest merits is that Egan was one of the first authors to write about real life, with insights into many ordinary people outside of Corinthian Tom and his friends. "Telling it like it is" would, I understand, be the appropriate modern expression.

Not only Egan's words made an impression. So did the coloured illustrations. Many years later Thackeray (no mean artist himself) went back to the British Museum to re-read "London Life" and wrote: "The pictures! – oh! The pictures are noble still!....and now we are at a private party, at which Corinthian Tom is waltzing (and very gracefully too, as you must confess) with Corinthian Kate, whilst Bob Logic, the Oxonian, is playing on the piano!"

This drawing of Corinthian Kate also remained in the mind of Rudyard Kipling. When he published an account of his 1889 travels he wrote: "I thought of the Oxonian in Tom and Jerry playing jigs....you have seen the old-fashioned plate?....while Corinthian Tom and Corinthian Kate danced a stately saraband in a little carpeted room."

I think I'd rather be in the company of Rudyard Kipling than the critics any day.

What of the artists responsible for this remarkable Plate, so alive with the high spirits of the Regency? The credit, as you will see, is to the brothers Isaac Robert and George Cruikshank and the critical judgement has been that it is among their finest work.

I would very much like to think that George Cruikshank (1792-1878) worked on this aquatint because he is generally considered to be Gillray's heir and the finest caricaturist of the Regency. But there is a snag. The authorship of this delightful caricature is unclear.

In the late 1840s George, wise man, saw the evil of his ways, foreswore the demon drink and became one of the most passionate campaigners of the Temperance movement (as my Grandfather carried the banner for the Salvation Army, my mother was a Primitive Methodist and I had to sign The Pledge before the age of ten, I quite understand).

One can see that a book like Egan's would then have been, well....a touch embarrassing. George declared that he had always had much doubt about the morality of Egan's book and, accordingly, had left two-thirds of the illustrative work to Isaac.

So was George hiding his light under a Temperance bushel? Or was this particular illustration all the work of Isaac Robert?

P.S.: You may wonder why the lady was called Corinthian Kate. The excellent Dr Brewer informs me that a Corinthian was a "fast man" and that to Corinthianize was "to live an idle, dissipated life". For ladies "To act the Corinthian" was to become a *fille publique*. Corinth was called the nursery of harlots because of the Temple of Venus, which was "a vast and magnificent brothel". Surely not Corinthian Kate? She doesn't look at all that kind of gel.

The Curious Case of the Cabinet Piano

Mrs Tibbs is surprised at night in the drawing-room, which is furnished with a handsome cabinet piano. Plate No.41.

If you look at enough artwork by George Cruikshank a curious feeling of déjà vu will eventually take over. There is one….and there is another….and another….and another.

What pops up surprisingly often is a cabinet piano and either Cruikshank kept coming across this type in different situations or he had a particular affection for its pictorial qualities, possibly because of the silk sunburst panel in the top.

You begin to wonder: Could he have had his very own cabinet piano, or was one owned by someone in his family?

Cruikshank first came to impudent fame as a political satirist, the acknowledged heir to Gillray. There are few scenes more poignant in art history than the moment when the print seller Mrs Humphrey introduced the young Cruikshank to the great Gillray, then suffering from mental illness and near the end of his life. Gillray looked at him and said: "You are not Cruikshank but Addison; my name is not Gillray but Rubens".

That Cruikshank succeeded in following the man he so much admired we may judge from a receipt in the Royal archives which reveals that George IV paid him £100 "not to caricature His Majesty in any immoral situation". This was an unscrupulous, cynical bargain by both parties but, since Cruikshank took the money and continued to satirise his Royal paymaster, we may take it that he had the ruthless streak required for the job.

But Cruikshank was to make an abrupt turn in his career by which he left political satire behind him.

It was claimed that, even at the age of 11, Cruikshank had supplied some designs to wood engravers for children's books and, from about 1819, he worked more and more as a book illustrator. No doubt this was a response to the growing number of new books published in Britain annually—estimated to have jumped from about 372 in c.1800 to some 2,530 by c.1853.

Illustration entitled "Mr Joseph Porter": Private theatricals in the home of Mr Gattleton the stockbroker, where Miss Jenkins sits at a cabinet piano with a sunburst top. Plate No.42.

The most driven of modern workaholics would have had difficulty catching Cruikshank. It is said that he illustrated over 860 books and that he was responsible for some 15,000 drawings, etchings, watercolours and oil paintings. Can you believe that? I'm not sure that I do but anything remotely approaching this scale made him an artist of prodigious industry.

Cruikshank lived from 1792 to 1878 and, as Michael Wynn Jones put it, his was a career that spanned three distinct ages, the Regency, the Reform and the Mid Victorian—and for much of that time he was the unchallenged No 1 illustrator, known in Europe as he was in the British Isles. He had an "inexhaustible abundance of grotesque invention", wrote Charles Baudelaire.

By the late 1830s Cruikshank could demand double the fee of any other illustrator of the day—he charged £12 for a single plate.

One would assume that with such an oceanic outpouring Cruikshank must have been a drudge, a hack, a seller of clichéd portions. It was not so. Original talent was the lead that filled his pencil.

You have only to see his illustrations to "Oliver Twist" to realise that it is to George Cruikshank that the modern film and theatre Directors owe their conception of Oliver, Fagin, Bill Sikes and the gang of child pickpockets.

Cruikshank not only illustrated Charles Dickens but such as Walter Scott, Daniel Defoe, Tobias Smollett, Henry Fielding, Oliver Goldsmith, Laurence Sterne, Cervantes, Harrison Ainsworth, Harriet Beecher Stowe, Robert Southey and, with equal facility, Grimm's fairy stories. I have a particular fondness for his illustrations to "Peter Schlemihl", the man who sold his shadow.

Some measure of Cruikshank's fame can be learned from a report in "The Spectator" of 1836 which declared Dickens to be "the CRUIKSHANK of writers". An unexpected reversal of roles for Britain's novelist supreme.

Customers, it is plain from the way the publishers advertised their wares, often bought the books more for Cruikshank's drawings than for an author's words and what we are given, in the process, is a slide show of the social history of the 19th Century. A panorama of domestic and public settings, of interior design and the fashion of the day.

It is inevitable that among these thousands of illustrations there should be reflections of the musical life of the nation but Cruikshank seems to show a special affection for music. Just find for yourself his wonderful view of the band playing at Vauxhall Gardens; the satirical take-off of George IV performing on his boasted cello; the orchestra pit in "The Last Song", depicting Grimaldi's final performance; or the row of young ladies with their guitars in "Steam Excursion".

But how much of music did George Cruikshank know? And did he play an instrument himself?

I cannot say, but, of Cruikshank's passion for song and love of all forms of theatre, there is much evidence. His delight was the singing and acting out of comic songs. "Pray heaven he hath not lost his voice singing of anthems!" wrote one friend.

In his youth, before he took The Pledge and became the passionate missionary of the Temperance movement, Cruikshank had been a man for the bottle and the roistering life; a risky progress "through coal holes, drinking dens, cider cellars and prizer's taverns". An early collaborator wrote that they could not complete a project "unless my friend Cruikshank will foreswear late hours, blue ruin *(gin)* and dollies". Odd indeed that, today, one of his best known works is the moralising parable of "The Drunkard's Children". Truly, a man in his time plays many parts.

Agricultural Distress.—From "The Comic Almanac" for 1850.

A cabinet piano appears to be the main possession of a debt-laden family shown in this 1850 scene, "Agricultural Distress", in which a top-hatted auctioneer disposes of their goods. Plate No.43.

From his early days, perhaps influenced by the theatrical portraits and song sheets his father engraved, Cruikshank toyed with the idea of making the stage his profession and he always exhibited a gift for mimicry and the dramatic. He is known to have gone to the opera and theatre with Dickens and he had a strong taste for both Drury Lane and the broader fare of the music halls. The great clown Joey Grimaldi had been a friend for whom his father engraved song sheets and, later, Cruikshank became a member of Grimaldi's crib-cum-club at a nearby public house.

Another childhood pal with whom he acted out dramatic scenes was Edmund Keane, the 19th Century Shakespearean idol and, later, Cruikshank joined Charles Dickens' troupe of amateur actors and toured the provinces as "Pistol" in "The Merry Wives of Windsor".

A view of the artist in his first guise was given by Charles Dickens: "George Cruikshank was perfectly wild at the reunion; and after singing all manner of maniac songs, wound up the entertainment by coming home (six miles) in a little open phaeton of mine on his head—to the mingled delight and indignation of the metropolitan police."

Apart from his vigorous dance of the hornpipe, Cruikshank's other favourite party piece was "The Loving Ballad of Lord Bateman", a song he had learned from a dustman known as "Brandy Tom". So popular was this in his circle that Cruikshank was encouraged to publish the song in 1839 with a set of drawings by himself and an anonymous introduction written, in fact, by Charles Dickens.

If Cruikshank was a compulsive singer was he ever accompanied by a piano? Impossible to think otherwise, especially as the manufacture of pianos rose to the scores of thousands and it became established as the resident instrument in so many 19th Century British homes.

Why Cruikshank was drawn to the cabinet piano particularly we can only speculate.

The cabinet piano was Patented by that most inventive of makers, William Southwell, in 1807 (though I have yet to see a single cabinet piano made by Southwell himself) and Britain's largest manufacturers, Broadwood and Sons, who had begun their production of the type in 1812, only ceased making cabinet pianos in 1856 with No. 8963.

That the cabinet piano had a vogue we may judge from the number that still turn up in auctions and these must have occupied a place in many a home long after fashion danced to new tunes.

I cannot claim to have made even a dent in the study of Cruikshank's alleged 15,000 works but the earliest of his cabinet pianos I have come across was in Dickens' first published book, the collected "Sketches by Boz". After a first edition was published in 1836, a second edition was published the same year in two volumes, illustrated by Cruikshank.

And, in fact, we are shown two cabinet pianos in "Sketches by Boz".

The first is seen in Dickens' word portrait of life in the genteel London boarding house run by the Tibbs family, which they advertise as "a cheerful musical home in a select private family".

When the three ladies of the Maplesone family arrive as paying guests we are told that "The young ladies have kindly volunteered to bring their own piano".

But in a highly embarrassing, and much misunderstood, scene the respectable Mrs Tibbs is discovered at night with a busybody named Mr Evenson *(illustration page 44)*.

The backdrop to this farce is the drawing room and the main ornament is a very showy cabinet piano with sunburst top and what looks to me like a cavetto pediment. We know it is a better quality instrument because of the cylinder front and twin columns with quasi-Ionic capitals, which would have cost extra.

The second cabinet piano in "Sketches by Boz" appears in the home of the stockbroker Mr Gattleton of Clapham Rise and we are told that "the whole family was infected with the mania for Private Theatricals" *(see page 45)*.

When the music is discussed it is said that "Miss Jenkins's talent for the piano was too well known to be doubted for an instant". But, as the night's entertainment descends into inevitable comic shambles, "The piano-forte player hammered away with laudable perseverance" until, as crisis succeeds crisis, she was "overpowered by the extreme heat of the room *(and)* fainted away".

From what is shown of this second cabinet piano we see that it, too, has a sunburst, radiated silk panel and twin, carved columns.

The next appearance of a Cruikshank cabinet piano I have found is in an illustration which stars not only the piano but Cruikshank himself.

Cruikshank had been satirised in print as an "eccentric man....The ludicrous and extraordinary fancies with which his mind is constantly teeming often impart a sort of wildness to his look, and peculiarity to his manner, which would suffice to frighten from his presence those unacquainted with him."

As might have been expected, Cruikshank's riposte was a comic drawing published in "The Omnibus" in 1841 in which the artist portrays himself as, literally, a hair-raising spectre and a musical gathering turns to him with horror as he enters the room.

Opposite Cruikshank is a lady playing a cabinet piano which has the fancy turned columns and a silk panel in the top but, we should note, one with fluted rather than radiated silk.

One of Cruikshank's most spirited drawings shows a lady at her cabinet piano playing for an enthusiastic group of singers but I have been unable to find when it was first published. Plate No. 44.

A cabinet piano drawn by Cruikshank makes another appearance in an 1844 publication "The Bachelor's Own Book", which relates the progress of one "Mr Lambkin (Gent.) in the Pursuit of Pleasure and Amusement". One of the flirtatious and "delightful" Swindelle girls turns away from her piano to talk to the innocent Lambkin.

But a more sorrowful scene *(see page 46)* has a cabinet piano as the centrepiece of an illustration titled "Agricultural Distress", which appeared in the "Comic Almanac" for 1850 and shows a top-hatted auctioneer disposing of the goods of some poor family. Chief among their possessions is the cabinet piano, which has the usual sunburst top and a cylinder fall but lacks the side columns and has distinctly ungainly supporting legs.

One of the most memorable Cruikshank drawings including a cabinet piano, but which I have been unable to date, has a lady playing while accompanied by a motley but enthusiastic group of fashionably dressed singers *(see page 47)*. The cabinet piano, once again, has a cylinder front and sunburst panel but, this time, we are shown that it stands on turned legs.

Yet another Cruikshank illustration with a cabinet piano, with the usual sunburst top, is "Skating", in which a drawing room has been turned into an ice rink. Plate No.45.

Another charming Cruikshank print with a cabinet piano with sunburst top is "Skating", in which a drawing room appears to have been turned into an ice rink *(shown on this page)*.

No doubt there may be other cabinet pianos in Cruikshank's oeuvre but even on this evidence we may make some deductions.

We learn, for example, that there were customers who were prepared to pay the extra money for a handsome case with all the trimmings, such as turned columns and a cylinder front. As far back as 1828 Broadwood and Sons would have charged 100 guineas for such a "Grand Cabinet" with carved pillars in a polished rosewood case. No small sum.

But, if we are to believe Cruikshank, the cabinet piano was a popular instrument of his time. And you might meet such examples, with all the trimmings, in any middle class setting, such as a stockbroker's home or a genteel boarding house.

How Six Legs Deceived Cruikshank

Cruikshank here tries to depict a square piano of 1798—but the six-legged style did not become popular until after c.1805-07, although Zumpe did produce an eight legged example in 1774. Plate No.46.

Although it seems to have been his favourite type, do not think that the cabinet piano was the only kind of keyboard instrument you will come across in the thousands of illustrations by George Cruikshank. Although there are fewer of them I have come across square, upright grand and grand pianos in his work.

In a well known drawing of a square piano by Cruikshank he is unknowingly guilty of a pictorial solecism.

A book published in 1845, written by W.H. Maxwell, tried to recapture the events of the previous century in "The History of the Irish Rebellion in 1798" and Cruikshank was responsible for some splendid illustrations.

One of these plates depicts "Rebels Destroying a House and Furniture" and the anarchic scene has a uniformed man hammering away at a square piano with his fists while two intoxicated insurgents dance a wild jig on top of the instrument.

But Cruikshank has deceived himself.

From the front view we see that he has given this square piano a pair of legs on the front corner, which probably means that the piano has six legs in all. But the six-legged style was a Regency fashion that did not become common until after c.1806.

The piano teacher asks the impossible—inviting an upper-class Chinese lady, with carefully cultivated curling finger-nails, to play a piano. Plate No.47.

Another fine Cruikshank illustration with a piano is "The Music Master Abroad" in which the teacher invites a Chinese lady to try her hand at the keyboard of what (from the lyre support underneath) I think is probably a grand piano.

Sadly, the lady holds out her hands with their very long fingernails to show why it is beyond her. If I remember rightly, the Music Master was asking the impossible—long finger nails had to be cultivated by upper class Chinese because they were the recognized mark of distinction by which they demonstrated that they did not perform manual labour.

Importing a piano into your home brought with it sexual danger, as Cruikshank spells out plainly in this illustration entitled "Jealousy". Plate No.48.

A clearer view of what I think is meant to be a grand piano, rather than a harpsichord, appears in a Cruikshank print titled "Jealousy" (not to be confused with another, and better known, Cruikshank print with the same title). In this illustration Cruikshank spells out plainly the sexual dangers that came when you imported a piano into your home.

These are just a few of many fond musical illustrations by Cruikshank but they leave us with a curious puzzle.

The upright piano, invented by Hawkins in 1800, had, certainly by 1850, become of increasing importance to the piano industry and was widening the customer base for the instrument to the less well off.

Why is it, therefore, that it is so difficult to find an upright piano in the illustrations of Cruikshank who, remember, was still working virtually up to his death in1878? Was it because he identified the upright with the lower class or, like many another ageing man, did he cling to dreams of his Regency youth when the cabinet piano was the more popular?

Little England in Bihar

"The Winter Room", by Sir Charles D'Oyly. Plate No.49. *Courtesy of The Yale Center for British Art (Paul Mellon Collection)*

I can almost hear you thinking: What a very English scene. Perhaps a Belgravia drawing room.

Not so. This is "The Winter Room in the Artist's House at Patna, September 11, 1824", by Sir Charles D'Oyly (1781-1845) and demonstrates the centrality of music to the cultural life of the Raj.

In many cases we are unable to identify the maker of the piano in such old paintings but, quite apart from the characteristic look, the official history of Broadwood and Sons identifies this particular grand as a Broadwood.

Such an attempt to recreate Little England in Bihar tells us, I think, much about Sir Charles for he belonged to that group, often despised by the Pukka Sahibs, that was native born to India. His father, an English Baron, was the Resident of the East India Company at the Court of Nawab Babar Ali of Murshidabad. So India was the real home of Sir Charles but, like those second-generation Indians living in Britain, he was trying to identify with his ethnic origin. Which cricket team do you suppose he supported?

In fact, Sir Charles belonged to one of the noblest British traditions, The Industrious Amateur.

All India should today be grateful for Sir Charles' prolific contribution as an artist (he took lessons from George Chinnery) for his body of work is of great importance in the history of the country. I was delighted to find that much of Sir Charles' early output was reproduced by "The Bahar Amateur Lithographic Press".

These paintings of Sir Charles were used to illustrate early books on "The costume and customs of modern India", "Indian Sports", "Views of Calcutta and its environs", "Oriental Ornithology", "Tom Raw" (a burlesque poem of the adventures of a cadet of the East India Company, complete with jokes at his friend Chinnery's expense) and other publications.

Apart from this painting we have another reminder of this gentleman amateur in a superb double portrait of Sir Charles and his second wife in masquerade dress, made by George Chinnery in 1819.

Modern Indians will be less sanguine about the career of Sir Charles. In an official life dedicated to the service of "Johnny Company" and the governance of the country, he held various posts as

Collector of Customs or Commercial Resident but, more controversially, he was "Opium Agent of Bihar" in 1821 and, lastly, "Senior Member of the Board of Customs, Salt, Opium and of the Marine" in 1833.

It may not be politically correct to say so but there is a fascinating watercolour of Sir Charles in top hat, looking completely over-dressed for the climate, "seated at a table, smoking a hookah, his clerks seated nearby, watching opium being weighed".

We are not told whether opium or tobacco has killed more people. Since cigarettes have just done for yet another of my old friends in journalism, I may be biased.

Amateur Night in Glasgow

"The Amateur Concert", by Heath. Plate No.50. *Illustration courtesy of Glasgow University Library*

The little dog standing against the leg of the piano is, presumably, trying to join in the perfect harmony of "The Amateur Concert", unlike the young man at the back who is desperately trying to snuff out the candle and bring the evening to a premature end.

This slice of Glasgow high life, at a time when that great City was approaching the height of its powers as a World trade centre, was shown in "The Northern Looking Glass" on November 28th., 1825 and, though meant as a comic satire, tells us much about piano fashions.

The lady in this drawing by William Heath, lithographed by John Watson, is playing a cabinet piano with turned legs at the front and it appears to have a painted nameboard. There can be no question, from such an unwitting contemporary source, that we have an accurate idea of the popularity of the "sunburst" silk panel in the top of cabinet pianos but we find, with slight surprise, that the silk has also been gathered in a hanging drape at the top with, at the bottom edge, a motif that is matched in the centre of the "sunburst" and at each side. Apart from the two turned finials, the rising centre ornamentation at the top is highly unusual and almost Continental in taste.

A Shrine to Beethoven

Bust of Beethoven owned by Broadwoods. Plate No.52.

Beethoven's Study, by J.N.Hoechle. Plate No.51.

The great composers inevitably had an effect on those who chose to take up the piano and of these I doubt that any was more central to British musical life in the 19th Century than one who was himself a pianist and so identified with the instrument, Ludwig van Beethoven (1770-1827).

The Beethoven cult was fostered enthusiastically by Britain's foremost piano makers, Broadwood and Sons, for a very good reason: Beethoven had accepted an 1817 Broadwood grand as a gift from the firm and it was with him till his death. In a letter often referred to by Broadwood, Beethoven wrote that his Broadwood grand was "an altar, upon which I shall place the sublimest offering of my spirit to the divine Apollo".

This piano, No.7,362, was transported to Vienna via Trieste and then over the Alps by cart. It had been tried by Clementi, J.B.Cramer and Beethoven's favourite pupil, Ferdinand Ries, all of whose names were inscribed upon it. "Beethoven set such value on it that he would allow no one but himself to play upon it and only as a great favour, used to permit Stumpff to tune it", we are told.

Beethoven's Broadwood grand is shown here in a poignant drawing by J.N. Hoechle (after which this lithograph was made) of Beethoven's study at his death in April, 1827. We see the piano in the light from the window, reminding one that just before his end a storm raged but, suddenly, the room was filled with light and the echoes of thunder.

Broadwood built what was effectively a shrine to Beethoven at their headquarters, complete with a bust of the composer presented to them by the London Philharmonic Society.

The Piano as a Portrait Prop

"The Sisters" by Sir William Beechey. Plate No.53.

Photo by courtesy of The Huntington Museum of Art, Virginia, U.S.A.

How romantic, you say and, indeed, this is a fine example of that school of British portraiture that reached some sublime standards in the Late 18th and early 19th Centuries, the age of Gainsborough, Reynolds, Romney and their skilled brethren.

The painting here, known as "The Sisters", is of such tender feeling, such evident filial affection between the young girls, that you may miss the subliminal message that accompanies the work.

What it tells you is that, quite apart from fashionable dress and aristocratic bearing, they are sufficiently important to belong to a family that owned a grand piano.

By this they are instantly separated from the mass of the population.

The painting was made c.1830 and by this time the (very expensive) grand piano was established beyond doubt as the favourite keyboard instrument of the Royal family; of fashionable society; and of the concert platform.

In all normal circumstances the grand was beyond the pocket of most people. In the 1828 price list of John Broadwood and Sons a square could be had for 36 guineas; an upright for 50 guineas and a cabinet for 65 guineas but the horizontal grand (and also an upright grand) were way above this in cost. The most basic model of the horizontal grand started at 100 guineas and normal variations could cost you up to 160 guineas. All these could be "ornamented to any given price".

When the piano first became popular in Britain, from the mid-1770s, you may find Zumpe-style square pianos depicted with evident pride in society paintings. After William Stodart patented the upright grand in 1795 you began to see this instrument in prints of fashionable settings. Another type, the cabinet, was invented by William Southwell in 1807 and features in some caricatures of middle class life.

But by 1830, I would suggest, it must have been increasingly rare to see any of these in the latest portraits or conversation pieces. By this time the grand piano was identified with the rich while the square, cabinet and upright grand, although still having a measure of acceptance, were on the wane. The mass market was beginning to move towards the upright.

So "The Sisters", we know from their grand piano, must be society ladies. Whether they were in truth sisters needs further clarification.

They have previously been stated to be the Misses Ann and Augusta Coventry, daughters of the Honourable John Coventry, son of the 6th Earl. An earlier Lord of Coventry, you will recall, was a main protagonist in the Godiva legend in which naughty Peeping Tom popped up to catch a glimpse of the nude lady on the horse. This led to a well known caricature of the 6th Earl of Coventry, a political as well as aristocratic figure, mocking the earl as "Peeping Tom" in "Miss W-ms and Peeping Tom of Coventry".

But the Archivist to The Croome Estate Trust tells me that the two daughters of the Hon. John Coventry were called Caroline and Anne and another Librarian informs me there is no trace of a daughter called Augusta. However, the Hon. John also had a son named John who, enthusiastic for matrimony, wed three times and managed to beget "numerous offspring". An obvious possibility is that the two girls in the painting were the grandchildren of the 6th Earl.

One look at the picture suggests that the two girls were closely related but it obviously needs further research.

The artist responsible for "The Sisters" was Sir William Beechey, R.A. (1753-1839) a man who worked so hard you wonder when he had time to breathe. Sir William, one of the most popular portraitists of the time, showed no less than 362 portraits at the Royal Academy over 64 years!

Sir William was patronized by George III, made portrait painter to Queen Charlotte in 1793, and lived much at Windsor where he was instructor to the Royal Princesses "who entertained the strongest regard for him to the end of his life". After 1830 he became Principal Painter to William IV.

Beechey's best work is always said to be his "Review of a Horse Guard with King George III and the Prince of Wales" (in the Royal Collection) and there is a fine portrait of his fellow R.A. Joseph Nollekens. Personally, I have always been interested in his picture of the actress Sarah Siddons, the "Queen of Tragedy", which is in the National Portrait Gallery.

One would very much like to know whether it was Beechey's idea, or the family's, to show the two girls with their grand piano but I suppose that is a question which will not be answered easily.

The Very Same Instrument...

Photo by courtesy of The Huntington Museum of Art, Virginia, U.S.A. Plate No.54.

For students of the possibilities of coincidence theory (as in Mr Nielsen and the decomposition of a coincidence set) I give you this Broadwood grand piano of 1811. When Mr George L. Bagby presented the Huntington Museum of Art with Beechey's painting of "The Sisters" he also gave them this grand piano.

According to the Museum's records: "When Mr Bagby presented the Museum with the piano, which is placed appropriately in front of the painting "The Sisters", he wrote that this piano was 'the identical instrument depicted in the painting'."

Presumably he was able to confirm this through the Broadwood Archives, which are now at Surrey History Centre at Woking.

How Mr Bagby acquired the piano I know not but, as they say, "There's nought stranger than life".

The Dangers of Piano Teachers

From a songsheet, "Fioravanti's Singing Lesson". Plate No.55.

The fellow at the keyboard hardly looks like a young maiden's dream of Casanova but (note the figure peering round the door) it was more than likely that there would have been an anxious mother, or watchful chaperone, somewhere close to hand. Piano teachers were, it appears, feared as a libidinous lot and, as parents might have muttered behind a hand, not quite gentlemen.

Of the tendency of impressionable young girls to fall for piano teachers there was no doubt. After all, Clementi married one of his pupils. So did Dussek. So did Hüllmandel. So did Schroeter. So did Steibelt. The list, one suspects, might be tediously long but, at least, when Sir Julius Killarney married a pupil, Miss Forty, it did produce a fine pun: "A union of piano and forte", they said.

In a brilliant essay on "Women Pianists in Late 18th Century London", Mr Nicholas Salwey tells us how in the case of Schroeter, the oft-praised German virtuoso fortepianist, 'His years in England provide a remarkable example of upper-class attitudes to the musical professional".

Schroeter first appeared in London in 1773 and when he then "eloped with one of his students, a young lady of 'good family', her father settled a yearly allowance upon him of £500 on condition that he abandon his career as a public performer, thus saving the family from the disgrace of having a professional musician as a family member."

There are echoes of such alliances to be found in du Maurier's literary portrait of Svengali and, surprisingly, it continues to have a resonance today in a film like Michael Haneke's "The Piano Teacher"—"shots of, predominantly, hands prancing over the ivories....Freudian sexual frustrations, abusive repression and barbaric lust". Not quite the picture I have of 19th Century piano teachers, especially as the one in the film is a lady.

Jaundiced and apprehensive some parents may have been at the approach of the music master but, to progress in society at that time and hook a husband, a young girl was often expected to have musical accomplishments. Ergo, a piano or singing teacher was vital.

The social status of such instructors was another matter altogether and usually ambivalent.

When Ignaz Moscheles moved to London he soon became a celebrity, musical impresario to the Rothschilds, Director of the Philharmonic Society and official pianist to Prince Albert but none of this saved him from the English class system.

One of the most fashionable music masters, Moscheles never charged less than a guinea a lesson but, arriving at the home of one milord, he was shown to the servants' and tradesmen's entrance. The matter was not rectified until the pianist went on strike.

That this was not an isolated attitude we may judge from a letter by the novelist Jane Austen to her sister in 1815: "The truth is I think, that they are all, at least Music Masters, made of too much consequence & allowed to take too many Liberties with their Scholar's time."

More demeaning was a correspondent of the "Quarterly Musical Magazine and Review" in May, 1824, who specifically referred to music masters as "these tradespeople".

Moscheles noted in his diary that in 1833 he gave 1,457 lessons. With 129 being gratis that made him £1,394/8s from teaching alone, a sum that would then have been enviable to many.

The teacher caricatured in our print (complete with customary howling dog!) could have been a contemporary. The drawing appeared on the front of a music sheet "Fioravanti's Singing Lesson, Newly arranged by Mr M. Moss", published by T. Williams of The Strand, London.

Williams was based at this address between 1818 and 1847 and a mid-way date of c.1830 is suggested for the print though, from the style of the drawing, you might think it earlier.

If any woman aspired to follow Moscheles' musical path she would have found the sex barrier as impenetrable as the class barrier—women teachers were paid only five shillings a lesson and the situation was yet worse for lowly paid governesses, social outcasts who were expected to supervise practice.

Those children who were put to the piano faced a Sisyphean mountain.

Mr Nicholas Salwey quotes one 18th Century source as saying: "Suppose your pupil to begin at six years of age and to continue at the average of four hours a-day only, Sunday excepted, and thirteen days allowed for travelling annually, till she is eighteen, the state stands thus; 300 days multiplied by four, the number of hours amount to 1200; that number multiplied by twelve, which is the number of years, amounts to 14,400 hours!"

But, as an educational manual of 1798 warned, it helped "to increase a young lady's chance of a prize in the matrimonial lottery".

In "Vanity Fair", Thackeray asks: "What causes them to labour at pianoforte sonatas, and to learn four songs from a fashionable master at a guinea a lesson….but that they may bring down some 'desirable' young man with those killing bows and arrows of theirs?"

No author described the anxieties and pressures that such young women suffered more evocatively than Jane Austen (1775-1817) not only the writer supreme but herself a pianist who went through the system. She was still taking lessons from a music master when she was 21 and practised every day.

For this author the piano was a standard prop of her books, an accepted part of the social fabric. That its main purpose was to forward marriage prospects and social advancement she seems to take for granted although the piano was to her a private consolation. In her letters she urged one niece to practise but when another married she wrote: "I am rather sorry to hear that she is to have an Instrument; it seems throwing money away. They will wish the 24 Gs in the shape of Sheets & Towels six months hence".

Contrast this with an account of how Jane Austen "began her day with music—for which I conclude she had a natural taste… none of her family cared for it. I suppose that she might not trouble them, she chose her practising time before breakfast—when she could have the room to herself—she played very pretty tunes I thought."

But Jane Austen was a maiden lady. The reality was that a great many women gave up the piano as soon as they had caught a husband.

In "Emma", where a Broadwood piano is crucial to the plot, one of the characters, Mrs Elton, says it is important for her to practise because "for married women, you know—there is a sad story against them, in general. They are but too apt to give up music."

And in "Sense and Sensibility", a Lady whose music was "brought into the family on her marriage….had lain ever since in the same position on the pianoforte."

For the thousands of girls who must have learned the piano in the late 18th and early 19th Centuries it was assumed that marriage was a sufficient career and that the pursuits of childhood must take second place to a wife's responsibilities.

High Society: The Natural home for a Grand Piano

"The Grosvenor Family", 1831, by C.R. Leslie *Photo by courtesy of a Private Collection and the Bridgeman Art Library.* Plate No.56.

To the glory that was Greece
And the grandeur that was Rome

To that list Mr Poe could have added a postscript: Not forgetting the Grosvenors of Park Lane. After all, how many families get to have over 500 roads, squares and buildings named after them?

This was about as high as High Society could reach and with the pocket money to indulge a fine artistic sensibility. The Lady at the piano in this painting of "The Grosvenor Family" is Eleanor, 1st Marchioness Westminster (aka Mrs Grosvenor) and she is surrounded by three generations of the Grosvenors– two Earls, a later Duke, assorted Lords and Ladies and not forgetting the family parrot.

The piano, we discern, is a completely natural part of the setting by the year 1831. The Marchioness, the most aristocratic figure in the room, commanding all with a glance, plays with the confidence that surely came from years of childhood practice under the eyes of a professional tutor. Would anyone have dared to ask Her Ladyship the question posed by Mrs W. in 1792: "And have women who have early imbibed notions of passive obedience, sufficient character to manage a family or educate children?" The look on the Marchioness's face rather reminds me of all the strong women in my own family, though I'm not too sure that my aunts, daily scrubbing the coal dust out of miners' work clothes, would have seen each other as sisters under the skin.

The Marchioness is here accompanied on the harp by the wife of the 2nd Earl Wilton. In front, two of the Grosvenor girls dance with style. This, we understand, was how the family took their ease and amusement.

The scene is Grosvenor House (tragically destroyed in the 1920s to make way for a mere hotel). We are in the picture gallery and two of the family's four Rubens' tapestries hang behind the columns, "Abraham and Melchizedek" and "The Fathers of the Church". Also on the wall is Velasquez's "Don Balthasar Carlos". The Collection then included other small baubles such as Gainsborough's "Blue Boy" and Rubens' "Adoration of the Magi".

In case you had not understood, the Grosvenors are (outside, presumably, of Mr Abramovich) as rich as any in the land and with a lustrous heritage. They have deep roots in Cheshire, where they were established by the early 12th Century and the family seat is Eaton Hall, near Chester, a borough firmly in their pocket for many years. The family fortune was earned in decent fashion by a series of clever marriages, which brought in Belgravia, Mayfair, Pimlico and the then rolling London acres.

Robert Grosvenor, 1st Marquess of Westminster, was known as a patron of the arts and the turf—"a great picture collector and racer". A follower of Pitt, he sat as an M.P. from 1788 to 1802, and thus became a Lord of the Admiralty and Commissioner of the Board of Control. But in 1806 he crossed the floor and left the Tories for the Whig cause. He rebuilt Eaton Hall in 1803; laid out Belgravia in 1826; and, along the way, "acquired by marriage the Egerton estates, 1794".

Already an Earl, Robert Grosvenor was made a Marquess on the Coronation of William IV in 1831 and this picture was commissioned to celebrate that elevation. The artist was an inspired choice and I doubt that Charles Robert Leslie R.A. (1794-1859) painted many finer pictures. His best known work was "The Queen Receiving the Sacrament after the Coronation" but here we have the reverse—not a State occasion but an intimate conversation piece, adroitly painted and cleverly grouped, with a keen eye to character, a delight in the beauty of the ladies and a refinement of taste.

I have no idea whether the piano shown in Leslie's painting was a Broadwood but there was a definite connection between the Grosvenor family and Britain's leading piano makers, Broadwood and Sons.

In the later Victorian period the Grosvenors had managed to add "The Duke of Westminster" to their titles and Broadwoods, with their West End headquarters and huge factory in Horseferry Road, were very much in Westminster territory.

The then Duchess of Westminster presented prizes to "F" Company of The Queen's Westminster Volunteers, a company inspired by the example of James Shudi Broadwood and comprising entirely of employees of Broadwood. The Duke of Westminster was Patron of a concert staged by the drum-and-fife band of the firm.

It can also be proved that Broadwood and Sons supplied at least two important pianos to the Grosvenors.

In 1883 the man who became first Duke of Westminster, a fine fellow named Hugh Lupus Grosvenor, commissioned a "special" from Broadwoods. The Duke was a man of far-reaching philanthropic effort who cared for hospitals, dumb animals, agricultural and technical education and much else, such as The United Committee for the Prevention of Demoralisation of Native Races by the Liquor Traffic.

It is a shame he backed a loser when it came to pianos. The instrument he asked Broadwood and Sons to make, was allegedly in "Louis XVI" style but, from photos, an article that might cause visual pain to the unprepared. No expense was spared to construct it of dark rosewood, with panelling, ormolu mountings, solid gold leaf and 500 mitres in the brass work but, to put the matter frankly, it was heavier set than a Clydesdale.

According to a report in "Music Trades Review" this grand was "destined for Grosvenor House and is similar to one now at Eaton Hall, made by Messrs Broadwood".

Bearing in mind the financial capacity of the Grosvenors, the size of the family and the spread of their establishments, my suspicion is that Broadwood must have supplied a number of other pianos to them.

The grand piano supplied to the Duke of Westminster by Broadwood and Sons in 1883 and still remembered and proudly shown in the firm's "Descriptive Album of Artistic Pianofortes", published in 1895. But not to my personal taste. Plate No.57.

Music Sellers to the Prince of Wales

D'Almaine's Piano Factory by T.H.Shepherd. Plate No.58. *Illustration courtesy of The Museum of London.*

In the ever-expanding World of the 19th Century piano makers, the acknowledged aristocrats were Broadwood, Collard and Erard (who, although a French firm, also established a London factory) but many ambitious entrepreneurs followed close behind.

Before 1800 there had been 45 piano making firms in London but by 1850 "There are at present between 200 and 300 in London alone, while there are makers in most of the capital towns in the United Kingdom".

With a number of these firms it is hard to say whether they were principally piano makers, music publishers or retailers, since their activities encompassed all three areas (I have found it particularly difficult, for example, to ascertain whether, or to what degree, Longman and Broderip actually made pianos themselves, or simply sub-contracted the work).

One of the firms who dabbled in all three areas was D'Almaine & Co., of 20, Soho Square, London, founded in 1785 as Goulding & D'Almaine by George Goulding. But that they were definitely piano makers can be proved beyond doubt by this watercolour by Thomas Hosmer Shepherd, now to be found in the Museum of London, and which shows the interior of the D'Almaine factory in Chilton Street, just off the Bethnal Green Road.

At one stage the firm were able to boast they were "music-sellers to the Prince and Princess of Wales" and they became well known for the publication of vocal and dance music, including "The British Minstrel" (1830) and a popular annual "The Musical Bijou", issued between 1829 and 1851.

Curiously, I see no obvious sign in Shepherd's picture of the firm's other manufacturing activities—they were also makers of organs and particularly known for wind instruments such as flutes and clarinets.

The drawing has been dated to c.1835 and the pianos we see are of particular interest because they barely reach the height of the gentleman's top hat. I think it is reasonable to deduce, therefore, that these pianos cannot be upright grands and yet they seem tall for "cottage uprights", or even "semi-cabinets".

An advert for D'Almaine and Co, c.1823, announced that they were "Manufacturers of Cabinet, Harmonic & Square Piano Fortes" and it is within my knowledge that the firm made cabinet pianos of 5ft 8in. The most likely explanation, therefore, is that all four pianos in the foreground are cabinet pianos.

The Factory of Britain's Mightiest Maker

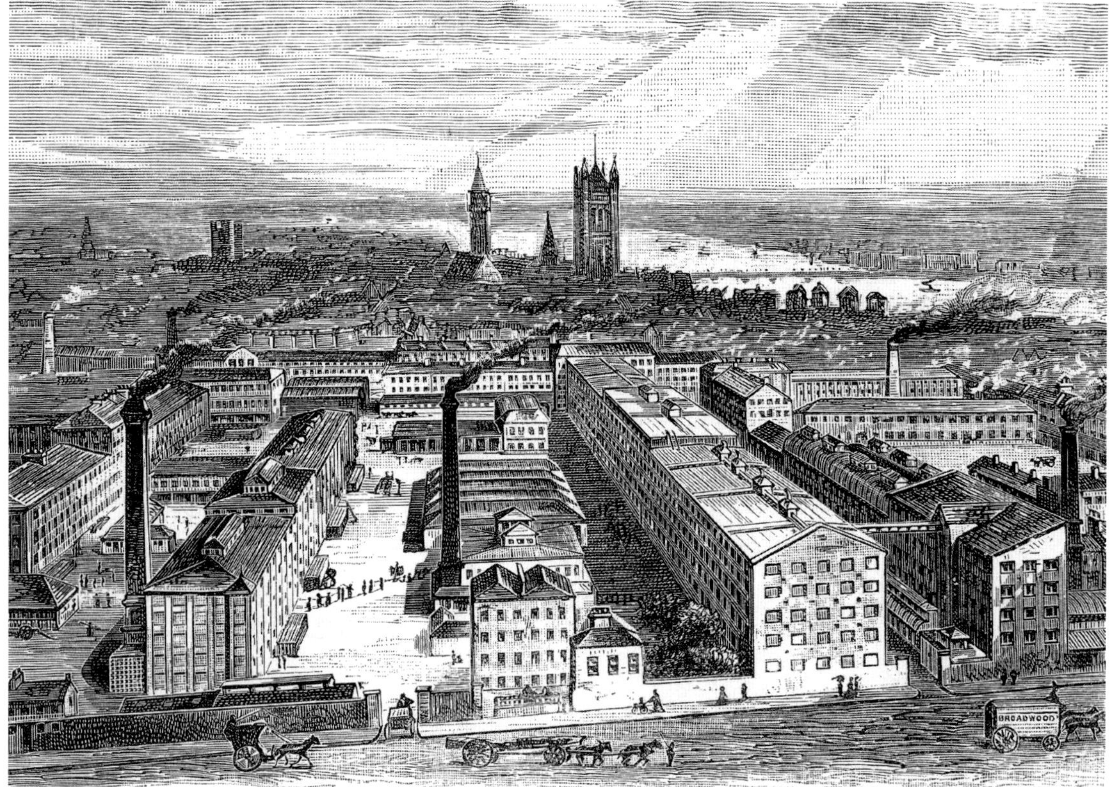

An exterior view of Broadwood's sprawling Westminster factory complex, shown in an 1895 publication. Plate No.59.

When the young Frenchman Camille Pleyel visited London in 1815 he wrote to his parents: "I went first to see the Broadwoods, who received me in a friendly way in the English manner, that is to say, without ceremony. They immediately sent one of their employees to help me look for a small flat and I live very near them. I pay 15s a week and that is the cheapest I could find and still live decently."

Young Camille was hoping to make a career as a concert pianist and, while in London, played with the Philharmonic and before the Queen and the Prince Regent. But Camille was also a Director of the family music publishing and piano making business and he meant to find out all he could of the London piano makers.

Soon he was writing back to the family: "Broadwoods are the best known, then Clementi, Stodart, Wilkinson, Tomkison, etc., etc. Up to the present I have had only a small square one of Broadwood, but they are supposed to send me a large grand piano today."

As reported in the research of Rita Benton, Pleyel found all the piano makers pleasant to him and Tomkison, in particular, made efforts to persuade Camille to play on one of his pianos in public.

But Camille wrote back to France: "On the basis of the instruments I have seen, Broadwood seem to me incontestably the first for grand pianos, Clementi for the small ones and Wilkinson for the cabinet pianos. I shall play on a Broadwood at the Philharmonic."

Another well known concert pianist, J.B. Cramer, "advises me to play on a Broadwood also, which I shall do, for in a large hall they are the best."

As he prepared to return home, Camille wrote that "If I had foreseen how things would develop, I would have got a grand piano of Broadwood or one of Wornum's cabinet pianos."

This small cameo of Camille Pleyel's experiences gives a fair reflection of the reputation of Broadwood and Sons in Europe and their standing within the British piano making industry. Within a short period of years they became the biggest and many believed them to be the best.

Just as indicative on the domestic front was the choice made by the great novelist Jane Austen when, in writing "Emma", she made the mysterious gift of a square piano a key point of the story. We are told that it was "a very elegant looking instrument" and had such soft upper notes that it was supposed the benefactor "either gave....very minute directions, or wrote to Broadwood himself".

An interior view of Broadwood's Horseferry Road factory from the "Penny Magazine", April, 1842. Plate No.60.

The British judged that, if you wanted the best, you went to the World leader: Broadwood and Sons. So did the Royal family, who kept giving them the accolade "By Royal Appointment". In the Broadwood archives there is a list of over 1,000 eminent musicians who had played a Broadwood, from Beethoven to Chopin.

So high was the Broadwood name that they often had to fight off forgers and near-the-mark operators trying to profit at their expense.

As early as 1803 Broadwood were forced to place an advertisement in Indian papers warning that they had received "authentic information that Instruments of very imperfect nature are sent out for sale to India and their name affixed as if manufactured by them".

Broadwood stated it was "necessary to acquaint the Gentry in India that none of the numerous Piano Fortes introduced into Asia by officers of Indiamen and others for sale within these 6 years last....are of their manufacture."

The success of the firm, and its expansion, hardly seemed to have a limit.

By April 1842, when the "Penny Magazine" published a lengthy account of a visit to Broadwood and Sons as "A Day at a Pianoforte Factory", they were at the height of their powers.

Adjusting the strings of a cabinet piano at Broadwoods, "Penny Magazine", April,1842. Plate No.61.

The small craft-based workshop of Shudi that had produced less than 20 harpsichords a year was far behind them. Now, it was reported, they had already manufactured between 80,000 and 90,000 pianos.

They still had their Great Pulteney Street, London, showrooms and workshops (which had grown to employ some 150 people) but, additionally, there was a massive industrial complex at Horseferry Road, Westminster, where many more hundreds worked.

Woodcuts which accompanied the article show us glimpses inside the Westminster factory.

According to the "Penny Magazine" there were four ranges of buildings, generally three stories in height and "there is an aggregate length of workshop truly enormous, in fact it considerably exceeds half a mile—an extent to which there are probably very few parallel instances in the metropolis".

Here were to be found giant tiers of choice timber, covering 300 feet of ground; special sheds for mahogany and lime-tree logs; and a "veneer store room" for valuable, fancy woods. Inside were shops for "case makers", "cottage case makers", "square-case makers", "cabinet-case makers", "desk makers", "fret cutters", "sounding-board makers", "belly-men", "key makers", "hammer makers", "hammer-rail makers", "bottom makers", "top makers" and "packing-case makers"; "fitters up", "cleaners off" and "polishers"; "cabinet-finishing" shops, a "turners' shop", a "stringers' shop" and others; a "cutting room", a "seasoning room", a "hot room" and an "engine house"; a range of "ten or a dozen" saw pits; and "four or five dwelling houses inhabited by the superintendents and foremen".

[Fret-cutter at work.]

A Broadwood fret-cutter, tool in hand, "Penny Magazine", April, 1842. Plate No.62.

The writer observed that the workshops "bear some resemblance to the shops of a cabinet-maker….The work benches, about three hundred in number, are placed in general transversely, with one end towards the windows".

What all this demonstrated was a sophisticated division of labour—essential to the new industrial efficiency but later detested by the Arts and Crafts movement because of the way it "degraded" human labour and dignity.

For much of the second half of the 19th Century Broadwoods continued to live off the

[Key-cutter at work.]

A Broadwood key-cutter at work, "Penny Magazine", April, 1842. Plate No.63.

great reputation they had established but, as the years ticked by, it looked less and less like glad morning. They faced strong Continental competition from such as Bechstein and a brash, fiercely capitalist American piano industry, led by Steinway, that seized on any means of improving mass production.

A portrait of John Broadwood (1732-1812), printed in "The Pianoforte Dealers' Guide", Oct 25th., 1882. Plate No.64.

Broadwood, meanwhile, suffered from the sins that afflict most companies once their dynamic founders have exited the stage. They grew conservative in their ways; they resisted innovation; and the later generations lacked the vitality of John Broadwood and his sons.

They remained the name for quality but it was more and more a fight for survival.

The Royal Blessing for the Piano

STAR
THE ROYAL PARTY.
"Guess___who he is"
Presented with No 6, of the TICKLER, Saturday Dec. 2nd 1837.

"The Royal Party", Plate No.65. *Courtesy of Her Majesty Queen Elizabeth II © The Royal Collection*

One of the biggest influences on British attitudes to the piano was provided by Queen Victoria (who had learned the instrument as a child and was skilled enough to accompany professional singers) and her husband, Prince Albert (if anything, even more devoted to music, both a competent performer on the keyboards and a composer). Throughout their marriage they welcomed pianists and composers of International renown to Buckingham Palace, Windsor Castle and other Royal residences and they commissioned pianos to be made for them by British, Continental, Empire and other manufacturers. This cartoon, "The Royal Party. Guess….who he is", was published in "The Tickler" on December 2nd., 1837, only a few months after Victoria ascended to the throne and beside her is Albert, whom she was to marry on Feb 10th., 1840. In the drawing Victoria is shown playing a Cabinet Piano (but did she ever own one?) with a silk panel in the top. And the supports to the keyboard already suggest a new French Rococo swagger that was to be yet more evident on other furniture at the 1851 Exhibition.

Gold and Glitter from The Mysterious Mr Blake

The Blake Grand. Plate No.66. *Photo by courtesy of the Metropolitan Museum of Art, New York*

I think we may regard George Henry Blake as the A.N. Other of the Designer world. When I first came across his name he was as mysterious to me as the author of the Muratorian Fragment or The Master of 1423. In short, I had never heard of him and nor could I find his name in any of the many sources I consulted.

At such a time one cannot help feeling ridiculous for, there before me, was incontrovertible evidence that this same Mr Blake of London was responsible for one of the most remarkable pianos of the 19th Century and which is now a prominent exhibit of the Metropolitan Museum of Art in New York.

How was it possible for Mr Blake to remain an unknown? The 19th Century is not, after all, the Dark Ages: It has been trawled by an Armada of ambitious design historians. And if Mr Blake was in demand for such high class work then there simply has to be other examples. Yet, of Mr Blake I could find no trace.

To make the matter yet more puzzling the provenance of the piano seems good. It is believed, and confirmed by a monogram and Baronet's coronet inlaid on the case, that this instrument was commissioned for the wife of a British aristocrat, Lord Foley, Baron of Kidderminster.

It is not as though the Blake grand piano, suggested to be c.1840, was some modest, reserved piece that would merge anonymously into the background. On the contrary, it is a gold and glitter job of audacious exhibitionism and I know of no other piano case like it in the British canon—in short, it is a Neo-Baroque paint and powder article that, one assumes instinctively, is in the Continental tradition, reminding me of an ancient Venetian harpsichord.

Described as "of unequalled magnificence" it has ornate casework with marquetry intarsia, gilded bronze, inlays of ivory and mother-of-pearl, coloured woods and lion masks. Dominant female heads peer out aggressively from the top of each leg midst gushing decoration while, underneath the main case, a figure of Apollo with his lyre poses on a lion's head, atop the heavily scrolled understretcher.

According to the Metropolitan's official Inventory description the piano case of Blake's lavish creation was made with a satinwood veneer over an oak and softwood carcass, decorated with marquetry of various dyed and natural woods, ivory, mother-of-pearl and metal.

In the centre of the lid is a trophy composed of "hurdy-gurdy, tambourine, viol and bow, lute, pan-pipes, hunting horn and French horn, sheets of music and volume of Beethoven's Symphonies".

The lid is "bordered with animal and human grotesques and floral sprays offsetting reserves containing representations in etched ivory of Persephone (Aphrodite), Ceres, Bacchus, woman and child warming themselves at fire, shepherd boy and dog and lion supporters of Foley shield".

The reserves are in ivory alternating with depictions in marquetry of rustic dancers and music-makers in 18th Century dress. The underbrace, music stand and pedals all have marquetry floral patterns.

Below the main body of the case is a spectacular "reclining statuette of Apollo with lyre in painted wood, resting on base overlaid with gilt leopard's masks".

The whole instrument has a heavy gilt wood edging in Louis XV style, incorporating flowers, scrolls, musical instruments, shells, masks of Bacchus, Apollo, Diana (crowned with crescent moon) and Venus (crowned with star) on knees of legs and mask of wind god blowing above pedals.

The inlays include holly, mahogany, burr-walnut, tulipwood and ebony.

On the front and back of the lid is a double "F" for Foley, entwined and surmounted by a Baron's coronet. The arms on the front of the lid in marquetry are probably those of Thomas, Baron Foley (1780-1833) but those of other members of the Foley family have also been identified. Supporting the heraldry is the Foley motto "Ut Prosim" (*That I may be of use*).

A scene that appears near the coat of arms has been identified as being after one of the "Fêtes Venetiennes" by Watteau.

In the judgement of the musical instrument historian Emanuel Winternitz: "This pianoforte is the most lavishly decorated Erard piano, and probably has the most exquisite intarsias of any musical instrument ever made....The vast profusion of detail is, in the end, rendered homogeneous and beautiful to the beholder by the rich golden hue of the satinwood case, which suffuses the whole instrument."

I was saved from my ignorance concerning George Henry Blake by the knowledge of one of the country's leading experts on furniture of the period, Mr Martin Levy, the Principal of H. Blairman and Sons of Mayfair.

Mr Levy was able to tell me that the Blake family were marquetry makers and probably cabinet makers and that a firm headed by Robert Blake was in business from 1826 until at least 1840.

"From 1842 the firm was known as George Blake & Brothers and after 1847 George Henry Blake is recorded at 53, Mount Street, London", Mr Levy told me. "There is a table in the V. and A. (formerly at Corsham Court) with the label of Messrs Blake, 130, Mount Street, Berkeley Square.

"George Henry Blake died in 1859 and Alfred Blake, presumably his brother, in 1866."

Although it is not to my personal taste it seems to me that Blake's grand piano must be ranked as the most outstanding British art piano of the half-century from 1800 to 1850.

The Swedish Nightingale, Jenny Lind

Photo by courtesy of The Royal Collection of Sweden and The Swedish National Museum of Art

This 1845 portrait of Jenny Lind by Louis Asher shows her playing a heavy Victorian style piano. Plate No.67.

A popular print of Jenny Lind showing her with what I presume to be an upright piano. Plate No.68.

Many played a part in the growing popularity of the piano: Queen Victoria and other members of the Royal family; the virtuosos of the keyboard; composers such as Beethoven, Liszt and Brahms who were also piano soloists of merit.

But there was also another group...the divas of the Opera House.

Of these, one of the greatest was Jenny Lind (1820-1887) for whom there ought always to be a special affection in Britain, since she gave as charitably to us as she took at the box office. They called Jenny "The Swedish Nightingale" and she was a Swedish superstar more than a century before we saw the blonde tresses of her compatriot Agnetha from ABBA.

Those who think life began in the 1960s should reflect on the following: When Jenny Lind left from Liverpool on the "S.S. Atlantic" for her first American tour, in 1850, thousands hurrahed her from the quayside; and when she landed in New York over 35,000 came to greet her. Such was the demand for seats at her first concert that some were auctioned. Did The Beatles match that?

The first steam locomotive on the London and Brighton Railway line, built in 1847, was named the Jenny Lind and so were the next 69 in the class. When Lindomania hit the United States the first opera house in San Francisco was called The Jenny Lind Opera House; a Jenny Lind Village was built in the Midwest; an island off the New England coast was called Jenny Lind Island; Jenny Lind streets appeared in a number of cities; hospitals, children's homes, scholarships and awards honoured her. They danced to the "Jenny Lind Polka" and the "Jenny Lind Waltz Quadrilles". They even named clothes and chairs after her.

She was on terms of friendship with the British Royal family as she was with Swedish and German Royalty. "The great event of the evening", wrote Queen Victoria in 1846, "was Jenny Lind's appearance and her complete triumph". It was an unparalleled happening when, on one occasion, the Queen threw her own bouquet of flowers at Jenny's feet.

So, with such fame, what must have been the reaction when they named pianos after her? When she herself was shown in portraits playing the piano? When she married a pianist? It must have helped.

At the age of 32, she found happiness with her piano player and settled down to life in... Wimbledon! In London she taught aspiring British singers and, as she had done throughout her life, continued to distribute her fortune to the unfortunate and the deserving.

She spent her final years in the peace of Worcestershire and is buried at Great Malvern.

The True Upright arrives at Last

This carved and gilded Revived Gothic upright is in the Collection of Holdenby Hall, Northamptonshire, where it is on loan from The Music Museum. Their catalogue description states that "This instrument is believed to have been manufactured specifically for the 1851 Crystal Palace Exhibition". But is it also, as evidence suggests, the missing piano designed for the Mediaeval Court at the 1851 Exhibition by a man who was the fountainhead of Gothic design in the 19th Century, A.W.N. Pugin? Plate No.69.

Photo by Simon Suckling Courtesy of Holdenby House and The Music Museum

The True Upright (I am tempted to say rather like this book) was a long time arriving.

It was in 1800 that John Isaac Hawkins and his rival, Mr Muller of Vienna, had each found the way to make a smaller, more practical piano that answered the needs of the mass market. But they were virtually ignored.

Then, with a series of brilliant innovations commencing in 1811 (and making some fine Regency cases along the way) Robert Wornum had turned Hawkins' upright into a commercial proposition. Yet, viewing such contemporary literature as is available to us, you do not get the impression that the upright was taking over the piano world in the 1820s, or even the 1830s.

I wish I had some facts so that I could be more specific but the records of most British piano companies have long since disappeared into the dustbin of history. Let us hope a horde of would-be PhDers can be persuaded to set out in search of the facts.

All I know is that when Broadwoods did an analysis of their historical sales records in 1842 it was stated that they had sold 9 "Cottages" (for which read Uprights) out of every 100 pianos they had sold. The square piano, by their records, had been far and away the most popular.

Which does not, of course, tell us what Wornum and his lesser imitators were selling by way of uprights to the lower end of the market at that time.

It was not until the half century that public recognition became universal.

The stage was the right setting. At that greatest of great occasions, The Great Exhibition of 1851, the True Upright announced its arrival. Hawkins' invention had (like the fax machine and so many other inventions) been a long time travelling but it left no-one in doubt of its presence at The Crystal Palace in Hyde Park.

It was claimed that over 1,800 musical instruments were on display but exactly how many of these were pianos and, even more

Photo courtesy of The Museum of London.
Here is the actual John Brinsmead upright in burr walnut, now in The Museum of London, which was an official entry at The Great Exhibition of 1851. Brinsmead stated that "The case permits the instrument to be placed in any part of a room". Plate No.70.

The Brinsmead Upright as it appeared in this illustration in the Official Catalogue of the 1851 Exhibition. The "1851" in the top panel is explained because originally there was an "Embroidered device in the central panel". Plate No.71.

problematical, how many were uprights, I find it impossible to say. The official catalogue was huge and a number of rival catalogues were published but the details were miserably inadequate.

What I know for a certainty is that the upright was given a higher profile than it had ever had before in illustrations in both the official catalogue and other publications. The interest was obvious.

The cheapest pianos on display were still the squares which were priced as low as 35 guineas compared to 125 to 135 guineas for the grand pianos. Uprights were priced from 45 to 70 guineas.

When you read the catalogues you are immediately struck by the evident Continental interest in the upright at this time: Aucher of Paris "two upright pianofortes"; Frey of Geneva, "Two upright trichord rosewood pianofortes"; Jastrzebski of Brussels, "Upright pianofortes"; Lichtental of St. Petersburg "cottage pianoforte"; Rumms of Hamburg "Upright pianoforte (piccolo)"; Seuffert of Vienna "Piccolo piano"… and so on. The French, in particular, showed a strong interest in this piano type.

Yet, they were matched by the British firms.

As you might expect, Robert Wornum exhibited his "Improved piccolo pianoforte". The most revealing comment came from "Newton's London Journal" which wrote that "it is to this gentleman we are indebted for the first introduction of the piccolo or small upright pianoforte which, from its capability of being produced cheaply, has had considerable influence in promoting our manufacture of pianos and indeed extending a knowledge and taste for music". Wrong, of course (credit, please, to Mr Hawkins) but a fair reflection of the regard for Wornum and his inventive mind.

In some instances it is hard to know from the catalogue exactly what type of pianos were shown but other British firms who exhibited uprights included Robert Allison, John Brinsmead, Robert Cocks, Abraham Dimoline, Charles Holdernesse,

This upright with its heavily carved cabriole legs at four corners and figures in the top panels, shown here in the Official Catalogue of the 1851 Exhibition, was yet another model in walnut. It was shown by Robert Allison of Regent Street, London, Plate No.72.

Frederick Hund, John Champion Jones, George Luff, W. Matthews, George Metzler, John & Henry Moore, Oetzmann & Plumb, George Peachey, William Rolfe, Smyth & Roberts and Towns & Packer.

It should not be thought that the grander British firms ignored these "cheapo" rivals: Collard &

Among the more unusual instruments at the 1851 Exhibition was this "double or twin semi-cottage, having two fronts and sets of keys, one on either side", by John Champion Jones of Soho Square, London. Mr Jones claimed that his walnut piano (shown here in the Official Catalogue) was "suitable for any number of performers, from one to six". Plate No.73.

Collard, the London factory of Erard, and Kirkman & Son, all showed uprights.

The 1851 Exhibition was a landmark of another kind also, because a number of the designers received credit for their work.

For myself, the greatest interest was in the two uprights shown by the piano makers Lambert & Co. in the Mediaeval Court, this latter being the subject of much controversy because of its commitment to Revived Gothic designs.

The force behind this Mediaeval Court was the man principally responsible for the Gothic Revival, the architect A.W.N. Pugin. In my view the evidence is overwhelming that Pugin was the designer of Lambert's two upright pianos.

Without here going into the details (I will leave that to a later Chapter) I think there is sufficient evidence to deserve further examination that one of these Pugin Gothic Revival pianos, surely one of the rarest survivors of British piano history, is now to be found in the Collection of Holdenby House in Northamptonshire, where it is on loan from The Music Museum.

When Pugin decided to give his talents to design such an instrument you may say that The True Upright had truly arrived. It might be the *Puya raimondii* of the piano industry but it was centre stage at last...and has never been shifted since.

Although Erard are identified with, and best known for, their connection with Paris, the French makers had a thriving London factory for many years and this "Elizabethan" upright (shown here in the Official Catalogue) was part of the London factory's entry at the 1851 Exhibition. It was stated to be a "grand oblique, ornamented in the Elizabethan style, adapted to extreme climates". Plate No.74.

Rows of Uprights in Luxurious Setting

Cadby's Showrooms in a print of c.1850. Plate No.75.

With the explosion in demand came Piano Showrooms fitted out to reflect the aspirations of their customers. Here we have a view of "C. Cadby's Show Rooms" c.1850 in which the serried rows of upright pianos are matched by a gallery of pictures hanging on the walls. The implication was, presumably, that if you bought a piano you, too, might be worthy of High Art.

The lofty ceiling and huge light fittings might give the illusion of a country mansion. The customers all have the smack of affluence and the salesman in the foreground, showing the instrument, dresses to a fashionable ideal.

The Charles Cadby Patent Pianoforte Manufactory had been been founded by its owner in 1839 off Tottenham Court Road and this is, presumably, their showrooms at 42, New Bond Street, London. Later, the dynamic Cadby bought an 82-acre site at Hammersmith on which to found a new piano factory. I have often wondered if there was a connection with Joe Lyons' well-known headquarters, Cadby Hall.

The Largest Pianoforte Gallery in Europe

CRAMER & CO.'S
PIANOFORTE GALLERY,
207 & 209, REGENT STREET,
THE LARGEST IN EUROPE.

Plate No.76.

When Cramer and Co. published this advertising insert, it is suggested in the 1890s, they claimed to have a Pianoforte Gallery that was "The Largest in Europe". Instead of the humble Cadby uprights we now see lines of grand pianos occupying the main ground, with the uprights banished to the walls.

Cramer could trace their lineage back to the pianist and piano maker Johann Baptist Cramer and had originally been founded as music publishers in 1824.

Menacing Pussies and the Victorian Psyche

"The Pianist", A stuffed cat exhibited at The Great Exhibition of 1851. Plate No.77.

The Victorians are a little over a Century away from us yet, I conclude, they seem already to be as far distant as Uranus or the truth about God. How does one explain their visions of piano-playing animals?

To the Victorian mind, apparently, Cats (especially) but also Dogs and, for all I know the entire animal Kingdom, were about to be translated into aspiring Mozarts or Chopins. Most of these pop up in 19th Century paintings and illustrations but others spring into queasy, trompe-l'oeil action as stuffed animals gruesomely posed above the keyboards.

If it were just some grand anthropomorphic joke we could comment on changed social attitudes and leave it there. But there is a great deal more to it than that.

I will not dwell on the common garden run of taxidermal, pipe smoking, poker-playing, Port-swilling squirrels imagined to be at their "Gentlemen's Club"; frogs who might have played Joe Davis off the table at billiards or, equally, doubled as your barber; rabbits who could with assurance teach the children how to read, or one's wife how to embroider; and cats dressed as brides and bridesmaids.

For the purpose of this book we can, I think, ignore the Victorians fascination with freaks such as two-headed lambs or the mind that could conceive a tableau of animals, themselves mounted on horses, engaging in a forest hunt. Readers of a sensitive disposition are strongly advised not to enquire further into the stuffed-animal activities of Dr Hughes, his "special", wealthy customers and his devotion to the Marquis De Sade.

Our concern is with pianos but, even here, some of the genre has a distinctly morbid, almost nightmarish, quality. An unmistakeable air of menace occasionally disconcerts. Some of the animals look altogether too assured and in control as though "Animal Farm" was a real happening. As if one's idle wondering as to why the well-organised ants do not take over the World had suddenly been translated into inexplicable reality.

Could it have been something to do with Darwin's explosive theories challenging established religion and people being forced to understand that we really were related to the Apes?

Or the first known stuffing of a bird in these Isles, the preservation of the Duchess of Richmond's African Grey Parrot in 1702?

The eccentric example of the Earl of Leicester, who frightened off the neighbours with his collection of taxidermy?

Perhaps the founding of the Natural History Museum?

Did Queen Victoria encourage this passion with her own avid collecting of stuffed birds?

Or was it a subversive kind of radicalism that led to the well dressed airs and graces of these Cats and Dogs, with the servants moving out from Below Stairs disguised as moggies or mongrels? Do we blame Marx, Engels and their predecessors for anarchic challenges to authority, expressed by way of metaphor? What would Freud have made of kittens dressed in frilly knickers?

As well seek the answer in Delphi. It is all frankly bizarre.

A crescendo of this anthropomorphic fixation was reached with The Great Exhibition of 1851 when no less than 14 different taxidermists showed their wares, one producing a worthy, life-size reproduction of the extinct Do-do.

But the foremost among them, judged by the enthusiastic public response, was unquestionably Herrmann Ploucquet of Stuttgart, in what is now modern Germany. Herrmann was the acknowledged master and received rave reviews.

One of the exhibits chosen from the Exhibition for reproduction in "Tallis's History and Description of the Crystal Palace", from Division 3, was Ploucquet's portrayal of "The Pianist", which I reproduce on page 71. Although by 1851 the Square Piano was on the way out in Britain, we see that the animal (I presume a cat), is modelled with a square piano. As this particular instrument has four legs, rather than the six legs of the Regency, we know that it was a late example.

But there is little that is comfy about this image, drawn by J. Mason and etched by T. Hollis. It is not the sugary stuff you might expect from a children's book. The cat sits on his (or her) chair with confident, tail-swishing authority and knows the music so well he does not have to read the music sheet, the paws in easy control of the keys.

The stuffed cat shown at the 1851 Exhibition is a maestro. The humans will have to practise a little harder to catch up. But if we want to rest a little easier in our beds we may comfort ourselves that such visions but reflected the enormous popularity of the piano.

A Lady Cat with Style

Illustration by courtesy of collectorsprints.com (also at Portobello Road, London). Plate No.78.

Where could you find such confidence, such style, such fine clothes....and such authority? Do not doubt who is in control of this imaginary (?) world—it is the Cats. The curious thing about this old coloured woodblock print, stated to be 1880, is that "Lady" Cat is playing, unmistakeably, a cabinet piano, a type that Broadwood and Sons stopped making in 1856.

The Kittens at Tea

"The kittens at tea". Plate No.79.

The German taxidermist Herrmann Ploucquet was, again, the inspiration for this piano playing soloist from the book "The Comical Creatures from Wurtemberg", presumably produced in 1851 to ride on the back of the publicity given to Ploucquet's stuffed animal tableaux at The Great Exhibition of that year.

The surroundings are very grand (pier glass and chandelier) and you might at first assume that the image was more comforting. The print, known as "The kittens at tea—Miss Pauline singing", depicts five cats grouped round a table having, apparently, taken up the civilised British custom of "5 o'clock tea". What we have this time, it would appear, is the comforting safety of a children's book.

Having no expertise in these matters I at first thought that the lady pianist (playing a square piano with four legs and, apparently, stretchers) looked more like a spaniel but an accompanying verse informs us that:

A young lady cat plays a tune in K flat
A strange key, of course, but the words come in pat

When you begin to study this print more closely you find that the other five cats are not quite what you might expect. There is none of the usual saccharine of conventional children's illustrations. These cats are no relation of the grinning Cheshire cat of modern times. They do not smile and are certainly not about to start purring.

Are they talking about the latest problems they are having with the human pets?

A Flavour of Gormenghast

Illustration from "Comical Creatures". Plate No.80.

The book that sprang from Ploucquet's success itself became so popular that it went into later editions as "Comical Creatures: A Picture Book for the Nursery" but how and why Victorian mothers believed this was suitable for tiny tots would be one for the analyst's couch.

As can be seen from this Plate the "Comical Creatures" often continued to be depicted as members of high society, complete with grand piano but study of this, and other Plates in the book, reveal the truth: This is not the World of Andy Pandy—more the flavour of Gormenghast and Mervyn Peake on "speed".

What you find is that the birds, like the cats, often have a reptilian, menacing aura. This is the cast list for a horror film, or the extras for a particularly nasty piece of science fiction.

I understand that the drawings are the work of the British illustrator Harrison Weir, a catofanatic who conceived the idea of the first Cat Show at Crystal Palace in 1871 and went on to become President of the National Cat Club. His best known work is "Our Cats" published in 1889 but he also drew poultry and the like.

I do not doubt the good intentions of either Mr Weir or his publisher. They must have believed that their work was ideal for the nursery. What does this tell us of the Victorian mind and their fondness for macabre, anthropomorphic translation? Why did they find it so necessary to depict animals with abilities that they themselves might have lacked? Behold, I shew you a mystery.

All I learn is that the Victorians loved pianos.

Maestro Mouse at the Palace

If a Cat could play the piano why not a Mouse? And, this time, why not a real life mouse pianist? Not having investigated the matter in depth myself, I can only repeat what the piano historian David Wainwright tells us in his book "The Piano Makers":

"Musical mice were a phenomenon of early Victorian London….drawn by George Cruikshank in 1847 when it was exhibited at Palmer's Hair Cutting Rooms in the Strand, evidently not only boasted a voice 'whose notes resemble those of a bird in Spring' but also played an early Victorian cottage piano."

"The singing mouse" by Cruikshank. Plate No.81.

What are we to make of this? By trade and inclination I start such (hardly tall) tales with a great many questions and a quizzical frame of mind….but always believing that I may, indeed, one day live to see a miracle.

Did Mr Wainwright write this on April 1st? Did Maestro Mouse have his own miniature piano? And, if so, with real keys and strings? Etc., etc.

I made a few cursory enquiries and became yet more sceptical when I discovered that Cruikshank's mouse drawing titled "The singing mouse" was one of a page of sketches by the artist which he titled "Humbugs of the Day".

Still, there seems to be a possible contender for The Singing Mouse in one who, I found, took to the London stage in 1843.

It seems that a housewife in Cripplegate was woken from her sleep by gentle singing which seemed to float around the room. When she set a trap she caught the mouse soprano "which is likely to prove a golden egg".

The Singing Mouse appeared at The Cosmorama Rooms and his fame was such that he was invited to Buckingham Palace to serenade the little Prince of Wales and the Princesses. It is said that the mouse could sing incessantly for 15 minutes and "its notes are low and clear, and not unlike that of the nightingale".

A doubting journalist from "The Globe" made the owner leave the room and studied the mouse's tremulous throat closely to ensure he was not the victim of a ventriloquist.

This fearless front-line reporter then revealed that: "I am one of those who believe in the transmigration of souls; and taking into consideration the neighbourhood, the song…all combined, I think I know who it is; it is John Milton".

Listening to him trying to explain away that one to Lord Hutton would have been a rare treat. "Such sweet compulsion doth in music lie" would have given the reporter a plausible, but double-edged, excuse allowing The Noble Lord to make an alternative reading….and deliver another of those historic, impartial judgements for which he is known throughout the land.

I can only add that when I was a lad, after the 1939-45 War, there toured a number of "Flea Circuses". I never saw such a thing myself and always wondered if you had to take your own magnifying glass, or even microscope (presumably flea powder would have been infra dig) but I read many accounts of these mighty fleas who could perform impossible feats.

If a mouse pianist why not, then, a flea pianist? The day of the nanotechnology piano can not be far distant but who is to play it? Perhaps someone should start training an amoeba.

The Battle of the Pianos

"The Battle of the Pianos", a "Punch" cartoon of 1855 by John Leech, in which rival households endeavour to drown out their neighbours. Plate No.82.

To have suggested that the piano was simply a musical instrument would have been as innocent as to believe that a diamond was but a small rock.

The piano might act as political springboard (Paderewski, from concert platform to Prime Minister), or as hostage in marriage (the young lady "in possession of means" who advertised in "Neue Nachrichten" that she was looking for a husband who should be pale, have black hair and be in possession of TWO grand pianos).

But, of course, as the piano rose to domination not everyone was happy—imagine the envious gatherings of First Violinists or frustrated xylophonists. And public authorities were not always simpatico: In Weimar, aspiring pianists were forbidden to play with their windows open, or later than 11 p.m., and in Vienna they proposed a piano tax.

All such amounted to mere side bars. One might as well proclaim that the object of the piano was the making of music.

Long before 1850 the piano had been apotheosised into Desirable Domestic Object. This, naturally, delighted West End furnishers, Designers in need of employment....and generations of 19th Century cartoonists.

None took to the task more gleefully than the artists of "Punch", who lovingly recorded the domestic and social chaos that followed.

"Punch" was launched on July 17th., 1841 and one of the earliest to make an impact (from their fourth issue) was John Leech (1817-1864), of whom their family friend Flaxman pronounced "The boy must be an artist; he will be nothing else or less".

And, after a false start as a medical student, that is the life that Leech pursued. Leech lacked the acid of Gillray, or the unique ability of Cruikshank and, personally, I find his drawing a mite rough but he had a gentle sense of fun and an acute eye for social foibles.

Today Leech is best known for his fond sporting illustrations to the novels of Surtees but he filled the pages of "Punch" for many a year with insights into Victorian life and that, naturally, included the impact of the piano.

Of these, his most remarkable, was "The Battle of the Pianos", published in "Punch" in 1855. On either side of a party wall, rival households have stationed their piano and fierce parents vie with each other to drown out the party next door.

Another upright was shown by John Leech in his cartoon "Juvenile Etymology", which illustrates a Victorian piano with pilastered columns. Plate No.83.

As one daughter pounds away as hard as she can, her father instructs her, "Play away my Dears! Silence the enemy's Piano if possible". In the "neighbouring" house a Mother tells her offspring, "Keep on Lottie! Here's Frederic coming directly with his Cornet".

Good fun but, for those interested in the progress of design, the drawing holds other insights. From what we can see of the piano on the right it is either a cabinet or a semi-cabinet. But on the left is what I would call a modern, or true upright, of the type introduced by Hawkins in 1800.

By the 1840s the upright had already begun to assume a heavier mien and might be decorated in various ways. By the 1850s it was a full-blooded, recognisably Victorian article that might be neo-Rococo or over-dressed with fret and carving. So the upright shown by Leech with, apparently, a plain, turned leg, might be of the "Cottage" type that gained ground from the 1820s.

The social status of the grand piano was reflected in this John Leech cartoon "Villikens in the Drawing Room", in which the Young Lady instructs: "Now, William, you are not low enough yet. Begin at 'He took the cold Pizen'." Plate No.84.

What we should also note is how long it took before the modern upright began to be seen regularly in 19th Century cartoons or illustrations. Was it because the upright was associated with the common herd and what people really longed for was the status that came with a grand piano?

Leech showed another, recognisably Victorian, upright with pilastered columns in "Juvenile Etymology" but the piano that shows up more often in Leech's drawings is still the cabinet piano and I also found four of his cartoons with a grand piano, such as "Villikens in the Drawing Room".

In Leech's work the upright was still the poor relation.

A Great Artist Paints his Upright

The Burne-Jones upright.
Plate No.85.

Photo by courtesy of The Victoria and Albert Museum

One of the most important British artist-painted pianos of the 19th Century, because it was one of the earliest produced by what I suppose I should term the Post-Pre-Raphaelites and their associates, must have been unknown to most of the general public, although it was seen by various artists and designers of the Arts and Crafts movement.

The piano was a simple upright made by Priestly but painted by Edward Burne-Jones, who not only transformed British painting but made constant efforts to reform the decoration and design of pianos.

The reason this piano was so anonymous was that it was the instrument used in their own home by the newly married Burne-Joneses, to whom it was given as a present in 1860.

According to Georgiana Burne-Jones in her book on her husband: "Mrs Catherwood gave us a piano, made by Priestly of Berners Street who had patented a small one of inoffensive shape that we had seen and admired at Madox Brown's house; we had ours made of unpolished American walnut, a perfectly plain wood of pleasing colour, so that Edward could paint upon it."

Georgiana was devoted to music and used to find pieces of classical music to fit the poetry that she loved. One was Rossetti's "Song of the Bower" sung to a Schubert waltz and another was Keats's "Drear Nighted December", "surprisingly and effectively mingled with the trio from the slow movement of Beethoven's Sixth Sonata".

The choice of subject by Burne-Jones for the decoration of his Priestly was weird to the point of being macabre—not everyone would choose to live with a piano showing the figure of Death, complete with scythe, waiting to gather in a group of innocent young girls listening to a musician in a garden.

You have to open the keyboard lid of this piano, now in the Victoria and Albert Museum, to find a figure in white robes representing Love, with a small chamber organ "a very early design for the 'Chant d'Amour'".

One of the visitors to the Burne-Jones home, where he found four or five fellow artists (Ruskin having just left) was the "Punch" artist and author of "Trilby", George du Maurier, himself an enthusiast for music.

George describes Burne-Jones as "such a stunning fellow" and writes of how he entered a "large studio with such marvellously coloured paintings—plain piano in wood on which he in his leisure moments paints designs which will make it very valuable some day."

How right he was but finance is but one measurement. The Priestly upright decorated by Burne-Jones is one of the key pieces in the development of the British Art Piano.

Sudden Mania to Become Pianists

Sudden Mania to become Pianists created upon hearing STEINWAY'S Pianos at the Paris Exposition.

"Sudden Mania",1867. Plate No.86.

A slice of (well justified) triumphalism from our Transatlantic cousins when they invaded Europe in 1867 to show the Old World just how pianos should be made. The result was gushing praise all round and this cartoon published in an American magazine: "Sudden Mania to become Pianists, created upon hearing Steinway's Pianos at the Paris Exhibition".

Of course, it is equally revealing about the passion for pianos at that time in both Europe and America.

Many thought the pianos shown at the 1867 Paris Exhibition by the two most important American piano makers, Steinway and Chickering, were superior to those from the Old World. They won Steinway the première médaille and Chickering another prize, plus the Imperial Cross of the Legion of Honour.

This cartoon, which appeared in "Harper's Weekly" on August 10th., 1867, was itself a skit on an original French lithograph drawn by "Cham".

It was, however, a true reflection of European enthusiasm for American pianos. The Jury praised their powerful tone and there was admiring comment from piano enthusiasts such as Hector Berlioz and Gustave Dore.

Frustrated Social Ambition

"Frustrated Social Ambition!". Plate No.87.

Throughout the Victorian period the leading satirical journal of the day, "Punch", had great fun at the expense of the new piano-owning classes and some of their jokes rested on the fame of Britain's most important piano makers, Broadwood and Sons. Here in "Frustrated Social Ambition!", published on November 8th., 1879, we have the hostess begging the great Virtuoso: "Herr Bogoluboffski, we thought you might perhaps like to try the new Broadwood". A Chorus of Ladies pleads "Oh do, Herr Bogoluboffski! Pray do!".

...and a Musical Duchess

"The Musical Duchess",1867. Plate No.88.

Other favourite targets of "Punch" cartoonists were the piano-accompanied, musical soirées of the aristocracy, leading to satires based on the "Musical Duchess". Here, in a caricature published on May 21st., 1881, titled "Distinguished Amateurs—The Musical Duchess", they record that "Her Grace always sings her own words, set to her own music. Her compositions are endless; and when once she begins, she doesn't like to leave off in a hurry". A suitably "appreciative audience" suffer nobly but "Her Grace's music invariably drives all the other Duchesses away".

A 19th Century Pop Star....

PUNCH'S FANCY PORTRAITS.—No. 41.

" IL DEMONIO " RUBINSTEIN-O.

Among the pop stars of the 19th Century were undoubtedly the great pianists, the subject of endless speculation in newspapers and magazines when their World tours inevitably brought them to London. And each was besieged not only by the public but a stream of piano makers promising them both cash and free pianos if they would but endorse a particular product. One of the biggest impacts was made by the Russian court pianist Anton Rubinstein, caricatured by "Punch" on July 23rd., 1881, as "Il Demonio Rubinstein-O", an "eccentric foreigner....said to have taken away ten thousand pounds English coin this season". He had, said "Punch", "also made De-Money-O"!

Plate No.89.

....And the Prince of Pianists

One of the biggest stars of all was Franz Liszt, the Hungarian "prince of pianists", who made his last tour of England in 1886 when he "was received with unprecedented enthusiasm and was invited to Windsor to play before Queen Victoria". During this visit he was celebrated in this cartoon, published on April 3rd., 1886, showing "Mr Punch" serenading the Abbé Liszt who had been given an honorary canonry. It was by way of a valediction—Liszt died the same year on July 31st., 1886.

Plate No.90.

A Byzantine Art Piano and its Tragic End

The Alma-Tadema "Byzantine" Grand. Plate No.91.

I cannot find "Art Piano" listed in either my copy of the "Dictionary of Music" or the "Shorter Oxford" and it is hard to know exactly how you would define such an article. But let us try:

An Art Piano is an instrument where, with regard to the exterior (and, with high quality work, it even stretches to the decoration of the usually unseen interior) the principal intention is to beautify the case. This may be achieved through artist painting; the choice of fine, contrasting veneers and exotic woods; the use of inlay or marquetry; the decorative employment of ormolu and other metal-working techniques; the application of rubies, pearls, garnets or other precious stones; the skilful application of gilding; the fitting of panels of stained glass; or cladding the surface with handsomely worked leather and the like. In fact, any material that serves the aesthetic, visual end purpose….Even plastic.

Whether any of these techniques necessarily add up to a successful Art Piano is, of course, another matter.

The decoration of musical instruments stretches back to antiquity, and one is entitled to ask whether this was not really veneration of an article that had the power to transfix human beings by producing sound. Both decoration and sound a form of magic, or is that too fanciful? Perhaps idolatry?

The Art Piano movement in Britain really gathered momentum in the second half of the 19th Century with this "Byzantine" grand piano, with a Broadwood works, designed by the artist Alma Tadema and shown in this illustration in "The Graphic" on August 16th., 1879. Its impact was immediate and it subsequently became known throughout the World. It was the first really famous British Art Piano.

The oddest thing about Alma Tadema's grand is that a man considered one of the foremost painters of his time chose to mainly decorate the instrument with gold, silver, ebony, ivory, lapis lazuli, tortoiseshell, mother of pearl, and rare woods.

Conspicuous consumption hardly describes the expenditure of precious materials on Alma Tadema's extraordinary piano. It had a mighty triumph, not least when shown at the Inventions Exhibition of 1885 but came to an end of Shakespearean proportions—blasted to destruction and immolated by German bombers when they hit the London premises of Maples the furnishers during the 1939-1945 War. If pianos could speak it might have been tempted to anticipate Cagney: "Made it ma. Top of the World!"

Burne-Jones and a Dream of Orpheus

The "Orpheus" grand. Plate No.92. *Photograph courtesy of Christopher Wood Gallery and The Mells Estate*

Both Alma Tadema and his great rival Edward Burne-Jones achieved the ultimate social recognition for a Victorian painter—the touch of the Sovereign's sword on the shoulders that dubbed them "Sir". And, in the kind of clash that reminds you of Mediaeval Knights meeting on The Field of the Cloth of Gold, each produced an Art Piano that inevitably led to a public critique of their abilities and reputation in the field of applied art.

If Alma Tadema's unconventional, Quixotic gamble on a bejewelled "Byzantine" grand was to result in the best known British Art Piano of that period it was to be challenged almost immediately by a very different venture—the "Orpheus" grand by Burne-Jones.

Each of these great men was lost beyond recall in a dream world of ancient days but where Alma Tadema plumped for his own interpretation of Byzantine style by the use of precious materials, Burne-Jones depended solely on the powers of his brush and a vision from the Underworld.

To what extent Burne-Jones was stung by Alma Tadema's success I do not know but, since he had already decorated another piano nearly 20 years before, it would have been perfectly understandable if Burne-Jones felt he had been first in the field and had somehow lost the recognition he deserved.

The "Orpheus", Burne-Jones' supreme achievement in the decoration of pianos, was completed between 1879-1880 but exactly how long he had planned such an undertaking I cannot say. Many of the artist's ideas were years in gestation and there is proof that the *subject* was in his mind c.1872—which does not prove that he was planning the piano at that time.

Major paintings were executed on each side of the lid and, round the sides, a series of eleven circular panels told the legend of Orpheus and Eurydice. The lid shows, on top, a Muse emerging from a winged circle to offer the poet a scroll. Underneath sits Mother Earth with her children spread around her and a sinuous vine winding round them.

Both Burne-Jones and Alma Tadema had a sincere concern to reform piano design and each carried out subsequent commissions for Broadwood and Sons. But these Art Pianos represent each man's main achievement in the field and remain the best known examples produced in Britain in the 19th Century, despite the attempts of subsequent imitators.

I'm to be a Great Pianist

"Removal". Plate No.93.

The importance of teaching children to play the piano (reinforced, on occasion, by the rap of a ruler across the knuckles) as a social asset and a cultural necessity, was a recurring 19th Century theme. In "Removal of Ancient Landmarks", published in "Punch" on June 25th., 1881, Lady Gwendoline tells the new Governess that Papa says she is to be a great artist, while Lady Edelgitha says she must be a great actress and "cut out Miss Ellen Terry". But Lady Yseulte, hand resting on the upright piano, tells her: "And Papa says I'm to be a great Pianist and play at the Monday Pops!"

Only the Daughters of Gentlemen

Plate No.94.

Perched alongside (of course) her grand piano, the dour Teacher assures the Doctor in this "Punch" cartoon of October 22nd., 1892, entitled "The Height of Exclusiveness", that "Under my care, I can assure you that your Little Ward will associate with daughters of Gentlemen only!" But the Doctor replies: "That, Madam, is to be select indeed; since I believe that Pallas Athene alone fulfilled such a condition".

The Boy Who Would Do Nothing but Play

Plate No.95.

Presumably meant as a skit on the six-times married pianist Eugène Francis Charles d'Albert, this portrayal of the (moustachioed?) "Master Charley D'Albert, The Boy who would do nothing but play", in "Punch" on June 5th., 1886, is equally a comment on child virtuosos who were trotted on to London stages regularly as the next would-be Mozart.

Will he Look for Garlands?

A SIREN.

Plate No.96.

Cruelty was not the norm in "Punch": Gentle japes, good natured fun and mild social satire was more their style. The Spirit of Wooster before P.G. Wodehouse came along, you might say. But, in one area, there was unthinking cruelty at the expense of one of the saddest classes in Victoria society: The Spinster Lady. Even the title of "A Siren", set against a portrait of a fat and ugly Plain Jane of uncertain age, shows the brutality that passed as humour when it came to women who were "left on the shelf". In this "Punch" cartoon of September 11th., 1886, the ever-hopeful old maid, thumping away at her upright, serenades herself with "Shall I wear a White Rose? Shall I wear a Red? Will he look for garlands? What shall wreathe my Head?"

How Come You've Never Married?

Even more vicious, if it is possible, is the smug, smiling satisfaction of the pretty, carefree, young married woman who has achieved the desirable respectability of marriage and who yet scores points off the aged, plain spinster. In this "Punch" cartoon of February 20th., 1892, The Young Wife declares "Oh, I'm so happy! How is it

PERFECTLY PLAIN.

Plate No.97.

you've never married, Miss Prymme?" To which the reply is, "My dear, I never have accepted—and never would accept—any offer of marriage". At which the wife starts playing on her upright piano the old Air, "Nobody axed you".

Captain Spinks Pops the Question

Plate No.98.

Sex and the Piano were never mentioned in the same breath in polite 19th Century society but of the piano as an aid to romance we are left in no doubt by either popular prints or the cartoonists. In "A Drama of the Drawing-Room", published in "Punch" on November 29th., 1879, Jones is being bored by a tale of illness but, at the grand piano, "Captain Spinks is Popping the Question to Clara Willoughby behind one of Chopin's Mazurkas".

A remarkable piano design by C.F.A. Voysey shown in "The Studio" in May, 1896, Page 218, although the design had been made in 1894. It seems to me it must have been influenced by the Noyon Armoire. Plate No.99.

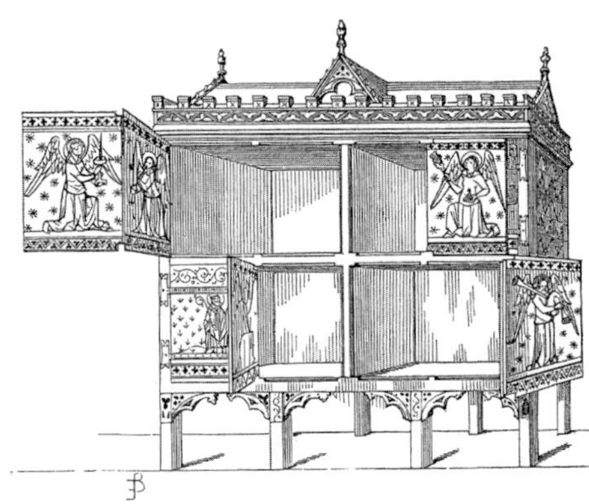

The Noyonne Armoire, a French Cathedral piece of c.1300, had a massive influence on 19th Century British designers from Burges onwards. This illustration in "Annales Archeologiques" and another by Viollet-le-Duc must have been studied by many of them. Plate No.100.

Voysey's Piano with a Roof

By the 1880s most of the big names of the British design World had already produced their own versions of the piano—men like A.W.N. Pugin, Bruce Talbert and E.W. Godwin. A host of other architects and trade designers added to a competitive mix.

In 1889 they were joined by another major figure, C.F.A. Voysey, whose design for an upright with a distinctive shelf above the keyboard and, presumably, painted panels, appeared in "The British Architect" on December 20th., 1889. I have to say that, by Voysey standards, it does not stir me, though perhaps I might change my mind if I saw the effect of the decoration in real life, rather than making do with this sketch.

Similar designs for an upright had already been produced by Erard in 1856 and Frederick Priestley in 1862, though whether Voysey had knowledge of these I know not.

Voysey produced a much more startling idea in 1894 that was shown to the public in an illustration in "The Studio" in May, 1896. It encompasses many of the standard Voysey ideas yet, unmistakeably, with its "roof", reminds you of a building…possibly a Church.

My presumption is that this remarkable design must have been translated into a real piano but whether it survives is, again, a mystery to me.

It seems to me that Voysey must have been influenced in his conception by a piece that just about put the hex on British designers from the 1850s onwards, the decorated Noyon Armoire of c.1300. From Burges onwards you can see them being hypnotised by its form and painted panels—I presume another part of the dream of a Mediaeval past where love and beauty reigned (so long as you didn't have to experience the real thing).

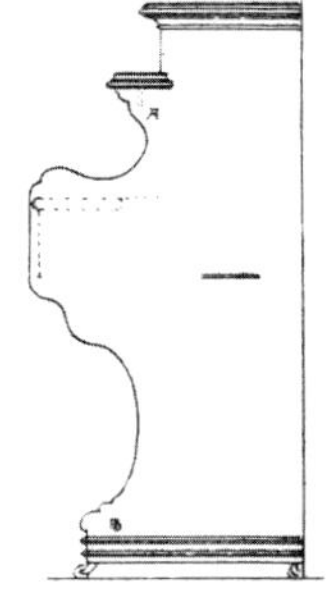

The first piano design by C.F.A. Voysey I have been able to trace was published in "The British Architect" on December 20th., 1889. By Voysey's standards it was fairly tame stuff. Plate No.101.

The Brass Neck of Mr Brinsmead

The huge Brinsmead factory in Kentish Town, London, shown in "Commerce", April, 1894. Plate No.102.

A firm who were prepared to publish a booklet in which their founder was described as "the Father of the Pianoforte Trade" when he wasn't even born until some 50 years after the golden age of Zumpe, Backers, Broadwood and the others had what I believe our American friends call "chutzpah" i.e. "unbelievable gall; insolence; audacity". Or, as we might say in old English, "a real brass neck".

You also have pause to reflect on the Munchausian powers of Brinsmead and Sons when the firm added that the founder, John Brinsmead, had been widely known by his "Father" title "Since the forties", by which they meant the 1840s. As Mr Brinsmead had, by his own account, walked to London as late as 1835 to begin work in "a piano factory as a journeyman case maker" his rise to pater familias and international fame must have been remarkable indeed.

But then, no-one ever accused John Brinsmead and his sons of being backward in self-promotion. They were, on this side of the Atlantic, King of the Puffs when it came to the piano trade.

Involved in a notorious court case of 1892 in which the frm was sued by a middleman who alleged that he was owed money for "arranging" to have flattering accounts of Brinsmead pianos inserted in various newspapers and magazines, the Brinsmeads were quite unfazed, despite judgement against them for £150 damages.

Talking of what he called "the gentle art of puffery", Thomas Brinsmead, the son and partner of John, blithely explained: "The aim of the advertiser is to secure the widest publicity possible. He is, moreover, entitled to employ every legitimate means to that end—to strike out, if he pleases, in new directions."

Brinsmeads were bold advertisers, especially in the fashionable journal "Illustrated London News". This full page ad of a lady soloist with three admirers appeared on February 16th., 1889. Plate No.103.

That wonderful phrase "new directions", one of the precursors of such modern gems as "Collateral damage", covered some innovative ground.

The middleman, or perhaps "fixer" might have been a more accurate description, one Barnard Morris, told the Court that "in order to further the Brinsmeads' interests" he had given presents to newspaper people such as "barrels of oysters" and "a silk dress".

Another Brinsmead full page advert showing children in period dress appeared in "Illustrated London News" on April 27th., 1889....with an upright of decidedly eclectic parts. Plate No.104.

Mr Morris, not I suspect a man who would enjoy your unalloyed trust, told a tale of getting Brinsmead pianos into the Royal Holloway College because it was known the Queen would be visiting; of how he had been "instrumental" in getting a Brinsmead piano accepted by Prince Leopold and had "worked the whole thing"; how he had managed to have an account of Mr Brinsmead's golden wedding, written by Mr Brinsmead himself, inserted in four daily papers; of a "laudatory puff of Mr Brinsmead and his pianos" in "Pall Mall"; how he had paid certain named papers for insertion of paragraphs. And numerous examples of promotional paragraphs in the Press.

When the Brinsmeads didn't like the judgement of the Jury at the 1885 Inventions Exhibition he had arranged for a letter from them to appear in various journals. This letter was from "One of the Jury" but, it was alleged, had been concocted in the offices of Brinsmeads.

The Court was told that Messrs Brinsmead had been "desirous of getting into the newspapers" items which were really advertisements "but which appeared to be ordinary news".

Morris's own Counsel described him as a man who "by reason of his great influence with the newspapers, they doing for him what they would not do for ordinary people, he had got into the papers paragraphs which would appear to be genuine to the ordinary readers."

After hearing both Mr Morris and two of the Brinsmeads swear on oath and then deliver contrary versions of events, Mr Justice Collins concluded that "both the plaintiff and the defendants had given their evidence (*and*) did but scanty justice to their respective cases".

What the public learned was the lengths to which the Brinsmeads were prepared to go to fight the piano sales war. And a trawl through the various media reveals that, for much of the firm's history, they were as successful as any other piano maker I could identify at getting the firm's name in print.

A view of the grand piano workshop in Brinsmead's factory, "Music Trades Journal", March, 1886. Plate No.105.

One can only marvel at an account of the founder appearing in the 1901 publication "Fortunes Made in Business" that began with the words: "The personality of John Brinsmead, splendid among workmen, the head and fine flower of his craft and maker of perfect pianos...."

Every possible effort was made to associate the Brinsmead name, no matter how remotely, with Kings, Queens, any variety of aristocrat they could find, concert pianists, singers and Exhibitions of every hue.

Despite such flummery and hagiography, it should be noted that John Brinsmead was a highly successful Victorian entrepreneur who, with vigour and push, built a major piano company, one of the big names of the Late 19th Century industry. From illustrations we can see that they had a very large factory at their one-acre site in Grafton Road, adjoining Kentish Town Station, London and a reporter noted 750,000 feet of timber in store and 33 workshops.

Just one half of the huge upright piano workshop in the Brinsmead factory, as shown in "Music Trades Journal", March, 1886. They claimed to turn out one piano every hour. Plate No.106.

In "old fashionable" Wigmore Street, in the West End, the firm also had handsome showrooms and warehouses designed by Leonard V. Hunt, complete with concert rooms for 150 people.

It was claimed (if you believe them) that they produced a piano every working hour of the year, except in the slack season.

By 1873 John Brinsmead had managed to make the pages of the "Royal Blue Book", a long way from his beginnings in Weir Gifford, North Devon, where he was born in 1814, the son of a farmer. The boy's attempt to become a flockmaster ended when his little band of 16 sheep was stolen and, he says, he became apprenticed to a Torrington cabinet maker for six or seven years.

Bending the case of a grand piano at the Brinsmead factory, as shown in "Commerce", April, 1894. Plate No.107.

Where John Brinsmead learnt about puffery I know not, but that his firm seldom missed a promotional trick can be seen by the introduction in 1887 of "The Cremona Pianoforte", conjuring up the names of the 17th Century Italian violin makers Stradivari, Amati, Guarneri, Bergonzi, etc. Their firm had, Brinsmeads explained, grappled with the secrets of Cremona violin making because of their "intimate conviction that it should be found possible....to recover this lost art".

Now Messrs Brinsmead begged "to say that they deem themselves fully entitled to affirm that they have met with a success". They had made a "close study of all parts of the violin, as well as of the constitution of the lustrous varnish, which by penetration into the pores of the wood so importantly affects its faculty of sonorous vibration".

Ah, the "lustrous varnish".

Brinsmead announced that they were able to "state with....confidence their expectation of being able to apply, in a similar way to pianoforte construction, this important discovery as to the violin".

A well varnished story indeed.

But just how good were their pianos as musical instruments? No one is less fitted than myself to make such a judgement.

The Brinsmead adverts quoted Nicolas Rubinstein as saying "The palm belongs to the Grand Pianos of the house of Brinsmead", And Adelina Patti as saying "I am charmed with the tone and touch of the Splendid Pianoforte made for me by Messrs John Brinsmead and Sons; and the case is lovely". Presumably both impartial, disinterested witnesses....unless they had been given a free piano, or benefits in kind.

The Examining Shop at Brinsmead's factory, shown in "Commerce", April, 1894. Plate No.108.

The modern piano historian Cyril Ehrlich puts the matter rather differently, stating that "an image of high quality was sedulously cultivated....But surviving instruments suggest that Brinsmead was never more than a good medium-class maker".

Mr Ehrlich explains that "Image and reality are peculiarly difficult to separate in the case of Brinsmead because of the elaborate and relentless nature of his puffing....an advertising agent....paid £16,000 during the 1880s to manipulate the press".

These cabinet makers, shown in "Commerce", April, 1894, seem to be working on the cases of the better class of Grand Pianos at Brinsmead's factory. Note the inlay on the case in the foreground. Plate No.109.

John Brinsmead, the determined Victorian entrepreneur who founded Brinsmead and Sons after, it is said, he walked to London from Devon. Born in 1814, he lived to be 93 and left an estate of £46,127. He was shown here in the 1901 publication "Fortunes Made In Business". Plate No.110.

My interest is purely in the design of the Brinsmead piano cases. The majority are not to my personal taste but any design historian is going to wish to study their contributions to the 1851 Exhibition (a wildly decorated upright is to be found in the Museum of London); the Paris Exhibitions of 1867 and 1878; and certain other exhibitions.

I am personally interested in an "Early English" (in reality Neo-Gothic) upright they made surprisingly late, in the 1890s and the pianos they produced for the grand liners of the P. and O. shipping line (each said to be "specially designed by some well known artist" but only one of which I have so far seen illustrated, that for the "S.S. Himalaya").

In commercial terms John Brinsmead was a success story of the Late Victorian era and, from the Broadwood cuttings book at the Surrey History Centre you learn what a jealous eye was kept on them by the greatest of British firms. With good reason: By 1900 Brinsmead employed more than 200 men and had overtaken Broadwood in annual production.

Few of them, however, seemed to sense the impending crisis that would overwhelm the piano industry in the 20th Century. After the Great War the firm, under John's less than successful descendants, were afflicted by labour and other troubles.

By January, 1920 they went into liquidation.

One of the most radical designs ever produced for the British upright piano came in 1893 from Walter Cave and was shown at the Arts and Crafts Exhibition of that year. This drawing appeared in "Furniture and Decoration", Page 166, November, 1893. Plate No.111.

◀

Two Radicals of the 1890's

The two most daring, and important, attempts to reinterpret the case design of the British upright piano were both made in the 1890s and, as you might have expected, came from two architects who were members of the avant-garde of the applied arts, The Arts and Crafts Exhibition Society.

One of the most radical was shown at the Arts and Crafts Exhibition of November, 1893 and was the work of Walter Cave, who came from a Bristol banking family. What Cave did was to support the keyboard with two elongated legs-cum-candle sconces which gave a completely new, dramatic, architectural and stark look to the piano. This was emphasised by a plain oak case, relieved only by large metal hinges across the piano lid.

Cave's piano was sold under the improbable name of the "Mediaeval English Upright Grand" which, I think, tells you more about the way the Society members had fallen for Morris's vision of a Lost England than it did about advanced design. Made by Bechstein, this was the most imitated piano design of its time.

But whether Cave pinched his ideas from C.A.F. Voysey is another matter altogether. Without question the design vocabulary was Voysey's.

The second major departure came from a splendid designer, M.H. Baillie Scott, under another unlikely name, "the Manxman" and this was shown at the 1896 Arts and Crafts Exhibition (although it had been announced to the Trade in June that year by its makers, Broadwood).

Again, one senses some longing for Olde England while, paradoxically, attempting to produce something modern. What Baillie Scott did was to totally enclose the top of the piano and turn it into what looked like a cupboard. Whether it was also intended to hide the true nature of the beast you may judge for yourself.

The first commercial models by Broadwood were stained dark green (harking back to Morris and Ford Madox Brown) and the plain oak relieved by four huge horizontal strap hinges. Later, Baillie Scott was to exploit the "canvases" of such pianos, the large flat areas he had introduced, with superb decoration of this basic model, in special commissions for the Grand Duke of Hesse and others.

Whether Baillie Scott's ideas were then stolen by Charles Ashbee is a matter we shall consider later.

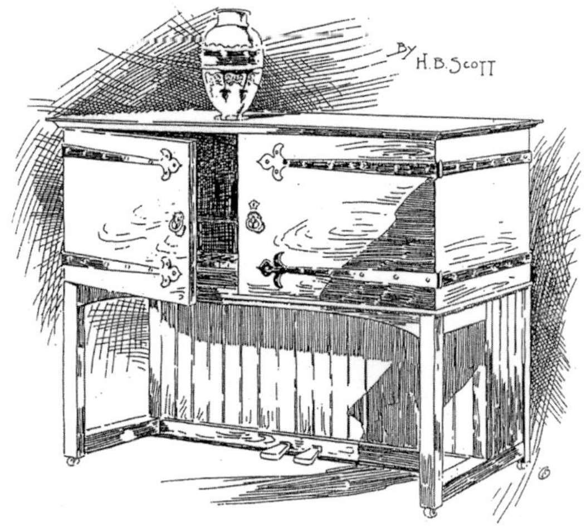

Another major attempt to reinterpret the case of the upright was made in 1896 by M.H. Baillie Scott and this illustration appeared in the "Cabinet Maker", Page 121, November, 1896. Plate No.112.

Making Sweet Music for the Mating Game

Postcard by unknown artist. Plate No.113.

With the dawning of the Edwardian age the relationship between The Piano and The Mating Game was made far more explicit. As these postcards (and one old song sheet) show it was generally a highly romanticised view that was put forward but sometimes it was translated into bawdy humour.

Song sheet cover by unknown artist. Plate No.114.

Postcard by unknown artist. Plate No.115.

Postcard by unknown artist. Plate No.116.

Postcard by unknown artist. Plate No.117.

The Amateur Pianist's Nightmare

Plate No.118.

Now what would Freud have made of this?

It is called "The Amateur Pianist's Nightmare" and the threatening figure perched like one of the James' Gang atop the grand piano, revolver in fist, is in fact Paderewski. He warns the would-be pianist: "You must play Chopin's Ballade in A flat major—and mind, the First Wrong Note—DEATH!"

The audience is, if anything, more terrifying. What we might assume to be the usual concert-goers turn out to be the deities and V.I.P.s of the world of music.

In the back row: Kubelik, Marie Hall, Frank Merick, Brahms, Handel, Sterndale Bennett and Sarasate.

In the middle row: Schubert, Rosenthal, Bach, Beethoven, Mendelssohn and Rubinstein.

In the first row: Pachmann, Liszt, Emile Sauer, Mozart, Backhaus, Sir George Grove and Herbert Parsons. At the front is Schumann.

The figure in the flower pot, decorated with musical notes, is stated to be Grossmith —could it possibly be George Grossmith the singer who appeared at the Opéra Comique and, later, in no less than eight of Gilbert and Sullivan's productions at the Savoy?

A clue might be Grossmith's headgear, looking suspiciously like an Aesthetic sunflower wilting in the heat of a new century. Which would have been an accurate, if painful, comment when this cartoon appeared in "Punch" on December 30th., 1903—"Patience" being by then but a quaint reminder of a social order subverted by the Decadents and about to be shell-shocked by Cubism and the like.

The caricaturist was R. C. Carter, a man who showed in his work that he knew enough about the latest developments in both the worlds of music and design to satirise each with an insider's knowledge.

Whether Carter had read Sigismund Freud's "The Interpretation of Dreams" we do not know but this disturbing work (the foundation of Psychoanalysis) had been published shortly before, in 1900. If Carter had come across it he must surely have studied Chapter Five, "The Examination Dream".

When we have such anxiety dreams, argued Freud, "These are the ineradicable memories of the punishments we suffered as children for misdeeds....When our student days are over, it is no longer our parents or teachers who see to our punishment; the inexorable chain of cause and effect of later life has taken over....we fear that we may be punished by some unpleasant result because we have done something carelessly or wrongly, because we have not been as thorough as we might have been—in short, whenever we feel the burden of responsibility."

Was it Al Capone who said "You can get much farther with a kind word and a gun than you can with a kind word alone"?

Call in the London Bobbies

Plate No.119.

Before the arrival of radio, television and The Beatles there were....The Great Solo Pianists. Strangely, Paderewski's first tour of Britain in 1890 was counted a failure but two things helped change perceptions: Queen Victoria's invitation for him to play before her at Windsor Castle and his "magnificent head and his mass of red hair....undoubtedly of great significance in his success". The Paderewski Fever was reflected here on November 11th., 1893, by the "Punch" cartoonist E.T. Reed, with the journal suggesting that three London Bobbies were needed by "Padded-Roomski" because of "devotees....who rush at, try to embrace, and deck with roses, a certain Master, whenever he appears". This was not simply a jest, "The Times" pointing out on November 1st that at his concert at St. James's Hall, London, "the usual farcical proceedings took place".

The Man who Started Long Haired Music

It has often been said that the description "Long Haired Music" (meaning highbrow) was first used about Paderewski. If so, it would be no surprise. Paderewski might have been one of the greatest pianists the World had ever seen but no-one (especially the Ladies) doubted that half his secret was The Hair.

"His long hair, red hair, inspired admiration and awe", says one writer. And other pianists tried to pinch the Paderewski style: Familiar top hat, long coat, long hair. They wrote that, when he sat at the piano, Paderewski gave the impression of a Botticelli or a Fra Angelico angel.

Plates Nos.120 to 123.

Sir Edward Burne-Jones saw him in the street one day and, not having the slightest idea who he was, rushed home and sketched him from memory. When Paderewski was brought to his studio subsequently, Burne-Jones exclaimed "You are my archangel!"

But "Punch", mischievous as ever, endeavoured to imply that the Maestro's hair was not all that it might seem. In their Almanack for 1894 they did a series of Paderewski cartoons titled "Musical Competition", showing fashionably dressed ladies fighting for a lock of the Maestro's hair.

But how could he have so much hair when so much was stolen? "Punch" claimed to reveal that when the tired Maestro retired to his bedroom he was, in reality.....bald! The key to it all was a row of wigs, they impishly suggested.

Bringing the Family Together

Plate No.124.

Plate No.126.

Before television the piano was the unifying influence in hundreds of thousands of British homes and, one might argue, since all the family could join in a singsong, a force for good. In these photos of anonymous interiors, from my own collection, you can see how central the piano was to everyday lives.

Plate No.127.

Plate No.125.

Plate No.128.

The Vital Element for the Home

More ghosts from an anonymous past come once more to vivid and touching life to demonstrate how much the piano was woven into the fabric of their lives.

Plate No.129.

Plate No.130.

Plate No.131.

Plate No.132.

Plate No.133.

Plate No.134.

The Search for The Child Prodigy

Mozart at a harpsichord. His fame as a child prodigy encouraged "The Mozart Effect" in child pianists. Plate No.135.

Myths and legends can, in our dreams, make heroes of us all and no illusion was promoted more assiduously by the piano trade than the concept of The Child Prodigy. For some tiny tots, even Beethoven, it turned into a nightmare…if legend is to be believed.

A number of accounts seem to agree that when Beethoven was four or five his father, who is described as "weak-spirited and (*who*) drank excessively", saw the child as a potential Wunderkind who could, with harsh discipline, be made into a concert pianist.

It is said that Beethoven's father "locked him in a room to practise for hours"; after long nights of drinking "would sometimes drag his son out of bed to practice the piano or play for guests"; and "caused humiliating scenes….trying to force genius into him".

As a child prodigy Beethoven failed to emulate Mozart's fame but nevertheless made his concert debut early, at about the age of eight it is claimed. And he did, of course, have a rather different success as the greatest composer of his age but I find it uncomfortable to believe that this was due to his drunken father's ill treatment.

One comes across hints of a similar harsh regime for other tiny children. An early, pre-1800 piano star in London was Elizabeth Weichsel, who was put on the stage at the age of six and it was said that "her father superintended her musical education with a degree of severity that could be scarcely justified, even by the proficiency of the pupil".

In a 1799 book "Strictures on the Modern System of Female Education", Hannah More reported eminent advice that: "Suppose your pupil to begin at six years of age and to continue at the average of four hours a-day only, Sunday excepted, and thirteen days allowed for travelling annually, till she is eighteen, the state stands thus: 300 days multiplied by four, the number of hours amount to 1200; that number multiplied by twelve, which is the number of years, amounts to 14,000 hours!"

Postcard by an unknown artist. Plate No.136.

Note that "only". I presume that would-be Wunderkinds were driven a lot harder than that.

Child prodigies had long been promoted, whether for parental pride or hard cash I leave you to judge, on a regular basis.

Britain's biggest piano makers, Broadwood and Sons, made sure to let the Press know in 1890 when they found the following advertisement in "The Morning Chronicle" of June 9th., 1785: "Mr Astley (of the Amphitheatre, Westminster Bridge) begs leave to inform the nobility, gentry, and others that he has engaged for twelve nights that amazing phenomenon the Musical Child from Newcastle-upon-Tyne. He is only thirty-six months old, has the judgement of the most professed theorist in music, and is allowed by all ranks of persons to be the most astonishing natural production that ever made its appearance in the known world. This infant is to perform in the centre of the school, on the Forte piano, several known airs, &c."

A likely story. Old hacks like myself would, within minutes, be setting out to check the Church baptismal records or see if it was an early example of the mechanical piano but it gives you a fair flavour of The Child Prodigy game. Someone's pockets were being lined.

But search and you will find other accounts of child prodigies around the turn of the 18th Century.

Dussek's sister, it was claimed, had a son who made his debut at the age of five; composed two fantasias dedicated to the Prince of Wales when he was seven; and performed a concerto of his own at the age of eight. He was described, in ludicrously inflated terms, as "Mozart Britannicus".

Few seem to doubt that the finest of all these Child Prodigies was Wolfgang Amadeus Mozart *(pictured on page 95 at the harpsichord)*. He was "that rare thing, an infant prodigy and an adult genius". Which did not prevent him dying in 1791, a penurious man in an unmarked grave, "harassed, miserable, overworked and poor".

It is claimed that when Mozart was three he could distinguish harmonic progressions; at four he was taught the harpsichord; and at five he was a composer (some of his earliest compositions were for the keyboard). As a child he was taken, with his sister, to perform at various European Royal courts where he was a universal sensation: "Received by the Emperor and kissed by Marie Antoinette".

Postcard of an anonymous child. Plate No.137.

But, as a biographer wrote, "his childish talents were exploited for the enrichment of his father and other impresarios".

Quite a number of composers first emerged as Child Prodigies.

It is suggested that the instrument shown here was a harpsichord but it was popular illustrations like this that helped inspire the search by Victorian parents for a piano prodigy. This is Margaret Dicksee's sugary offering for the 1893 Royal Academy Exhibition, "The Child Handel", said to have been discovered playing in the garret. Plate No.138.

"Royal Academy Pictures", 1893

Chopin, described as "Little Chopin", was claimed to have given public concerts by the age of seven, when he had already written two polonaises. Mendelssohn took piano lessons at six and is said to have appeared in public at nine. Albéniz, it was claimed, first performed at the age of four. Bizet, they claimed, was able to enter the Paris Conservatory at the unheard-of age of nine. Saint-Saëns was another early starter. Such claims, I would suggest, need careful checking.

I read with interest that, today, some modern classical pianists start training as early as three years old and a suggested definition of a child prodigy is one who, by the age of ten, "displays expert proficiency in a field usually only undertaken by adults".

A study of gifted children, using the latest M.R.I. scanning methods, showed that those in the field of mathematics were achieving blood flow to parts of the brain at six to seven times the typical flow, it was reported.

The myth of The Child Prodigy appears to be as strong today as it ever was.

One Internet site has a section devoted to "Boy Musical Prodigies". A competition for "International Piano Prodigies", open to children from 11 to 13, was staged in Utah and attracted over 70 applicants. A veritable production line of child players is emerging from the East and "China's one-child policy has created a culture where parents invest heavily in children's education—a boon for piano makers like the Pearl River Piano Co."

One does not know whether to weep, laugh or rejoice at a story headed "Giving birth to a piano prodigy and profiting from it", which tells how a Chinese mother listened to countless hours of classical music while she was pregnant, hoping to transmit the rhythms to her foetus. Subsequently, the family spent half their yearly income to buy a piano for their baby son, and the father took his child to the big city for training, which meant the couple were separated for the next 12 years. Now the small child has grown into an International performer.

So persistent are such attempts to transform an infant into a musical genius that today there is a name for this hypnotic visitation. It is known as "The Mozart Effect".

For my own part I do not look with pleasure at any adult prepared to make money off the back of a child but am realist enough to know that the World is full of committed parents who wish to live out their own failed dreams through their offspring. As long as there is a Mr and Mrs Smith who see their little Jimmy or Joan as the star of the Albert Hall, so will more Child Prodigies be manufactured.

As that very nasty man, John Ford, said through the voice of a very good man, Ransome Stoddard: "When the truth becomes legend, print the legend". Thus, thousands of proud parents believe that The Myth of the Child Prodigy has to be, must be, can only be, their reality.

And, who knows, one day we may see another Mozart.

The Bonfire of the Square Pianos

The Old Square of the Past (Was $450, Now $15)

Its Future

As Harry Edward Freund geared up for his campaign to obliterate the old square piano, he published these two propaganda cartoons in his journal "The Musical Age", on November 28th., 1903. Plates No.139 and 140.

One of the most notorious episodes in the history of the piano, still guaranteed to reduce square piano enthusiasts to apoplexy and, for all I know, paroxysms of tears, was The Bonfire of the Square Pianos at Atlantic City, America, on May 24th., 1904. Of the squares offered for sacrifice, one particularly ornate, veneered square of 1876 was covered entirely with white paint; was proclaimed "The White Elephant"; and then exposed to public ridicule. It was daubed with "poetic" doggerel that ended "I'll feed the flames by the salt sea air".

Perhaps William Holman Hunt chose the wrong subject for his morality painting "The Scapegoat".

Hard as it might be to imagine, this publicity stunt was organised by a music journal. More specifically, it was the wheeze of one Harry Edward Freund, Editor of the "The Musical Age" (to our shame, born a Londoner in 1863) who, after a relentless campaign, organised a pyre that was built with the specific aim of obliterating the innocent and hapless square piano. A fair idea of Freund's propaganda can be gained from the above cartoons that he published in advance of the bonfire.

Mr Freund's journal was the self-proclaimed organ of the National Association of Piano Dealers in America. And he told them it was all for their benefit.

If you believe Mr Freund (and I would suggest a large measure of caution with such a Barnum-like figure) 1,000 square pianos were thus destroyed at the annual convention of the Association, each dealer being urged to contribute "from three to five of these instruments".

If they followed such a practice "for, say, a period of ten years, 15,000 to 20,000 squares would be out of existence", he boasted. The problem, it was claimed, was that the old squares damaged profits because, often, dealers had to take them in part exchange.

Press coverage of the planned event, as Freund had schemed and encouraged, was International and one wit wrote: "Musical instrument makers are going to make a bonfire of 1,000 pianos at Atlantic City. By any happy chance, do these include the pianos in the adjoining flat, the flat overhead, and the flat beneath?"

Not everyone in the music business agreed with Freund's plan and even his own brother attacked him in print, suggesting that it was a scheme "whose futility as well as ridiculousness are apparent".

Freund told the American dealers that "The old squares are a bugbear in the piano business....The destruction of a couple of thousand of these old boxes would rid the trade of a considerable nuisance....They constantly crop up in retail piano transactions, much to the disgust of piano men."

It was certainly true that America had kept faith in the square piano long after the Europeans had deserted this form for the upright piano and that, consequently, there must have been many, many thousands still housed in homes across the U.S.A.

As far back as 1860 Henry Fowler Broadwood, head of Britain's largest piano makers, had ordered "Discontinue all Squares which are not made solid for the tropics". The very last Broadwood square, No. 64,161, was produced in 1866.

But in that very year, 1866, squares still made up 97 per cent of American piano production, according to H.E. Krehbiel. It was not until 1888 that America's best known company, Steinway, ceased production of squares and by the 1890s they were largely out of fashion, though a few were still made after 1900.

What the trade wanted in 1904, Freund urged at every opportunity, was simply the sale of shiny, new, expensive pianos with no irritating after-thoughts.

Suggestions that they should simply give the old squares to the poor were ignored. After a pantomime episode involving the Mayor of Atlantic City, Fire Brigade, Police and angry insurance men frightened of the risks, Freund managed to stage his bonfire, complete with the singing of "Hot Time in the Old Town Tonight".

Thanks to the impressive research of Professor William E. Hettrick of Hofstra University (from whose thorough dissection of the 1904 episode I garnered most of these facts) we know that Freund claimed "a thousand old squares pianos" were burnt; the President of the Piano Dealers said there were "a great many"; the Mayor's office thought about 300; a local paper said "about 15"; and some rivals muttered about "The spectacular fake of the week", another suggesting that "not more than a half dozen squares" had been burned.

Freund himself lit the bonfire and reported that it was a "mountain of instruments….in the form of a pyramid fully fifty feet in height". To complete his publicity campaign he arranged that each delegate who attended the Association's celebration dinner would receive a burnt relic with a tag that recorded it as a souvenir of The Bonfire of the Squares.

At a subsequent auction, held in St. Louis, twenty square pianos sold for fifty cents each and a prominent dealer proudly commented that: "When old square pianos sell at fifty cents, it is a silent tribute to the great work which The Musical

The message is unmistakeable in this cartoon in "The Presto" of May 26th., 1904: "The Square is Dead. Long live the upright". Plate No.141.

Age accomplished for the benefit of the trade by burning the old squares at Atlantic City in 1904".

Like it or not, Harry Freund's self-promoting stunt loudly broadcast the end of a mass market for the square piano in America—to such a degree that it also caused some very uncomfortable moments for the Trade. No less a journal than the "New York Times" scented something more in the air with this event: It caused them to print an editorial headlined "The Passing of the Piano".

According to the New York paper there were indications "that as an article of usual household furniture the piano is passing into innocuous desuetude….the proportion of those in normal use which remain silent for three hundred to three hundred and sixty-five days in the year is steadily increasing.

"The burning at Atlantic City recently of a small mountain of square pianos which could not be sold and perhaps could not be given away was indicative of something more than a change in domestic architecture which makes the old shape inconvenient."

Throughout the 19th Century, in my opinion, the piano was the most important item of furniture in a great many homes. But now, the times they were a' changing.

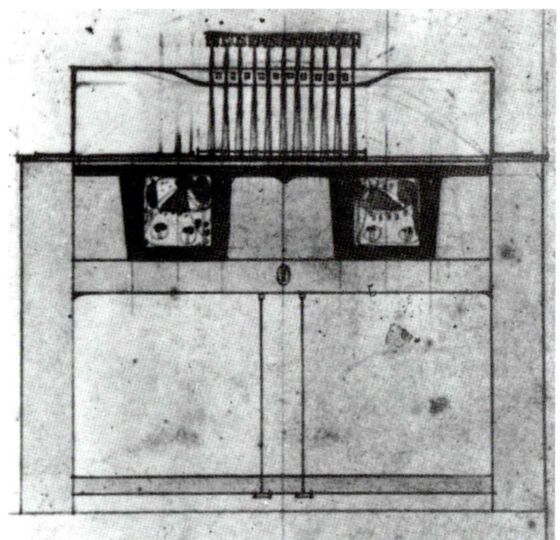

A revolutionary he undoubtedly was but Charles Rennie Mackintosh could not resist an attempt to design his own version of a familiar Victorian friend, the piano. This upright was conceived for the Wärndorfer Music Salon, Vienna, in 1902. Plate No.142

Photo by courtesy of Glasgow University Library

Enter Mackintosh the Giant

When 1799 melded into 1801 you could, in terms of the piano case, hardly see the joins. But c.1900 was nothing but artistic chaos: Decadents, Symbolists, Post Impressionists, Soon-to-be Cubists and, in design terms, Art Nouveau, Free Style, the Cotswold School, etc., and even, ugh!! Unbroken Acres of Repro and Bankers' Georgian.

Across this landscape strode Charles Rennie Mackintosh, the greatest Art Nouveau designer produced in these Isles and, of course, thus unappreciated in this country and ending his days in obscurity.

You might have expected that such a revolutionary (in one of whose buildings I had the honour to work) would tackle the motor car, or at least the gramophone. Instead, like most of the other radicals in The Glasgow School he turned to a safe, familiar old friend of the Victorian scene, the piano, an instrument in decline in a market of saturation and over-production.

It was to the piano's benefit.

This design was part of a legendary commission for The Wärndorfer Music Salon, Vienna and, originally, it is suggested, the completed piano contained two brilliant decorative panels by his wife, Margaret, "Opera of the Sea" and "Opera of the Winds".

Mackintosh made at least one further design for a piano.

One of Mackintosh's followers, but an outstanding furniture designer in his own right, was George Logan, who devoted much of his life to creating furniture for the Glasgow firm Wylie and Lochhead.

In Logan's work, in my opinion, you often find the flavour of Mackintosh (unless you wish to argue that there was something in the Glasgow air that affected them all simultaneously) but he was always far more of a romantic than Mackintosh.

Logan published this design for "The White Boudoir", complete with grand piano, in "The Studio" in November, 1905 and there is a related "Design for a Music Room" by him, also c.1905.

Was it ever carried out? I suspect it was.

Another leading member of the Glasgow School, George Logan, published this romantic vision of "The White Boudoir", complete with grand piano, in "The Studio", November, 1905. Plate No.143.

A Piano Gravestone for Lost Love

Harry Thornton's piano memorial as it stands today. Plate No.144.

This, I feel, should be the final, self-evident comment on public attitudes towards the piano and the meaning of the instrument to so many people. For a moment you wonder if a ghost-like figure will emerge to make those stone strings come to life.

The inscription tells of a woman's love and belief in her dead husband's talent: "To the memory of my beloved husband Harry Thornton, age 35. A genius who died Oct. 19th, 1918".

It was painful to go to Highgate East Cemetery and find that the widow's grief and devotion was to some no more than a chance to play Rollerball. Byron's Young Barbarians had been all at play before me and the top of the monument was smashed.

I could no longer see what had appeared from an old photo to be a plaque of a man shown at the keyboard. Of the lid there remained but a jagged, broken slab laying inside the "case".

Still surviving, however, was a passage from Puccini carved on the side:

Sweet thou art sleeping
Cradled on my heart
While we must weep apart

Perhaps some musical benefactor will one day think it proper to restore the grave.

As I stood there, I wondered: Was Harry Thornton really as good a pianist as his wife so fondly believed? Could he have been indeed the stuff of genius? What did the audience miss?

I did not have the time to investigate his background further but pondered on whether, having died in 1918, he was another of those millions who went "over the top" and sacrificed their lives for their country. If so he would have been one of the really unlucky ones, since the Armistice was signed on November 11th.

Whatever the truth, Thornton's memorial remains a poignant statement of faith and, if I do not stretch fancy too hard, perhaps a broken reminder of all those other young musicians who marched off merrily to fife and drum and left their bones at Mons, Ypres, Cambrai, Arras and the like.

Harry Thornton's memorial before it was desecrated. Plate No.145.

Effectively, too, Thornton's memorial marks for us the end of a century in which the piano had dominated much of British domestic life, the very "orchestra of the drawing room".

After the blood and terror of the First (but not the last) World War, a new generation wanted to put the past behind them and the piano found serious competition from the gramophone, the radio, the motor car and other new toys.

Sadly for the piano makers, in a World already overflowing with pianos, they never equalled the car industry's ability to convince many of the people, most of the time, that life was not possible without a new motor every year.

It needs new research to investigate the exact numbers of pianos produced in Britain after 1900 and give a detailed account of the contraction of the once mighty British piano sector but I think the number of firms who disappeared tells its own story.

Not so much the lost chord as the lost industry.

This is a painting which, I believe, has much to tell us about Mid Victorian attitudes to furniture design and what many reformers believed should be the moral principles that governed such matters. The painting, "The Awakening Conscience" of 1853-1854, is a morality picture by one of the founders of The Pre-Raphaelite Brotherhood, William Holman Hunt and there is not a single element in the work which does not have some symbolical meaning. It is my view that Holman Hunt chose to portray a rosewood veneered piano not as an object of beauty but because he earnestly believed it to be a despicable and false commercial production, reflecting debased values. Plate No.146.

Photo by courtesy of The Tate Gallery, London.

Attitudes to Piano Design

Chapter Three

It is my belief that in a single Victorian painting you will find not only illumination of the human condition and a test of sexual morality but, strangely indeed, insight into piano design and a questioning of the ethics of those who designed and sold such instruments.

In the present age of knowingness and supermarket secularism there will be those who dismiss this painting, with a press of the mental "remote", as just another overdose of Victorian saccharin. To do so is to underestimate the 19th Century intelligence and forget that few things can be more subversive than art.

I can already see the ghosts of Peter Cook and Dudley Moore gleefully queuing to ridicule such pretentious rubbish in Pseuds Corner but I assure you it is so and can be proven to be so. The trick is to read the language of a different age.

Before television, the dreams of many Victorian small householders were fired by reproductions of paintings of the day.

Through them they learned that the piano was high fashion.

I do not know whether there were popular prints of the sumptuous Zoffany, of 1775, showing Earl Cowper and the Gore family,[1] in which Her Ladyship plays a square piano that looks very much like a Zumpe. Neither do I know whether they could have seen a magical salon painting by C.R. Leslie of 1831, "The Grosvenor Family"[2] in which another aristocratic lady sits at a grand. Some of the more aesthetically inclined must, surely, have acquired framed prints of Whistler's "At the Piano"[3] of 1859, or may have been lucky enough to have seen Arthur Melville's luscious "The White Piano"[4] of 1897.

But, of a certainty, many must have had knowledge of one of the most popular and controversial of all Victorian morality paintings, Holman Hunt's "The Awakening Conscience", shown at The Royal Academy in 1854 and now in The Tate. It was described by the modern critic, author and professional nasty, Evelyn Waugh, as "perhaps the noblest painting by any Englishman".[5]

If you came to this picture without any information you might assume it showed a married couple relaxing in domestic harmony. What we are really being presented with, however, is a vile seducer striking the piano keys "carelessly with his gloved hand".[6]

The great mistake is to think that the piano, so central to the picture, is just an elegant accessory to this tale of a poor girl ruined by a smarmy society gent, with his curling mustachios and slicked back hair.

But nothing is as it appears in this picture. It must be read[7] like one of those portraits of the Virgin Queen, where the very jewels denote the virtue of Elizabeth.

Here, in Holman Hunt's parable, you will see that the kept woman, in her glossy room of assignation complete with fashionable piano in the latest style, has many rings on her fingers....but no wedding ring.

The music that lies on the floor is for the song "Tears, Idle Tears". The torn bird has been clawed by the cat, itself a known metaphor for a sexual predator. The man's other glove is cast on the floor as a fallen woman might be cast off. The books have been embossed and are thus "vain and useless". The tapestry is gilded. The tangled embroidery threads on the carpet are trapped as the young girl is trapped. The wall decoration shows vine and corn left unguarded by slumbering watchers so that "the fruit is left to be preyed upon by thievish birds". The pure white hem of her dress may be soiled by the city's dirt. The picture on the wall is of the woman taken in adultery.

The song on the piano is "Oft in the Stilly Night" and some chance words have numbed the maiden's heart. Outside the house lies the safety of the garden but the flowers, too, have a message:

"Hope not to find delight in us, they say,
"For we are spotless, Jessy—we are pure".

The very frame of the picture bears marigolds as emblems of sorrow, bells for warning and a star to represent "the still small voice" of spiritual revolution.

As Robert Upstone[8] of The Tate puts it: "Every item in the room, and every action, is symbolic of the moral turpitude and possible redemption that faces the woman".

It is a savage and bitter joke upon Holman Hunt that he chose to base his moral lecture to others on the apparently innocent face and form of wayward Annie Miller, an originally lice-infested but beauteous girl from "the foulest of courts", for whom he conceived a hopeless and devoted love, to whom he became engaged and promised marriage. He also, in best Eliza Doolittle style, tried to turn her into a Lady.

Perhaps more foolishly, when he went on a trip to the Holy Land, he left her in the care of his friend, the philandering Dante Rossetti, who repaid his trust by taking her to "places of amusement". Annie deserted both for the arms and bed of a notorious rake, Lord Ranelagh, who made no bones that she was his mistress.

Holman Hunt's claim to be originator

What, you wonder, did the Bible-quoting Holman Hunt sense of her slide to sin when he chose her as the vehicle for his parable for "The Awakening Conscience"?

The piano in the picture is just as fickle a jade, made up to deceive. Hunt's friend, the critic John Ruskin,[9] said: "There is not a single object in all that room, common, modern, vulgar (in the vulgar sense, as it may be) but it becomes tragical, if rightly read.

"That furniture, so carefully painted even to the last vein of the rosewood—is there nothing to be learnt from that terrible lustre of it, from its fatal newness; nothing there that has the old thoughts of home upon it, or that is ever to become a part of home?"

The "fatal" rosewood piano was a symbolical part of an interior which the contemporary critic F.G. Stephens said was shown furnished by the seducer's wealth "for the luxury of a woman who has sold herself and her soul to him".

I believe, logically I think, that Holman Hunt intended this particular type of piano to convey a message, as do all the other minute items in the painting. And that his ally, Ruskin, knew this well.

But my assumption rests on more than the painting itself.

Holman Hunt was not just one of the founders of the Pre-Raphaelite Brotherhood. He was also a furniture designer who had Crace make pieces for him and of the year 1855-56 Hunt wrote: "In furnishing my new house I was determined, as far as possible, to eschew the vulgar furniture of the day... After this the rage for designing furniture was taken up by others of our circle until the fashion grew to importance."[10]

Holman Hunt, therefore, saw himself as the originator of the reform movement in British furniture design subsequently taken up by the William Morris circle: all equally opposed to "vulgar" fashions of the time.

This reform movement had strict principles and two of the things it was against were veneer and glossy polish, both denounced on moral grounds as much of those of taste.

Veneer hid faults and tried to conceal the construction: Therefore it must be false. French polish and the like were again methods of gulling the customer.

As Bruce Talbert put it: "It is to the use of glue that we are indebted for the false construction modern work indulges in: the glue leads to veneering, and veneering to polish".[11]

A celebrated designer and critical authority, Dr Christopher Dresser, told the public: "Another falsity in furniture is veneering—a practice which should be wholly abandoned. Simple honesty is preferable to false show in all cases; truthfulness in utterance is always to be desired."[12]

Charles Eastlake, while rejecting a moral judgement, wrote that veneering was employed "To cover inferior work completely....thin and fragile joints must be used, which every cabinetmaker knows are incompatible with perfect construction". He said he had had a substantial oak table made to his own design for "much less than what I should have paid for one veneered with rosewood".[13]

As the architect and piano designer T.G. Jackson was later to tell the Society of Arts, he "could not understand why all modern pianos were put into those hideous rosewood cases which made such ugly black blots in a room."[14]

That these were shared attitudes we may judge from the words of a man who devoted much time to a determined attempt to change the design of the Victorian piano, the painter Edward Burne-Jones.

In a private letter to his collaborator Kate Faulkner he wrote: "I have been wanting for years to reform pianos....so hideous to behold mostly that, with a fiery rosewood piece of ugliness, it is hardly worth while to mend things".[15]

I believe that Holman Hunt was trying to show his public the very sort of piano they should NOT be buying—that, as with much else in the picture, the piano itself was, surprising as you may find the idea, morally reprehensible. But did his superb technique, depicting the rosewood piano with such brilliance, have the opposite effect?

Whatever Holman Hunt intended to convey, I suspect it was a case of "No publicity is bad publicity", especially for the more innocent. This was an age when such paintings could draw audiences of thousands. If the star of the work was a sinful but seductive piano then there were many likely to desire one for their own homes.

What the Public Wanted

At the beginning of the following century one of the top men at the piano makers Broadwood and Sons, George Rose, told the Society of Arts that: "It was no use asking why the piano was always made of rosewood and polished like a boot. It was simply that the public wanted it and would not buy if it were made of anything else."[16]

The German critic and architect Hermann Muthesius, who spent some years in Britain to study the latest methods, wrote for his German audience that Bechstein and Bluthner were, as he saw it, outrivalling Broadwood in Britain but "these instruments are all sold to England in rosewood instead of the black polish that is in general use with us".[17]

Looking back now at the earliest days of British piano case design, after the introduction of the first squares, c.1766, it seems virtually impossible to know what 18th Century piano "designers" or customers thought of such matters.

Until 1800, and for some years after, the piano was the new toy of those with money. Their writings show their delight in a welcome advance in music making but of comments on the actual case there are precious few.

It is from the actual cases that we must infer most about 18th Century attitudes to design.

We can tell from two unique pianos by Frederick Beck that a tiny number of specially commissioned cases were, at the highest cost, given all the luxurious treatment of Palace furniture; although two other exceptional 18th Century British designs, by Robert Adam and Thomas Sheraton, were both for foreigners.

From a number of surviving square pianos in the fashionable Neo Classic style, around the late 1770s to 1805, we can tell that the socially ambitious were prepared to pay for rare veneers, inlays, tapered legs and even painted decoration on the nameboard. Though how many plain cases were made at the same time for those of simpler tastes, or lesser means, it is now impossible to say.

But as the 19th Century progressed and instruments began to be made, literally, by the scores of thousand, the aesthetics became an increasing concern. The years became punctuated by attempts to beautify the looks of the piano, to make the case conform to the latest theories of design, or simply to vulgarise the decoration if that was what it took to sell.

All such efforts were accompanied by a constant "Mrs Grundy" wailing about the lack of success—if the piano designers and their critics were in the wings you had no need of a Greek chorus.

How odd this seems when set against two of the most impressive achievements of the Victorian period: the success of the piano in mechanical and commercial terms. The bright endeavours of the inventors enabled the participation of millions. Commercially, John Broadwood and Sons became a dominant World power in piano manufacture, chased by other British firms such as Collard and Collard.

How the Queen led Fashion

The public deification of the piano was much encouraged by Royal favour.

Throughout the Georgian period the piano received Court patronage and, for example, George IV installed a number of magnificent grand pianos in his Brighton Pavilion.

But the distribution of popular prints and illustrated magazines showing two of the most devoted home music makers in the kingdom, Queen Victoria and Prince Albert, must have reached many. In one[18] print the Queen herself plays a cabinet piano with the Prince standing alongside. In the newspapers, all could read of the many famed pianists, pop stars of the day, invited to Buckingham Palace or Windsor Castle.[19]

Accounts of how the Royals kept commissioning pianos with specially designed cases were reported. Where the Queen led, Society was bound to follow. And fashion and the general public behind them.

Piano makers trying to cater for the growing mass market and design the best piano case had to fight on two fronts: Against musicians who thought the looks of the instrument a complete irrelevance and aesthetes who believed the piano so cumbersome it could never make a good vehicle for design.

The attitude of those who scorned attempts to prettify the case and who wished only to make sweet music is best summed up by the declaration made by Cramer & Co. at the top of their list of pianos for sale: "The BEST instruments only dealt in. The inferior, showy Instrument entirely excluded".[20]

Nevertheless, the tendency to apologise for the piano's, perhaps ungainly, shape started early and was unceasing, the tone becoming ever more hostile and irrational.

One of the most important design books of the 19th Century, J.C. Loudon's "Encyclopaedia of Cottage, Farm, and Villa Architecture", published in the mid-1830s, presumably reflected public attitudes when it discussed attempts to make the piano "harmonise with the general forms of drawing-room furniture".[21]

More specific objections were made in the "Encyclopaedia" by the architect Edward Buckton Lamb[22] who considered that the grand piano "presented the greatest difficulties to surmount: the form prescribed by its uses, the great space required for it in a room and the very unarchitectural character it assumed, set me to consider whether some alterations could not be made, so as to embrace all the utility of the present instrument with more beauty".

In Lamb's view, although the grand piano was "the most perfect instrument now in use" it was of an awkward shape; "almost impossible" to imbue with any expression of style; and occupied so much space in "a moderate-sized house" that it had generally been replaced by the upright grand piano.

In 1847, Henry Whitaker, author of the "Treasury of Designs" with its menu of seven different styles, put forward his own design as the answer because the Grand Pianoforte was "a piece of furniture which has hitherto set designers at defiance, and which, although an expensive article, has always been unsightly".[23]

A critic of The Great Exhibition of 1851, while praising carvers, inlayers and gilders, declared that "we miss any attempt to give a more elegant and uniform shape to the grand pianoforte, which is so much to be desired".[24]

At the Philadelphia Centennial Exhibition of 1876 it was said that: "It is one of the anomalies of art that the piano, which contains the soul of harmony, is generally the least harmonious and ungraceful appearing object of the modern drawing-room. It is usually bow-legged and veneered, badly shaped and worse decorated. The old-fashioned spinet was decidedly superior."[25]

One of the finest designers of the 19th Century, E. W. Godwin, told his fellow architects in 1876 how he had carefully designed all his own furniture for his Chambers but "....as I cannot live without music, I spoilt a really light and pretty effect by introducing that conventional lump of pretentious ugliness, a modern piano. Some time after I found it not such a difficult matter to alter the ordinary piano case in such a manner as to render it so far from displeasing that it should at least not be out of harmony with its surroundings."[26]

The Piano "Remains Unshapely"

Commenting on pianos at the 1885 Inventions Exhibition, "Illustrated London News" said: "It is a curious fact that though the style of furniture has greatly improved during the past five and twenty years, this improvement has not extended to pianofortes, which remain almost as unshapely as ever".[27]

In 1890[28] "Furniture and Decoration" was still asking: "Why are the designs of piano cases such eyesores?" and gave its

"Music and Aesthetics", "Punch" cartoon, Feb 16th., 1878.

The triumph and acceptance of the Upright Piano is confirmed in this cartoon of an imaginary fashionable gathering of the 1870s though, effectively, the battle over the square and other forms had been won well before.

What is of more interest to design addicts is the way George du Maurier's knowing eye has emphasised two things: The growing cult among artists for painting their pianos and the use of the sunflower as decoration for the end of the upright, the sunflower being a favourite motif of the Aesthetic designers.

Here the adherents of the Aesthetic movement are the target. When the songs of Gilbert and Sullivan lilted o'er the land, W.S. Gilbert advised those aspiring to the high aesthetic ideal to "Walk down Piccadilly with a poppy or a lily in your mediaeval hand" and famously, in "Patience", poked fun at the "greenery-yallery, Grosvenor Gallery, foot-in-the-grave young man".

"Patience" was not staged until 1881 but "Punch" had tuned in well before that, as is proven by "Music and Aesthetics", which they published on February 16th., 1878. Few knew as much about new art movements as the cartoonist and novelist George du Maurier for whom the Aesthetes provided endless fun (he was accused by Charles Hallé of bringing contempt on the Aesthetic Movement and helping ridicule it out of existence) and here some of the audience blanch as the young lady, more New Woman than love-sick maiden, steps up to hammer (that surely, must be the right word) out a tune. Plate No.147.

own answer: "Firstly, because the makers still follow the patterns of fifty years ago, when the art of designing furniture was at its lowest ebb, and secondly because the construction of the cases is neither truthful nor calculated to do its work in the most straightforward way.

"The furniture of the period fifty years ago was coarse and ugly, and the piano makers of the time followed the fashion and have seldom since changed their designs, except in a very few instances.

"They have, indeed, added to the faults by using veneer in place of the solid wood and by increasing the amount of coarse carving—sometimes tawdrily gilt—and miserable fretwork displayed on the cases, which has become more meaningless every day".

This, of course, was the voice that echoed through the later Victorian era, especially from members of the Arts and Crafts Exhibition Society, pleading: Fitness for purpose.

The polemic published in a respected magazine, the "Art Journal" in 1894, by John F. Runciman[29] was both scornful and bucolic.

Runciman wrote that: "Like the patent medicines, you should always have it in the house....where shall you place it? If your drawing-room be sufficiently spacious, say not less than sixty by forty-five to fifty feet, it is a question easily answered....you will realise what an intractable leviathan it is. It stands there in the most helpless and ponderous manner....without a beautiful line about it....so long as it is in view you are painfully conscious that it rests heavily on its ugly legs....Was ever such a hotch-potch devised since Adam delved and Eve span! Of all forms of furniture invented by man it takes the palm for obtrusive lack of adaptability."

The piano was, in Runciman's view, "a masterpiece of ugliness". As for the cottage piano, "there seems no more possibility of making it elegant than there is of making a household pet of an elephant."

His solution, however, had logic: What he wanted was "first, a smaller piano".

Of the efforts of the British Art Piano movement, Runciman was simply dismissive.

His verdict[30] was that "so far all the 'artistic pianos' have been failures. Sir E. Burne-Jones painted a series of pictures on one exhibited at the New Gallery some time ago; Mr William Morris covered one with a wall-paper design; and Mr Alma Tadema did nothing in particular to his.

"Who is responsible for the Paderewski 'thousand pounder' I do not know. But it—and the attempts of the above-named masters—failed, and were bound to fail, for they did not strike at the root of the evil—the form of the instrument.

"We know that no amount of detail beauty will save a badly-composed picture, no amount of gorgeous colour make a building of weak design beautiful. In the same way all Sir E. Burne-Jones's fancy, Mr Morris's industry, and Mr Alma Tadema's striving have come to nought!"

An intriguing contrast with Runciman is provided by Hermann Muthesius, who sympathised with progressive British designers and did much to make their work known on the Continent.

Writing a few years later, Muthesius's judgement was that: "In England too during the past thirty years there have been all kinds of attempts to give the piano an artistic form. All the artists who design furniture have tried their hands at pianos.

"There have been a number of successful solutions, among the best being those of Morris, who decorated the casings of his pianos with inlay or gesso, and Burne-Jones.

"But most of the other attempts, especially those of the London Arts and Crafts group, suffer from their rustic character. The mistake has been to consider a casing put together like a barn-door suitable to a delicate mechanism like that of the modern piano."[31]

In 1895 "The Realm"[32] claimed that: "It (*the piano*) remains the one object unaffected by the aesthetic movements of the century, and if a hundred years hence it be not, as now, ugly and unsatisfying, then indeed must the Orient have resumed its supremacy over the Western World."

The Repro-bates Answer

The "Cabinet Maker"[33] demanded: "Why is it....that the artistic aspect of this instrument has been so neglected? The quality and purity of tone, the question of touch, and every other detail of internal construction, have been considered, and improved year by year, until, today, they seem to be as near perfection as human ingenuity can bring them; yet, in the cases, a deadly monotony reigns supreme.

"We can tell, almost to a nicety, when visiting any pianoforte showroom, the class of design we shall see—the same old forms, with their turned supports, or brackets; their incised and gilt 'decoration', or inlaid panels; their over-elaborated gilt sconces, and inevitable burr-walnut".

The art journal of the middle class, "The Artist", argued that "The keyboard is an excrescence from the main body of the piano".[34]

The voice of the architectural enthusiasts, "Architectural Review", judged in 1901 that "With the exception of a few daring artistic Radicals belonging to the Arts and Crafts Exhibition Society, scarcely anyone has attempted, until quite recently, to dispossess the public of the idea that a 'grand' must necessarily be a clumsy tripod and a 'cottage' a tall box with a shapeless excrescence in the middle."[35]

But then went on to praise Lutyens for a grand "in the Jacobean style"; Arthur Blomfield for a grand in "Georgian" style; Charles Allom for a grand "in Louis XVI style"; and George Henschel for a grand "in the Early Flemish style"! Thus did the Repro-bates point the way forward for British design.

Even after a century of attempts to better the beast, a lecturer to the Society of Arts was

Presumably with unconscious irony, a Victorian song sheet titled "Airs and Graces" shows us what was the most desirable accessory for this fashionably dressed lady: A GRAND Piano. This illustration of 1854 also demonstrates how Victorian makers set out to bolster and inflate the impression made by the instrument.

The Georgians had relied on an innate good taste and an understated approach to the design of the grand piano, depending on the beauty of wood and a number of cross-banded panels round the main body of the case.

It can be said with certainty (relying on the evidence of a Broadwood grand in the Metropolitan Museum of Art, New York) that a crucial change had taken place by the year 1827, in which cross-banded panels were abandoned. The shaped panel shown here appears quite different to the traditional "Tabel" panel.

In their place came, with the more expensive instruments, an ever-increasing reliance on rich carving and ostentatious decoration, as shown here in the carving on the scrolled cheek and leg. An altogether heavier, more demanding presence, a tendency which the introduction of the iron frame and extra strings only encouraged.

But such a grand was an instrument for the wealthy and the growing upper middle class thrown up by the Industrial Revolution. For the musically aspiring working classes there had to be another answer. Plate No.148.

to pronounce as late as 1907 that the piano was "an object which by common consent is not artistic".[36]

This came from a well known authority, William Dale, F.S.A., who lamented that, after iron bars and iron framing came in, "the case of the piano had to be made increasingly strong. Its elegant proportions vanished, and the legs soon became elephantine in size".

New miniaturised forms such as the "Mignon", "Bijou" and "Baby Grands", were "ugly in inverse proportion to the sweetness of the names they bear".

How did the public respond to the interminable sourness of the critics? I think it had one unfortunate effect.

Hostile public attitudes to piano design led to a growing constituency of those who wished to disguise the piano and deny its existence. What such owners wanted was to "prettify" the piano into something else. In effect they were trying to deny its existence by giving it a new identity (much as Stodart had done with his Upright Grand "in the form of a bookcase").

Nothing reveals this mind set better than the writings of the Victorian author on style Jane Ellen Panton, daughter of the painter William Powell Frith. She said she found the piano a "very ugly piece of furniture" but explained that she made her way around the problem by making "a very pretty frame for hers out of sage-green silk worked with rosebuds", although she had considered "a turquoise-blue material worked in pale yellow campanulas".[37]

The efforts to disguise the true nature of the piano started in the 18th Century and continued throughout the 19th Century. This illustration put out in 1900 by Moss Brothers of Halifax shows how they thought the back of an upright piano ought properly to be hidden. Plate No.149.

A Piano Complete with Fountain

Such attempts at disguise were taken to their *outré* limits in 1886 with the offer of a bamboo structure to go over the piano which "will please the many who desire to gracefully hide....the ugly back of the cottage piano". This provided "A combination of glistening bevelled plates, flower dishes in bamboo, made to fill the desired space, but the special feature is that in the base of the article a pretty fountain plays when desired."[38]

As the iron grate was disguised by the ornamental fire screen when unlit, toilet tables encircled with a muslin petticoat,[39] or tables draped with long table cloths, so the back of the cottage piano was often dressed in yellow or pink pleats, the top hidden with an elaborate needlework drapery, a tasselled cloth or purple velvet[40] and loaded with china or bric-à-brac.

When offering Cottage uprights to the public in 1862, the makers Knoll and Co. took a two page advert in the "Musical Directory" to boast that their pianos were "Silked and Fluted behind and so finished that they may be placed in the centre, or in any part of the Drawing-Room."

All this was a form of denial of the piano's identity, I feel, and such prejudices were long-lasting, as demonstrated by a competition for piano design launched by "The Studio" in 1894. The magazine might be the very voice of the avant garde but one of the entries by Arthur Ernest Shaw of London "has a somewhat novel feature in curtains hung between the legs".[41]

It is only just to the Victorians to record that one expert provides an alternative explanation for their passion for dressing the instrument in silks, tapestry and the like. He suggests that textile coverings showed the desire to protect a valuable instrument from dust rather than any Victorian prudery. But surely this was not the whole story?

I have always doubted the old myth that the Victorians covered even piano legs because the sight of these wooden uprights might carry sexual innuendo and corrupt the innocent.

It was probably Capt Frederick Marryat who started this particular urban legend[42] with "A Diary in America" in 1839 when he told how a young middle class American maiden was shocked by his use of the word "leg". The word he should have used was "limb".

The good Captain was told: "I am not as particular as some people are, for I know those who always say limb of a table, or limb of a piano-forte".

As is the way of these things the legend multiplied through theatrical satire, a "Punch" cartoon and, worse, reputable modern historians. But where is the credible evidence of an authentic case of the special covering of a piano leg, for reasons other than safe transport?

What there can be no doubting is that throughout the century, even to 1900, the concern to beautify or improve the looks of the piano never ceased.

A trade paper reported that "Pianos with solid silver cases have occasionally been made", one of these for an Indian Prince.[43] An architect argued that for piano legs "ormolu or silver fittings should be the only embellishments".[44]

One piano[45] in a case of ivory, superbly carved, was stated to be in the possession of the Dowager Countess of Dudley and a second, veneered with ivory, had been made for Prince Albert.[46] Another, said to be the most beautiful example of its kind, was "garbed in paper, delicately embellished" and was owned by the Duke of Devonshire, who had paid 500 guineas for the instrument.[47]

According to a trade source, pianos had been made of "bronze, aluminium, glass, porcelain, and, in combination, mother-of-pearl".[48] Papier-mâché pianos were exhibited[49] in 1851 and in 1865 a patent[50] was taken out for the cases, frets, trusses and legs of pianos and organs to be made of the same material or "paper other than papier mâché". Sheet metal,[51] celluloid veneer[52] and plastic were other alternatives. One optimist even tried to make piano cases of concrete.[53]

At the Great Exhibition of 1851 George Aggio of Colchester exhibited a "Pianoforte, fitted up in plate-glass case".[54] Later a patent was taken out for "the cases of pianofortes &c.

Caricature poking fun at Art Nouveau, with Baillie Scott's Broadwood piano in background, "Punch", 1903

Quite apart from the exotic piano in the background this is, from the furniture design point of view, one of the most important cartoons ever published by "Punch". The work of the Bristol artist and humourist Rubens Charles Carter, it appeared on March 11th., 1903.

At a casual glance you might think that the cartoonist has merely dreamt up some imaginary, up-market room, complete with Society couple in evening dress, to gently mock the Art Nouveau enthusiasts. Such an impression is apparently reinforced by the caption: "The Latest Style of Room Decoration. The Home Made Beautiful".

What gives the game away is a tiny sub-caption "According to the 'Arts and Crafts'."

The artist, Rubens Charles Carter, must have had a very detailed knowledge of *avant-garde* furniture design for I recognise most of the caricatured furniture as well known pieces and I therefore assume it must be true for much of the rest of the decor.

Quite apart from The Arts and Crafts Exhibition Society, Carter had a specific target in his sights: the architect Mackay Hugh Baillie Scott. For those in the know there were some telling jokes. Note the cats trotting round the frieze: they have no tails. That is because they are Manx cats and Baillie Scott had previously been in practice in the Isle of Man.

Not only that but Broadwood, who made most of Baillie Scott's piano designs, had launched a basic upright piano by him, under the trade name "The Manxman".

The one depicted by Carter, however, is not just any old production line piano. This one bears a striking resemblance to a highly decorated upright which was part of an Internationally known commission by Baillie Scott for The Grand Duke and Duchess of Hesse in Darmstadt, which had been illustrated in "The Builder" on November 5th., 1898.

There is one final joke: Lionel Lambourne has suggested in "Utopian Craftsmen" that the figure sitting in the "Quaint" armchair in the "Punch" cartoon is meant to be none other than "Baillie Scott, who sits nervously reading the paper".

The cartoon tells us one final thing: That the artists and designers of the day still considered the piano an essential component for modern living....and were blissfully ignorant of the coming impact of the radio, the gramophone and the motor car. Plate No.150.

wholly or partially of glass, with suitable holes to insulate and transmit the sound".[55] Such a "see through" grand piano was made in relatively modern times for the liner "Queen Elizabeth II" but, inevitably, in acrylic.[56]

One inventor patented the idea that "imitation animals" might be inserted between two sheets of glass, which would then be used to decorate the piano.[57] Another brainwave was tortoiseshell decoration "inlaid with pearls, ivory, &c".[58] A patent was taken out for printing decoration on pianos in bronze, silver, gold or coloured inks on the wood or veneer used for instruments.[59] Wax flowers,[60] lace, silvered glass,[61] embroidery,[62] Indian rubber[63]—the list was endless.

In 1894 Brinsmeads could tell their public that the only difference between a 100 guinea and a 500 guinea piano was "merely one of extra ornamentation"[64] and, despite the hostility of the critics, there was evidently still a market for such conspicuous display.

The majority of paying customers felt that the taste for music, and the taste for a piano case that was pleasing to their eyes, went hand in hand, no matter what the purists might say.

Photo by courtesy of Warwickshire Museum

The Hermann Tabel harpsichord of 1721, the only surviving instrument by this maker but one which instantly proves, by comparison, that Tabel's distinctive style was the "Father" of virtually all 18th Century British grand piano cases. The design of the main case is unmistakeable—a series of panels each outlined by a contrasting band of veneer. It was later adopted for the grand piano by two rival firms founded by former employees of Tabel, Messrs Shudi and Kirkman. Plate No.151.

Style, Fashion and the Early Piano

Chapter Four

The most sardonic and memorable comment made about the piano by a designer came from Halsey Ricardo, a luminary of The Arts and Crafts Exhibition Society, who observed that "it has the size without the handiness of an African elephant and the elegance of a mammoth toad….if no home is to be complete without a piano, let us at least have a presentable tyrant, instead of an awkward monster".[1]

While the inventors proceeded from triumph to triumph in their improvements of the piano action and its tonal qualities, the furniture designers were often in despair as they struggled to fight against the straight-jacket imposed by the strings and the problems inherent in the size of the instrument.

Never have so many gallant pencils been sharpened for the fight, only to retreat from the drawing board in defeat. In the first part of the 19th

The way in which his one-time employee Burkat Shudi copied his old Master, Hermann Tabel, when it came to the panelled style of the main case, can be seen in this 1771 harpsichord by Shudi that was kept in Broadwood and Sons' own Collection. It was illustrated in "The Connoisseur" in September, 1928. Plate No.152.

Photo by courtesy of Messrs Sotheby's of New Bond Street, London

That another leading British harpsichord maker and former Tabel employee, Jacob Kirkman, also copied the style of the main case from his former Master is obvious in this Kirkman harpsichord of 1763 auctioned by Messrs Sotheby's as Lot 278 on November 10th., 2004. The supporting stand is later. Plate No.153.

century they groaned at the results of piano design and at the end of the century the cries of the experts were piteous. In retrospect such flagellation was, I think, a mite overdone.

Despite the critics, select British Art Pianos and the choicest of their multitudinous brethren, the Designer Pianos, were to become unlikely objects of desire, the first through fine artists such as Sir Edward Burne-Jones and Sir Lawrence Alma-Tadema, the latter by the guileful skills of A.W.N. Pugin, Bruce Talbert, Charles Bevan, Walter Cave, Baillie Scott, C.R. Ashbee, C.F.A. Voysey and many another.

But the piano could no more free itself from the 18th and 19th Century wars of fashion and style than could the rest of the furniture world. The result was, often, scornful confrontation between aesthetic idealists and those prepared to dress the piano up like a maypole if it could but turn a profit. Dedicated musicians suggested both were an irrelevance.

It needs an 18th Century specialist to investigate further the stylistic origins of the first British pianos cases but, having looked at the question in a limited way, my main conclusions are:

- That the progress of the two principal type of pianos of the 18th Century, the grand piano and the so-called "square" piano (in reality oblong) was, in design terms, quite different and this was because the "square", the poor relation, did not cling to tradition in the same measure.

- That the grand piano, the product of men who had previously been harpsichord makers by trade, inherited the mantle of the British harpsichord with hardly a scintilla of change in case design. And this harpsichord style, restrained and Classical in taste, can be traced back to one man working in the early part of the century, Hermann Tabel.

- That the 18th Century square piano adopted the guise of its predecessor, the small clavichord but, in terms of case design, found its own identity much sooner, proceeding by way of Functionalism to become a protagonist of elegant Neo-Classicism well before 1800.

The grand had been invented in Florence before 1700 and there are accounts of a piano being brought to Britain about the 1730s-1740s and another made in London about 1756 but, if so, neither the actual instruments nor illustrations can I find.

Believed to be the earliest surviving British grand piano, this instrument of 1772 by Americus Backers lets us know immediately it is the stylistic descendant of Hermann Tabel, as surely as if one drew up a family tree. The series of veneer panels along the main case are instantly recognisable.

Now to be found in the Russell Collection in Edinburgh it is numbered 21 and it seems reasonable to believe that the others made by Backers would have had the same panelled sides. One can trace the style in an unbroken line of descent from Tabel through the harpsichords of Shudi and Kirkman to Backers' piano.
Plate No.154.

Photo by courtesy of the Director of St. Cecilia's Hall: Copyright University of Edinburgh

Enter Hermann Tabel and the Veneered Panel

The earliest surviving British grand piano, and the only known example of his work,[2] is by Americus Backers, who is shown to have been making such instruments between 1767 and 1772. It needs only a moment's comparison between Backers' grand and the harpsichords produced in previous decades by rivals Burkat Shudi and Jacob Kirkman, to establish they all inherited the same design genes.

These undoubtedly came from the man both Shudi and Kirkman worked for in London, their Master, Hermann Tabel, whom we first hear of in 1716 but who, it has been suggested, may have been making instruments in Britain either from "about 1700" or "somewhere about the year 1710".[3] The layman might be tempted to say, instinctively, that the Tabel style was quintessentially British in character and it is enlightening to discover that Tabel was from the Low Countries, possibly Flemish, Shudi a Swiss immigrant and Kirkman from Alsace.

The principal characteristic of Tabel's approach was to achieve a decorative effect by the use of a series of veneer panels round the side of the main case and these were outlined and contrasted by cross-banding. This was underpinned by a measure of reserve and good taste, a rejection of conspicuous ornament, and a reliance on the grain of fine quality wood for effect.

The intoxicating love of fine woods, the insistence on promoting the sensual beauty of nature while retreating from the artifice of man, seemed to allow the sober British to put on a show without a welter of guilt. Nature, it might be deduced, was the Creator showing his hand and its beauties free of either sin or vanity.

It would thus follow that the unique patterns and textures of veneer and timber were permissible on the largest scale without apology but the slightest sign of glitter and garter smacked of wicked excess and damnation.

One is reminded of the 18th Century customer who ordered a London piano with the words: "I wh *(sic)* to have it Plain in every Respect and the case of handsome wood".[4]

This devotion to the purity of wood and faith in the truth of honest method seems from earliest times to have been a British constant, adherents attempting, with varying success, to fight off Continental and other fashions. As in life and dress, so in piano design we can trace from the 18th Century the swings between the Puritans and the Free Thinkers.

If you doubt the analysis you have only to spend a day studying the architecture of British Chapels and Churches of the 19th Century which immediately announce the temper of each faith—from plain walls and hard benches all the way to smells and bells.

Flemish or not, Tabel was in tune with the native spirit of these Isles at that time. His cross-banding, the nearest he came to overt display, was not as sophisticated as you find on later instruments but it was inevitable that those who followed would refine his technique. The inventor is the genius, not those who tread in his steps.

As with Backers, fate has allowed just one example of Tabel's work to survive, a harpsichord of 1721, which is numbered 43 and is now in Warwickshire Museum. This enables us to say that Tabel's style had already reached maturity.

Donald Boalch describes it as having "Case veneered in walnut with cross-banding; inside sycamore with walnut stringing. Finely chased brass hinges. Gilt rose including a viscount's coronet".

Only in his use of walnut for the main case of this particular instrument was Tabel markedly different from later 18th Century piano makers, who followed fashion towards mahogany. Thereafter, walnut stuttered along and it was not until the Victorians that there was to be, once more, an enthusiasm for walnut.

It was about 1715 that mahogany began to be imported regularly into Britain[5] and Raymond Russell states that it was first used for harpsichord lids but "gained in popularity and was soon applied as veneer (*usually on an oak carcass*) sometimes alone, sometimes as cross banding for walnut panels. Walnut itself quickly lost ground and disappeared in the 1770s, except for special uses such as burr walnut as decoration round the keyboard."[6]

Another leading expert of the piano world[7] told me that from around 1770 to 1840 the best mahogany used in British pianos was "darker than the darkest Port wine, and heavier than oak"; the next grade was "rich in colour but not as dark….nor so heavy"; and another, also known as Bay Wood, was softer, "about half the density, much paler in colour and is so different it could really be a different species".

Contrary to much written by earlier furniture historians, Mr Adam Bowett suggests that the best mahogany was, in fact, from Jamaica itself and not from Cuba.[8] In 1770, Jamaican mahogany ("right Jamaica wood") was sold in Britain at between 12d and 16d per foot, as against Honduras at 4½d per foot and Cuban at 6d and 7d per foot.

Just where might the Tabel style have come from? Could it have been entirely his invention? I can provide no certain explanation and, so far, can myself find no earlier harpsichord that exactly matches the Tabel casework of 1721.

I have consulted experts[9] who tell me they cannot recall any earlier British harpsichord with cross-banded panels of wood prior to Tabel.

One possibility occurs to me.

It is known that, before Tabel, there was a British method of harpsichord decoration which employed "faux" panels along the sides—artist painted to give the illusion of panels.

One example of this I came across is a harpsichord of 1700 made by Joseph Tisseran of London and now to be found in The Bate Collection at Oxford. Some believe its imitation panels were painted on c.1710.[10]

The well known historian of the harpsichord, Professor Edward L. Kottick of the University of Iowa, told me there were other, older instruments "redecorated with faux panelling" and drew to my attention a 1646 Ruckers with "a painted finish imitating cross-banded wood panelling. Although I have no direct evidence, I always assumed that instrument had been redecorated in England".[11]

A number of writers have suggested[12] Tabel trained in Antwerp with the Couchets, the successors to the best known family of harpsichord makers in the World, the Ruckers. But it seems to me that Tabel's case style rejected the gleeful use of decoration adopted by so many Continentals and was more obviously related to the British tradition than any other.

Is it too fanciful to wonder if Tabel had worked with another harpsichord maker when he first came to London? Someone who was skilled in "faux panel" decoration? If so, could this have inspired Tabel to translate the painted illusion into real panels made with cross-banded wood?

This is but guesswork.

One strong pointer, I feel, is that cross-banding, in use earlier, became increasingly popular in general British furniture making after c.1710 and cross-banding was an essential element of the Tabel approach. Perhaps, in this regard, he was following fashion.

My conclusion is that Tabel, although a Continental, took forward a British tradition already outlined by the makers of plain but superb late 17th Century bentside spinets, one that was classically British in its dependence on understated Good Taste.

Photographs by
Dr Hélène La Rue
Courtesy of The Bate Collection, Oxford

▲

If, as I feel certain, Hermann Tabel was the originator of the style subsequently adopted for the decoration of British grand pianos, how on earth did he conceive such an idea?

Should we seek the answer in the kind of panel shown in the accompanying photo?

At first glance it seems to be just another inlaid panel but it is nothing of the sort. What we have here is illusion: A "Faux" panel painted on to the wood.

The painting is one of a series of such painted panels along the sides of one of the most important harpsichords in the country, now to be found in The Bate Collection at Oxford.

This instrument was constructed by Joseph Tisseran in 1700 and the "panels" are suggested to have been painted on in work carried out c.1710.

We know only one fact about Tisseran but it is crucial: He was Joseph Tisseran of London. And London is the city where Hermann Tabel set up business when he came to this country "somewhere about the year 1710" or, at any rate, by 1716.

Was it the sight of one such painted panel that gave Tabel the idea to copy the device in inlay and transfer illusion into real wood? Was this to lead to the characteristic "British style" of decorating the main cases of so many British pianos? Plate No.155.

The Tisseran harpsichord of 1700 in The Bate Collection, Oxford, which has a series of artist-painted "faux" panels along the sides of the main case. Plate No.156.

▼

This grand piano of 1799 demonstrates how Broadwood and Sons continued to employ, right until the end of the century (and beyond), the panelled sides that took their inspiration from Hermann Tabel's harpsichords of the early part of the 18th Century. Plate No.157.

Photo by courtesy of The Royal College of Music.

How they copied Hermann

Tabel's "British style" was copied, and I do not think that "copied" is too strong a word, by both Shudi and Kirkman for their harpsichords before re-appearing in the guise of their firms' later 18th Century British grand pianos.

The way Tabel's method spread through the British Isles can be studied in a harpsichord c.1775 by the best known maker in Dublin, Ferdinand Weber (another from the Continent, born in Saxony) which has the familiar veneered panels.[13]

And the universality of the style is apparent in a spinet of 1780 by Longman and Broderip in the fine Collection of the Royal College of Music.[14] Like most British spinets (I doubt that our makers have ever produced a keyboard instrument more beautiful in appearance) it has a case of elegance with a distinctive sweeping curve but even here the sides have the typical Tabel series of veneered panels—in this instance mahogany outlined with sycamore stringing.

An early scholar of case design, William Dale, pointed to an essential difference between the British and Continental traditions when he commented: "It is somewhat strange that neither of the Shudis attempted any decoration of the cases of their instruments other than that of skilful cabinet work….nor did the English makers follow the custom of putting mottoes inside."[15]

Mr Dale also believed the British style of piano was derived from the harpsichord but suggests these early grands "being somewhat smaller than the harpsichord, their lines were

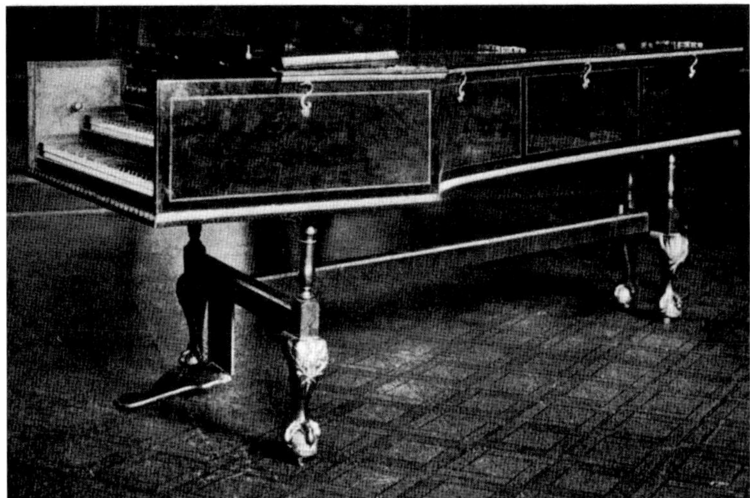

◄
Occasionally the British harpsichord makers produced an out-of-the-ordinary stand for their instruments with a highly distinctive dropped cabriole leg but this embellishment was to have little influence on later piano makers. On the contrary, the Late 18th Century piano makers moved ever more determinedly in the direction of a plain supporting stand of pronounced angularity. This Shudi harpsichord, c.1765-1766 and illustrated in William Dale's 1913 book "Shudi, the Harpsichord Maker", is said by Dale to have been made for an Emperor, Frederick the Great. Plate No.158.

►
A close-up view from William Dale's book of the idiosyncratic dropped cabriole legs on the harpsichord said by Dale to have been made for Frederick the Great by Burkat Shudi (I have also seen an example of this type by Kirkman). Even on harpsichords such supporting legs were an "extra" and the quality of the work is immediately evident—such special carved work for special V.I.P.s must have cost a Princely sum. But if the Emperor was granted the unusual accolade of dropped cabriole legs we note that he still had to accept a main case in the traditional British style of veneered and outlined panels. Plate No.159.

Photo by courtesy of The Deutsches Museum, Munich

◄
A transitional instrument, a rare British piano-harpsichord of 1780, demonstrates the move towards a supporting stand of pronounced angularity but, unusually for a London-made instrument, has a decorated stand. This piano-harpsichord is by that remarkable man Joseph Merlin, the Celebrated Inventor and this example, now part of the impressive collection of The Deutsches Museum in Munich, was shown at the great Merlin Exhibition in London in 1985. As can be seen, the main case has the familiar British veneered panels with the sort of decorative matching stand you might find on satinwood crossbanded pianos. However, you usually find the stand of the grand piano of this period left unadorned. Plate No.160.

The familiar veneered panels of mahogany on this Kirkman grand piano of c.1800, sold by Sotheby's as lot 289 on March 20th., 1980, demonstrate that the Tabel style was almost universally employed by British firms making grand pianos in the Late 18th Century. Plate No.161.

Photo by courtesy of Messrs Sotheby's of New Bond Street, London

better, and this was particularly noticeable in the curve of the bent side."[16]

As you might expect, Shudi's son-in-law, John Broadwood, adopted the "house" style when he took over the family firm and came to make grand pianos. The Kirkman family, likewise, continued to follow Tabel's design when it came to pianos. The Stodarts (the founder, Robert Stodart, had worked for Broadwood) and even minor makers, followed suit.

The way Tabel's style impregnated the British grand piano for the rest of the century and carried strongly into the 19th Century did, I am tempted to say, amount to a vernacular tradition. It was so distinctive in character it would be easy to confuse the casework of one maker with another. As the piano historian David Rowland wrote: "Most English grands of the late eighteenth century looked much like the Backers grand of 1772".[17]

A similar view is taken by Michael Cole of Cheltenham, author of "The Pianoforte in the Classical Era", who observes: "The oldest surviving Broadwood grands....Like most of Stodart's, are externally very similar to the Backers piano, veneered and cross-banded in mahogany with plain, rectangular section legs to which the two pedals are affixed with the oddly pigeon-toed appearance that Backers devised."[18]

A good description of the general run of these early grand pianos is provided by the noted collector and expert, C.F. Colt, who wrote that "from the 1780s the earliest Broadwood grands had plain mahogany cases with cross-banded edges to the case, with a white line of box or sycamore. The sides were carefully chosen veneer, the top lid usually solid mahogany with no cross-banding, but a boxwood line inlay. The legs were plain....the nameboard was of sycamore with the name inscribed in Latin."[19]

One can only add: The cross-banding so arranged as to give the effect of a series of outlined, even dramatised, "panels" along the sides.

Another defining trait of these 18th Century British grands needs to be mentioned.

Although British harpsichord makers occasionally produced instruments with a distinctive, dropped cabriole leg (almost certainly for special customers—the Prince of Wales had one of them and so did Emperor Frederick the Great) the early piano makers largely rejected such ostentation and showed a preference for the plain square leg and a supporting stand of stark and pronounced angularity. This naturally tended, by contrast, to reinforce further the decorative effect of the veneered panels above.

Instruments such as the Merlin piano-harpsichord of 1780 in The Deutsches Museum, Munich, with a decorated stand, were unusual. I have not inspected this instrument but have read nothing to suggest the stand is not original.

A rare bird indeed....out of context and out of time. While most of the piano makers stuck to the Tabel style of veneered panels in a Neo-Classical manner, John Crang Hancock produced this grand piano with baluster-turned legs making it look like a refugee from a previous century. Part of the explanation for Hancock's unusual case, suggested to be between 1775 and 1781 and now to be found in the splendid Colt Clavier Collection, may be that Hancock had previously been a maker of spinets. Plate No.162.

Photo by courtesy of The Colt Clavier Collection, Bethersden, Kent

Six Exceptions to the Rule

Pre-1800 examples of British grand pianos which did not conform to the Tabel template do exist but such survivors are of great rarity. I can think of six immediately but they are very much curiosities.

The first is a grand, attributed to Crang Hancock and given a date of c.1775-1781, which is now in The Colt Clavier Collection.[20] The main case is elaborately inlaid in a unique manner and it is suggested that a Continental craftsman may have been employed.

Another "spinet-shaped" grand, again by John Crang Hancock, appeared as Lot 26 at Christie's on June 26th., 1987, when it was described as having a "cross-banded mahogany case with figured walnut interior, on trestle stand".

The third is a grand piano of 1782, again by Crang Hancock and once more in The Colt Clavier Collection[21] but as different from the first as you could imagine—it looks as though it might be a refugee from the 17th Century. This has a walnut case instead of the more usual mahogany and, bizarrely for the date, turned legs of baluster shape. The explanation, perhaps, lies in the fact that Crang Hancock was earlier a maker of spinets.

The fourth is a Robert Stodart grand, 1784, now at Heaton Hall, Manchester, which is prominently decorated along one side with inlays of Classical figures in statuesque poses. Though, this feature apart, one can see its relationship to "The British Style". Michael Cole suggests this Stodart was "probably designed specifically to blend tastefully with the décor of an Adam-style interior".[22]

The fifth, and best known,[23] is Thomas Sheraton's grand pianoforte of 1796, which was built by Broadwood, at great cost, for a Spanish grandee and decorated with Wedgwood cameos and Tassie's medallions. It stands on thick, tapered legs though these, says John Koster, are "not original". This is, from the point of view of the case, the most important grand piano of the 18th Century being Sheraton's only provable furniture commission.

The sixth, another Wedgwood-decorated grand of 1798, was a more modest interpretation by Broadwood of the Sheraton design of two years previously. The Wedgwood plaques were set above the piano keys and the rest of the case was, yet again, very much in The British Style.[24]

But these, in the light of the known evidence, were exceptions. You would be hard put to find other British 18th Century grands not built in the Tabel manner.

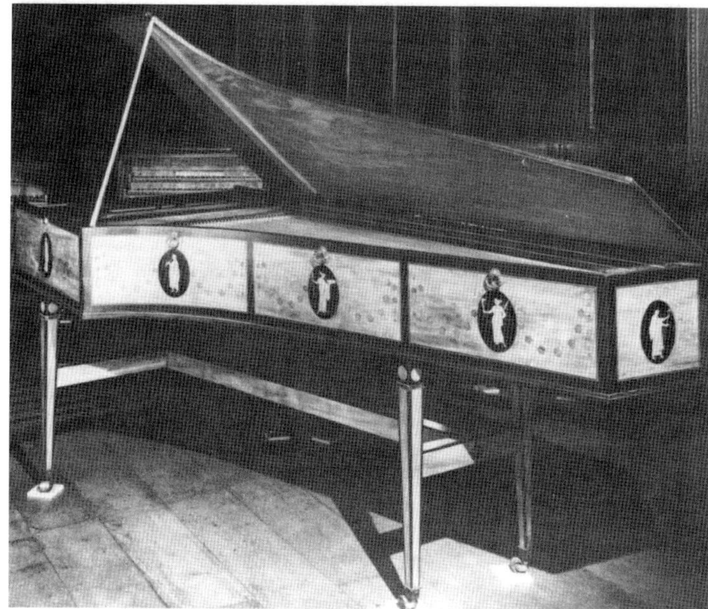

Photo by courtesy of The Colt Clavier Collection, Bethersden, Kent

Was it the work of a Designer, or did the piano maker Robert Stodart simply buy in these highly decorative, Neo Classical oval insets from a sub contractor who specialised in such work? I have no answers.

What one can say is that this is one of the most remarkable British grand pianos of the pre-1800 period, one of the tiny number that were not built in the accepted Tabel style. You can be certain it was a "Special" for a moneyed client and I know of no other authentic pre-1800 British grand in this manner (there is a Broadwood with decoration of similar flavour but that, as they say, is another story).

Although he may never even have known of the existence of this Stodart the indelible 18th Century presence of Robert Adam is felt as a background influence to the decoration of Classical figures which are meant, I suspect, to represent The Nine Muses.

Formerly in the Colt Clavier Collection and now to be found at Heaton Hall, Manchester, the piano is inscribed "Robertus Stodart Londoni fecit 1784 Wardour Street Soho". It is made with a mahogany veneer over an oak carcass and garnished with satinwood and other veneers.

It is my judgement that the most important pre-1800 British grand from a decorative point of view is the "Don Godoy" Sheraton grand. Not all agree.

The respected expert Mr Hugh Gough told a meeting of the Royal Musical Association in 1951 that this Stodart grand is "by far the finest English grand of its period that I know and I think it surpasses the celebrated piano made by John Broadwood in 1796 for Don Manuel de Godoy". Plate No.163.

I can think of six unusual grand pianos which do not conform to the pre-1800 norm but the rarity of such instruments becomes ever more apparent when you reflect that it was just these kind of "specials" that were most likely to be saved when the owner had a clear-out. It was the ordinary kind that were most likely to be put on the bonfire.

David Hunt, a leading restorer of the early piano, told me: "I am sure that decorated instruments survive in greater proportion to the ratio when built."

The grand shown here is one of a group of at least three "Specials" decorated with Wedgwood pottery and produced by Broadwood around the end of the 18th Century, this grand piano of 1798 has been described by a lady expert as "enchantingly pretty". The Wedgwood plaques and medallions are indeed remarkable (they include, for example, subjects modelled after characters from Laurence Sterne) but it can be seen immediately that, in all other respects, the main case follows the Tabel tradition. Plate No.164.

Photo by courtesy of The Albany Institute of History and Art, New York

This famous 1767 example of a square piano by Zumpe, the man who introduced this type to Britain, demonstrates with clarity the almost rustic character of the trestle stand on which the instrument sat. It is plain, angular and well matches the temper of Zumpe's casework. Note Zumpe's favourite black "string" inlay on the main case. Plate No.165.

Photo by courtesy of the Victoria and Albert Museum

As fashion moved further and further away from the austerity of Zumpe's early instruments the "English square" quickly developed a completely new identity. This Late 18th Century example by Christopher Ganer, some of whose cases are superb, has the new "French frame" kind of stand and shows the abandonment of Zumpe's plain and simple approach. It was put up for auction as Lot 166 by Sotheby's on Nov 17th., 1994 and was stated to be in mahogany with satinwood cross-banding and chevron and tulipwood stringing. Plate No.166.

Photo by courtesy of Messrs Sotheby's of New Bond Street, London

Zumpe and the Plain Squares

During this same time the square piano was following a more individual path.

A (comparatively) cheap and cheerful rival to the grand piano, the "English Square" enjoyed immediate popularity when introduced to British customers on a commercial level by Johann Christoph Zumpe, c.1766.

Zumpe managed to reduce the price of his little square, just over 4ft long, to 16 guineas[25] and, to attain this end, the instrument case was purely Functional. Every frill was cut and it was, in effect, a simple box enclosing the works, being meant to sit on a stand or table.

They were usually in mahogany with an oak or spruce back and few more portable pianos can have been produced. Indeed, a dealer's catalogue of 1789 seems to suggest that such square pianos might be "conveyed and....performed upon in a coach".[26]

Some of the earliest known Zumpe squares have no decoration at all,[27] other than the small brass hinges, a reduced version of those on English harpsichords and spinets. If he thought of such matters at all, Zumpe can only have depended on the glory of the broad boards of mahogany to make a visual impact, set against the polished, fancy brass of the hinges.

When Zumpe did introduce decoration it was but a severe black, thin "string" inlay near the edge of the case which, again, made for the illusion of a panel. But this very simplicity and restraint gives the Zumpe squares their own appeal, especially for that strong constituency prefering Puritan values.

In the words of a former officer of the Victoria and Albert Museum, Philip James, the early English square "though simple....did not lack the fine proportions which are one of the chief characteristics of contemporary English furniture".[28]

Photo by David Hackett. Courtesy of the Hackett Collection

The knowledgeable expert C.F. Colt dated the earliest "French frame" he came across to 1778 on a square piano by Christopher Ganer. The "French frame" spelled the end for Zumpe's rustic trestle stand (though some Zumpe-type examples were still made for years to come) and endorsed the introduction of a Neo Classical style for the cabinet work of the Late 18th Century square. This "French frame" shown here is the support for a square by William Rolfe, c.1805, in the Hackett Collection. Plate No.167.

The Puzzle of the "French Frame"

As other makers such as Pohlmann, Beyer and Haxby, followed Zumpe into the profitable business of making squares they adopted Zumpe's approach to the casework. But such Puritanism did not endure and the key to an emphatic switch of taste was a new type of stand known as "the French frame".

In place of the rustic trestle stand made by Zumpe the "French frame" introduced tapered, slender legs, usually on brass castors with decorative brass paterae at the top of the leg (to hide bolt heads) and, an occasional added feature, a music shelf under the keyboard with the leading edge cut away to provide knee-room. This frame was often constructed with a "lip" so that when the actual piano was dropped in it gave the illusion of being one article.

To the layman's eye the new stand gives such square pianos a distinctive "splayed" look but this was achieved on some early examples by tapering only the inside of the leg. Later examples might be subtly tapered on the outside also.[29]

It was inevitable that the main case of the Late 18th Century square piano would itself be garnished with decoration to match its new companion, the "French frame". Altogether a more sophisticated piece of cabinet-making and recognizably Neo-Classical in taste (even to the motifs on the brass) a tendency that was to be reinforced by important designs.

Photo by David Hackett. Courtesy of Bonham's of Montpelier Street, London

The "French frame" was constructed to give the illusion it was part of the piano it supported. It is shown here, in its proper place, holding up the William Rolfe square piano, c.1805, now in the Hackett Collection. But by 1805 the "French frame" and the Neo Classical square were both about to be overtaken by history, the Regency ushering in a new style with a turned leg. Plate No.168.

The result was a Late 18th Century square far more likely to be a decorative object than the grand pianos of the same period.

Precisely when this change of style occurred in the square piano is a matter of debate.

Not only was the "French frame" jointed but it was often held from the side by a formidable bolt (so called by square piano enthusiasts although, to the layman, it looks like a giant wood-screw), the decorative brass patera being introduced to hide the head of the bolt. This photo by Mr Hackett demonstrates how the bolt (which connected with a threaded iron plate) on this William Rolfe square, c.1805, was put in as additional reinforcement. Some "French frames" might appear not to have such a bolt but close inspection often reveals that they have been glued, or supported with corner blocks, after a failure of the screw thread. Plate No.170.

Another photo by David Hackett shows the bolt being inserted from the side to connect the "French frame" on his c.1805 William Rolfe square. The bolt fits into a threaded iron plate visible on the inner face. Plate No.171.

The square piano enthusiast and collector David Hackett very generously agreed to "deconstruct" a "French frame" for me and photograph the constituent parts. This fine close-up of the top part of a front leg on a William Rolfe square, c.1805, shows the meticulous workmanship of the inlay. Originally it would have looked more colourful and, if any of the woods were originally dyed, the effect would have been even more vivid. Mr Hackett tells me that the front legs are of mahogany inlay on an oak core and he believes the edge banding to be in satinwood with a broad stripe of boxwood edged with ebony. "The detail of the inlay banding is incredibly fine", said Mr Hackett, "I just can't see how it was done." Interestingly, the two rear legs are of solid mahogany but inlaid on the forward and outward facing sides only. Plate No.169.

The connected joint of the "French frame" of this c.1805 William Rolfe square shows the wooden peg on top (one of four) that will hold the actual piano when it is put in place. Some square pianos have the peg arrangement and some a "lip with recess" into which the instrument fits (I have been told of one, a Houston, where triangular corner blocks help locate the piano). A brass patera on this Rolfe now hides the bolt head and provides a decorative disguise—hardly fitness for purpose. Mr Hackett tells me that the brass patera is of the right date but was transferred from another piano. Plate No.172.

All photography by David Hackett. Courtesy of the Hackett Collection

Philip James argued that until about 1780 square pianos "varied little and there was no great change in their construction save for a gradual increase in the size of the case and the abolition of the trestle-stand in favour of the 'French frame' with its four taper legs".[30]

William Dale likewise argued this change occurred "soon after" 1780.[31]

C.F. Colt had a slightly different view: "The earliest squares and grands invariably had trestle stands but, quite early on, more elegant squares would rest on a French stand: Ganer squares as early as 1778 and a Broadwood square by 1787. These 'French' stands consisted of four elegant, tapered legs which could be taken apart for easy transport".[32]

I cannot discover when the description "French frame" was first used but an expert pointed out to me[33] that there were a number of references to such an article in the 18th Century records of Broadwood. The earliest he identified was 1794 but he suggests this meant it was already a known term in the London trade and "I think we may reasonably infer that they thought it originated in Paris, or at least to them it represented French style".[34]

The expert is right when he suggests it was already a known term because a list of pianos imported into India in 1786 reveals that a Longman and Broderip piano brought in by the merchant ship "Walpole" had "a French frame".[35]

There is one perplexing aspect to this term "French frame", which Mr Dale describes as "a stand with tapering legs of Louis Seize pattern" (which has obvious implications).[36]

As C.F. Colt wrote, "the name 'French stand' seems a contradiction in terms, since the French used screw-in, tapered turned legs for their pianos at least fifteen years before the English and one rarely sees French instruments with 'French stands'."[37]

Some indication of the influence of French ideas can be gained through the work of Thomas Chippendale, who published the first edition of his "Director" in 1754. Chippendale himself used the term "in the French taste" and in the London Trade at that time they employed such descriptions as "French foot", "French mattress" and "French elbow chair".[38] As late as 1851, William Stodart was advertising "Cottage" pianos with "French front and mouldings".[39]

And, of course, there was "French polish" introduced to Britain after the Napoleonic wars.

The brilliant Scots architect Robert Adam, a designer of both pianos and an harpsichord, suggested "The French style... is best calculated for the convenience and elegance of life".[40]

When Americus Backers started making his first grand pianos in London in the late 1760s the French were themselves emerging from the second phase of Rococo and entering into their own version of Neo-Classical, otherwise Louis Seize, which was to last into the 1790s before being consumed in the Revolution and its Directoire Style.

Louis Seize was characterised by the abandonment of the curves of Louis Quinze, a surrender to the discipline of straight lines and geometric patterns, an embrace of Neo-Classical ornamentation. So far as the French could manage it, a measure of restraint.

"In furniture in general the very earliest experiments with Neo Classicism, in either France or Britain, were in the 1750s, and by the mid-1760s Neo Classicism was a definite fashion in both countries though still not necessarily the dominant one", says Ms Lucy Wood, Senior Curator of the Department of Furniture at the Victoria and Albert Museum. "French and British architects and designers borrowed ideas, selectively, from each other".

The wilder waves of French Rococo, which ebbed and flowed to the very end of the 18th Century and beyond, never quite overwhelmed the British, though you could see evidence of its earlier infiltration in the work of Chippendale himself. The Victorians later flirted with this exotic foreigner more ardently than earlier generations but even here Revived Rococo was to an extent tamed and tailored to the native temperament. Never to be confused with actual French work.

Photo by courtesy of Bonham's of Montpelier Street, London

The development of piano case design was often dictated by the shape of the mechanical works and thus highly idiosyncratic. But it must not be thought for a moment that the piano could exist separately from the fashions and styles of its time. I have often been struck by the relationship between the "splayed leg" look of the Neo Classical square piano and the same "splayed leg" look on certain Georgian tables. This example of a George III serpentine serving table, described as standing on "square tapering legs", was auctioned by Bonhams of Montpelier Street, London, on June 11th., 2002, as Lot 78. Plate No.173.

Photo by David Hackett. Courtesy of the Hackett Collection

This photo by David Hackett shows what he believes to be a genuine cast brass, decorative patera from an 1806 Broadwood square. Such paterae, which were likely to be casualties of wear and tear and often replaced, were introduced to hide the head of a bolt inserted from the side to reinforce the construction of a "French frame". Mr Hackett suggests, correctly I am sure, that such paterae were generally "bought in" from specialist metalware makers. Plate No.174.

Photo by David Hackett. Courtesy of the Hackett Collection

Here we have the brass patera from a Clementi c.1815 square (strangely reminiscent of later Art Nouveau design) which, again, David Hackett believes to be original. Such paterae were generally of gilt brass and of two basic types—cast or stamped. This Clementi patera, secured by a soldered centre pin, is stamped but, as you might expect with such a fine maker, of heavy quality. Some of the thinly stamped paterae were flimsy. The fashion for such paterae remained a convention long after the need no longer existed and some brass paterae on later squares are there simply for symmetry or decoration and serve no practical purpose. Plate No.175.

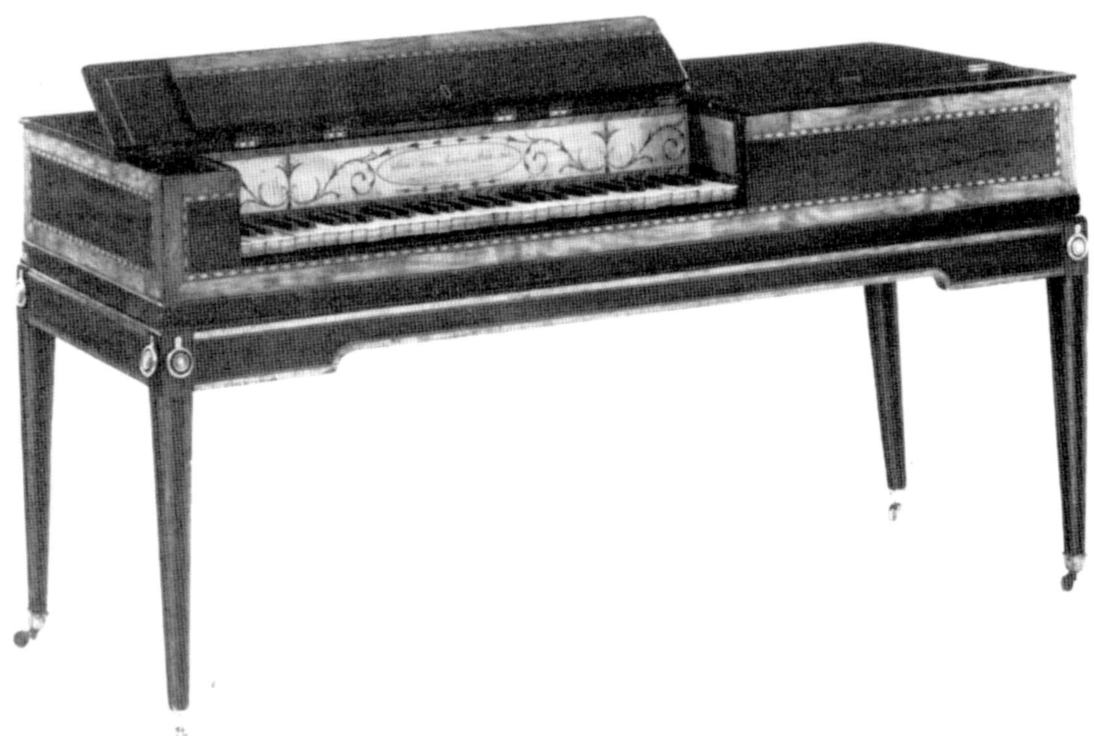

Photo by courtesy of Sotheby's of New Bond Street, London

The degree to which the English square adopted a new character can be judged from this instrument, bearing the date 1795 and the name of Joshua Done, which was sold by Sotheby's on July 19th., 1979. Sotheby's stated that the main case was in mahogany with satinwood crossbanding and a satinwood nameboard that has tulipwood cross-banding, harewood swags and boxwood and ebony stringing. Note the "splayed" legs; the disappearance of Zumpe's trestle stand; the modest brackets under the keyboard; the brass fittings; the decorated nameboard; and the inlay "en suite" to sides and legs. Plate No.176.

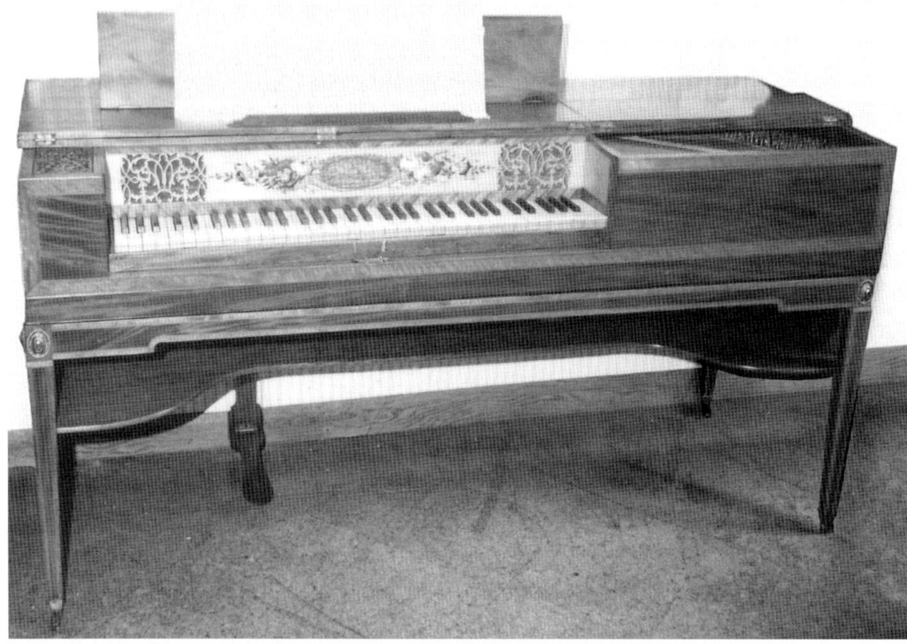

Photo by courtesy of the Colt Clavier Collection, Bethersden, Kent

One would never guess from this photo of an elaborate English square by William Rolfe, given a date of c.1805, that the Neo-Classical style was about to disappear in the embrace of the Regency. Here the Neo-Classical style of the square has reached maturity: A main case in mahogany with cross-banding and stringing in lighter veneer; straight legs with brass paterae; music shelf underneath and modest brackets above; highly decorative floral painting on the satinwood nameboard (an identical pattern to one found on a Clementi upright grand); and complex fretwork panels at either end. Plate No.177.

Photo by courtesy of The Deutsches Museum, Munich

Of course you may find exceptions and, of course, some instruments continued to be made along traditional Zumpe lines but, by the late 1780s, the British square piano was acquiring a recognizable Neo Classical character. This style was at the height of its popularity throughout the decade of the 1790s and continued until c.1805, when it was vanquished by the Regency, disappearing with remarkable speed.

During this period Broadwood established their position as Britain's most important piano maker and impressive quantities of the square piano issued from their works. What one sees in the Broadwood square are the hallmarks of the firm's style: Quality above all, fine wood and other materials but married always to a certain mainstream conservatism so far as the case was concerned. Not for Broadwood the artistic flourishes of a Ganer, a Rolfe or a Southwell. The tone is almost invariably more sober.

One of the stylistic keynotes of the Broadwood approach to the square became a broad band of inlay round the edge of the case and Michael Cole says the firm's records show you could buy a plain version for 20 guineas or inlaid (usually with satinwood) for 24 guineas. I have seen similar inlay on early squares by Ganer and others sold under the name of Longman and Broderip. The square shown here, signed "Johannes Broadwood Londini Fecit 1786" is to be found in the Deutsches Museum, Munich. Plate No.178.

Photo by courtesy of Messrs Sotheby's of Amsterdam

The broad band of inlay round the edge of the Neo Classical main case can be seen again in this Broadwood square that appeared as Lot 146 at Sotheby's of Amsterdam on March 27th 2002. It was claimed to be "in the manner of Thomas Sheraton" and inscribed "Johannes Broadwood Londini fecit 1793". Plate No.179.

Photo by courtesy of Messrs Sotheby's of New Bond Street, London

Again we see the established Neo Classical character of this Broadwood square of the 1790s, which appeared at Sotheby's as Lot 67 on January 25th 1979. Bearing the serial number 2636 it was dated 1795 on a boxwood plaque and stated to be in mahogany with fruitwood stringing and satinwood crossbanding. The satinwood nameboard had fruitwood stringing and mahogany crossbanding. Plate No.180.

Photo by Mr Laurence Libin *Courtesy of The Palace of Pavlovsk, Russia*

This remarkable square piano of 1774, by Zumpe & Buntebart, was discovered in The Palace of Pavlovsk in Russia by Mr Laurence Libin, Research Curator of the Metropolitan Museum of Art. He believes it to be the square piano designed by Robert Adam in the same year and lost sight of for some two centuries. Plate No.181.

The First Identified British Piano Design

Whether or not we believe French fashion was the major factor in the development of the British Neo-Classical square (an alternative view might be it was a response to Adam's unique re-interpretation of a medley of Continental designs) there is, in my judgement, incontrovertible proof, both in design drawings and an actual example, that a major shift in the style of the English square took place in 1774, to be immediately reinforced by another key design of 1775 and a third in 1777.

The assertion this change had taken place by 1774 can be proven by design drawings[41] which still exist in Sir John Soane's Museum and are, I believe, the first known design for the British piano. They are by Robert Adam, who towers over the history of 18th Century design and was the populariser and inspiration of so much of the Neo-Classical movement.

It was in 1774 Adam made two designs (suggested to be alternatives) for a square piano for Catherine the Great, Empress of Russia and, as you might expect, both are virtuoso displays of Adam's mastery of Classical detail.

What he believes to be the actual Zumpe and Buntebart square made to one of these designs has been discovered[42] in a Russian Palace by Mr Laurence Libin, Research Curator of the Metropolitan Museum of Art and, since it is dated 1774 and covered with Neo-Classical inlay, it would appear to give added confirmation that fashion, and the square, had changed direction by this date.

The surprise is to find the man associated with such a new fashion was none other than the prophet of austerity himself, Johann Christoph Zumpe though, by this time, he had been joined in partnership by Gabriel Buntebart and I find it impossible to decipher the exact part played by each.

Despite three proven examples of a new fashion in the 1770's, square pianos in "Old Zumpe" style continued to be made by a number of firms. One can speculate that a more definite shift took place c.1780.

William Dale believed the changes resulting from the new Neo-Classical style meant "the homely square piano was worthy to rank as a decorative object", introducing "Satin and tulip wood, and that beautiful wood, now so little known, called hare wood (*in fact, stained sycamore or maple, sometimes known also as "silverwood"*) ....for decoration, and some little brass work.... sparingly added."

Photo by Mr Laurence Libin
Courtesy of The Palace of Pavlovsk, Russia

A photo showing the right hand side of the case and top of the paired front legs (there were eight in all) of the 1774 Zumpe & Buntebart square piano discovered in The Palace of Pavlovsk by Mr Laurence Libin. Plate No.182.

A Classical head shown in a detail from the main case of the Zumpe & Buntebart square piano of 1774 discovered by Mr Laurence Libin. Plate No.183.

Michael Cole, not only a piano historian but a gentleman who works at the bench and has studied in close-up the cases of hundreds of such pianos, tells us how, after Zumpe's Spartan approach, the first decorative efforts of other makers were "confined to the use of contrasting inlaid lines of boxwood and ebony".[43]

This was followed by the use of rich veneers around the keyboard, or of an exotic timber like kingwood as a cross-banding, set against a lighter-coloured key well.

Satinwood of a golden colour became more general from c.1780, says Mr Cole and "Purpleheart was a favourite for cross-bandings around keyboards. Yellow boxwood, pink-striped tulipwood and green-stained 'airswood' were high on the list of other timbers used for decorative effect."[44]

As Mr Cole points out, the golden satinwood, a favourite choice, must have made "a perfect foil for dark red mahogany... The colours of some of these pianos when new must have been quite startling".[45]

Ralph Edwards, one of the authors of the mighty "Dictionary of English Furniture", wrote: "These small pianos from 3 feet 6 inches to 4 feet 6 inches in length were soon increased in size to cover 5 feet, and by the case-maker's skill decorated, in accordance with the prevalent taste of the period, with veneers in panels and bandings of satin and tulipwood, swags of painted husks and inlaid lines and medallions; the plain 'stand', copied from that of the spinet and harpsichord, gave way to the 'French frame', with square taper legs and brass 'furniture'."[46]

Photo by Mr Laurence Libin *Courtesy of The Palace of Pavlovsk, Russia*

Drawings reproduced by courtesy of Sir John Soane's Museum, London.

These three drawings, to be found in Sir John Soane's Museum, show details from the alternative designs by Robert Adam for a square piano for Catherine the Great, Empress of Russia, in 1774. When it became better known Adam's Neo-Classical decoration, such as this, was to inspire much of the furnishing trade in the Late 18th Century. Plate Nos.184, 185 and 186.

The Domination of Robert Adam

What caused the sudden switch in the style of the square in the 1770s? Undoubtedly French fashion was greatly admired in Britain but you have to consider not simply Adam's piano designs for the Empress of Russia (whether or no these were seen by other piano makers) but his absolute domination of the last three decades of the 18th Century which "became a truly national idiom affecting the work of virtually every British cabinet-maker and designer".[47]

Critics might counter this by arguing that Adam, the creator of the interiors of Syon House, Osterley Park and the library at Kenwood, was himself but a vehicle for the reinterpretation of ancient Roman and Etruscan styles. To which I would reply: Seen through an Adam's prism with the eye of genius, the end result unique.

It needs a systematic comparison of the decorative motifs used by, particularly, the Late 18th Century square piano makers against the motifs introduced by Robert Adam to see exactly to what extent he influenced such decoration. The question, I admit, needs further investigation but my feeling is that Adam was the important exemplar.

Hepplewhite's work was not published until 1788 and Sheraton's until 1794 so, unless there was some special access to workshops where their work might be seen at an earlier date, these two designers cannot have affected matters before those dates.

G.B. Cipriani, the decorative artist, likewise, did not begin his own publication in London until 1786.

However, Robert Adam did not stand alone.

The motifs used by J. Carter for the decoration of ceilings, sides of rooms and "sundries", in a book published in 1774 by a society of architects, are certainly worth studying.

As is the work of George Richardson in "A Book of Ceilings in the style of the Ancient Grotesques" 1776 and in 1781 "A New Collection of Chimney-pieces, ornamented in the style of the Etruscan, Greek, and Roman Architecture".

But it has been pointed out that Carter's designs "seem to be based on the Adam lines" and are also similar to Richardson's.[48] In short, both shared something of Adam.

Rather more tentatively, I think you would also have to put a question mark against the decorative designs of Francesco Bartolozzi (who came to England in 1764).

A far more difficult question is the possible input of Michael Angelo Pergolesi, who published "Designs for neoclassical ornament", in parts from 1777. It has often been claimed that Pergolesi, who had worked for the Adam brothers in Italy c.1760-1763 was, like Cipriani, influenced to come to London by Robert Adam.

Pergolesi was then further commissioned by the brothers in Britain (he is proven to have worked on Syon House interiors) and his designs, to the layman, would seem to share many Adam qualities. So it is legitimate to ask so far as the ornamental motifs are concerned: Which came from Adam and which from Pergolesi?

Amongst his vast range, Pergolesi designed musical trophies, marquetry, arabesques, urns and vases, sphinxes, gryphons—in short the gamut of "Adam-style" ornament.

However, if you look at the "New Style" Late 18th Century square pianos of, say, Christopher Ganer, or William Southwell, or Longman and Broderip, or Joshua Done, or John Preston, you wonder: did they not owe something to Robert Adam?

And do not forget Adam began publication of "The Works in Architecture" in 1773.

A good hard look at Adam's design for both his square pianos and harpsichord for the Empress of Russia provides a strong basis for comparison with later piano design.

The first thing you notice about the alternative conceptions for a square piano provided by Adam in 1774 is the tendency to a slimmer line and feeling of lightness when compared with previous squares. These were to become, with ever more emphasis, the essential qualities of the later 18th Century British square pianos, long before Sheraton appeared in print.

And if you study those Adam swags and drops you will not have to look far to find their match. Like the other motifs used so often by Adam, the urns, the vases, the paterae and ribbons, the spandrel fans and all the rest, these were to be copied by both furniture and piano makers. It could, of course, be suggested the French too, at this time, were providing a plethora of Neo-Classical ornamentation but I believe that British piano makers were more likely to consult British pattern books rather than, say, J.-F. Neufforge, who published between 1757 and 1777.

A convincing case[49] has been made, for example, that Adam was, as early as 1767, the man who introduced the lyre motif to Late 18th Century British households. Subsequently, it was adapted not only for general furniture design (as splats in the backs of chairs, or supports for small tables) but also in place of legs to support the main body of some special, post-1800, grand and square pianos that were evidently made for wealthy clients.

Whether one can withstand an unvaried diet of Adam decoration is another matter. While I do not share Joseph Gwilt's hysterical antipathy[50] to the "vile taste of Robert Adam, a fashionable architect whose eye has been ruined by the corruptions of the worst period in Roman art", I am certainly in sympathy with Stanley Ramsey when he writes "After a time one tires of those ornate ceilings and endless arabesques; the very brilliance of the artist dazzles and fatigues".[51]

However, I think Adam's influence was potent and I shall continue to believe Robert Adam has the honour of being the first known British piano designer unless and until better evidence emerges.

Few of the general public (or even the Trade?) can have known of Robert Adam's designs for a square piano for Catherine the Great, Empress of Russia, in 1774. Or perhaps I have not done my homework well enough since I can find no contemporary public references to these designs.

However, a great many people must have known of Robert Adam's far grander design, made the same year, for a Harpsichord for Catherine the Great *(shown here)*, since this became a published Adam design during the 18th Century. When Volume 1 of "The Works in Architecture" appeared in 1778 it was described as "Design of a Harpsichord inlaid with various-coloured woods executed in London for the Empress of Russia". Plate No.187.

Photo by courtesy of Christie's of New York

This is one of two outstanding Neo-Classical pianos known by the London piano maker Frederick Beck but expert opinion is now coalescing round the view that the casework was by a Swedish immigrant, Christopher Fuhrlohg. This one, dated 1777 and decorated with a Classical figure playing the lyre, was auctioned by Messrs Christie's of New York as Lot 345 on October 17th., 2001. Plate No.188.

Two Extraordinary Pianos by Beck

That a climate of change was affecting other London piano makers at exactly the same time we can prove from two further pianos of Neo-Classical exuberance that were produced immediately afterwards by Frederick Beck. In my judgement there is absolutely no question but that a Designer was again involved with each.

These two Beck designer pianos, one of 1775 and the other of 1777, are extraordinary to behold but both have been classed[52] as square pianos, although they look little like my conception of a square and much resemble high class drawing room furniture.

The question to which I can make no answer is: When we consider how many 18th Century pianos have disappeared over the years, is it possible that Beck made other such pianos before 1775?

I am certain there was a third, later, Beck piano of the same remarkable quality but it has long ago been lost. The evidence for the existence of this third instrument is very strong.

Among the 62 harpsichords and 64 pianos, all "les plus rares, par leur perfection", which were seized during the French Revolution there is a written account of at least one other exceptional Beck instrument.[53]

Only in a few instances was any mention made of the monetary value of the instruments seized from the aristocrats but one Beck piano of 1779 was stated to be worth 600 francs and another by Beck of 1788, "belonging to Debrange, emigré, rue de Sevres", was estimated at no less than 5,000 francs and was, by a margin of thousands of francs, more valuable than any other on the list. I believe that Debrange's piano, made by Beck, must have had a case of superlative quality.

The apparent absurdity of Beck's work, and a fact very hard to comprehend, is that some of the ordinary square pianos he made and sold to the general public have been criticised in modern times for "rushed cabinet-work, poor key-carving, and even in one case an adze-mark on the wrestplank".[54]

How could this man have also been responsible for two of the most remarkable pianos of the 18th Century? Pianos of the most sophisticated cabinet work. Pianos with inlay panels which must have been about as good as you could get in Britain.

In Beck's 1775 instrument, which is totally enclosed rather like some huge, super-ornamented Christmas box, there are ormolu borders and extensive inlays of coloured woods, with a herring-bone pattern of harewood and wood lines dyed green. A figure in the middle of the front panel, seated in a landscape with tambourine, is suggested to be derived "from an engraving after Angelica Kauffman's 'Triumph of Venus' and is made to represent the Muse Erato by the addition of a tambourine".[55]

Convincing evidence has been put forward that the Swedish immigrant Christopher Fuhrlohg was the originator and inlayer of the casework of Beck's piano of 1775.[56]

The second decorative Beck piano, dated 1777, which appeared at a Christie's auction in New York, in 2001, was similar in character to the 1775 instrument and a little (but not much) more practical, being stood on four legs.[57] Many people might assume it was a commode.

The 1777 piano showed a similar inlaid Classical figure playing a lyre, suggested to be "a seated figure of Erato, Muse of lyric poetry". The sides were inlaid with urn medallions and the case was in "Satinwood, amaranth and marquetry", with gilt-bronze mounts of goat heads and marquetry incorporating sycamore, harewood, satinwood and rosewood.

If Christopher Fuhrlohg was responsible for the casework of the first then he must be the man who did the inlay for the second, was the inevitable conclusion. These two pianos, I would suggest, represent a high water mark of the Neo-Classical movement and are among the important furniture designs of the period.

What we know of Fuhrlohg is that he was said to have been born in Stockholm, c.1737 but spent a period working for Paris cabinet makers about 1764-67. One suggestion is that he was in the employ of Simon Oeben.

A number of his countryman had, however, already moved to London and Fuhrlohg followed them there, initially working for John Linnell before establishing his own business. He is known to have had premises in Tottenham Court Road between 1769 and 1776.

On one of his trade cards Fuhrlohg was described as "Ebeniste to his Royal Highness the Prince of Wales" and a later card stated he was "Cabinet Maker, Inlayer and Ebeniste to His Royal Highness the Prince of Wales, makes and sells all kinds of Inlaid Work". In a third card he was described as "Cabinet Maker in the Modern Grecian and Chinese Taste".

What is particularly important from the point of view of the Beck pianos is that Fuhrlohg is proven to have exhibited at the Society of Artists in 1773 "A bacchante, in inlay" and his partner and half-brother, Johann Christian Linning, subsequently showed with the Society in 1775 "The Muse Erato in different coloured Wood", giving his address as "At Mr Fuhrlogh's, No 24, Tottenham Court Road.

Photo by courtesy of The Beurmann Collection, Hamburg

It seems extraordinary how, after c.1780, the new style, Neo-Classical English square developed in the late 18th Century and how completely they abandoned the austerity of the early Zumpe instruments. If we accept Mr Cobbe's hypothesis that Southwell may have introduced the painted nameboard technique in the 1780s, then this Longman and Broderip in the noted Beurmann Collection, with a date suggested of c.1786, appears to show how soon others took it up. I have not personally inspected it but from the photo we see spirited painting of roses that decorate either side of a central oval containing the name of the firm. Plate No.189.

Nameboards: An End to Puritanism

The most love, care and skill in the best Neo-Classical square pianos went on the embellishment of the nameboard which might be inlaid or cross-banded with contrasting veneers of satinwood, tulipwood, boxwood, ebony, harewood and fruitwood. Alternatively they might be painted with garlands, swags, floral leaf, berry motifs and the like. Sometimes oval enamel plaques were affixed on which to paint the maker's name and I have seen it suggested that some of these were "Battersea enamel".

In this exuberant fashion Puritanism was put behind them and there was unrestrained joy in a surrender to the beauties of decoration.

Surely specialist craftsmen, perhaps sub-contractors who did only this kind of work, must have been involved and such nameboards must have demanded high skills and artistic sensibilities.

Who began this fashion for painting the nameboard of the square?

Mr Alec Cobbe, of the famous Cobbe Collection, points to two early William Southwell squares and states: "In both these instruments the decorative features include flowery swags painted on the nameboard... These features are entirely uncharacteristic of the London pianos of the time".[58]

Fretwork was sometimes introduced in two matched panels on these nameboards, usually with a silk backing to heighten the effect. Again, Mr Cobbe suggests Southwell's squares of the 1780s[59] as a possible origin for piano fretwork which is said to have come into more general use from around 1795.[60]

Southwell's early squares demonstrate that he was another who was incapable of producing a piano that was boring: Here was a case with a more architectural flavour than those produced by most of his rivals,

Illustration by courtesy of the Hackett Collection, Photo by David Hackett

Surely the piano makers of the Georgian period must have employed specialist craftsmen for the highly intricate and skilled work that appeared on the nameboards of their square pianos. This painted decoration on the nameboard of a c.1810 square by Clementi is in the Hackett Collection. Plate No.190.

Illustration by courtesy of the Hackett Collection, Photo by David Hackett

Another development in the Late 18th Century square where Southwell was certainly one of the early innovators, was the introduction of fretwork panels. This developed into a convention of a pair of matching fretwork panels either side of the nameboard, such as this one on David Hackett's c.1810 Clementi square. I have seen virtually identical fretwork panels on a Longman & Clementi square given a date of c.1800 and an eminent restorer tells me he believes this particular fret design "died out c.1813". Plate No.191.

plus fretwork and with an attractively decorated nameboard.[61]

From my own enquiries it seems to me likely that the artist painting of square pianos by decorating the main case and not simply the nameboard, must have begun[62] by 1776 (a Pohlmann square of that year, now lost, is said to have had "paintings on the cover") but, again, this must have been very rare, the British preferring, possibly on grounds of cost, to rely on inlay for decoration.

Photo by courtesy of Sotheby's of New York

Not having inspected it personally I can make no intelligent comment on this remarkable piano other than to say I know of no other Late 18th Century British piano with such Chinoiserie decoration nor, indeed, anything in this form. The piano was put up for auction by Sotheby's of New York as Lot 457 on October 22nd., 1999, when it was described as "An important George III black lacquer and parcel-gilt piano in the manner of Thomas Chippendale" with a suggested date of "third quarter 18th Century". Plate No.192.

Black Lacquer and Chinoiserie

Another highly unusual piano, again looking more like a piece of cabinet furniture than a square, appeared at an auction in New York in 1999 when it was stated to be "An important George III black lacquer and parcel-gilt piano in the manner of Thomas Chippendale". A date has subsequently been put forward of "c.1776".

Again, I have not been able to study this piano personally and can offer no opinion on such matters but its most remarkable feature is its ornate Chinoiserie decoration, being "decorated all over with....figures at various pursuits, birds and foliage, within floral borders".

So far I have not come across any other pre-1800 British piano with Chinoiserie decoration (there is a Stodart grand that might be thought to qualify but I am advised[63] that although the piano is pre-1800 a question mark remains regarding the date of its Chinoiserie decoration).

A smaller, but again unusual, pre-1800 piano is the instrument stated to have been made in 1786 for Jane, Duchess of Gordon, by Richard Horsburgh of Edinburgh and which is now in the delightful Goodwood House collection. This has a case made down to the floor, with a highly decorative concave front, in satinwood veneer with mahogany crossbanding, the nameboard in walnut veneer with sycamore inlay.[64] Was the design of the case simply the work of a highly skilled cabinet maker, or was he working to an architect's drawing?

Another rare square of the period, one of unusual shape and fascinating casework, was made by George Froeschle of London in 1776.[65] It has a curious and elegant serpentine end but this was not just intended to make the case more attractive—Michael Cole tells us that it was made in this form to give room for longer bass strings. In 1774 Froeschle had paid for a number of announcements in the "Public Advertiser"[66] to inform the public he had made a piano "on a new construction"; that this had the qualities of a large harpsichord; and it was approved by the best music masters. My presumption is that this was probably of his 1776 type.

We may conclude that few piano cases reached the heights of the two Beck articles but the period to just after 1800 showed a confirmation of the Neo-Classical tendency of the square and its makers sometimes produced cabinet making of a high standard.

The decorative casework of such as Christopher Ganer, William Southwell or William Rolfe is always worthy of attention and, although they are often described as dealers who sold pianos from other makers, I have found a number of pianos with the Longman and Broderip name to be of interest, their instruments having a distinctive "house style".

In 1798 the great pianist Muzio Clementi took over Longman and Broderip and, if anything, improved on their case work. It seems to me that Clementi can seldom have produced anything that was mean or dull.

A couple of pianos I have seen by George Astor have casework of real interest and individual instruments with the names of Joshua Done, George Garka, William Cope and Lucas have also seemed to me to be of merit.

With time, the legs of the supporting French frame of the square became yet more tapered and refined, the brass paterae almost obligatory and, often, with modest brackets. Broadwood, whose work was always sound, began to adopt a distinctive band of broader, light inlay round the edges of the main case and there were variations on this by other makers who thus gave their squares an individual character. In the best examples the sides and the legs were inlaid or decorated to match the decoration of the front of the main case.

Courtesy of Goodwood House, Goodwood, Chichester
Photographs by Ken Wormald

A close-up of the sophisticated arrangement of inlay on the piano stated to have been made in 1786 by Richard Horsburgh and now in the collection of Goodwood House, Sussex. The case is in satinwood veneer with mahogany crossbanding and the interior shows a nameboard veneered in walnut with sycamore inlay. Plate No.194.

◀

A highly unusual piano displaying the arts of the cabinet maker, this instrument was stated to have been made for Jane, Duchess of Gordon, in 1786, by Richard Horsburgh of Edinburgh. The case is in satinwood veneer and is now to be found in the fine collection of Goodwood House in Sussex. Plate No.193.

Photo by courtesy of The Metropolitan Museum of Art, New York

This is a well known example of an artist painted square in the wonderful Collection of the Metropolitan Museum of Art, New York but the judging of artist painted furniture is the trickiest game in town—and certainly beyond the competence of an amateur like myself. The Preston square has a suggested date of c.1790-1805 and is decorated, according to the Museum's official description, on the sides with "floral garlands and other elements including antique busts in beaded ovals"; and on the lid with "a rectangular panel surmounted by griffons flanking an urn, the ovals and central panel depicting women and boys playing a variety of classical instruments, all painted somewhat in the style of Angelica Kauffmann". Plate No.195.

The Tricky Problems of "Artist Painted"

Painted furniture produced by the followers of Robert Adam presumably encouraged the same development on pianos and a finely painted Longman and Broderip square of c.1790, decorated with swags of flowers on the front, sides and top, was illustrated by Philip James, who commented: "The cases of English pianos were sometimes decorated with paintings when this form of embellishment for furniture became fashionable towards the end of the eighteenth century; but it is not often that such fine quality of painting is found on musical instruments as we see on this square piano."[67]

Around the turn of the century a tiny number of artist painted pianos appeared and the work on some is associated with the popularity of prints after Angelica Kauffiman and her world of Classical figures.

Although I have not been able to study it, the Chris Maene Collection in Belgium has a Clementi grand c.1798-1799 with, particularly for a grand, an unusual nameboard decoration of an allegorical figure inside an oval, matched by a second figure with lyre, accompanied by a Cupid.

In the Metropolitan Museum of Art, New York, is a Broadwood square of 1801 which has "painted decorations in the style of Angelica Kauffmann"—a painting of the "Judgement of Paris" with another "painted scene of reclining Venus with two cupids, in grisaille within border of painted beads".[68]

The Met also has an upright grand of 1801 by William and Matthew Stodart with doors "decorated with painted birds, flowers and musical instruments".[69]

A third instrument in the Met is a John Preston square, with dates suggested from 1790 to 1805, which has "busts in beaded ovals and (on the lid) two beaded ovals flanking a central rectangular panel surmounted by griffons with an urn, the ovals and central panel depicting women and boys playing a variety of classical instruments, all painted somewhat in the style of Angelica Kauffmann".[70]

In the private collection of Mr Otto Rindlisbacher of Zurich, there is an upright grand of c.1806, by the Royal makers Jones and Co., with three artist painted scenes above the keyboard including a Cupid and what appears to be a musical group.[71]

Dating such paintings is a risky game and I can offer no opinion on whether all these are contemporary with the case on which they appear. Where they can be proved to have the same date one must emphasise the uniqueness of the instruments but the genuine are rare birds indeed.

Photo by courtesy of Sotheby's of New Bond Street, London

Although most British "square" pianos were made in an established oblong format, there were a few exceptions. This elegant and distinctive "square", made by George Froeschle of London in 1776, was put up for auction by Sotheby's as Lot 173 on November 20th., 1980. The most obvious characteristic is the serpentine sweep to the left hand side, which the piano historian Michael Cole points out was necessary to accommodate longer bass strings. The case is in mahogany with boxwood and ebony stringing. Froeschle advertised in 1774 that he was making an instrument of new construction that had the qualities of a large harpsichord and was approved by the best music masters. Plate No.196.

Photo by courtesy of the Musée des Instruments de Musique, Brussels

Another exception is this very rare Upright Square, suggested date c.1780-1790, by the inventor Joseph Merlin of London, with a short, stubby upright extension but note the quality of the cabinet work, especially the concave ends of the main case. It is made in mahogany with distinctive cross-banding and the top decorated with three panels. I know of no other piano like this one, which is in the collection of the Musée des Instruments de Musique and the maker's approach is quite different to the solution devised by William Southwell for his Upright Squares. Plate No.197.

◄

Two innovations that were to have an important influence on the case design of the British square piano were painted decoration of the nameboard and the use of fretwork, the latter mainly in panels at each end of the nameboard. The question is: Where did these ideas come from and when were they introduced? This early William Southwell square, now to be seen at Croft Castle, with its painted garland of foliage and open fretwork panels backed by silk, proves that this maker was already making use of both ideas by an early date. Plate No.198.

By courtesy of The National Trust
Photo by Robert Anderson

►

William Southwell's use of painted decoration on the nameboard and silk-backed fret panels can be seen yet more clearly on this superb Southwell square of the George III period, sold as Lot 365 by Adam's of Dublin on March 15th., 2005. The expert Mr Alec Cobbe wrote in the "Irish Arts Review Yearbook" that Southwell's earlier use of painted decoration in the 1780's was "entirely uncharacteristic of the London pianos of the time". Plate No.199.

Photo by courtesy of Adam's of Dublin

Photo by courtesy of Sotheby's of New Bond Street, London

Among the most brilliant examples of pianos transformed into combination furniture in the Late 18th Century are a small number of demi-lune (or half-moon) instruments produced by that most wonderful of piano makers, William Southwell and the cabinet work has often been suggested to be the work of a Royal maker, William Moore of Dublin. This one, taking the form of a side table, the hinged top inlaid with satinwood and yew wood, appeared at Sotheby's as Lot 167 on November 17th., 1994 and the date was given as c.1785. Plate No.200.

"Half Moon" Pianos by William Southwell

The grand and the square were not without competition from other forms in the 18th Century.

One of these was a remarkable series of "exceptionally beautiful"[72] inlaid, demi-lune, Neo-Classical pianos made by William Southwell of Dublin, which, at first sight, appeared to be high quality 18th Century "half moon" tables. Michael Cole suggests these have "the external appearance of a beautifully proportioned side-table in the classical style of Robert Adam".[73]

Such piano-tables were typical of combination furniture in which the piano served a dual purpose and about six by Southwell are known,[74] variously suggested as being between c.1785[75] and c.1794-98.[76]

An example with a date given as c.1785 and inscribed "Southwell fecit", appeared at a Sotheby's auction on November 17th., 1994, when it was described as having "a central shaded half-paetera with outer segmental veneers in satinwood banded in yew-wood, with an inner lobed border of amaranth, the frieze set with three oval

Photo by courtesy of The Colt Clavier Collection, Bethersden, Kent

That the demand for combination furniture was established early in the musical world we may judge from this Kirkman harpsichord of 1781 in the famed Colt Clavier Collection at Bethersden. The main case with its familiar veneered and cross-banded panels is faithful to the Tabel style but underneath we find a row of matching drawers has been introduced. Mr Colt suggests that the drawers may have been added specially by an outside joiner, presumably at the request of the customer. Plate No.201.

yew-wood panels, raised on square tapering legs also set with yew-wood panels".[77]

This was very fine cabinet making of the period and expert opinion usually attributes the casework of these pianos to a Royal cabinet maker, William Moore of Dublin."[78]

It is hard to find any Southwell piano which is not of interest from a cabinet making perspective and this is so with another pre-1800 form of piano which he devised but which had a relatively short life before being overtaken by new inventions: The Upright Square.

Southwell produced an alternative to other piano forms by turning the usual square piano on its side to produce an instrument standing on legs but only some 4ft 10in high, a design he patented in 1798.

A very small number of these upright squares have survived and we see once again the design and quality of Southwell's cabinet work. The Classical influence of the times is obvious.

An example that appeared at Sotheby's in 1980 sat on four tapered legs and was "richly veneered in mahogany and satinwood with bands of geometrical stringing in various woods". A central oblong panel was "inlaid in marquetry with a musical trophy" and a pierced gallery surmounted the instrument with small vase finials.

What is also described as an "Upright Square" is in the Collection of the Musée Instrumental de Bruxelles and this is by a remarkable 18th Century figure, the Ingenious Mr Merlin, otherwise John Joseph Merlin, the celebrated inventor who produced a number of keyboard instruments. The date is tentatively put forward as 1780-1790.[79]

Compared to Southwell's version the case has but a stubby, rising appendage at the back. However Merlin, as usual, has gone to some trouble with his cabinet making, the case not only having the "new style" look of the square but elegant, curved sides and three distinctive, outlined veneer panels across the rising top. The veneer is of mahogany, with other contrasting wood and the front has been banded to reflect the decoration of the top.

After William Stodart introduced his version of an Upright Grand "in the form of a bookcase" very late in the 18th Century, on January 12th., 1795, the instrument was to corner a niche market for the next 30 years or so—surprising when you think of the main trend towards miniaturisation. This Stodart upright grand (suggested to be c.1810 but believed by at least two experts to be later) is unusual but it illustrates perfectly the limited bookshelves left inside after the strings are accommodated. It has pronounced (possibly unique?) cabriole legs and is in rosewood with plentiful Regency influenced brass inlay and a sunburst silk panel in the top. Plate No.202.

Photo by courtesy of The Eddy Collection, Duke University, North Carolina, U.S.A.

A Piano Like a Bookcase

Another alternative to the grand and the square was the so-called Upright Grand, patented by William Stodart on January 12th., 1795, in which the grand piano was turned on end and perched, somewhat threateningly, on four legs, the strings starting upwards from the keyboard.

This was not a new idea, upright harpsichords and later, but similar, Continental pianos being known for many a year but Stodart gave his upright grand a character of its own by registering it as "an upright grand piano in the form of a bookcase" and the limited space not occupied by the strings was turned into bookshelves.[80]

Since the design was, in effect, rendered obsolete very quickly by the cabinet piano and the Hawkins modern upright, it is curious that Stodart's upright grand was copied by a number of other makers and, we are told, continued to have some popularity as late as 1830.[81] Perhaps its longevity was due to its loud, resonant sound.

The earliest upright grands I have seen I would class as Georgian mainstream "brown"

Photo by courtesy of Sotheby's of New Bond Street, London

A latecomer to the 18th Century scene, and an unusual one at that, was William Southwell's short-lived Upright Square, which he patented in 1798. Southwell, as inventive a piano maker as you could find, tried to produce a smaller upright by simply turning the square piano on its side—a smaller, but unsuccessful, rival to Stodart's upright grand. Despite its late appearance we see immediately, in this rare and superb example, c.1800, auctioned by Sotheby's as Lot 172 on October 9th., 1981, that Southwell is still firmly in the grip of Neo-Classicism. In pianos like this Southwell's attention to cabinet work was keen and the end result fine quality from its mahogany veneer to its central marquetry panel with musical trophy. Plate No.203.

furniture of modest Classical influence, though different fashions inevitably affected later models.

Much as the suggestion may pain musicians, I suspect that part of the appeal of Stodart's upright grand was due precisely to the fact it did NOT look like a piano. Its stated aim was to appear like a more conventional item of normal household furniture: A bookcase.

This was a phenomenon which showed itself regularly through the 19th Century because of dissatisfaction with the shape of the piano. What we have with Stodart's design is the piano in disguise, an instrument presented incognito for owners who could not face the real article.

Instead they now owned a piano that appeared to be a prestige piece of furniture, usually in mahogany and giving full rein to the cabinet maker's art, employing cornices and other embellishments.[82]

As William Dale observed, the upright grands had "an imposing cornice on the top, quite architectural in its character and not unlike a Chippendale bookcase—though generally the appearance was spoiled by a wealth of silk curtain fluted and radiated from the centre".[83] A few I have studied have had the silk draped rather than radiated.

It may seem that, by 1800, there was already a wide choice of different types of piano but if there was one thing the piano makers were never short of it was new ideas. In the 19th Century patent after patent was filed by ambitious entrepreneurs and yet more new kinds of piano were to be introduced. With organised factory production the instrument was to become affordable to a mass market and, the more the century progressed, the more they attempted to produce decorated piano cases that would ride the latest fashion wave.

Main Sources

In my opinion the piano was the most important item of furniture in many thousands of 19th Century homes, so it seems odd that, despite an avalanche of books devoted to the instrument, so little regard has been given to the decoration and design of the British case.

However, a number of pioneers (from whom I have learned much) have explored different facets in a number of essays and articles and we must pick the bones of more general piano histories.

In modern times we have to thank, especially, Michael I. Wilson of the Victoria and Albert Museum and I would draw attention, particularly, to three of his articles: "The Case of the Victorian Piano" in "The Victoria and Albert Museum Yearbook", 1972, Vol No 3, Pages 133-153; "Burne-Jones and Piano Reform", in *Apollo*, Nov, 1975, Pages 342-347; and "Updating the Ivories" in "Country Life", Jan 22nd., 1976, Pages 198-199.

Although he does not specifically set out to cover decoration or design, I gained some important insights by reading odd comments in C.F. Colt's book, "The Early Piano", published by Stainer and Bell in 1981, which is wonderfully illustrated.

Again, you may learn much from the asides of Michael Cole in a modern classic "The Pianoforte in the Classical Era", published Clarendon Press, 1998 but I would draw particular attention to passages such as "External appearance", Pages 79-80; comments on the cases of Zumpe, Pages 55-56; "Aesthetic considerations", Pages 255-256; valuable references to the woods used, in "Materials", Pages 285-287; etc. His picture captions should also be studied since Mr Cole is the voice of accuracy. Those who have a more specific interest in square pianos will want to study Mr Cole's recently published "Broadwood Square Pianos" (pub Tatchley Books, 2005) another detailed, authoritative work.

Some brief notes on pianos in the Victoria and Albert Museum's collection appear in Peter Thornton's "Musical Instruments as Works of Art", published H.M.S.O., 1982.

An important article that makes a number of points concerning the casework of the early square is by Philip B. James, "The Square Piano and its Origin", "The Connoisseur", September, 1928, Pages 4-9.

A passage on pianos appears in a furniture historian's classic, "The Dictionary of English Furniture" by Ralph Edwards, 2nd Revised Edition, Vol 2, published by Country Life, 1954, Pages 378-379.

Kathleen Purcell contributed "The Design of Grand Pianos" to a well known book "The House and its Equipment", Edited by Laurence Weaver, published Country Life, 1911 edn., Pages 61-66.

A leading Victorian art critic, Aymer Vallance, was responsible for two earlier articles from which one may learn much of contemporary attitudes: "The Decoration of the Grand Piano" in "Magazine of Art", Vol 25, 1901, Pages 204-210; and "The Decoration of Upright Pianos" in "Magazine of Art", Vol 25, 1901, Pages 544-550.

In the same year Hugh B. Philpott published "The Piano Aesthetically Considered" in "The Artist", 1901, Vol 32, Pages 181-187.

More of a curiosity is Wallace L. Crowdy's "Is the Pianoforte 'A Thing of Beauty'?", in "The Artist", October, 1894, Pages 387-389 but the three illustrations are of much interest.

Another article of great value because of the illustrations, which include the work of Alma-Tadema and Kate Faulkner, is "The Piano as a Work of Art", in "Cabinet Maker", January, 1896, Pages 188-189.

One of the early historians of the piano was the Victorian scholar William Dale, who published a number of articles and whose best known work is the book "Tschudi, the Harpsichord Maker" but, for our purposes, I must draw special attention to his major essay "The Artistic Treatment of the Exterior of the Pianoforte", in "The Journal of the Society of Arts", Feb 15th., 1907, Pages 364-373.

Photo by courtesy of The Metropolitan Museum of Art, New York

It is my opinion that this Broadwood grand piano, proven to be 1827 at the latest, represents a significant turning point in the design of the mainstream British grand piano, the point at which the piano world finally abandoned the Tabel style... unless someone can show me a more important example of earlier date. For over a century the Tabel approach, with its veneered and cross-banded panels along the side of the main case, had been the standard method of decoration of British harpsichords and grand pianos. Here we see immediately that the panels have been completely eliminated and a new style established. The Designer, and there must have been a designer, is unknown but the Broadwood record books show that on October 18th, 1827, grand piano No.11186 was "delivered at Mr McIntosh, 39, Bloomsbury Square *(London)*". To what degree the designer was influenced by two Astor grands and a Clementi grand, all of which had curved "cheeks" and are suggested to be of the 1820s, is an interesting question. Plate No.204.

1800-1850: Three Major Changes

Chapter Five

Although there were other fads and fancies, the period between 1800 and 1850 in Britain was dominated by three major styles: The existing Neo-Classical Georgian that carried over from the previous century for a few years; the Regency, much influenced by French Empire style; and Early Victorian, the latter part fathered by French Rococo.

Piano design moved to its own rhythm but it is my opinion that, in terms of the piano case, these fashions can be seen to have had three significant impacts—around the years c.1805-7, c.1809-10 and c.1827-28.

It is true that in the half century after 1800 you will find a bewildering *à la carte* of other furnishing styles, oscillating from Greek Revival to Archaeological Gothic and "Elizabethan", with a brief aperitif of Chinoiserie, an hors-d'oeuvre of Egyptian, plus repeated ladles of French influence. And you will come across isolated pianos that reflect such fashions.

But most piano case design followed the mainstream. What becomes apparent is that:

- The piano entered the new century still largely clothed in Neo-Classical Georgian garb.

- That subsequently the square, from c.1805-1807, was the first to throw itself at the charms of the Regency but the grand, remaining faithful to tradition, resisted longer, until about 1809, changed but in small measure and was never wholly seduced.

- That, from around 1827 for the grand and, so far as I can discover, approximately 1829 for the square, these two instruments began to make the transition from Regency but, while the grand initially picked its way with careful reserve, the British square sadly slid into a bourgeois and unconvincing middle-age, lacking the confident "power dressing" of its American rivals.

I do not suggest in any way that these dates represent the height of new piano styles, or that you will then necessarily find appealing decorative examples: Simply that around these years you can first detect a new approach to piano case design.

Surprisingly, the 18th Century styles of the grand and the square had survived the opening years of the 19th Century despite the emergence in 1800 of a rival of modest mien but unsuspected potency: the modern upright piano.

The upright, at first intended as a portable instrument, started slowly on a utilitarian note; had a short but splendid Regency period, certainly between 1810-13 but quite possibly longer; evolved into a somewhat safer, more mainstream 1820s; and then exploited, more successfully than any, the many possibilities of Victorian eclecticism.

After 1850 (and possibly before, but I lack the facts) the upright came to be the market leader of the piano world and it now seems extraordinary that its first 50 years were so long in gestation but my impression is that, in its early period, it had little influence on the case design of rival piano types.

The upright grand in its bookcase form, which had only been patented in January, 1795, seems to me to have had a sober, restrained approach to design, with the two extraordinary exceptions of the trend-setting Regency upright grand of 1807 by Thomas Hope and the "Gothic" upright grand made in 1808 by Jones and Co. for the Prince of Wales. Because fewer examples have survived than other main types it is hard to measure what effect Hope's design had on others. But there is an unusual Regency flavour to the Stodart (suggested to be c.1810, but believed by two experts to be later) in Duke University in America, which is in rosewood with characteristic brass inlay, highly unusual cabriole legs and (I would like to know how usual this was for an upright grand) a sunburst panel in the top.

Its smaller rival the cabinet piano, patented by William Southwell in 1807 must, I presume, have had something of a Regency character from the very beginning but I have found it impossible to identify cabinet pianos of such an early date.

The earliest cabinet piano design I have seen published, of 1812 by Wilkinson & Wornum, shows a superb Regency conception and I have come across some other fine Regency specimens.

The Regency proper was not official until 1811 but the term "Regency" is used today by design historians[1] to indicate a longer period, say from about 1805 to 1830 and this must be generally true in design terms. One writer, in an article entitled "Regency Taste 1790-1830", has even suggested that the Prince's influence "began in the 1780s".[2]

It was through the adaptable square that we see early evidence of the impact of The Regency.

It is comparatively easy to find square pianos up to 1805 which still have the square tapered, "splayed" Neo-Classical look of pre-1800 but my sense is that a major switch to a turned leg must have occurred around 1805-07.

The eminent furniture historian, Ralph Edwards, evidently saw Thomas Sheraton as being a large influence when he wrote that the new style squares might have "the turned legs so frequently shown in Sheraton's designs".[3]

Although I have not personally inspected the instruments concerned, at least three square pianos described as having turned legs and given dates of c.1805, are known.[4] Whatever reservations one may have about the description "Circa" it seems to me likely that a number of others could be found of slightly later date which might reinforce this suggestion.

William Stodart patented his Upright Grand in the form of a bookcase in 1795 and this example of 1804 in the Haags Gemeentemuseum shows the instrument in its first guise: Restrained, understated and in Good Taste with a Neo Classical tinge. Note particularly the straight legs carried over from Late 18th Century design. Plate No.205.

Photo by courtesy of The Haags Gemeentemuseum, Den Haag, The Netherlands

Photo by courtesy of The Smithsonian Institution (N.M.A.H)

Other firms besides Stodart made the Upright Grand and this Broadwood of c.1815, in the Smithsonian Institution, shows this type in its second guise—with the turned legs that were adopted by the square piano c.1805-07 and by the grand piano, c.1809. The case itself is still very basic in shape but has now acquired a lyre support underneath and the Regency influence shows itself in the plentiful brass inlay. Plate No.206.

Photo by courtesy of The Colt Clavier Collection, Bethersden, Kent

Further sophistication is shown in this mahogany Upright Grand by the makers Clementi, which also has a suggested date of c.1815. Now we see that the piano has acquired a cylinder fall which, a nice quality touch, has been decorated on the inside to match the exterior. The legs are now finely reeded, turned and tapered with brass decoration at the top of the leg and under the frieze. Plate No.207.

Wornum, who had miniaturised every type of piano he made, produced this "Piccolo Grand", suggested to be "after 1832"—very much at the end of the Upright Grand's reign. The smaller mahogany case, said by Mr C.F. Colt to be at least 1ft 6in lower than the usual version, is once again fairly plain (except for the green panel in the top) and, although the legs have been reeded, they look more substantial than the earlier Regency versions. Plate No.208.

Photo by courtesy of The Colt Clavier Collection, Bethersden, Kent

Photo by courtesy of Messrs Sotheby's of New Bond Street, London

From a period commencing about 1812 Robert Wornum and his partner George Wilkinson produced a series of Uprights with cases of distinction. It seems to me plain that these must have been based on Wornum's patent of 1811 and I have yet to see a bad one from this series. This example, from c.1812, was put up for auction by Sotheby's as Lot 158 on March 30th., 1989 and was in mahogany with a pierced brass gallery, with two mirrors either side of a panel of grey pleated silk, the panels edged with gilt mouldings. The two front legs were turned and reeded with brass collars. Plate No.209.

Photo by courtesy of The Colt Clavier Collection, Bethersden, Kent

Quite when Wornum's adventurous Regency-style approach to the design of the upright, as shown in his pianos from c.1812, came to an end I have not been able to determine. Wornum's partnership with Wilkinson was short-lived, ending in 1813 and I find it impossible to say how long these early Regency cases went on being made. What we learn from the upright piano photographed here and made by Butcher of London, is that, subsequently, design of uprights was safer and more mainstream—what dealers tend to call "Good brown furniture". Plate No.210.

The Cabinet piano was born to the Regency style and this refined specimen is part of the huge Collection of the Haags Gemeentemuseum. Made by David Loeschman of London c.1820, one notes immediately the fine spiral turning of the legs; the typical inlay to nameboard and the frieze; the decoration of the flat cornice; the beading round the bottom doors and base; the sunburst panel in the top. Plate No.211.

Photo by courtesy of The Haags Gemeentemuseum, Den Haag, The Netherlands

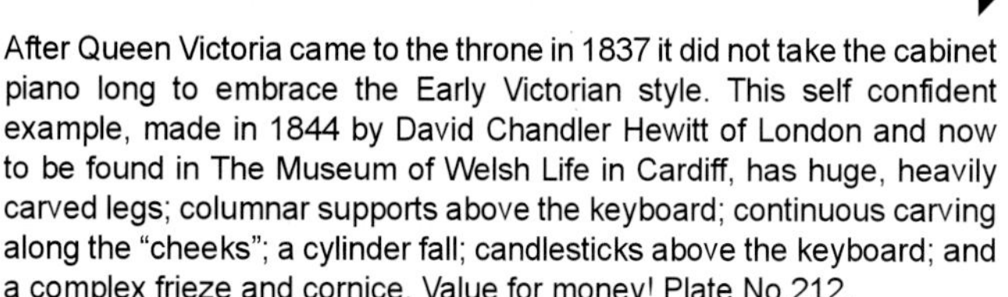

After Queen Victoria came to the throne in 1837 it did not take the cabinet piano long to embrace the Early Victorian style. This self confident example, made in 1844 by David Chandler Hewitt of London and now to be found in The Museum of Welsh Life in Cardiff, has huge, heavily carved legs; columnar supports above the keyboard; continuous carving along the "cheeks"; a cylinder fall; candlesticks above the keyboard; and a complex frieze and cornice. Value for money! Plate No.212.

Photo courtesy of The Museum of Welsh Life, St. Fagans, Cardiff

To look at this decorative William Southwell square, attributed to c.1805 but with features strongly in the Late 18th Century Neo-Classical tradition, it is hard to think that this style was virtually at the end of the road at this date. Here we still have the tapered, straight legs but all this was soon to change. This instrument, with its satinwood case, delightful arabesques, inlaid urns and foliage and the rest, was auctioned by Sotheby's as Lot 517 on May 15th., 1981. Plate No.213.

Photo by courtesy of Messrs Sotheby's of New Bond Street, London

What a difference a few years make. This square by the Royal makers Jones and Co. is given a date as early as c.1807 by Mr C.F. Colt yet the case has undergone important changes, the major one being the introduction of six turned and fluted legs instead of the traditional four straight legs. It was somewhere around this date, c.1805-1807 that this change was introduced into the design of the English square—the grand piano was much slower to change. Plate No.214.

Photo by courtesy of The Colt Clavier Collection, Bethersden, Kent

The Square Acquires Six Legs

There is another square in the Colt Clavier Collection, suggested as c.1807, with a radically different kind of case—SIX turned and reeded legs in a design that gives the instrument a wholly new character. Produced by the Royal makers Jones and Co., who are known to have been working between at least 1800 and 1813, this is described by Mr Colt as "a typical square of the period", in mahogany with satinwood cross-banding.

These developments in the square, which I hypothesize as starting c.1805-1807, meant that the almost delicate, fastidious, near anorexic instruments of the 1790s began to give way to an equally sophisticated but often more embellished and substantial looking case, the most obvious change being the use, increasingly, of six legs.

With this new type you might find legs either turned, reeded, or even spiral turned but some latter-day purists believe that the introduction of the turned leg marked a regression. "This change from the square taper leg to the turned leg marks the decline of the square piano as a pleasing and well-proportioned piece of furniture", argued Philip B. James.[5]

Metal work became more boastful. Banding of inlay and other forms of decoration received more emphasis. No lack of self-confidence here.

This resulted in some highly accomplished, decorative cases of individual character such as the square of c.1812 by the piano maker to King George IV, Thomas Tomkison, which is in the Colt Clavier Collection. Made in figured rosewood, with cross-banding and satinwood legs it is assertive and certain, standing on six turned and tapered legs with the added refinement of drawers under the keyboard. The over-emphatic veneer a mite too much for my taste but undoubted quality.

Many other splendid examples of the six-legged variety were produced by such as Muzio Clementi, William Southwell, Isaac Mott, Broadwoods, the Stodarts, George Dettmer, William Rolfe and others.

Photo by courtesy of The Colt Clavier Collection, Bethersden, Kent

If there is a better example of "Buhl" work on a British square to be found in the whole land than this Clementi piano then I have yet to come across it—obviously the very best of craftsmanship, it is inlaid in brass with figures of dancing maidens and "Pan" at the corners. With a suggested date of c.1825 it is, in terms of the case, one of the shining jewels of the Colt Clavier Collection and, to quote the late Mr C.F. Colt, "the brass inlay is so grand and costly that one cannot help wondering whether it was made for somebody very important indeed. It must be one of the most elaborate square pianos ever made." At around this time Clementi's firm were advertising their top of the range square as being "in rose or albuera wood cases, either plain or superbly ornamented with buhl work" for between 65 and 120 guineas. But, of course, you could always pay for more. Plate No.215.

I do not, of course, suggest that every square piano produced after c.1805 suddenly started to sprout six turned legs and some firms must have been slower to make the transition.

For example, photos of a Clementi square in a Brussels museum, with a suggested date of "c.1810", show it sitting on a Neo-Classical frame (is the frame original?) but other Clementis are recorded with six legs and suggested dates of 1810. Certainly from 1811 you will find a procession of Clementi squares, such as that in the Bad Krozingen collection, which have six turned legs and a convincing Regency manner.

With so many pianos now being made, there were always those who had different ideas.

One apparent example is the Goulding, D'Almaine, Potter and Co. square of c.1815 in the Yale University Collection which marries both styles, adopting six legs but each of these square sectioned and tapered. It is suggested by the University as being "in the Hepplewhite style" and is in satinwood with rosewood borders with an inlay band of ebony and holly. In addition it is artist-painted, decorated inside with a classically dressed figure.

I have also come across an apparently unique example of a square that does not depend on either four or six legs. This is an instrument of c.1810, again by the great Clementi firm, that stands on lyre supports at each end, with canted corners and an equally fine, inlaid and decorated nameboard. Yet another fine case by Clementi.

The Effect of Boulle on British Pianos

One important facet of Regency taste that showed itself in British pianos was the adoption of "buhl work", a form of predominantly curvilinear brass and tortoiseshell inlay said to have been favoured by the Prince of Wales. It must have been expensive but it was occasionally employed with surprising abandon.

Originally said to have been an Italian process from the 10th Century, the method was brought to perfection by a Frenchman, Andre-Charles Boulle (1642-1732) who inspired the subsequent revivals. Oddly, British piano makers of the 19th Century, who must well have known that they owed much to Monsieur Boulle,

Photo by courtesy of The Colt Clavier Collection, Bethersden, Kent

Most Broadwood grand pianos that I have seen which date after 1800 and up to c.1809 retain the straight legs that had prevailed for most of the Late 18th Century, as can be seen here in this Broadwood grand of 1806 in the Colt Clavier Collection. And what was true for Broadwood was true for a number of other British firms. In this example the legs are now perhaps a trifle tapered; there is a "square collar" near the top; and a lyre frame holding the pedals....but the case is recognisable as being in the usual 18th Century Tabel panelled manner. Plate No.216.

Photo by courtesy of The Colt Clavier Collection, Bethersden, Kent

It is immediately evident that there is something different about this early 19th Century Broadwood grand. Where is the usual joined stand with the connecting stretchers?

What we have here is a major change of direction and, although the Tabel panels are retained along the sides of the main case, there is an undoubted Regency tinge to the whole article and a feeling of further refinement, especially in the reeded and turned legs which now support the case.

The big question is the date. The late Mr C.F. Colt, one of the most respected figures of his day in the piano world tells us that it is 1810 and the judgement is endorsed by Martha Novak Clinkscale.

Mr Colt writes in his 1981 catalogue that this is: "The earliest of the 'new models' I know of....The 1810 must have been a very advanced model with turned legs and, generally speaking, is very Regency in style. It has, however, the slightly lighter casework of the 18th century instruments and yet it looks almost identical to one of 1819. Satinwood fascia like an 18th Century instrument, not rosewood, as is usual with this model." However, I am told by the eminent restorer and Broadwood expert, David Hunt, of an even earlier Broadwood grand with turned legs, No. 4773, now in Munich and in The Broadwood Archives there is mention of a grand with four reeded legs on Aug 30th., 1809. Plate No.217.

referred to work in this style as "buhl" and I suspect this spelling has a German derivation.

Few in the piano world did this kind of buhl work better than Clementi, Collard and Collard who, in 1824, were advertising[6] a square pianoforte "in rose or albuera wood cases, either plain or superbly ornamented with buhl work" for up to £120, a cabinet with buhl for £150 and a grand in rosewood and buhl for £250.

A masterpiece of buhl work is the Clementi square of c.1825, in the Colt Collection and described by Mr Colt as "one of the most elaborate square pianos ever made". The brass inlay, evidently the work of a top craftsman, represents one of the high points of this style in the decoration of pianos, with its inlaid figures of dancing maidens and "Pan" characters set against the rosewood case. The Clementi, which has six elaborately turned, spiral legs is one of the star turns of the Collection.

An important repercussion of the "buhl" style was that, for those who could not afford the full treatment, piano makers of the period introduced small areas of decorative brass inlay on different types of instrument, usually on the nameboard. As is the way with the British the wilder swirls of "buhl" were here eliminated, the design being tamed and subdued, often in a tight geometric pattern.

Changes in the Grand Piano

It is through the grand piano that we can identify two of the other major shifts in design—those of c.1809 and c.1827.

For much of the half-century to 1850 the grand piano sailed serenely on, little given to adventure and secure in its position at the top of the market. The style of the grand immediately after 1800 was much the same[7] as the grand before 1800: In other words the Tabel, or British Style, prevailed, complete with outlined, veneer panels.

It is true that, around 1807-1809, Broadwood were responsible for at least three unusual grand pianos which, although they had the Tabel-style main case, stood on lyre end supports rather than conventional legs. But these were quite obviously "specials" and seem to have had no effect on the firm's main production of grand pianos.

The first major shift in the design of the British grand, around 1809, was however, also concerned with the supports for the main case.

In the Colt Clavier Collection there is a Broadwood grand of 1810 in which the legs are now found to be turned and reeded and there is no sign of a stretcher. I have identified other, similar examples c.1811-1813. In the Broadwood Archives they record one with reeded legs on August 30th., 1809.

Since the square piano had switched to the turned leg c.1805-1807 this reveals (providing no similar pre-1809 examples of the grand can be found) the more conservative approach to the design of the grand and its resistance to change.

Mr Colt wrote[8] of his 1810 Broadwood grand that it was "The earliest of the 'new models' I know of....The 1810 must have been a very advanced model with turned legs".

Elsewhere[9] he commented that "after 1810...there were four turned legs, two in the front and two about two feet from the tail. This system continued until about 1830, when only one back leg was retained at the tail."

Mr Colt also said that with Broadwood: "More elaborate grands with rosewood cross-banding were being made from 1810 onwards, so in these cases the black line (*the so-called Nelson "mourning" inlay*) was not used."

To what degree these changes were affected by technical considerations I do not know but the eminent authority John Koster observes that the five-and-a-half octave model by Broadwood "became standard in England by the mid-1790s" and, I am told, lasted until c.1812.[10]

William Dale puts forward the theory that: "The pleasing shape of the harpsichord and its appropriate stand, disappeared (*from piano design*) early in the following century owing to the extension of compass and the increase in weight".[11]

But it is important to stress that, despite changes to the legs of the grand, the Tabel Style of veneered panel for the main case, outlined by cross-banding, continued to be used for many grands after 1810 with only minor "tweaks" to the type of banding, or woods employed. The new turned legs apart, many of these might still stand comfortably alongside the harpsichords of Shudi or Kirkman and be recognised as a brother.

The Regency seldom overwhelmed these British grand piano designers. Instead, they usually assimilated certain facets of Regency design. A very good example of this was an 1814 Broadwood grand[12] where the panel inlay became more geometric and the ornamentation more redolent of the Regency but, otherwise, the flagship of tradition could be seen sailing placidly onwards.

I could point you to extravagant exceptions of highly individual, or even eccentric, character, especially those made for the Royal family such as the Mott grand of 1817 or the Tomkison grand of 1821, both owned by George IV. But that is just what these are—Regal, extraordinary instruments made for a King and in no way to be confused with mainstream production.

Photo by courtesy of Mealy's of Castlecomer, County Kilkenny, Ireland

Isn't there always an exception that proves a rule? And what a magnificent exception! This Broadwood grand has neither straight legs, nor turned legs but, instead, stands on lyre supports. It is one of a tiny number of "specials" made in this style by Broadwood about 1807-1809 and this one is stated to have been commissioned for Sheringham Hall, Norfolk, by Humphrey Repton. It was auctioned as Lot 1186 by Mealy's of Castlecomer on November 13th., 2002. Plate No.218.

A rare bird indeed, a square piano shown standing on lyre supports, with a suggested date of c.1815-20, and produced by the Clementi firm. It has, also, unusual angled corners with decoration reflecting the highly decorative metal inlay on the nameboard. I have personally seen but one other square in this style, by the American maker Joseph Hiskey. An expert on 18th Century furniture, Mr Clifford Musgrave, wrote in his book on Adam and Hepplewhite furniture that the first known structural use of the lyre motif (for a chair) was by Robert Adam in 1767. Plate No.219.

Tabel is Abandoned

The second major change to the British grand is represented by a Broadwood grand of 1827 in the Metropolitan Museum of Art in New York and this demonstrates a far more decisive turning away from the past.

After a run of more than a century it signalled the complete abandonment of Tabel's veneer panels, first identified in his sole surviving harpsichord of 1721, together with the distinctive cross-banded inlay that habitually outlined them.

From other instruments that followed thereafter we know that this significant change must have occurred somewhere around this date and, unless a significant, earlier example emerges, this would appear to represent a crucial piece of evidence.

As with almost all pre-1850 British pianos we can only speculate as to the identity of the designer of the 1827 Broadwood but I believe that the detailing of the case proves it was the work of a professional.

If Broadwood had simply decided to eliminate the veneered panels they would have been left with an instrument of stark nature, *à la Zumpe* and this cannot have been to their taste. So the designer dramatised the main case by scrapping the rectangular lines of the "cheeks"[13] alongside the keyboard and introducing in their place a curved end with a double scroll, embellished with a heavy and florid, but fine, piece of carving.

Instead of the familiar mahogany of most early British grands we now had a case in rosewood veneer and, in the absence of the panels, this was highlighted by a continuous line of prominent, carved egg and dart moulding along the bottom of the main case and the edge of the lid. This egg and dart continued even in front of the keyboard. As a counterpoint, the designer introduced carving in a circular pattern at the top and bottom of each of the four legs.

This piano was presumably a "Special" but its effect on the design of other grand pianos was immediate. Broadwood, the largest maker in the country, began to manufacture other grands with variations of this design.

I know of two Astor grands and a Clementi grand, all suggested to be 1820s, which had curved "cheeks" but none went quite as far as the Metropolitan example.

I have also seen a photo of a Broadwood grand of 1832 that has a similar main case but is perched on three extraordinary, carved cabriole legs, joined in such a way that it reminds me of a bird about to take flight. Though perhaps a bustard rather than a sparrow.

And there is an even grander grand, said to be by Broadwood and made in 1833, which uses the same stylistic device.

In each instance the familiar two legs at the "tail" had now been replaced by one.

Another modified and plainer version of the 1827 design, a Broadwood of c.1835 which I presume must by then have been a fairly standard model, can be seen in the Manx Museum.

Mr Colt observed that "By 1830 the practice of dividing the lid and sides into panels, either by cross banding or inlay, was abandoned in favour of more elaborately grained wood, with the grain on the sides laid vertically instead of horizontally".[14]

At precisely what date other makers started copying features of the 1827 Broadwood I do not know but similar modified features can be seen on a Wornum "Pocket Grand" of 1837[15] and a Stodart grand of pre-1840[16] and I do not doubt there must be other examples of similar date. I have also seen a Continental example of around the same date and later American grands which "adopted" these British ideas.

The Wornum "Pocket Grand", which was 5ft 6in in length and 3ft 9in in width, shows the pressures there must have been to produce smaller versions of the grand. Mr Colt states that "Wornum seems to have started manufacturing this type of instrument in about 1830".[17]

The Victorians Assert their Identity

In the world of the more commercial piano makers the general production of models for the mass market became permeated by a distinct Victorian spirit the nearer they approached the half century.

In the grand piano this trend can be identified, for example, in the chubby legs of an 1840 Broadwood grand and, to the point of weirdness, in the wildly bulbous appurtenances of an 1838 Wornum Imperial grand.

All the possibilities of Victorian eclecticism had begun to open up.

Now here are two mysteries awaiting a modern-day piano detective.

First, this highly unusual grand, poised as though about to launch down the runway at Heathrow, is a tantalising bird altogether. The photograph was drawn to my attention by one of the most assiduous and dedicated researchers I know on piano history, Bill Kibby of PianoGen, who has files on many hundreds of piano companies.

It shows a Broadwood grand of 1832 restored by John Paul years ago and, from the photo, the quality seems self-evident. It looks for all the world like a "Special" but who was it made for? And, more important, who was the Designer?

The design of the legs in particular is eye-stopping. The carving of those exaggerated cabriole legs is elaborate but the shape has been stretched to the very bounds of possibility, and the now single rear leg reversed. Plate No.220.

And here is an even more puzzling customer.

Again I am indebted to Bill Kibby of PianoGen for drawing this one to my attention. It is suggested to be a Broadwood grand of 1833 but the photo has been floating round the Internet and, as to its origin and the accuracy of the information, no man has spoken.

We ponder: Could the same Designer have been responsible for the 1827 Broadwood grand in the Met, the 1832 Broadwood grand restored by John Paul and this one as well? The only thought I can offer, and there is not a vestige of proof to support any such suggestion, is that Broadwoods employed George Morant as one of their Designers for the 1851 Exhibition. Plate No.221.

If our two mystery grands were indeed made in 1832 and 1833 who, then, could have known of them? Might they, for example, have been seen by our American cousins?

The grand piano shown here was constructed on the same basic premise as our mystery grands: three dominant cabriole legs, the rear one in reverse. It was made by one of America's most respected piano companies, Chickering of Boston, who claimed in one of their own official publications that it was "The First Chickering Grand".

Jonas Chickering, we are told in the firm's Centennial publication, constructed a grand in 1837 "after years of experiment" and realised "his dream of producing a grand piano scientifically constructed". But nowhere do we learn how he arrived at such a case design, or who his Designer might have been.

It is logical to ask: If the two mystery grands were indeed made in the early 1830s then did they influence Chickering's subsequent design? Plate No.222.

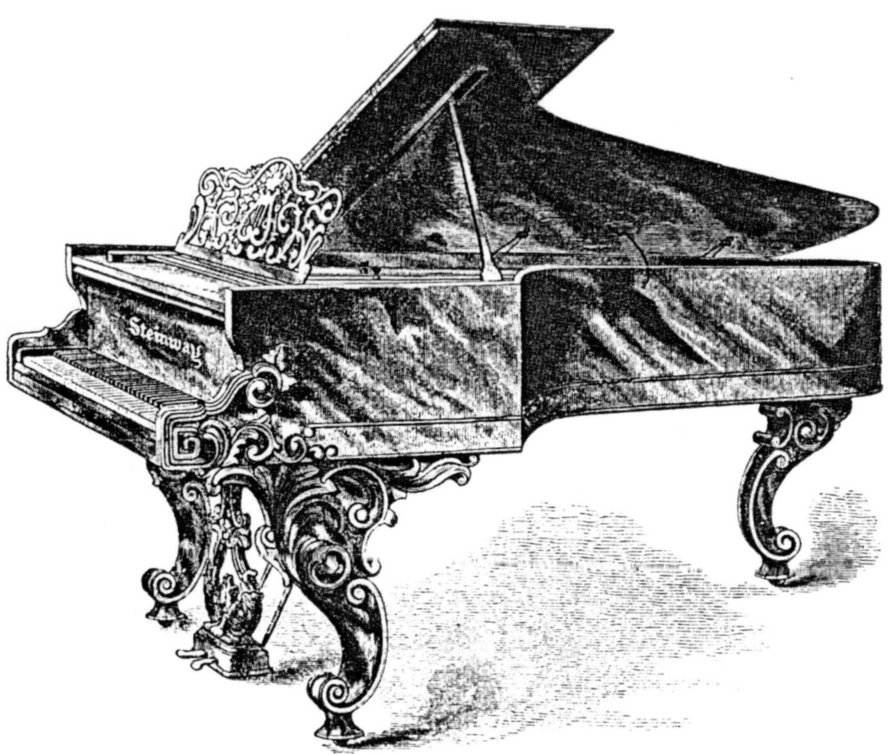

And here, surprise surprise, is the official entry to the 1876 Philadelphia Exhibition by America's best known piano makers, the house of Steinway...complete with reversed rear cabriole leg. A similar style Steinway grand of 1857 is in the Smithsonian Collection. Plate No.223.

It is my view that the 1827 Broadwood grand in the New York Met is a vital clue to the changes that took place in British grand piano design about this date but this theory can easily be proven by comparing two examples from another maker, William Stodart. This first Stodart grand of c.1820, auctioned by Messrs Sotheby's as Lot 271 on Nov 10th., 2004, has the usual square "cheeks" to the keyboard; panelled sides; turned and reeded legs with brass collars that have not yet taken on a Victorian girth. This is recognisably in a tradition going back to Tabel, except for the turned legs and lyre support. Plate No.224.

Photo by courtesy of Messrs Sotheby's of New Bond Street, London

The changes in style that overcame the British grand by 1827 are evident in this second and later William Stodart grand, which I am told must be pre-1840, auctioned by Messrs Sotheby's as Lot 117 on May 3rd., 1979. The panelled sides have disappeared (just as they have on the 1827 Broadwood grand in the New York Met) the "cheek" is now curved and the legs are now much heavier and heavily carved. A beading is now used round the bottom of the entire main case. To reinforce the point I should mention that there is a similar Stodart grand, given a date of c.1830, in the Kuntsthistorisches Museum, Vienna and I have seen another example of c.1835. Plate No.225.

Photo by courtesy of Messrs Sotheby's of New Bond Street, London

Other types of piano were more prey to stylistic changes than the grand.

When Regency ideas fell from fashion, the cabinet type soon assumed a Victorian persona.

The year Queen Victoria came to the throne, 1837, she was already portrayed playing a cabinet piano of a florid, Revived Rococo style. Further confirmation of the Victorian manner of later cabinets is provided by the huge carved legs on the instrument made by Daniel Chandler Hewitt in 1844, now in The Museum of Welsh Life at Cardiff.

The Victorian age saw the modest square piano puff itself up until its pompous illusions simply burst.

A new iron frame,[18] claimed as a big improvement in 1825, did much for the tone of the instrument but became yet another reason why the instrument was forced to grow

Photo by courtesy of Mr David Winston and The Period Piano Co.

I may write all day about my theories on changes in piano case design but some pianos just appear to break all the rules. A date of c.1825 is suggested for this grand but, while mainstream design in this decade evolved through the use of the turned leg, this instrument seems to have arrived at something quite different—a supporting device of three central pillars. The effect is to give the piano a stark architectural quality quite unlike any other I know. The nearest "relative" I can think of is the Mott grand of 1817, made for King George IV, which stands on a triangular pillar. Although I suppose I should add that I have seen an American square by Sturm & Miller that stands on a pedestal base. The piano shown here bears the name of one of the finest makers in Britain, William Stodart and the nameplate boasts "MAKER to His MAJESTY and the ROYAL FAMILY". Plate No.226.

like Topsy. From the 59 keys first employed by Zumpe it now expanded to 85 keys.

I am satisfied that the British grand piano underwent a major change of style by at least 1827 and it would make sense that the square piano would be similarly affected by new fashions.

The earliest example of a square of a new kind that I have so far been able to discover is a Broadwood of c.1829 in the Haags Gemeentemuseum[19] that has four legs instead of the familiar six of the Regency and these of far more solid, bourgeoise reassurance. I am a little surprised that I cannot find an earlier example, from 1827 or 1828, as I half expected.

As the Victorian style took hold the severely functional Zumpe box of the mid-1760s, sometimes criticised as "crude",[20] was replaced by a pretentious square piano that threatened to

◀

With the grand piano I believe that the 1827 Broadwood in the New York Met gives us a good idea of when the grand began to change its established style but it is surprisingly difficult to identify the moment when the English square began its transition from Regency to William IV to Victoriana. I am sure there must be other examples (I have heard of one example of 1818) but the earliest I know of is this Broadwood square of c.1829 in the remarkable Collection of the Haags Gemeentemuseum. One is struck immediately by the fact that the six-legged Regency style has here given way to four legs and there is, generally, a much heavier "feel" to the case. Plate No.227.

Photo by courtesy of The Haags Gemeentemuseum, Den Haag, The Netherlands

▶

Thomas Tomkison, who supplied a unique grand to King George IV for his Brighton Pavilion, was a maker of pianos with cases of quality and sometimes brilliance. This Tomkison, a solidly built square in rosewood, suggested to me to be c.1845-50 (this maker very rarely dated his instruments) shows the change of personality that came over the English square as it began to transform its character totally. Earlier, Tomkison had been making six-legged squares but here the instrument sits on four sturdy legs of a different nature. It seems likely to me that Tomkison must also have been commissioned to work for either Queen Adelaide or Queen Victoria, since a late piano bore the inscription "Maker to Her Majesty". Plate No.228.

Photo courtesy of The Museum of Welsh Life, St. Fagans, Cardiff

Photo by courtesy of The Metropolitan Museum of Art, New York

I feel that the later generation of British square pianos, the biggest of which became known as "Grand Squares", never carried this extravagant role with conviction so far as the case was concerned. When it came to using power and size with confidence (as, for example, in skyscrapers and post-War automobiles loaded with chrome and tailfins) few could compete with the Americans. This bravura rosewood casework by Nunns & Clark of New York, in-your-face and without the slightest apology, clothed a square that was made in 1853 and is probably the outstanding example of this kind of American piano. It has been illustrated many times and is one of the prize exhibits of the Metropolitan Museum of Art. Plate No.229.

Photo by courtesy of The Colt Clavier Collection, Bethersden, Kent

What legs! The stylistic earthquake that was to hit British grand piano design before 1850 needs no explaining when you see this extraordinary, rosewood Wornum Imperial Grand of 1838, now in the Colt Clavier Collection. Just one year into Queen Victoria's reign and those remarkable, heavily carved, bulbous legs (presumably original) and the Gothic support for the pedals announce that there will be new ways for a new Queen. The oddest thing is that such a large grand seems to run completely counter to Wornum's philosophy of miniaturisation, both with the upright and his "Pocket Grands". Plate No.230.

rival the grand. Its ambitions became clear when it was styled the "grand square"[21]

The American versions[22] especially (some of which are intriguing from a design point of view) became positively Baronial in their ambitions and grossly inflated in importance. British makers were not immune to the fashion but, in the end, their inhibitions could not match the convictions and chutzpah of our Transatlantic cousins when it came to embracing size and power.[23]

Typical of this British type was a Collard and Collard square of c.1840, shown to have already developed a thickening waistline and, instead of six legs, now supported on four clumsy but, needs-be, grossly thicker, baluster turned legs.

It was the unlovely side of Victoriana, more lumpen bourgeois than functional grace. And the square lost the battle.

If around 1825 the square was thought to be "undoubtedly the favourite type"[24] of piano in Britain then, before 1850, it was, along with the upright grand, the cabinet and other archaic forms, on the way out.

William Dale[25] explained it this way: "….as the construction of the square piano improved, to meet the musical requirements of succeeding generations, its size and unwieldiness increased, until it was finally improved off the face of the earth."

The future belonged to The True Upright and, for the wealthy, the traditional horizontal grand.

Whatever the misgivings of those who believed they should rely on musical qualities alone, most makers understood that to sell to the general public they had to make the case attractive. The appeal had to be to the eye as well as the musical ear.

From the ancient Venetians to Robert Adam we see this desire to beautify musical cases but always, it must be said, in the face of, at best, uneasy tension and, at worst, downright hostility from a section of piano makers, experts or musicians who considered the case an irrelevance to music as an art form.[26]

Despite such creative friction the period after 1850 was to become the golden age of The British Art Piano and The Designer Piano.

Illustration by courtesy of The British Library

A.G. Pugin, or Welby Pugin...or both? Modern scholars are still at odds over exactly who was responsible for the design of this grand piano, which was revealed in this illustration in the "Repository of Arts", on July 1st., 1826 but what is certain is that it was either Pugin the father, or his young son, or both working together. At the age of 13 Welby Pugin, the genius who led the Gothic Revival, was already making designs for his father and, at the age of 15, he undertook a major commission to design furniture for the Royal family for Windsor Castle. Plate No.231.

The Emergence of the Designers

Chapter Six

As the ambitions of fine artists such as Lawrence Alma-Tadema and Edward Burne-Jones led to the painted or specially ornamented form of the British Art Piano, these were matched and eventually eclipsed by a new breed who came to dominate the look of 19th Century furniture: The Designers.

In the 18th Century the piano had been a late developer and the harpsichord a long time dying. As the pattern books prove, during The Age of the Cabinet Maker there can only have been a tiny demand for professional piano case design before 1800.

The entry of the Piano Designers was publicly signalled on July 1st., 1796, when the engraving of Thomas Sheraton's design for the "Don Godoy" grand piano, uniquely decorated with Wedgwood cameos, was published by Inigo Barlow[1]. But I cannot say how many of these prints were produced and only one surviving copy is known.[2]

In the view of a British pioneer of research on the design of the piano case, Michael I. Wilson, when Sheraton provided his grand piano for the Spanish grandee Don Godoy, made by Broadwood, he was "the first known English furniture designer of stature to have produced an idea for a grand piano".[3]

This design by Sheraton is of supreme importance in another respect, in that it is Sheraton's only proven direct commission for a client.

To what extent other British piano firms might have taken their lead from Thomas Sheraton's "Cabinet-Makers' and Upholsterers' Drawing Book", published in parts between 1791 and 1794, which was concerned with general furniture designs, we can but guess.

But it is revealing that three harpsichord makers and three other musical instrument makers were among the subscribers to Sheraton's epic work.[4]

Reinforcing an existing trend, one of the significant effects of Sheraton's designs was to make furniture lighter and more portable, as had already become evident in many Late 18th Century square pianos.

I have been unable to find any other pre-1800 published piano design such as Sheraton's but there is absolute proof that he was NOT the first British piano case designer.

Thanks to original design drawings which have been discovered in Sir John Soane's Museum (although they seem to have been little known in their time) we can prove that that honour belongs to an even more important Designer than Sheraton and one of the foremost architects of the 18th Century, Robert Adam, who designed a square piano (in fact, two alternative designs for a square) for Catherine the Great, Empress of Russia, in 1774.

A figure of repute among modern piano historians, Mr Laurence Libin, Research Curator of The Metropolitan Museum of Art, has traced a British square piano in a Russian Palace which he believes to be the very piano made to Robert Adam's design for the Empress.

A fact as startling as any other about this highly ornamented square piano in Russia is that it was made by the austere Zumpe, though by this date working with a partner, Gabriel Buntebart. I know of no other "Zumpe & Buntebart" piano of such an extravagant nature.

But hopes of coming across other early, original piano drawings like Adam's, or a printed design such as Sheraton's, are slim indeed. So what may we deduce about the pre-1800 piano designers from other clues?

One could, I think, put forward a strong argument that Johann Christoph Zumpe, who introduced his "bare bones" square piano to Britain in the 1760s, was the first Functionalist of the piano world, a man who demonstrated how the ideas of Marc-Antoine Laugier and Carlo Lodoli could be applied to the instrument.

But it seems unlikely to me that, when he built his plain box case, Zumpe had heard of either of these contemporaries and, if he ever produced actual designs, then I have found no trace of them.

◀ In my opinion the first known British designs for a piano were in 1774 by the great architect Robert Adam, who was commissioned to design a square piano for Catherine the Great, Empress of Russia. The original drawings (Adam provided two alternatives) are now to be found in Sir John Soane's Museum, London. Plate No.232.

Drawings reproduced by courtesy of Sir John Soane's Museum, London.

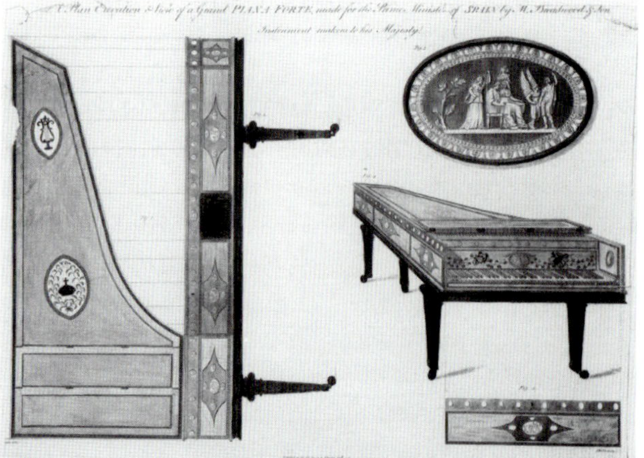

▶ The first publication of a grand piano design that I can trace is also Thomas Sheraton's only provable furniture commission—his design for the 1796 Don Godoy grand. This piano was profusely decorated with Wedgwood pottery and, as early as 1774, Josiah Wedgwood had written to a friend mentioning "such pieces of furniture as our Encaustic paintings and Cameos have been introduced into". Plate No.233.

Photo by courtesy of the Museum of Fine Arts, Boston, Cluett Collection

Photo by courtesy of the Lady Lever Art Gallery, Port Sunlight

It may look like the largest Neo-Classical Christmas box you ever saw but this is, officially, a square piano. All I can say is that I do not know of another square piano even remotely like this and that adjectives hardly seem equal to this quixotic treasure of the Lady Lever Art Gallery at Port Sunlight. The hidden piano action is by Frederick Beck and dates to 1775 but the case is, without question, by one of the best 18th Century makers. Much scholarly detective work (sadly, all by people other than myself) suggests, very convincingly, that it was the work of Christopher Fuhrlohg, a Swedish cabinet maker who established himself in Tottenham Court Road, London. Plate No.234.

Christopher Fuhrlohg's Christmas Box

Just one year after Robert Adam made the first known professional British piano design a quite remarkable "square" appeared, though it seems to me a strange use of language to call it a "square" when it looked so much like a piece of conventional drawing room furniture.

That a designer was involved in the making of Frederick Beck's (or should I say, more correctly, Christopher Fuhrlohg's?) piano of 1775 with its Neo-Classical figures and aggressive herring-bone patterning, and another Beck piano of 1777 made in similar Neo-Classical taste, I do not doubt for a second.

Judged not simply as pianos but as furniture, this was 18th Century British cabinet work of the most important kind, the ornamentation superb. Stuff for the history books.

All the available scholarly evidence suggests that the casework of these two Beck "square" pianos was by Christopher Fuhrlohg, a Swedish cabinet maker said to have been born in Stockholm c.1737, who had spent a period working in Paris, about 1764-67, possibly in the employ of Simon Oeben.[5] He then moved to London, where a small group of his fellow Swedish cabinet specialists had already established themselves and, initially, he worked for John Linnell before setting up his own business. He had premises in Tottenham Court Road between 1769 and 1776.

Fuhrlohg exhibited examples of his marquetry panels in London and I think there must be a strong inference that he was himself the designer of the two Beck pianos although, naturally, there is always the possibility that Fuhrlohg was working to an architect's drawing, or that someone else in his workshop was responsible.

An interesting speculation might be whether any similar Beck-Fuhrlohg pianos were made before 1774 and thus beat Adam to the honour of being Britain's first known piano designer.

If so, they have long since disappeared into history's maw and we are left with question marks hanging in the air.

A piano of great interest but on which I can make no personal judgement, never having seen it in the flesh, is a Chinoiserie lacquered square for which a date of "c.1776" has subsequently been suggested.

This piano appeared at a Sotheby's auction in New York in 1999 when it was stated to be "An important George III black lacquer and parcel-gilt piano in the manner of Thomas Chippendale" and dated to "third quarter 18th Century".

This Chinoiserie piano, having a concave well in the middle and twin bow-fronted ends, looks little like a conventional square and is "decorated all over with….figures at various pursuits, birds and foliage, within floral borders".

It stands on "leaf-tip carved legs ending in reeded ball-form feet" and, taking these fine details in conjunction with the sophisticated shape, leaves little doubt that a designer was at work.

I know of no similar Chinoiserie British piano of pre-1800 (there is one other example of a genuine piano with Chinoiserie decoration but I am advised that the decoration is of later date).

John Crang Hancock produced a number of pre-1800 pianos with eccentric cases that were out of sync with his times—among them a 1782 "throwback" grand[6], now in the Colt Clavier Collection, with a case much like a spinet of a previous century; and an unusual transverse grand[7] of 1799, with a delightful double curve. There is also another grand, with a date of c.1782[8] and attributed to Crang Hancock, that has an elaborately inlaid main case with geometric motifs, suggested to be the work of a Continental craftsman.

Such pianos show a guiding mind behind the appearance of the case but, somehow (which is hardly the scientific approach to history) you feel it was more likely to be someone in the Crang Hancock workshop rather than an outside designer.

A really fascinating piano case can be studied on a Robert Stodart grand of 1784[9] which has its own personality, being inlaid with oval panels of Classical figures, as well as foliate swags although, in other respects, it is recognisably a traditional British grand.

But was this the work of a designer, or did the piano maker simply buy in decorative panels from a specialist sub-contractor at the behest of a customer? Who is to say?

This photo shows a detail of one of the panels of the Beck square piano, 1777, that appeared at Christie's of New York on October 17th., 2001. The relationship to the work of Christopher Fuhrlohg seems obvious. Plate No.236.

Photos by courtesy of Christie's of New York

This is the second Beck square of 1777 that is, it seems to me obviously, related to the Beck square of 1775 in the Lady Lever Art Gallery. This Beck square appeared as Lot 345 at Christie's of New York on October 17th., 2001 and scholars have, likewise, linked it to the work of Christopher Fuhrlohg because of the similarities in the high quality casework. Plate No.235.

The Ghosts of Anonymous Designers

We look at each of these pre-1800 pianos and wonder: Was this the product of a Designer's imagination? There are no answers…yet.

Apart from the two certain instances of Robert Adam and Thomas Sheraton (and probably Christopher Fuhrlohg) I find it impossible to give the name of another single British piano designer of the 18th Century.

Yet, besides their known designs, other pianos were produced of pronounced individuality. And a number of piano workshops were owned by men who were themselves trained cabinet makers. Did they try their hands at designing?

Study of the work of splendid people like William Southwell and Christopher Ganer would soon cause you to ponder. And the "house style" of a firm who were supposed to be but retailers, Longman & Broderip, is not only elegant but suspiciously consistent. Was there a single mind controlling their output?

One must hope that more evidence will emerge.

Quite unlike 18th Century British grand pianos made by other firms this piano, by John Crang Hancock, c.1775-1781, would seem to be in the style of a previous century. Plate No.237.

Photo by courtesy of The Colt Clavier Collection, Bethersden, Kent

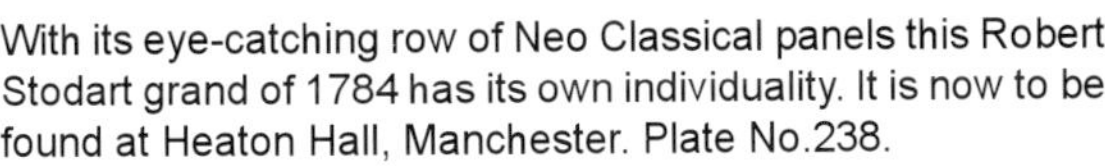

With its eye-catching row of Neo Classical panels this Robert Stodart grand of 1784 has its own individuality. It is now to be found at Heaton Hall, Manchester. Plate No.238.

Photo by courtesy of The Colt Clavier Collection, Bethersden, Kent

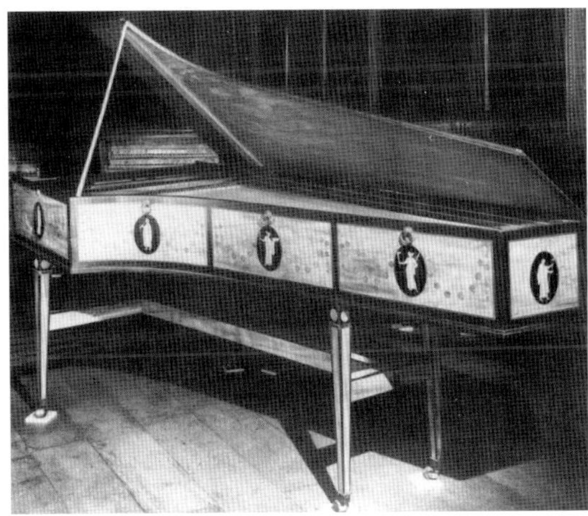

Described as "An important George III black lacquer and parcel-gilt piano in the manner of Thomas Chippendale", with a suggested date of "third quarter 18th Century", this piano was auctioned by Sotheby's of New York on October 22nd., 1999. Plate No.239.

Photo by courtesy of Sotheby's of New York

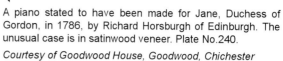

◀ A piano stated to have been made for Jane, Duchess of Gordon, in 1786, by Richard Horsburgh of Edinburgh. The unusual case is in satinwood veneer. Plate No.240.

Courtesy of Goodwood House, Goodwood, Chichester
Photo by Ken Wormald

▲ This Broadwood "Special", with its Wedgwood pottery decoration, was made by Broadwood in 1798 and plainly derives from Sheraton's "Don Godoy" grand. Plate No.241.

Photo by courtesy of
The Albany Institute of History and Art, New York

▲ One of the handsome demi-lune pianos produced by William Southwell. This one was put up for auction at Sotheby's as Lot 167 on November 17th., 1994 and the date was given as c.1785. Plate No.242.

Photo by courtesy of
Sotheby's of New Bond Street, London

▶ William Southwell patented his Upright Square in 1798. This example was auctioned by Sotheby's as Lot 172 on October 9th., 1981. Plate No.243.

Photo by courtesy of Sotheby's of New Bond Street, London

The gulf between William Southwell and most other 18th Century piano makers is immediately apparent in the design drawing he submitted for his 1798 invention of an "Upright Square". Who can look at this Neo Classical design, with its fine detailing of the case, and doubt for a second that this is not the work of a Designer. But who was that Designer? Plate No.244.

The Genius of William Southwell

I think we are on rather firmer ground with the piano cases of a very remarkable man, a genius of the piano world, William Southwell of Dublin. Because he patented a number of his piano inventions and, in some instances, lodged detailed drawings of these at the same time, we know instantly that Southwell was much concerned with the appearance of the case.

But were these drawings his own work? Did he employ a professional designer? Or did he rely on a Master Cabinet Maker? Questions, questions...

My opinion is that much of Southwell's early known casework was Neo Classical in conception and influenced by Robert Adam's designs—by which I do not mean they were the work of Adam himself.

Tragically, I know of no drawings concerning some of Southwell's earliest and most important work: A series of superb, semi-circular, table-pianos[10] produced from c.1785. Speculation has long been that these demi-lune pianos, looking almost identical to the conventional Georgian semi-circular tables of the time, were the work of the Royal cabinet maker William Moore of Dublin.

Southwell, "one of the most inventive of all piano builders"[11], devised the "Square Upright" of 1798 (an attempt to introduce a small upright) and continued to have an impact on design into the new century. He patented both the "Cabinet Piano"[12] in 1807, which was to become a commercial success, and another that tipped over into obscurity, the "Piano Sloping Backwards"[13] of 1811.

Judging by the elements gathered together in such an assured way in the drawing for the case of his "Piano Sloping Backwards" my assumption is that it had to have been done

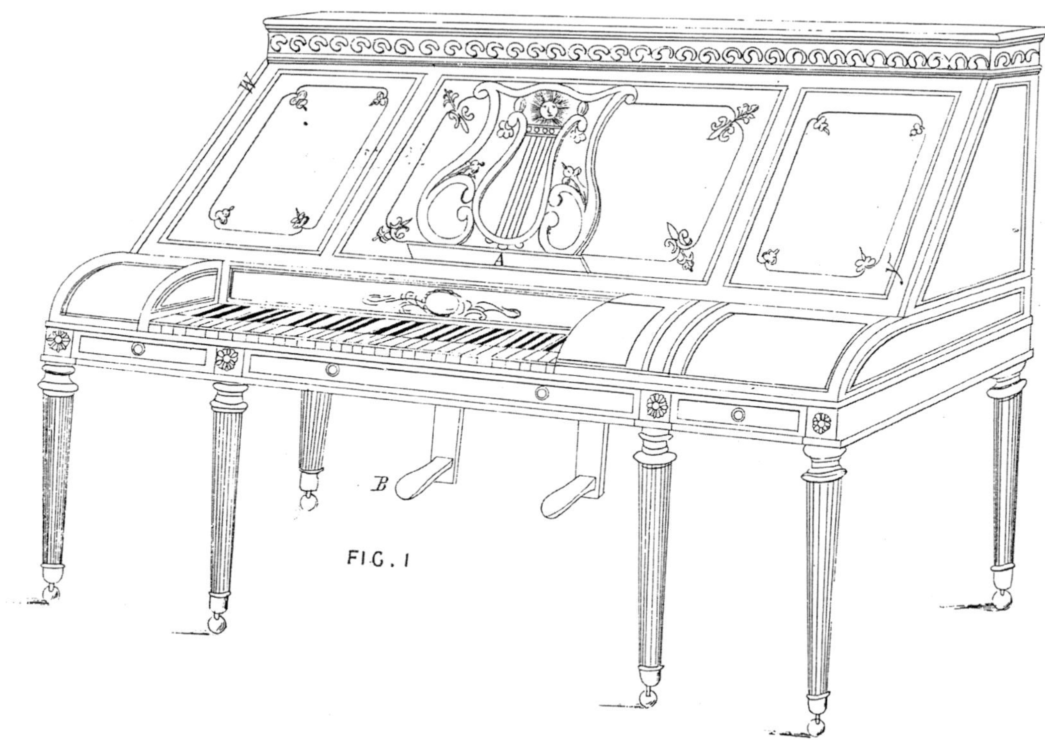

Although I cannot find a single surviving example of William Southwell's "Piano Sloping Backwards" we learn from this Patent drawing of 1811 that it had the usual Southwell sense of style involving, surely, the services of a case Designer. Whether that was Southwell himself or A.N.Other, who can tell? His 1811 invention was, said the piano historian Rosamond Harding, "a square placed on its side on a stand but the shape differed from his earlier one of 1798 in that the strings and sound-board sloped away from the performer". Once more we see Southwell's careful attention to cabinet detail but, this time, he was to lose out to Wornum and his development of Hawkins' ideas for The True Upright. Plate No.245.

The central panel of Southwell's drawing for an Upright Square of 1798 shows two love birds in amorous flight, surrounded by a garland of leaves. Southwell was an innovator of advanced piano mechanics but this design demonstrates his love also of fine cabinet work. Plate No.246.

◀ William Southwell began his illustrious career as a piano maker in Dublin and his 1798 design for an "Upright Square" showed an Irish harp in each of the two side panels, though I'm not sure how many of his countrymen would have approved of the Royal crown above. Plate No.247.

by someone with a knowledge of design and it seems to me certain that an accomplished designer was at work.

But immediately we are faced with the question that bedevils every piece of piano research in the pre-1850 period: Was the piano maker also the case designer, or someone else?

My belief is that, until the 19th Century, pianos conceived by specialist Designers were rare (unless you count the actual piano makers themselves, a number of whom were trained cabinet makers, as Designers).

Some individual pianos by makers such as Christopher Ganer, William Rolfe and others had such pronounced and individual character that they could never be looked at as simply a repetition of a vernacular tradition.

Though you wonder if some notable features on square pianos of the 1780s and 1790s, such as inlaid and decorated nameboards, did not owe as much to highly skilled, specialist craftsmen in a workshop as to the controlling hand of a designer.

Photo by courtesy of The Smithsonian Institution (N.M.A.H), Washington, U.S.A.

This is the piano that changed the music world: The True Upright, invented by an English civil engineer, John Isaac Hawkins, in 1800. Hawkins was a great traveller and divided his life between England, America and Austria but there is no question but that his first models were made while he was living in Philadelphia—this one is marked No. 6 and was constructed in 1801. Hawkins described his invention as a "Portable Grand Pianoforte" and, to serve his purpose, the whole case has a pleasing utilitarian air, complete with folding keyboard and handles on the side. It was presumably the work of one of the skilful Philadelphia cabinet makers. Plate No.248.

Photo by courtesy of Sotheby's of New Bond Street, London and the Marlowe A. Sigal Collection

From simple functionalism to the sophisticated artifice of the Designer and the cabinet maker—but this, too, is the work of John Isaac Hawkins. The evidence seems to indicate strongly that Hawkins must have been arranging to have other of his pianos made in England because this one, c.1803-05, bears the Royal Arms with a holly garland and, now, an address in City Road, London. After the uncompromising functionalism of Hawkins' upright in The Smithsonian this example comes as a total surprise—Hawkins's little portable transformed into an elaborate essay "in the form of a chiffonier in the Egyptian taste". Plate No.249.

Hawkins' Egyptian Adventure

Because of growing industrialisation, the subsequent rise of the Designers in the 19th Century was both inevitable and unstoppable, for they could do what individual fine artists could not—supply the needs of the expanding mass market.

Compared to the 18th Century we know a little more, but still a pitifully small amount, about British Designer pianos of the period 1800 to 1850.

This lack of knowledge may, of course, simply be a deficiency in my research. The Dark Ages, so far as piano case design is concerned, is the period up until The Great Exhibition, due to the lack of trade papers and other evidence. Going in search of facts is indeed to take up "Lucky Dip".

The very opening year of the new Century brought with it a cataclysmic change to the piano world but, as on many other such occasions, it passed by with few signs of public recognition.

In 1800 a Taunton man, John Isaac Hawkins, who lived alternatively in Britain and America, patented his version of an Upright Piano—a concept that had been tried before but without much success. The name he gave his new instrument sounded very unlikely: He called it the "Patent Portable Grand". [14]

But for many other early forms of the piano it was to prove a death sentence. What Hawkins had invented was what a piano historian has called "The True Upright",[15] the version of the instrument that was to become its most popular form.

Mainly by starting his piano strings from near floor level, instead of keyboard level, Hawkins reduced the 8 to 9 feet high of the Upright Grands to a modest and manageable 3ft 7in.

Judging by two of the very few surviving pianos by Hawkins, all his early uprights were probably made with utilitarian cases, I presume in co-operation with a cabinet maker. They have, I feel, an honest, functional appeal.

But, perhaps seeking a more fashionable market, Hawkins went on to produce a piano c.1803-1805, which was given the full design treatment and a far more sophisticated case in the Egyptian style.[16]

Hawkins's first pianos were certainly made in America (during a period when his father continued to represent his interests in Britain) but this "Egyptian" version bears not only Hawkins's name but the Royal Arms and an address in City Road, London.

However, as to the case designer responsible, I have no evidence.

Sadly, Hawkins, one of the most prolific inventors of his time, did not make his fortune from his new upright piano and the instrument only began to make its real impact gradually over the next half century.

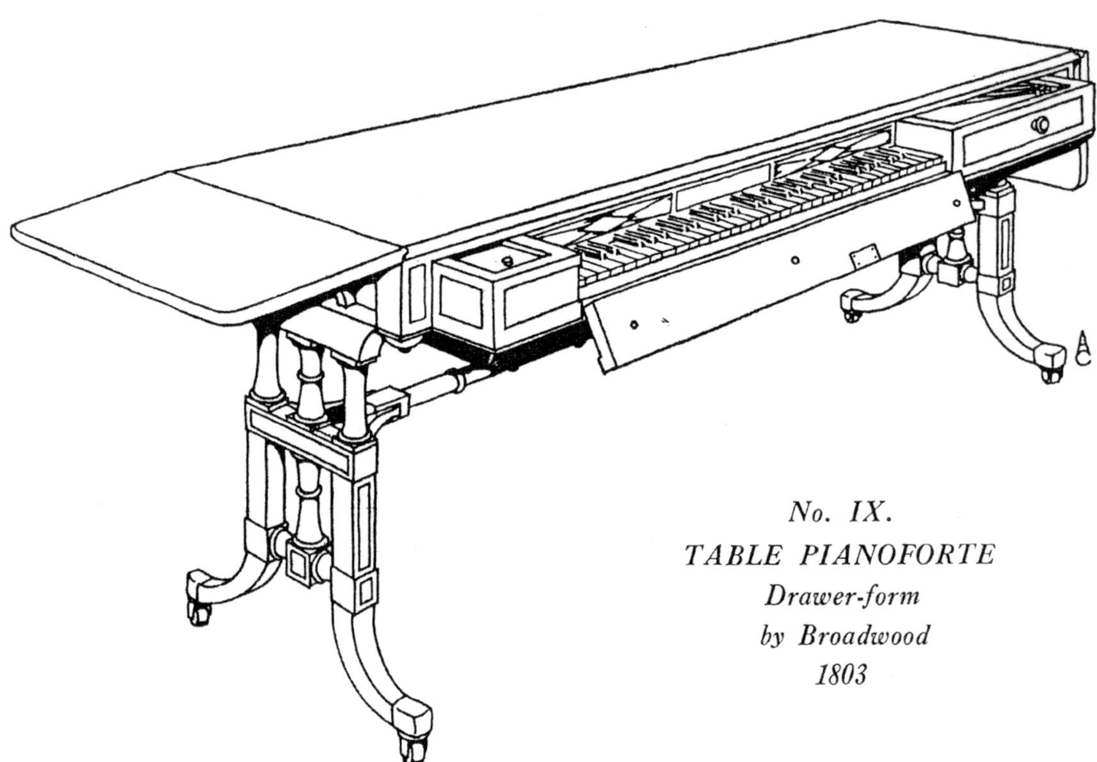

No. IX.
TABLE PIANOFORTE
Drawer-form
by Broadwood
1803

It is a long stretch from Zumpe's plain box to artfully disguising a Georgian mahogany sofa table to accommodate a square piano that will slide in and out like a drawer—but was it the work of a specialist Designer or a highly skilled cabinet maker working to a commission? All we know is that at least two were made in this style by Broadwoods and this drawing subsequently appeared in an official publication put out by the firm. Such pianos represented the desire both to hide the piano's true identity and turn it into a piece of combination furniture. Plate No.250.

Pianos Hidden in Sofa Tables

In the late 1800s, *vide* Southwell's demi-lune table pianos, there had already been a proportion of customers who either wanted to disguise the piano or convert it into a piece of combination furniture.

This trend persisted in the 19th Century and, for example, Broadwood made at least two square pianos, in 1801 and 1803, disguised as sofa tables.[17] These were done with assured panache the instruments having drop-leaf sides, two drawers, and an "elaborately tooled pedestal stand on four curved legs, connected by turned stretcher".

Quickly climbing into the leading position among British piano makers, Broadwood's emphasised quality and, generally, were safe, predictable and conservative in their treatment of the case but, from about 1807 to 1809, they made at least three "Specials" that were innovative and sparkling.

These were superior examples of the Broadwood "house style" which kept to the traditional Tabel-inspired main case but sat on very unusual supports.

Instead of the old conventional stand, or a fashionable, new style leg, they perched on eye-catching lyre ends.

One of these was a Regency grand "Commissioned for Sheringham Hall, Sheringham, Norfolk….by Humphrey Repton",[18] the stand with its three lyre supports sitting on brass lion paw feet. It may sound doubtful but it was done with conviction.

Repton, the leading English landscape designer and would-be architect, "collaborated with his son John on the landscapes of Sheringham Hall, Norfolk (1812-19)", according to Professor James Stevens Curl.[19]

What role, exactly, did Repton or his son play in the commissioning of this grand? Or the others in the series? It is impossible to say unless some evidence emerges.

Another well known example of this limited series "on trestle stand with three lyre supports", No. 3992 and dated to Nov 5th., 1807, is to be found in the Cobbe Collection.[20]

I know of no Broadwood squares built after this fashion but there is a Muzio Clementi square[21] of c.1810 and an American square by Joseph Heskey, c.1825-35, that both have similar lyre supports.

The lyre became a recurring motif in British piano design, used decoratively but also in a structural sense in that it became a convention to support the pedals for the grand from a lyre frame.

As you might expect, the lyre motif was also associated with furniture necessary to music making, such as music stands[22] but I have also met with lyre supports on conventional Georgian sofa tables[23] and games or work tables,[24] though more often built into the backs of chairs as splats.[25]

So the question occurs: Did the makers of such furniture borrow this decorative device from musical instruments, or was it the other way round? In any event, when did it first occur? Edward Joy, writing of chairs, mentions "some early specimens of about 1775 which had lyre-shaped backs".[26]

But I think we can take it back a few years before that.

No less a one than Thomas Chippendale had made a set of six chairs for Nostell Priory library, invoiced on January 22nd., 1768, that had lyre backs and which he described as "in the antique taste". Nor was this an isolated example—Chippendale later provided lyre back library chairs for Brockett Hall about 1773.[27]

It is not Chippendale we should look to, however, but our old friend Robert Adam.

An expert on Adam's furniture, Clifford Musgrave, says that Adam supplied a set of lyre backed chairs for his Osterley Park commission and these were "executed presumably in 1767".[28]

Mr Musgrave states that this Adam design is "the first known design for a lyre-back chair", though I have seen suggestions that the Byzantines had chairs with lyre backs. And Renaissance artists also used the motif.

Photo by courtesy of Mr David Winston and The Period Piano Co.

One of the famous Broadwood "Lyre" grands of c.1807 was owned by Mr David Winston, who kindly provided me with this photo. Plate No.251.

Although I can find no absolute proof that Thomas Hope ever transformed his design for an upright grand into an actual piano, I have no doubt that he did indeed do so.

The design appeared in 1807 as Plate XXIII in Hope's "Household Furniture and Interior Decoration" and what we note immediately is the sub-heading on the title page: "Executed from Designs by Thomas Hope". This could have meant the Plate was from a Hope design. However...

In Hope's own remarks in the Introduction he says: "....having occasion, a few years ago, to appropriate a little repository *(Hope surely means the annexe to his London town house)* for the reception of a small collection of antiquities, Grecian and others, I determined to make a first attempt towards....the few articles of furniture, required for this purpose....

"I was thus obliged to depend in a great measure on my own inadequate abilities for the accomplishment of my purpose; and to employ that feeble talent for drawing which I had thus far only cultivated as the means of beguiling an idle hour, in the laborious task of composing and designing every different article of furniture, which I wanted the artisan and mechanic to execute."

Hope captioned his piano design as: "Upright piano-forte. Two genii, contending for a wreath form a group round the keyhole".

Many of Hope's furnishings must have been dispersed far and wide but, occasionally, they have turned up in surprising nooks and crannies. It will be a tragedy if the great Regency designer's idea for a piano did not survive history's battering. Plate No.252.

Hope: A Great Regency Designer

Few may have been aware of Adam's and Sheraton's 18th Century designs but I suspect a great many more people, both professionals and the dilettante, were aware of Thomas Hope's Regency design for an upright grand when this was published in 1807 as one of the illustrations of his "Household Furniture and Interior Decoration".[29] There is reason to believe that a piano must have been constructed to this design but, if so, I have no clue as to its fate.

For me Hope was the quintessential Regency designer, the man who set the agenda for those who followed.

By Hope's standards the decoration of his upright grand was restrained. Two lion masks sat over each of the tall, arched doors which were presumably backed by taffeta.

Under the doors Hope's two "genii" fought for their wreath while a decorated line swirled away on each side to form a circle. The "genii", of course, were the tutelary spirits that the Romans believed attended them from cradle to grave, one good and the other evil. Good luck came from the "good genius" and ill luck from the "evil genius".[30]

Thomas Hope must have had a serious interest in music because, in addition to his design for an upright grand, it can also be proved that he designed a very large, handsomely decorated organ for his Picture Gallery with details "copied from the exquisitely beautiful specimen displayed in the temple of Erctheus (*presumably Erechtheum*) in the Acropolis of Athens".

It is my belief that Hope must also have designed and had made his own square piano.

When Hope published "Designs of Modern Costume" in 1812 it showed many of the figures set against Hope-style furniture.

In Plate 14 are three society beauties, one of whom sits playing a square piano. Although you do not see the whole of the square piano in the Flaxian-style sketch we can discern that there are two "lion"-type masks, typical Hope motifs, and the arabesque decoration on the right hand side again has a Hope feel to it.

By 1812, when this book was published, this type of square with straight legs would already have been out-of-date and I think that Hope was copying from a square he probably had made before 1805-07. Plate No.253.

It is my belief that Thomas Hope also designed a square piano.

One of Hope's other passions, apart from furniture design, was costume and in 1812 he published "Designs of Modern Costume". In all but a few cases the figures in the 20 Plates are set against furniture and this so prominent you might think it was, equally, a book of furniture designs.

In Plate 14 of this volume we find three society beauties, one of whom sits playing a square piano on which we can discern "lion"-type masks, typical Hope motifs, and arabesque decoration on the right hand side.

Since the piano shown has the straight, Neo Classical legs of a style that would have been out-dated by 1812, what Hope is showing us is a square that would probably have been made before 1805-07.

I think there is reason to believe that Hope drew such furniture from his own previous designs and my working hypothesis is that this square piano may well have been among his personal possessions.

In his 1807 book "Household Furniture and Interior Decoration", Thomas Hope also provided three designs for Lyres. Plate No.254.

Where do you start with this extraordinary "Gothick" piano?

Firstly, I would ask: Was this the tallest piano ever made in Britain? It is 9ft 1in high and, personally, I do not know of one taller.

Secondly, I would suggest that it is the most exotic of the surviving British upright grands. I would very much like to have seen a possible competitor, the upright grand designed by Thomas Hope but I fear it must have come to a sad end since I have had neither sight nor sign of it during my research.

It is impossible not to rejoice at the adventurism of this design. I cannot think of any British piano type that opted more cautiously for safe, middle-of-the-roadism than the upright grand and this one is a refreshing change.

But then, it was a Kingly instrument, made in 1808 for a rash voluptuary, George IV, when he was still Prince of Wales. The cost may sound less than the price of a good television set today but, at the time, £680 was quite beyond possibility for most in the nation.

You may see this remarkable piano now at The Museum of London where it is on permanent loan from Her Majesty The Queen. It was made for Prince George by R. Jones and Co. of Golden Square, London, to be part of the furnishings of the Gothic library created in Carlton House.

Even the makers seem to have been astonished by the enterprise since their invoice described it as "A curious fine toned Six Octave Upright Grand Piano Forte/ in black Ebony Case, designed from the antique/ Supported by four Strong Gothic Columns".

It has been suggested by a modern piano historian, Philip James, that "it is not unlikely that the gilt and black Gothic case was made by George Smith, who published a book of designs in the same year as this piano was made which he dedicated to the Prince". Plate No.255.

Photo by courtesy of The Museum of London and Her Majesty Queen Elizabeth II

The Tallest British Piano?

I am told that one important piano made in 1808 for The Prince of Wales was, that very year, illustrated in a British journal but I have so far been unable to trace the print.

This piano was a 9ft 1in high Upright Grand by R. Jones and Co. and must be the principal contender for the tallest British piano ever produced. No other Upright Grand looked remotely like it.

It was always going to be a "wall climber" because, in the upright grand, the strings had to start upwards from the piano keyboard rather than the ground.

"These early uprights were dangerously top-heavy, especially when the fronts were covered with mirror-doors, as one was when made for the Prince of Wales", wrote the piano historian David Wainwright.[31]

Conceived in the "Gothick" taste and decorated in contrasting black and gilt, it cost £680, a very substantial sum at the time and I do not doubt that most of the money was lavished on the case.

Photo by courtesy of Mr Otto Rindlisbacher of Zurich, Switzerland

What a contrast this c.1806 upright grand by Jones and Co. provides when measured against the Gothic instrument of 1808 which the firm made for the Prince of Wales only a couple of years later. But could a designer have been involved in this one, or did they simply work it all out in Mr Jones' cabinet shop?

The two instruments are so dissimilar that you might wonder if they were by the same maker but the c.1806 upright grand, now in the Collection of Mr Otto Rindlisbacher of Zurich, Switzerland, has its own merits.

Made in mahogany, Mr Rindlisbacher's piano has four highly distinctive turned and reeded legs at the front, with paw feet and matching brass metalware above. The turning tells you immediately that this piano belongs to the Regency, as the turned legs only became usual after c.1805-07.

Of considerable interest are the three paintings above the keys. Genuine artist painted pianos are as scarce as principled politicians and, as I have not made a personal examination, I can make no comment on these but photos show paintings rich with musical references and occasional hints of Kauffman and Bartolozzi. Plate No.256.

We are fortunate that the original 1808 invoice[32] gives us such an exact maker's description: "A curious fine toned Six Octave Upright Grand Piano Forte/ in black Ebony Case, designed from the antique/ Supported by four Strong Gothic Columns; Moulding/ and Cornice formed of the best Workmanship/ Carving & Gilding the Columns, Moulding and/ Cornice; in Burnish and Mat Gold,/ Ivory Balls Rosets & Orniments (*sic*) for do/ Japanning the Inside of the Case a Royal Crimson/ Fine Locks Water Gilt and Hinges/ Silk Curtains made full with gathered Heads for do/An Elegant Bookcase Complete in all respects to/Match the Piano Forte".

The maker of this unusual piano, now on long-term loan to the Museum of London from Her Majesty The Queen, was R. Jones and Co. of Golden Square, London and the instrument was made, together with matching bookcases, as part of the furnishings of the Gothic library[33] created in the basement of Carlton House.

A modern scholar, Philip James the expert on early keyboard instruments, has suggested[34] that "….it is not unlikely that the gilt and black Gothic case was made by George Smith, who published a book of designs in the same year as this piano was made which he dedicated to the Prince, describing himself on the title-page as 'Upholder Extraordinary to His Royal Highness The Prince of Wales'."

George Smith, you might say, was a man who followed in the footsteps of Thomas Hope and published his own book of designs, much influenced by Hope.

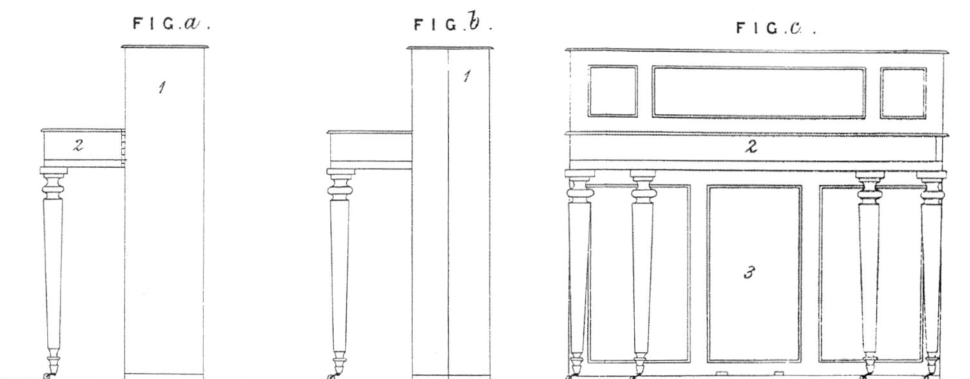

Compared to the careful detailing of William Southwell's drawings this design, submitted by Robert Wornum in 1811 for his innovative "Unique", looks thin indeed but Wornum (in partnership with Mr Wilkinson) was to produce uprights that had real Regency style. In his patent application Wornum went into minute detail concerning his "improved upright" but said not a word as to who might have been responsible for the case. Plate No.257.

Despite the skeletal appearance of Wornum's 1811 drawing the real article can be instantly recognised and turns out to be even better when seen in the flesh. This Wornum upright of 1811 is about as authentic as you can get since it was donated to The Museum of London by Wornum's grand-daughter and, in correspondence, was stated to be "the fifth upright ever made" *(by Wornum)*. Plate No. 258.

Photo by courtesy of The Museum of London

Wornum's Regency Uprights

Another piano maker whose work can be traced from the original patent drawing was a prolific inventor and important figure, Robert Wornum.

The drawing for Wornum's innovative upright of 1811, the "Unique", is skeletal compared to the more polished drawing of Southwell but is sufficiently distinctive to be instantly identifiable with the actual pianos made to this design.

Robert Wornum the younger (1780-1852)[35] was one of those men of remarkable mechanical ingenuity brought forth in Britain by the development of the piano—but he had more practical effect on the market than some who were ideas men but lacked a business brain.

Wornum was responsible for major technical innovations in the small upright, with his patents for the "Unique" in 1811,

That prolific genius and proven piano maker, William Southwell, was the man who invented the cabinet piano in 1807 but I had no more success in tracing a cabinet piano with Southwell's name on it than I had in trying to find an example of his "Piano Sloping Backwards". The earliest design for a cabinet piano that I can trace is this illustration printed in the "Repository of Arts" in February, 1812, of a cabinet piano by the short-lived partnership of Wilkinson & Wornum. It has a multitude of sophisticated touches from the concave well under the keyboard to the elaborate detailing of the cornice (the top panel with its drapes rather than "sunburst" is, on my evidence, unusual for a cabinet). Plate No.259.

Photo by courtesy of the Director of St. Cecilia's Hall: Copyright University of Edinburgh

After a great deal of searching I finally found a cabinet piano that has one major feature in common with the 1812 Wilkinson & Wornum illustration...but this instrument was made some 20 years later by John Broadwood and Sons! The Broadwood piano, which has a fine quality case in rosewood, is now in the famous Russell Collection in Edinburgh and was formerly owned by the Danish concert pianist August Hyllested, Constructed in 1834 it has the same type of distinctive, concave well under the keyboard, though the top panel and cornice are different in nature. Plate No.260.

the "Harmonic" in 1813 and the "Piccolo", which he patented in 1826. His ideas were widely copied on the Continent from 1815 and it has been suggested[36] he may have licensed Pape and Pleyel, the latter calling his version of the upright the "pianino". It is frequently claimed that the term "Cottage piano" was first coined in connection with Wornum's "Harmonic" but I have been unable to pin this down.

Although I can find no examples where Wornum tried to compete with the Neo-Classical extravagance of Beck, or the Wedgwood decorated grands of Broadwood, there is much appeal in the Regency influenced, early uprights produced by the brief partnership of Wilkinson and Wornum. One of the pair had the secret ingredient: Taste.

A cabinet piano of 1812 illustrated in the "Repository of Arts", was another fine example made during Wornum's short-lived partnership with George Wilkinson c.1810 to 1812. This appeared in February, 1812, as part of a series called "Fashionable Furniture" and would have been seen by people of culture and education throughout the British Isles and the Continent.

To what degree this published design, with its concave well behind two reeded

Photo by courtesy of The Colonial Williamsburg Foundation, Virginia, U.S.A.

One Wornum piano, more than any other upright I have seen by this maker, seems to confirm the conclusion that Robert Wornum must have had something to do with case designers. This is the highly decorative Wornum upright now to be found in the fine Collection of The Colonial Williamsburg Foundation.

It is a case design of subtlety and sophistication—a little masterpiece of a piano.

Originally given a wide-ranging date of c.1813 to 1820, it now has a suggested date of c.1815, by which time Robert Wornum would have gone his separate way from George Wilikinson.

The case of this Wornum upright radiates its quality. Just take a look at the sides to see the way the inlay pattern has been mirrored from the front. The brass beading at the bottom; the brass gallery round the top; the geometrical decoration below the keyboard reflected in the keyboard lid; the fluting, turning and interesting "cap" at the top of the leg; most especially the way the anthemion motif in the knee panel is reflected in the detailed carving on the legs

I think that the three panels in the top tell us immediately of its relationship to Wornum's upright design of 1811, though the different arrangement of the legs give it a new character. Just when did people begin identifying the "Cottage piano" with this particular type of Wornum upright? Plate No.261.

legs and textile top panel with tasselled gatherings, influenced other piano makers I do not know but it is the earliest design I can trace for a cabinet piano.

Curiously, the nearest matching cabinet piano that I could identify was made some 20 years later, by Broadwood. Dated 1834 this is now in The Russell Collection.[37]

"The cabinet piano-forte represented in the print", says the caption writer in the "Repository" of 1812, "is a specimen chosen from among the extensive variety composing the stock of Messrs Wilkinson and Wornum, whose improvements have procured it a very high degree of reputation, so that it is now becoming an article of general and fashionable request."[38]

According to the "Repository": "The general approbation of piano-fortes, as instruments of refined entertainment, and the elegance with which they are finished, in the different manufactories of the metropolis, have long rendered them as indispensable articles for apartments, furnished, as well in the simplest, as in the most costly style."

They went on to say that this cabinet piano was "an instrument of much elegance....Its height varies from six to seven feet two inches; its width is three feet eight or nine inches; and its projection twenty-one inches....Instruments of this kind, finished in mahogany, are highly ornamental, but if in rose-wood and brass, they may be pronounced truly superb. They may be inspected, finished in various ways, at the manufactory of Messrs Wilkinson and Wornum."

But who designed the 1812 cabinet piano? Mr Wilkinson, Mr Wornum, or a specialist designer?

The Wilkinson-Wornum partnership, according to a member[39] of Wornum's family, ended when their factory was burned down in 1812 but it was far from being the last of either man in the piano business.

Wornum set up on his own in the following year and became famous for his later development of the small upright piano, his "Piccolo" especially being treated as though it were itself a new invention. He also tried to miniaturise the grand piano by developing what he called the "Pocket Grand", which was just 5ft 4in long.[40]

After 1812 Ackermann's "Repository" published further drawings of pianos and, following 18th Century practice, other Designers put out their own Design Books a number of which showed the latest fashion of piano.

Photo by courtesy of Her Majesty Queen Elizabeth II © The Royal Collection

It can hardly come as a surprise to find that Royal pianos are, usually, of the finest quality and high distinction. Do you really need me to tell you that this grand piano, made in 1817 by Isaac Mott, can only have been the work of a Designer?

The client was George IV when he was still Prince Regent.

This grand is supported on an unusual triangular base (it is hard to think of its equivalent outside the work of Mott) and is in walnut veneer with inlaid brass foliate bands. Today it is normally on display in the Green Drawing Room of Buckingham Palace.

Mott, a man of parts who had shops in Pall Mall, London, and in Brighton, was himself a composer and played in the Royal band. Plate No.262.

Royal Pianos: A Class Apart

Before the 19th Century was ended the Designers, led by luminaries such as C.F.A. Voysey, were to develop principles and theories by which to manufacture furniture and offer people new lifestyles in packages providing for the design of everything in a house from the very knives and forks to the chimney pots.[41] For Voysey[42] and many others that included a design for a piano.

Those less high-minded were also, in an age of rampant capitalism, in a position to respond quickly to what Prince Albert called "the unreasoning laws of markets and fashions".[43] In other words, large piano factories needed specialist piano designers who could speedily turn out a new case outwardly "dressed" according to the demands of the latest fad, such as "Grecian" or "Italian".

What Prince Albert didn't mention, of course, was that many of these fashions were set by Royalty themselves—most often in clothes but in music also. King George III and especially his wife Queen Charlotte, King George IV and the Royal couple Queen Victoria and Prince Albert all did much to encourage the art.

The British Royals and their extended families bought piano after piano, after piano, after piano. You certainly needed a few Royal residences to house them and patronage was widely distributed among British, Continental and American makers.

The Royals themselves followed few rules except one: Hire the Very Best.

Few did it with the artistic style of that wicked fellow King George IV and some of the most exciting pianos made for him ended up in his exercise in costly fantasy, The Royal Pavilion at Brighton.

Photographs by courtesy of The Colt Clavier Collection, Bethersden, Kent

A Royal rake he may have been but George IV was a handsome-spending Patron of the Arts and a man of taste, responsible for commissioning some of the finest Royal pianos. The most eccentric of these was certainly this opulent instrument of 1821 by Thomas Tomkison, a piano maker always recognised for the quality of his casework.

The Tomkison grand, now in the Colt Clavier Collection, is so distinctive it can easily be identified in Nash's print of the Entrance Hall of the Brighton Pavilion. Decorated with little regard to expense it is carved in solid rosewood with elaborate brass Boulle inlay and mythical figures sitting either side of the keyboard. The arrangement of the legs is very unusual and reminds me of Sheraton designs.

But who could have been the designer of this one? Plate No.263 and Plate No.264.

That designers were responsible for two of the most exceptional of these Royal pianos is certain; but, again, I have no idea who they were.

As regal as any Royal was the grand piano created for George IV in 1817, when he was still Prince Regent, a symphony of brass inlaid rosewood which can be seen in its original setting in an aquatint published by John Nash, showing the furnishings of "The Music Gallery" at Brighton.[44]

This was made for the Prince by a member of his own band who was also a maker of pianos of the highest possible quality, Isaac H.R. Mott. A versatile man, he was also a composer who sold his own music in his shops in Pall Mall, London and in Brighton.

The Mott grand, now normally on display in the Green Drawing Room at Buckingham Palace, was constructed with walnut veneer and inlaid brass foliate bands, supported by an unusual triangular base, on castors concealed by patinated bronze shell and acanthus scrolled mounts.[45]

A matching music stool is probably that shown in the Nash aquatint and is "of oak painted with alternating anthemion and lyre motifs in gold on a green ground".[46]

At least two additional grands in this magnificent manner are known to have been made by Mott.

Another most characterful Royal piano for George IV was by Thomas Tomkison of Soho, London, a man much respected for his cabinet making. "Tomkison pianos are characterised by their unusually fine casework", it has been written.[47]

This grand, of real individual personality, "opulent and lavishly decorated", can be seen in Nash's print of the Entrance Hall of the Pavilion.[48] It was carved in solid rosewood with elaborate brass Boulle inlay and mythical figures sitting either side of the keyboard, with the legs specially ornamented.

Tomkison's Royal grand is now to be found in the Colt Clavier Collection and the greatly respected expert, the late C.F. Colt,

Photo by courtesy of The Colt Clavier Collection, Bethersden, Kent

Presumably because they were Britain's best known firm of piano makers and had such a long association with the Royal family, Broadwood and Sons were also asked to make a grand piano for George IV's Royal Pavilion at Brighton.

Once again we have to go to the outstanding Colt Clavier Collection at Bethersden, Kent, to study the piano that they supplied, c.1821. As you might expect it is of the finest Broadwood quality but, on this occasion, I have the feeling that Broadwood solved the problem "in house" rather than go to an outside designer.

What we have here is a safe and familiar Broadwood grand enlivened by distinctive brass inlay. It cost 185 guineas and was made "in rio" (Rio Rosewood). Plate No.265.

judged[49] that "Of the....Pavilion pianos, the Tomkison is, perhaps, the strangest in design....this one has legs reminiscent of an earlier era. They are carved out of solid rosewood and reflect Renaissance taste rather than the oriental splendour of the Brighton Pavilion interior. The rest of the casework, on the other hand, is perfectly in keeping with the marine residence."

Mr Colt stated that the three unusual pairs of legs were "decorated, inverted lyres". To my mind they are reminiscent, though more formalised versions, of the twin, animal-type legs that Sheraton used in some of the designs for his "Encyclopaedia", perhaps in turn deriving from Piranesi.[50]

A note on the Tomkison grand written in Indian ink, which came to light when the action was removed, says simply "For the King, December 21st., 1821".

Who could have designed these two wondrous pianos? Answer have I none.

As you might expect, Britain's best known piano makers, Broadwoods, were also commissioned to supply a grand piano for The Royal Pavilion but they did not permit themselves to succumb to the exotic fever. Only in the more complex design of a band of brass inlay that surrounded the case, matched with brass trim, is there the hint of a loosening of the shackles.

This Royal Broadwood, c.1821, was eventually acquired by the Colt Clavier Collection and research uncovered the original record, which stated "His Majesty—an elegant six octave grand piano in rio (*Rio Rosewood*) 185 guineas—no. 8948—delivered at His Majesty George IV's Pavilion, Brighton".[51]

That description of "an elegant six octave grand piano in rio" is of special interest.

We know the word "rio" meant a particular kind of rosewood but what did "Elegant" mean?

It may sound simple but there is nothing simple about it. Reaching for the "Oxford" will not solve the problem.

Anyone who wishes to volunteer for the piano "anorak" ranks and spend his time reading 19th Century piano price lists will

Thomas Tomkison's 1821 Royal grand "For the King" can be instantly identified by the unusual "double leg" shown in this Nash print of the Entrance Hall of the Brighton Royal Pavilion. This unique piano is now in the Colt Collection. Plate No.266.

soon discover that the word "Elegant" in this context must have had a very specific meaning for these Georgians. But what?

From at least 1815 Broadwood price lists offered certain pianos with an optional "Elegant" decoration.

For example, in 1815 Broadwood offered a "Square, elegant" for £26—but you could have had a "Square with single action" for £17 6s 0d or a "Square with double action" for £18 3s 0d.

What was so special about the "Elegant" that it should cost more than any other square piano?

The same description was used by both Collard (at least until 1832) and Wornum (at least until 1838).

Collard offered a square "elegant, with rounded corners" for £40—but this was more expensive than six other sorts of square piano and less expensive than three other types.

Wornum's "Elegant" piccolo of 1838 was offered as a middle of the range "Elegant, with trusses" for 38 guineas, or, alternatively, as the most expensive of six types, listed simply as "Elegant…from 46 to 50 guineas"

How do we now de-code their use of the word "Elegant"? Could it, for example, have meant buhl or other inlay?

I have spent a good many hours on the issue and am little the wiser. Any advice from cryptologists gratefully accepted.

The late Mr C.F. Colt evidently felt there was a possibility that another fine quality piano in his Collection, a Kirkman grand of 1820, was also from the Royal Pavilion at Brighton. A record still exists of an Inventory of the Royal pianos at Brighton made in 1833 and this mentions a Kirkman grand.

"Unfortunately the illustrations in the archives are not as clear as that of the Tomkison grand piano in the Entrance Hall", wrote Mr Colt. "It is therefore impossible to be absolutely certain that this instrument is in fact a Royal one".

What we learn from Mr Colt's Kirkman of 1820 is that the design is conservative in approach and of the finest quality. It is in a rosewood case and, comments Mr Colt, "the unusually elegant casework would certainly have fitted it for such an exalted residence". Plate No.267.

Photo by courtesy of The Colt Clavier Collection, Bethersden, Kent

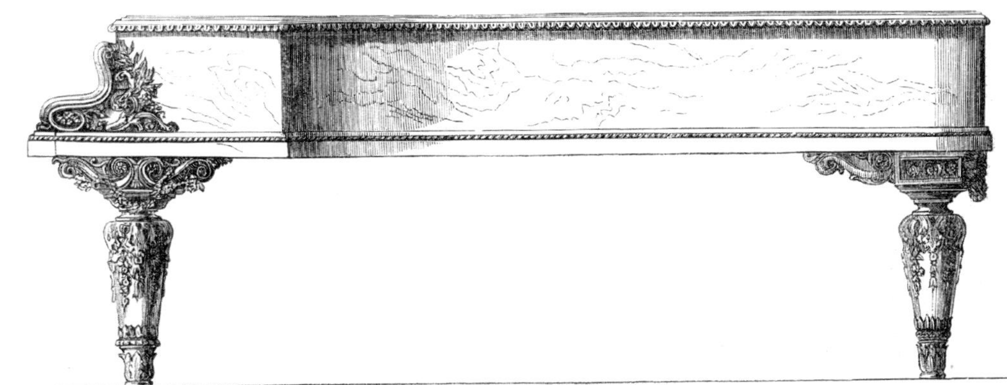

Might George Morant, or the Morant firm, have had anything to do with the design of a succession of Broadwood "Specials" in the 1830s? I confess it is the wildest speculation, with not a hint of evidence outside my imagination. Morant was an officially named Designer by Broadwood with this entry for The Great Exhibition of 1851 shown in the "Art-Journal Illustrated Catalogue". One sees immediately the prominent characteristics that had been the hallmark of the Broadwood grand since 1827—the curved and carved "cheek"; the unbroken horizontal veneer, etc. Interestingly, it was stated that the decoration was in "the rich style of Italian ornament". Plate No.268.

Broadwood: The Mystery Designers

An slightly enlarged view of the front leg of the George Morant design for a Broadwood grand exhibited in 1851. This was published on Page 201 of "An Illustrated Cyclopaedia of the Great Exhibition of 1851". Plate No.269.

It is one of the most remarkable facts of piano history that prior to 1850 we do not appear to know the name of a single Broadwood case designer for Britain's greatest piano firm, other than Thomas Sheraton.

We know that Sheraton designed the first of the Wedgwood grands[52] for Broadwood in 1796—and that E.M. Barry and George Morant, half a century later, conceived totally different kinds of "specials"[53] as the firm's exhibits at The Great Exhibition of 1851. And that is about it.

Could it be that they never employed a designer during that time, or did not have to produce special, custom-made instruments for other rich clients?

Impossible.

To pose another obvious question: If the founder of the firm, John Broadwood (1732-1812), really had "learnt his craft of joiner and cabinet-maker from his father"[54] how could a cabinet maker not have involved himself in the question of case design?

John Broadwood is believed to have started making square pianos[55] c.1778 and grand pianos[56] from 1784. So, effectively, he would have been the deciding voice on the firm's case design until the first decade of the 1800s.

I think we must look to John Broadwood himself as probably the most potent influence on his firm's designs until 1812—and a continuing influence on the house style even after his death.

Did John Broadwood himself design any piano cases? We can only speculate but, while he was in the forefront of mechanical advance, the dominant characteristic of his rule, so far as the case was concerned, was an adherence to tradition.

The series of "Wedgwood" grands they made around 1800 and the "Lyre" grands around 1807 were idiosyncratic exceptions, not the rule.

As the 19th Century opened most Broadwood grands still displayed the characteristics of the "Tabel", or British, Style: Veneered panels in mahogany round the sides of the case.

"Mahogany with crossbanding and boxwood stringing; satinwood keyboard surround" was the description[57] of a Broadwood grand of 1805—and one that could fit many other Broadwoods.

But according to a Sotheby's musical instrument expert: "After the news of Nelson's death arrived in England in late 1805 Broadwood changed the boxwood stringing to ebony."[58] I have no idea whether this was so (I fear I am a born doubter) but it explains why it has since been suggested that we should call such Broadwoods "Trafalgar Grands".[59]

The designers of other pre-1850 Broadwood "specials" remain a foggy mystery.

A highly unusual mahogany Broadwood square[60] of 1807 that was in an American collection had four turned legs with the appearance of architectural columns borrowed from a Classical building.

If the legs, topped by gilt collars and sitting on small, square bases, were original to the design (and I do very much wonder) then this certainly had out of the ordinary qualities. I was tempted to say there could be few like it but the journal "Cabinet Maker" published a drawing[61] of a square piano, given a date of 1833, on which similar unusual legs were fluted and there are a number of Continental examples.

Some other exceptions in the Broadwood *oeuvre* have been noted by that assiduous piano historian Martha Novak Clinkscale.

Circa 1810, she reveals, Broadwood supplied a grand piano[62] in "Mahogany veneer with maple and green-coloured wood stringing, four tapered legs with bronze Empire-style ormolu.... nameboard and support decorated with intarsia of flowers and ornaments; group of musical instruments inlaid in the centre".

Somewhere between 1820 and 1825 the firm made a cabinet piano,[63] in satinwood with ebony stringing and ebony mounts, the "centre top of case with cast and entwined snakes on ebony block".

Other unusual Broadwoods could be cited but most especially the series of "Specials" that began by at least 1827 with the ground-breaking design of the grand piano in the Metropolitan Museum of Art, New York, that effectively junked the Tabel style main case.

The familiar, British-style Tabel panels were eliminated as one might press "Delete" on a computer keyboard; the profile of the "cheeks" was completely altered; heavy carving was introduced; so was pronounced beading; the display of the veneer was treated in a new fashion.

Someone had decided to throw away a century and more of tradition and go back to the drawing board.

It is infuriating that we cannot name the designer (and have not the slightest doubt that there was a designer) of this important piano. Unless and until someone can show me an earlier grand that incorporates all the features of this 1827 Broadwood, delivered to Mr McIntosh of Bloomsbury Square, London, I shall continue to work on the hypothesis that this was a crucial marker of the point when British piano design veered in a new direction.

In place of the old we now had a heavy, dark rosewood main case of unbroken veneer, with carved and scrolled "cheeks", complemented by continuous egg and dart moulding.[64]

There was an almost immediate effect on the ordinary run of Broadwood grands which, if not including all the expensive new features, introduced the new style in a modified form.

But, within a few years, there appear to have been at least two other Broadwood "specials" taking their lead from the 1827 grand. I use the word "appear" with caution because I have

Mystery Designer: The designer responsible for the Broadwood grand of 1827 that changed the whole style of the British grand piano is unknown. It is now in the Metropolitan Museum of Art. Plate No.270.

Mystery Designer; We have no clues to the Designer of this 1832 Broadwood grand, drawn to my attention by Bill Kibby of PianoGen. Plate No.271.

Mystery Designer: For the third time I must report "Designer Unknown" for this ornate grand piano said to be a Broadwood of 1833. Again I have to thank Bill Kibby of PianoGen for drawing this to my attention. Plate No.272.

images but, as the old country saying might have it, not a fact worth a spit.

Thanks entirely to that most assiduous of piano researchers, Bill Kibby of PianoGen, I have been shown two illustrations.

The first depicts a Broadwood grand, given a date of 1832 and restored many years ago by John Paul. It is an extraordinary sight, reminding you of something about to launch itself into the air.

In most respects this case follows logically on from the new style set by the 1827 design but the legs are totally different.

The visual hint of an airborne bird comes from three extraordinary, heavily carved cabriole legs (the rear one reversed) which have been manipulated into bends so extreme that you wonder if they might not break under the strain of supporting the main case.

The illustration of the second of these "Specials", an ornate, gilt-covered grand which is said to be an 1833 Broadwood, has been floating round the Internet, so I cannot vouch for a single fact concerning it. Nevertheless, one has to say that it incorporates certain features, such as the curved and carved "cheek", pioneered by the 1827 Broadwood grand.

Again, we now find three heavily carved cabriole legs, the rear one reversed but the spirit of these is different again. These have more of a Neo Classical feel.

One automatically asks: Could the same Broadwood designer have been responsible for all three grands, the instruments of 1827, 1832 and 1833? If so, who might this have been?

Like Mr Burton I am a plain, rude writer and I call a spade a spade, so I must confess that facts have I nary a one. "Attributions" I regard as the work of the Devil and idle speculation without evidence a game for fools.

Nevertheless, I look speculatively over the horizon at two of the earliest Broadwood designers whose names I can prove, E.M. Barry and George Morant, who were each responsible for Broadwood grands shown at the 1851 Exhibition. Might they have been around in 1827?

The architect E.M Barry we may dismiss immediately. He was not born until 1830 and was but a young whipper-snapper when he designed Broadwood's main 1851 exhibit.

Morants were important 19th Century furnishers who became established in Bond Street but of George himself and other Morant designers I know but little. So I have fallen into my own trap of foolish speculation.

But the question nags away: Who was Broadwood's 1827 designer?

Thanks to Martha Novak Clinkscale we know there was a later, 1842 Broadwood of potential interest, an upright "Extremely ornate with gesso, perhaps decorated in Paris".[65] And there is another ornate Broadwood grand of 1848 in the "Finchcocks" Collection.

Were all such "Specials" left to the individual judgement of Broadwood craftsmen? I think not.

The foreman of a cabinet shop can be a powerful figure—I have watched such a man rough out a reproduction design, full scale on plywood for one of his craftsmen, straight from his head without a drawing in sight. But trying to imagine the standing of such men between 1800 and 1850 is difficult.

It is my view that, post 1800, Broadwoods tended to be more adventurous with the design of upright and cabinet pianos than their grands but, even allowing for such, you will find more provocative contemporary examples of the cabinet maker's art in the pianos of Tomkison,[66] the Mott[67] family, R. Jones and Co.,[68] Muzio Clementi and Co.[69] or even Robert Wornum[70] who, more famous for his mechanical innovations, yet managed casework of simple elegance in his early instruments, before they began the melt-down into Victoriana.

While Broadwood generally retreated to safety in case design a firm like Clementi were prepared to embark on the buhl adventure that resulted in the startling square piano of c.1825, in the Colt Collection, a masterpiece awash with brass inlay of dancing maidens and "Pan" characters let loose across the rosewood surface. Which rash buccaneer did they hire who was prepared to discard all inhibitions and design what is, surely, one of the most remarkable British square pianos?

The extent of buhl work on British pianos and the effect of Regency influence in this area is worth a study in itself, not least the way in which British reserve translated the mad swirls and curls of the Continentals into tight little geometric patterns on nameboards, or around the sides and tops of cabinet pianos.

Illustration by courtesy of The British Library

Oh dear! What can one say when one of the recognised names of the design world gets it so wrong? This cabinet piano was illustrated in the "Repository of Arts" on October 1st., 1826 and was unsigned but later appeared as the 16th illustration of "Pugin's Gothic Furniture" in 1827.

I find it hard to conceive that Welby Pugin could have been responsible for such a dog's breakfast and assume it must have been the work of his father, A.C.N. Pugin, the man responsible for the 1827 book. Plate No.273.

Pugin: The Work of a Child?

Thanks to the increased publication of Design Books in the 19th Century we can now begin to identify a tiny few of these mystery piano designers of the 1800-1850 period.

It is through such publications that we learn of Thomas Hope's upright grand of 1807; the piano designs shown by John Claudius Loudon in his magnificent "Encyclopaedia of Cottage, Farm and Villa Architecture and Furniture"; and the later piano designs by men such as Michael Angelo Nicholson and Henry Whitaker.

But for me the most interesting mystery of the pre-1850 period is whether two piano designs of the 1820s were the work of the Gothic specialist Augustus Charles Pugin or his son, Augustus Welby Northmore Pugin. Or, as has been speculated,[71] might they have been jointly responsible?

Pugin the elder established a dynasty of Pugins connected with architecture, at least seven of them entering the profession.[72]

The French-born Augustus Charles Pugin hinted at an aristocratic background by occasionally calling himself "de Pugin" and floated suggestions that he was really Comte de Pugin who "fell fighting for the king, and was thrown with some hundred bodies into a pit near the Place de la Bastille, whence he managed to escape by swimming across the Seine".[73]

He had fled to England to avoid "that death which befel (*sic*) his father and brothers, as their position was sufficiently high to make them considered enemies".

Another romantic version had it that he fled France after fighting a duel.[74]

Or, perhaps, he entered England as an early economic migrant, since one biographer could find no trace of a title and the family arms had, unfortunately, been "burnt in the Revolution, in terror of their being discovered".[75]

But Pugin senior was a man of resource and talent, becoming an assistant to John Nash, making a fine reputation as a draughtsman and author of architectural books, besides establishing himself among the leading watercolour painters.[76]

Pugin senior can be proven to have been a furniture designer and a man of sufficient standing to have his work reproduced many times in a well known journal and to have been approached to supply furniture for the King.

Such was his repute in matters Gothic that it is said that George IV sent his *chef de cuisine* to Pugin senior for advice on the proper Gothic manner in which the Royal table should be decorated.[77]

So far I have identified two early piano designs which must be the work of one of two people—A.C. Pugin himself or his son, A.W.N. Pugin, then barely into his teens. The degree to which either was responsible for certain Gothic designs is a debate that has already drawn in the leading scholars in the field and there is still no final proof either way.

A number of modern authors have questioned who should have the credit for the designs in "Pugin's Gothic Furniture", the book published by Augustus Charles Pugin in 1827 (and often confused with his son's later book of 1835, "Gothic Furniture in the Style of the 15th Century").

"On 1 June 1825, when the first plate appeared, A.W.N. Pugin was just thirteen years old, but we do know that he had already executed drawings for his father's publications", reveals one of the Pugin specialists, the late and much lamented Clive Wainwright.[78]

If the possibility still seems barely credible we must judge it in the light of proven fact: That, at the age of 15, Pugin the younger undertook a major commission to himself design Royal furniture for Windsor Castle.[79]

So, evidently, a child prodigy in his own field to rival the tiny tots who appeared on the concert platforms of Europe, though Pugin was still not quite so young as Chopin, said to have appeared in public at the age of eight.

Not until there is further evidence regarding Pugin senior's work for the "Repository of Arts" (not easy because many plates gave no clue to authorship), or his possible furniture designs for architects, will we get a better measure of the man.

One of the surprises of the 1827 book is to discover that "Gothic Furniture" contained designs for both a grand piano and a cabinet piano.

The design for "An Horizontal Grand Piano Forte", with its accompanying music stool, was especially ambitious and was first published in Ackermann's "Repository" on July 1st., 1826. Although unsigned it was later to become the third plate in "Pugin's Gothic Furniture" of 1827.

An accompanying caption in the "Repository" said this piano "from its size, would be the leading feature in any apartment". Readers were told "that musical instruments are almost become an essential part of furniture, and among them we can reckon none more frequently used than the piano".

The Pugin grand, with elaborate Gothic decoration, had a total of eight legs joined by stretchers, the sides panelled and with traceries of arches and diamonds.

It was explained that the instrument "being totally unknown to our ancestors, and only invented within the last half century, we can merely decorate the given forms by traceries and other Gothic ornaments best calculated to assist the sound".

At this point one must turn to the expert advice of Clive Wainwright.

Writing[80] of the early furniture of Pugin Junior, he said: "The most satisfactory answer

Photo by Simon Suckling

Courtesy of Holdenby House and The Music Museum

Is this one of the long sought, missing treasures of Welby Pugin? According to the catalogue of a Holdenby House exhibition: "This instrument is believed to have been manufactured specifically for the 1851 Crystal Palace Exhibition". There are serious grounds for considering whether it is, in fact, an upright made for the Exhibition to the design of Welby Pugin. A matter, I think, for further scholastic research. Plate No.274.

would seem to be that at this period the design characteristics of the work of the father and young son, who he had trained, were so close as to be indistinguishable.

"I would suggest that it is not perhaps particularly fruitful or useful to attempt to separate the work of one from the other at this early period in A.W.N. Pugin's life."

Fact is lacking and, at this stage, we can only rely on that most dangerous of evidence, stylistic differences.

The grand piano revealed to the world in July, 1826, was soon followed in the "Repository" by an "Upright Piano-Forte, Music-Stand, and Chair" in the issue of October 1st., 1826. Again, the plate was unsigned but later appeared as the 16th illustration of "Pugin's Gothic Furniture" in 1827.

The "Upright" shown was, of course, not a true upright but a cabinet piano.

Revealing how early were concerns about the size of pianos, the accompanying caption stated that "it is admirably calculated for a small apartment, in which a horizontal piano would be heavy and inconvenient; it has also a very pleasing appearance when placed in a recess, such as that formed by the projection of the chimney".

Sadly, I have to report that I have not come across any real life piano that looked like either of these Pugin designs but one would dearly like to know what contemporary piano makers thought.

The Rise of the Designers saw an increasing publication of design books, some of which now began to include illustrations of pianos.

When Michael Angelo Nicholson published his "Practical Cabinet Maker" in 1826 it included this elaborate "Upright Gothic Piano Forte" that might have passed as the frontage of a Cathedral...or possibly a wedding cake. Despite the four sturdy legs at the front the case comes down to ground level behind them. But if the Gothic arches were cut-outs, was it an upright grand or a cabinet piano? Plate No.275.

Michael Angelo Nicholson: Gun for Hire

Another well known Gothic piano design of this period[81] *(shown above)* was presented by Michael Angelo Nicholson in 1826 in his "Practical Cabinet Maker" but from its "icing sugar" detail to its reach-for-the-sky pinnacles you would be hard put to know whether it was a wedding cake or, more possibly, a church. A layman could not be blamed for thinking it might be the frontage of a French Cathedral.

Nicholson himself described it as an "Upright Gothic Piano Forte" but one is tempted to say: First find your piano.

One of my correspondents[82] suggests that it might be compared with details of the long side elevations of King's Chapel, Cambridge, or perhaps the West porch of St Luke's, Chelsea.

"Given the buttresses at the upper half of the piano, its pinnacles seem a logical completion for the top", he writes. "If they were steeples, the crockets up to the tips would be far out of scale.

"At first glance the whole composition might be taken for an Early Victorian altar and reredos.

A second illustration of what is again described as an "Upright Piano Forte" appeared in Michael Angelo Nicholson's 1826 volume, "The Practical Cabinet Maker, Upholsterer and Complete Decorator" but, without a blink, Nicholson this time offered the polar opposite of his "Cathedral Gothic". What we have this time is a venture in Neo-Classicism: In place of the buttresses and pinnacles we now find Classical columns supporting the top and a Greek-style mask at the centre. Is there a hint of Thomas Hope behind this Nicholson design? Plate No.276.

"I don't suppose these 'Gothick' designers had period-authenticity for their ideal….the arches in the lower stages might be Dec (Middle Pointed), while the parapet looks Perp (Third Pointed) after c.1340."

That it was a remarkable confection is quite certain but, as with other such designs, you wonder: Was it actually translated from paper to real life?

Nicholson's design has four sturdy legs at the front but a side elevation definitely shows the case behind these coming down to the ground. Nevertheless, because it is unclear whether the gothic arches in the base are applied tracery or "cut-outs", I find it impossible to judge whether it was a cabinet piano or an upright grand.

Besides his "Church Gothic" piano, Michael Angelo Nicholson also designed a Neo-Classical piano[83] that was illustrated in the same 1826 volume, "The Practical Cabinet Maker, Upholsterer and Complete Decorator", on which he collaborated with his father.

Again described by Nicholson as an "Upright Piano Forte" this was the complete opposite of his Gothic design being in a Classical style, with columns supporting the top and a Greek-style mask at the centre of what seemed like a radiating silk panel. It smacks very much of the Regency, I think.

Nicholson, I conclude, was the complete pro and gun for hire: Gothic or Neo Classical as the customer demanded.

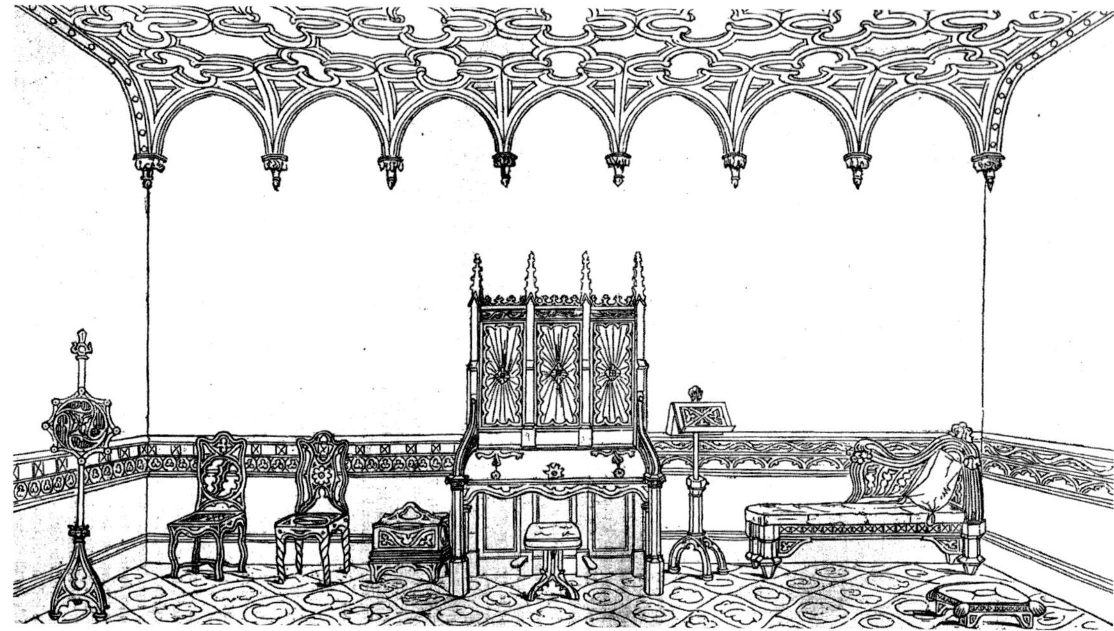

The architect Edward Buckton Lamb is stated to have been responsible for an ambitious piano design that appeared in the "Encyclopaedia of Cottage, Farm and Villa Architecture and Furniture" as part of a room setting.

This piano dominates a Gothic drawing room and here Lamb, presumably drawing on Church architecture, presents us with a cabinet piano with crocketed pinnacles, "sunburst" silk panels and a curved piano lid with ornamented hinges. Below are three panels and, at the front, two hefty columns supporting the keyboard. Plate No.277.

The New Ideal: Lamb and Wornum

When John Claudius Loudon came to publish his mighty "Encyclopaedia of Cottage, Farm and Villa Architecture and Furniture" ("the crucial document of 1830s middle-class taste", said Simon Jervis[84]), packed with furniture designs, he paid especial tribute[85] to the previous work on pianos by both William Stodart and Robert Wornum.

But were the Principals of these two well known firms responsible for their casework; did they develop from a vernacular tradition; or did they employ Designers? We simply do not know.

Anonymous designer ghosts hover over so many of these intriguing pianos of the period, tantalising us with unanswerable questions.

In his "Encyclopaedia" in which, with total shock, one comes across one of the most radical chair designs[86] of the century, Loudon (1783-1843) discussed attempts to make the piano "harmonise with the general forms of drawing-room furniture".[87]

Already established as a multi-talented workaholic, Loudon, architect, botanist, linguist and "Designer of Rural Improvements", recruited nearly 50 architects and cabinet makers to contribute additional designs to his "Encyclopaedia".

Illustrations of their work reveal the pragmatism and practicality of Loudon's judgement—the "Encyclopaedia" was an eclectic's handbook and the designs aimed not at a wealthy few but a Middle Class version of the Common Man.

The way in which Loudon divided the furniture styles of his day gives us a freeze-frame of contemporary attitudes.

An early proponent of "the principle of unity of expression",[88] Loudon believed that the kind of furniture you bought should relate to the design of your house.

He maintained that 1830s furniture could be divided into four principal styles: "Grecian or modern style, which is by far the most prevalent"; "the Gothic or perpendicular style, which imitates the lines and angles of the Tudor Gothic Architecture"; "the Elizabethan style, which combines the Gothic with the Roman or Italian manner"; "and the style of the age of Louis XIV, or the florid Italian, which is characterised by curved lines and excess of curvilinear ornaments".[89]

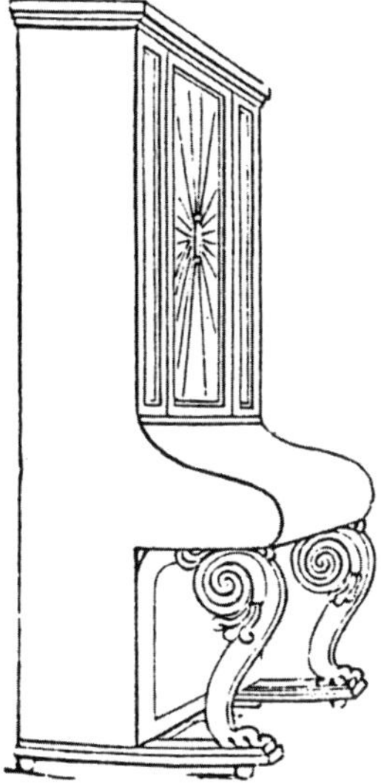

Two further designs illustrated in the "Encyclopaedia of Cottage, Farm and Villa Architecture and Furniture" ("the crucial document of 1830s middle-class taste") were of pianos by Robert Wornum, one of the most important makers of the period 1800-1850. They appeared in a chapter headed "Grecian and Modern Villa Furniture".

This one was a very simple, outline design for a cabinet piano by Wornum that stood 6ft 6in tall and cost between 50 and 100 guineas, depending on specifications.

The "Encyclopaedia" was re-issued ten times within 30 years after beginning publication in 1832 and I believe these Wornum designs were likely to have influenced other piano makers. Plate No.278.

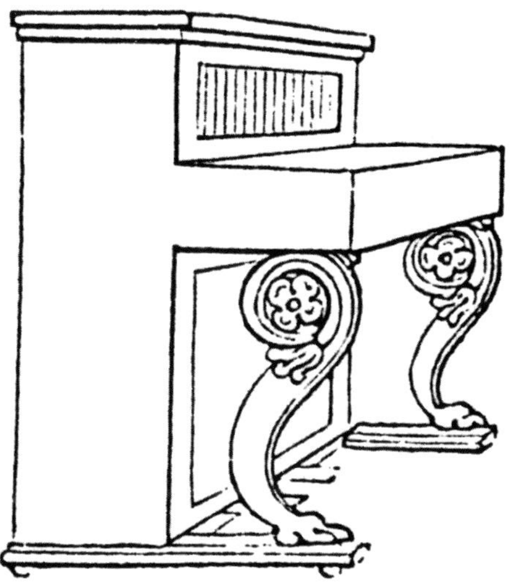

The second Wornum design that appeared in the "Encyclopaedia" was for one of his famous uprights and this, it was stated, was one of the maker's "most frequently used" sizes. The instrument stood only 3ft 4in and was one of the smallest made, costing between 36 and 55 guineas but it had more obvious Victorian lines than his earlier, elegant Regency productions, boasting cabriole legs with heavy, exaggerated scrolls.

The Victorian author William Pole said Wornum's first uprights had varied from about four to five feet high but, in 1827, he introduced the "Piccolo", standing "only about three feet six inches from the ground. This has served as the model for many others under different names." Plate No.279.

In his "Encyclopaedia" Loudon provided four illustrations of pianos.

If I decipher Loudon's text correctly, two of these pianos were by Robert Wornum and the third definitely by Loudon's collaborator and principal illustrator, Edward Buckton Lamb. The fourth has been subsequently credited to Lamb.

Included in a chapter headed "Grecian and Modern Villa Furniture" were the two Wornum instruments—a cabinet piano[90] with radiating silk top panel and a modest upright,[91] each bolstered by cabriole legs with heavy, exaggerated scrolls *(see above)*.

As you might expect for the date, both were transitionary heralds of the approaching Victorian age. Nevertheless, the simplicity of approach and evident intent to cater for a general public is obvious.

The "Encyclopaedia" proved to be a publishing event of wide influence in Britain and America (first appearing as a part-work from 1832, the volume was re-issued ten times within 30 years) and I do not think there is much doubt these two piano styles were copied.

"The forms of piano-fortes have been lately much improved, so that they now harmonise with the general forms of drawing-room furniture better than they ever did before," it was said in the "Encyclopaedia".[92]

After praising "the manufacturer Stodart" for "the first step in the road to this desirable end", the edition I studied went on to reveal that, in 1833, Wornum had "exhibited a piano-forte that could hardly be distinguished from a library table".

The two Wornum pianos shown in the "Encyclopaedia" were, says Loudon, the maker's "most frequently used" sizes.

The upright, at 3ft 4in, was one of the smallest made and cost from 36 to 55 guineas. The larger cabinet, standing at 6ft 6in, cost from 50 to 100 guineas.

"The advantages of Wornum's instruments are, that, with the same degree of tone and excellence, in a musical point of view, as the horizontal pianos, and with the convenient form of the upright pianos, they are finished behind in such a manner as to have a handsome effect whichever side is presented to the company", it

When I first saw this illustration I thought it might be some sort of monument in stone but it is, in fact, the architect Edward Buckton Lamb's idea (if I have interpreted the matter correctly) of a "Grecian or modern" piano that he intended to be made in wood.

Lamb's design appeared in the "Encyclopaedia of Cottage, Farm and Villa Architecture and Furniture" in the 1830s and was the expression of Lamb's ambitious ideas for the piano. He wanted it to be a "hint to manufacturers" and primarily intended it to be smaller than a grand piano while being "superior as an article of furniture." Plate No.280.

I knew that I had seen somewhere else an illustration of a piano that looked as though it had been carved of stone and thought that Edward Buckton Lamb might have "borrowed" his idea.

In fact the other piano design I was thinking of was from 1872 by a later, and very great, Victorian designer, E.W. Godwin, who also experimented with Anglo-Grecian style.

Godwin, like Lamb, was designing for wood but wrote that his printed illustration was "unfortunate, as it gives this design a heavy look, more like stone than woodwork. This, however, is not the case in reality". Plate No.281.

was said. "The old upright and cabinet pianos were generally placed against walls."

The distinguished expert Philip James blamed Wornum's upright for introducing "a type in which ugliness found its apotheosis in the Victorian age"[93] and, since Victoria came to the throne in 1837, I suppose we must take it that James meant post-1837. But the Victorian era was long-lived—Wornum and Sons continued until 1900 and I think it a harsh judgement, made in 1930 before there had been any serious reappraisal of the different strands of Victorian design.

The third piano[94] illustrated by Loudon was a very strange animal indeed, unmistakably architectural in inspiration but so well disguised you might think it was the base of a building, or perhaps a sideboard, even a fitment for a conservatory. You might imagine it built of stone, rather than wood. Anything but a piano.

From the Classical allusions one can only presume this was meant to be an exploration of "Grecian or modern".

But, despite its monumental look and whatever one may think of the realisation of his ideas, there were some very important theoretical considerations behind this design by Edward Buckton Lamb.

What Lamb intended, we learn from his comments,[95] was a revolution in which manufacturers would move away from the grand piano to small instruments that would fit into most houses; that could be placed in any position in a room; would look good from all directions; might be "constructed in the most simple manner, or….can be richly decorated"; and, particularly, would be made small enough for the purposes of a singer whose voice could ring out over the top of the instrument.

In this design, wrote Lamb, "the whole body of the instrument is….kept below the performer, which renders it equal to the horizontal grand piano; while it occupies much less space than the latter instrument, and it is superior as an article of furniture."

Lamb argued that: "As all the sides could be finished alike, it can be placed in almost any situation, so that the performer can face the company, and thus the full effect of the voice can be heard; and, if surmounted with vases of glass or alabaster, bronze figures, candelabra, or other ornaments, it would form an agreeable acquisition to the drawing room."

His design was intended, he said, "as a hint to manufacturers" because he considered the grand piano "presented the greatest difficulties to surmount: the form prescribed by its uses, the great space required for it in a room and the very un-architectural character it assumed, set me to consider whether some alterations could not be made, so as to embrace all the utility of the present instrument with more beauty."

In Lamb's view although the grand piano was "the most perfect instrument now in use" it was of an awkward shape; "almost impossible" to imbue with any expression of style; and occupied so much space in "a moderate-sized house" that it had generally been replaced by the upright grand piano.

This upright grand, he said, was certainly more compact and much might be done with it by way of decoration but it was "seldom distinguished by any marks of judgement or good taste".

If an upholsterer made the design the proportions were "inconsistent" and "the cornice is a crowning absurdity of massive ovolo and turned beads". To produce "fitness of expression" it was not necessary to have columns.

But Lamb had another serious objection to the upright grand because, he argued, "the dulcet tones" of the singer were lost in the silk that faced them on the top half of the instrument.

"All this is known and acknowledged to be a defect by all makers", he wrote. "I am surprised that no remedy for the evil has been attempted by keeping the whole body of the instrument below the head of the performer."

Lamb saw the way ahead when he pointed out that "Cabinet, cottage, and other small pianofortes, are sufficiently below the voice generally for all the purposes of a singer".

What these comments showed was the essential designer's approach of an architect thinking of form, use, space and the position of the piano within a room.

But I have to confess that when I first saw Lamb's "stone piano", I had a curious feeling of *déjà vu*. Could he have stolen the idea from someone else?

Not so. I realised it had reminded me of a later design—although they are not identical, there is a similar, monumental feeling in the illustration of an 1872 piano[96] by E.W. Godwin, who also experimented with Anglo Grecian. It is no surprise that Godwin, one of the foremost designers of the century, felt that the published drawing of his piano was "unfortunate, as it gives this design a heavy look, more like stone than woodwork. This, however, is not the case in reality".

The fourth piano design in Loudon's "Encyclopaedia" *(see page 192)* was quite different but again, according to the furniture historian John Gloag,[97] was by Lamb.

This was a tall, dominating "triple division" cabinet piano[98] seen as the most important piece in a Gothic drawing room, hardly Gothic as we know it but, unmistakably, Lamb's very own interpretation.

No doubt taking inspiration from Church architecture, Lamb gave his cabinet piano four crocketed pinnacles, sitting over three "cloudburst" silk panels and a curved piano lid with large, ornamented hinges. Below were three panels and, at the front, two hefty columns supporting the keyboard. There was also a matching stool.

Photo by courtesy of The Colt Clavier Collection, Bethersden, Kent

Throughout his career Robert Wornum seems to have tried to miniaturise the instruments that he made and the grand piano was no exception.

This Wornum "Pocket Grand" of 1837 in The Colt Clavier Collection is of special interest on a number of fronts, especially as one of the early attempts to reduce the size of the traditional grand: This one being 5ft 6in in length and 3ft 9in in width.

Mr C.F. Colt believed that Wornum began manufacturing "this type of instrument in about 1830".

The question is: Did Wornum employ a Designer, or was the final form the inevitable result of his mechanical efforts, with a few stylistic flourishes added in his cabinet making shop? Plate No.282.

Photo by courtesy of the Metropolitan Museum of New York

It is my view that this piano by George Henry Blake, c.1840, is the outstanding British art grand piano of the period 1800 to 1850, although not to my personal taste. For once history does not leave us scratching our head—Inset in the lid is a silver plate stating "Designed and Executed by George Henry Blake, London". Described as being a grand piano "of unequalled magnificence", it was made for the wife of Lord Foley, Baron of Kidderminster. Plate No.283.

Blake and a Remarkable Art Piano

One rare instance where we can give certain proof of the designer of a highly decorated pre-1850 piano and see the finished article concerns an Erard[99] from the firm's London factory which was the conception of George Henry Blake".[100]

This grand piano "of unequalled magnificence" and stated to have been made for the wife of Lord Foley, Baron of Kidderminster, is in my view the most important British Art Piano of the period 1800-1850 although, personally, I care for it not. A mite gaudy for this old (aesthetic) Puritan's taste.

The Blake grand is as sumptuous as any created by a British designer, though a mirror to Continental fashion, in which dominant female heads surmount the top of each leg, bursting forth from swirling decoration as though an Art Nouveau designer had decided to visit the Planet 50 years early.

Poor old Apollo, a mere male, is put firmly in his place underneath, a midget with lyre perched on a lion's head, atop the heavily scrolled understretcher.

Suggested to be c.1840, the Blake grand is now in the Metropolitan Museum of Art, New York and bears monograms of the Foley family, one of which is probably that of Thomas Henry, Baron Foley.

Some might think it over the top but it cannot be denied that the Blake grand was the grand gesture: Aristocratic taste indulged for its own sake. One is reminded of Vanbrugh: "Quality always distinguishes itself....women of rank always buy things because they have not occasion for 'em".[101]

In the view of the expert on musical instrument decoration, Christoph Rueger, although the design was by Blake it was "a product of the first wave of neo-Baroque that swept France after 1830....before spreading to Britain. The instrument is clearly a child of the famous French parent company *(Erard)*."[102]

While Mr Rueger's comment is controversial it cannot be denied that that there are historical Continental precedents where sculptures were carved underneath the main case of keyboard instruments—the 18th Century Venetian harpsichord[103] in the Musikhistorisk Museum, Copenhagen, which has two overgrown putti and a winding acanthus; and, unquestionably one of the finest decorated musical instruments in the world, the Italian harpsichord[104] of c.1650, now in the Metropolitan Museum, New York, where three golden tritons bear the instrument on their shoulders, a putto carried by dolphins rides behind and life-size matching statues sit on either side.

Words seem insufficient to describe this marvel.

I have no doubt that Blake also set about trying to make a large splash.

As another expert wrote, his instrument has "Extremely ornate casework with marquetry intarsia, gilded bronze, inlays of ivory and mother-of-pearl, coloured woods; lion masks" and "female heads in large medallions at top of each leg".[105]

Bearing in mind the cascading opulence of this piano and the fact that it was made in association with one of the world's best known piano firms, Erard, we are left with a curious mystery: Who was George Henry Blake?

Of Blake's part in the making of this extraordinary art object, now sitting in one of America's great museums, there can surely be no doubt: Inset in the lid is a silver plate stating "Designed and Executed by George Henry Blake, London".[106]

The British origins of this spectacular instrument are further confirmed by the ink signing in the keywell of a workman's name "Wm Barnes" and the name "Nettlefold" stamped on a lock with "VR/ Patent" below a Crown.

Given that Erards worked with internationally known artists in the creation of such "specials" I presumed it would need but the simplest check to supply Blake's history. How wrong I was.

The Royal Academy has no knowledge of George Henry Blake. He does not appear in any of the standard reference books. Neither could I find him in the many lesser known works through which I trawled.

Two piano firms named Blake were in existence somewhere around this period but neither of them is so far known to have included George Henry Blake.

I had the uncomfortable feeling I had somehow missed the obvious. How would it be possible for such an artist or designer not to be recorded somewhere?

Fortunately I have been saved, just as I was going to Press, by the impressive knowledge of Mr Martin Levy, the Principal of H. Blairman and Sons of Mayfair and one of the country's leading experts on 19th Century furniture.[107]

Mr Levy was able to tell me: "The Blake family were marquetry makers as well as probably cabinet makers. There was a Robert Blake at 8, Stephen Street, Tottenham Court Road, London, from 1826 until at least 1840.

"From 1842 the firm was known as George Blake & Brothers and after 1847 George Henry Blake is recorded at 53, Mount Street, London. There is a table in the V. and A. (formerly at Corsham Court) with the label of Messrs Blake, 130, Mount Street, Berkeley Square.

"George Henry Blake died in 1859 and Alfred Blake, presumably his brother, in 1866."

Subsequent research by Mr Levy[108] has identified a marquetry table at Goodwood House, Sussex, that is almost certainly by Blake and it appears that the firm carried on until at least 1880.

According to the Metropolitan's official Inventory description the piano case of Blake's lavish creation was made with a satinwood veneer over an oak and softwood carcass, decorated with marquetry of various dyed and natural woods, ivory, mother-of-pearl and metal.[109]

In the centre of the lid is a trophy composed "of hurdy-gurdy, tambourine, viol and bow, lute, pan-pipes, hunting horn and French horn, sheets of music and volume of Beethoven's Symphonies".

The lid is "bordered with animal and human grotesques and floral sprays offsetting reserves containing representations in etched ivory of Persephone (Aphrodite), Ceres, Bacchus, woman and child warming themselves at fire, shepherd boy and dog and lion supporters of Foley shield".

The reserves are in ivory alternating with depictions in marquetry of rustic dancers and music-makers in 18th Century dress. The underbrace, music stand and pedals all have marquetry floral patterns.

Below the main body of the case is the "reclining statuette of Apollo with lyre in painted wood, resting on base overlaid with gilt leopard's masks".

The whole instrument has a heavy gilt wood edging in Louis XV style, incorporating flowers, scrolls, musical instruments, shells, masks of Bacchus, Apollo, Diana (crowned with crescent moon) and Venus (crowned with star) on knees of legs and mask of wind god blowing above pedals".

The inlays include holly, mahogany, burr-walnut, tulipwood and ebony.

On the front and back of the lid is a double "F" for Foley, entwined and surmounted by a Baron's coronet.

The arms on the front of the lid in marquetry are probably those of Thomas, Baron Foley (1780-1833) but those of other members of the Foley family have also been identified. Supporting the heraldry is the Foley motto "Ut Prosim" (*That I may be of use*).

A scene that appears near the coat of arms has been identified as being after one of the "Fêtes Venetiennes" by Watteau.

In the judgement of the musical instrument historian Emanuel Winternitz: "This pianoforte is the most lavishly decorated Erard piano, and probably has the most exquisite intarsias of any musical instrument ever made....The vast profusion of detail is, in the end, rendered homogeneous and beautiful to the beholder by the rich golden hue of the satinwood case, which suffuses the whole instrument"[110]

Mr Winternitz supports the attributed date of c.1840 on the basis that the lock was made during the reign of Queen Victoria (who had come to the throne in 1837) but that the arms of the 4th Baron Foley do not yet include those of his wife, whom he married in 1849.

The Blake piano is such a sumptuous art object that I think this is a clear instance where one can argue that the Designer piano has translated itself into an Art Piano. Such pianos demonstrate that you did not have to depend solely on the paint pot for eye appeal.

But, of course, implicit in that judgement is the same criticism that can be levelled at the artist painted pianos: That art objects like the Blake grand could never be produced for even a modest proportion of the population.

George Henry Blake was creating what was presumably his greatest work for a minority of one. Just imagine what the cost of such a piano would have been.

As a writer in "Chambers's Journal" was to recognise a few years later, they might have "pianos adorned in richest carvings, built of costliest woods and illustrative of all the wealth, ingenuity and tastefulness of the age" but "better still, little Quaker-like pianos of white wood, fine tone and most moderate price".[111]

You might have thought Blake's creation was so out of the ordinary that it would have made a splash in artistic, architectural or musical circles. If so, I cannot so far discover any lingering impressions. Perhaps it remained hidden in the drawing room of a country house.

Even if they had known of it there is not the slightest doubt that its Louis XV trappings would have been anathema to Morris and his fellow Goths.

The Blake grand must at least have remained a folk memory to those at Erard's London factory but, if so, no obvious proof remains that this particular instrument influenced contemporary piano design.

Yet the pervasive spirit of Louis XV and the florid gilt of French taste lived on in British homes in a stream of reproduction pianos and furniture well into the following century. For cynical British makers who lacked fresh ideas it was always a profitable banker.

Photo by courtesy of Mr Tony Bingham

I was forced to revise my ideas about Dr John Steward when, thanks to the well known dealer in ancient musical instruments, Mr Tony Bingham, I was given a set of photos of a piano I had no idea ever existed...an UPRIGHT version of the "Euphonicon". That it comes from Dr Steward there seems no doubt since it bears the inscription "Euphonicon Boudoir Invented by John Steward Esq. and manufactured by Beale & Steward. 201 Regent St. London". From its unusual deep blue and brown colour scheme to its Rococo swirls you know immediately that this was the work of a designer. But who? Plate No.284.

Photo by courtesy of The Victoria and Albert Museum

Some designs spring, so self-evidently, from the mechanical conception that you wonder whether a furniture designer was ever needed (rather like a beautiful motorway bridge with a flying curve, which hardly needs an architect). Here we have Dr John Steward's 1841 invention, the "Euphonicon", in which the overt display of part of the works dictates the unusual shape and appearance of the piano. What I should have taken more into consideration was the careful design of the fretwork below. Plate No.285.

Dr Steward the Inventor

Apart from design books and magazines, another way of identifying some piano designers came when ingenious inventors patented their ideas.

Thus we learn of Dr John Steward, the man who invented the "Euphonicon" of 1841, with its harp shaped, exposed metal frame and strings. But with men like Dr Steward, one feels, any subsequent aesthetic was the addendum to the invention, though sometimes none the worse for that.

The "Euphonicon", though still intriguing, was design on the Richard Rogers principle, the piano works exposed to the air much as our architect now places his lifts and gas pipes on the outside of buildings. With Dr Steward's instrument I believe his primary intention was the quality of sound thus obtained.

But I am having to revise my ideas of Dr Steward. Perhaps I underestimated the gentleman.

Thanks to a remarkable personality of the music world, Mr Tony Bingham, the well known Hampstead dealer in old musical instruments, I have managed to acquire a set of photos of a piano of which I can find no previous illustration: An UPRIGHT "Euphonicon" on which the nameboard clearly reads "Euphonicon Boudoir Invented by John Steward Esq. and manufactured by Beale & Steward. 201 Regent St. London".

I know of no other like it and the case, with its careful detailing, immediately announces itself as the work of a designer. It is in a most unusual deep blue and brown colour scheme and, although it is a conventional upright shape, there are wild Rococo curls at the sides and similar supports under the keyboard.

In the cases of A.G. Pugin and Nicholson we have pre-1850 designs for Gothic pianos but no sign of any actual piano made to their drawings. Here we have that unusual article, a real-life, pre-1850 Gothic piano of merit but no clue to the identity of the Designer. What we can say is that it was made by a quality firm, Collard and Collard and is given a date of c.1845 by the Victoria and Albert Museum. From various points in the design it seems possible to me that the design was made by a follower of Welby Pugin. Plate No.286.

Photo by courtesy of The Victoria and Albert Museum

Pugin's Anonymous Follower

One Gothic design that we can judge from the real article is a Collard and Collard upright of c.1845, now in the Victoria and Albert Museum.[112]

It has an undoubted touch of quality in the workmanship and that it was the work of a designer can be seen immediately.

If the date of c.1845 is accurate then we must immediately enquire: To what degree might this have been influenced by the publications and furniture of Welby Pugin?

The intricate tracery of the panels above the keyboard reminds you of some of Pugin's work and, more so, the linenfold panels at the bottom because, although originally an ancient device, Pugin dearly loved his linenfold panelling.

But what is one to make of the roundels placed amidst the carving, each with its own portrait head? My learned correspondent says: "I think the four head-roundels….are definitely an early-Renaissance motif; and if they were wainscoting I would think of its five upper sections as having the frames used for 'fielded panels', a post-mediaeval treatment."[113]

It might be remembered, however, that according to Clive Wainwright: "A considerable number of his (*Pugin's*) pieces are inspired by Renaissance prototypes rather than just mediaeval ones as might be expected."[114]

Does one presume that this piano was designed by a Pugin follower?

At much later dates Collard and Collard worked with designers of the quality of Charles Bevan and C.A.F. Voysey and the firm could trace their descent from previous owners who proved their taste for quality cabinet making, Muzio Clementi and, prior to that, Longmann and Broderip. But the mystery designer of this 1845 upright remains another of our puzzles.

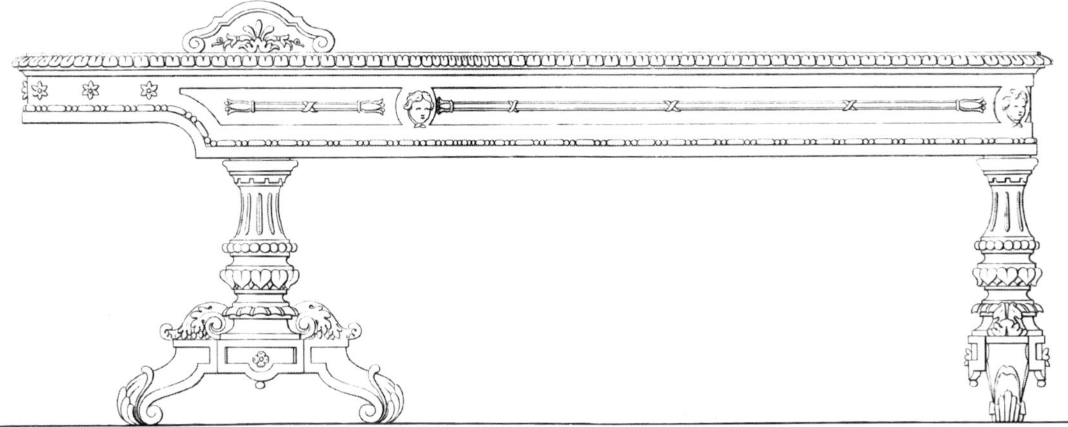

Illustration courtesy of The Bodleian Library

The Designer Henry Whitaker must have been an unusual article in pre-1850 Britain: He was hostile to French ideas and convinced of the superiority of British ways. Which, paradoxically, did not prevent him having great faith in his own interpretation of the Italian style. In his 1847 book, "Practical Cabinet Maker and Upholsterer's Treasury of Designs", Whitaker provided this design for a grand piano "in the Italian style". Plate No.287.

Henry Whitaker: British is Best

It should not be thought that the Late Regency and Early Victorian Goths had the field to themselves with piano design. To earn a living, designers had to follow fashion (often French) and prove their mastery of different styles.

For example, Collards themselves produced a very ornate Rococo grand, designer unknown, c.1835, with cabriole legs.[115]

Another prominent designer who turned his attention away from Gothic was Henry Whitaker but it seems unlikely you would find him trying to imitate the French.

Author of books including "Designs of Cabinet Upholstery Furniture in the Most Modern Style" (1825) and "Practical Cabinet Maker and Upholsterer's Treasury of Designs" (1847), Whitaker was the man who believed that British was best and had an evident hostility to French design.[116]

Paradoxically, he saw nothing wrong with the "Italian style", presumably so long as a Briton was responsible for the interpretation.

In his "Treasury" of 1847 Whitaker provided designs for a grand piano[117] and a cabinet piano,[118] both "in the Italian style".

Firms with whom Whitaker collaborated were Holland and Son and Bantings and his clients included the Dukes of Devonshire and the Marquis of Exeter.[119]

His conviction of the superiority of British design over the Continentals was demonstrated in a long letter he wrote to "The Builder" during the staging of the 1851 Exhibition, in which he maintained that "there is not a foreign article....that could give our upholsterers a single new idea, or help to raise the mind of the artist or artizan employed by them....the British furniture department is infinitely more elegant than the foreign".[120]

From his 1847 book it is obvious that Whitaker had given much thought to piano design, describing the instrument as "a piece of furniture which has hitherto set designers at defiance, and which, although an expensive article, has always been unsightly".

Whitaker's "Italian" grand piano, which the caption states was "for Burttinyoung's Patent Works", showed elaborately carved supports and further carving round the case, including profile heads. Clinkscale states that a piano inventor named Frederick Handel Burkinyoung was a "gentleman of Baker Street" who registered patents in Britain and France.[121]

The cabinet piano by Whitaker was described as a "Vertical Piano in the Italian Style" and, again, was much decorated with what looked like carving, especially in the

Illustration courtesy of The Bodleian Library

A second design offered by Henry Whitaker in his 1847 book was this design for a cabinet piano, which he described as a "Vertical Piano in the Italian style". Whitaker, who is known to have worked with Holland & Son and Bantings, had evidently given much consideration to piano design saying that it was "a piece of furniture which has hitherto set designers at defiance, and which, although an expensive article, has always been unsightly". Plate No.288.

elaborately scrolled supports and cheeks for the keyboard. It seems possible that the oblong panel above and arched panel below may have contained silk—but this is not certain.

When Whitaker makes specific reference to his grand piano design being for "Burttinyoung's Patent Works" it is hard to believe that he was not working in direct association with a piano inventor and that this did not result in actual pianos being made. If so, I have yet to see them.

Instead, when I traipse through auction rooms or private piano collections, I come across mysteries of the opposite sort: fascinating pianos actually constructed by famous firms... but we have not a clue as to who might have designed them.

From my sampling of the literature and records, and travels round auction rooms and Museums, I am satisfied that there were significant British piano designers of the period 1800-1850 who have yet to be identified and given credit for their work.

Many of these Designers were brave enough to reject Reproduction and bring forth pianos that were not only practical but also sold on eye-appeal. Such products constituted an open challenge: Was it the Fine Artists or the Designers who could provide the future of the British piano?

Photo by courtesy of The Smithsonian Institution (National Museum of American History)

To the old-time hot gospellers all lessons were "salutary" but, for those about to set out on the trail of Early English Artist Painted Pianos, I assure you that none come more "salutary" than this mysterious, highly decorated British grand.

At first glance it looks fascinating. Across its painted panels pose three goddesses, draped around with floral garlands and under the lid are further goddesses in a pastoral scene.

Now to be found in the Collection of The White House, Washington, it declares itself to have been made in 1799 and to be the work of Britain's most respected maker, John Broadwood and Son.

But expert opinion says: The nameboard is doubtful; the piano may have been made either c.1806 or c.1810; and that, "because of the apparent fakery with the nameboard, the decoration is suspect". Plate No.289.

Early British Artist Painted Pianos

Chapter Seven

Anyone foolish enough to contemplate writing about Artist Painted Pianos ought to be given a health warning: This subject may destroy beyond redemption any hopes you have for credibility, or what may pass as your reputation.

The situation was best set out by Professor Edward L. Kottick, writing about harpsichords: "Describing the decoration of outer cases is problematical, since they are frequently redecorated, sometimes many times over, and often were not original to the instrument. It is also possible that some cases were not painted at all, receiving their decoration years later."[1]

All this applies equally to pianos.

Fortunately for the student, in the Victorian period there is often abundant contemporary evidence of the artist painted pianos of such as Sir Edward Burne-Jones but the earlier the piano the more you should question and, I should add, there is certain proof that the late decoration of early pianos (for whatever motive) was still being practised after 1900.

So with that proviso and considerable trepidation, I venture forth....

Unless it has suffered the fate of many an old cassone or harpsichord and had its paintings ripped out to make into pictures for our walls[2] then, somewhere out there, may be Britain's first artist painted piano.

I must confess that trying to identify this particular piano is rather akin to practising hepatascopy—one may, like the Ancient Greeks, see signs and omens but there is a noticeable lack of facts.

In short, I do not have any certain answer to the question despite some years of effort.

I suppose that one should first define one's terms. By artist painted I do not mean merely decorated with Classical swags or Rococo scrolls, trailing flowers, ornamented bands, festoons, arabesques, or a cartouche, however appealing or skilled these might appear and no matter that painters were employed.

In the late 18th Century, in Britain, such efforts were most often relegated to a subsidiary role, usually on square pianos and confined to the nameboard above the piano keys. Or, like blooms in a secret garden, sometimes mysteriously painted on the interior.[3]

Just when and where did the decorated "nameboard" technique re-emerge for the newly introduced piano?

Such subsidiary painting can be seen on an early square by William Southwell of Dublin which has flowery swags painted on the nameboard, designed in a way "entirely uncharacteristic of the London pianos of the time".[4] But other firms were to become associated with nameboard painting, such as Rolfe, Astor and Clementi.[5]

Southwell is suggested to have supplied the retailers Longman and Broderip with pianos[6] and it is tempting to look for a link between the Irish maker and square pianos sold by Longman which have nameboard painting.[7]

A piano that demonstrates the great charm of this technique is a Longman and Broderip square of c.1786 in the Beurmann Collection, Hamburg, which in photos shows artist painting of what I take to be roses on either side of the central inscription.

In 1798 the composer and piano soloist Muzio Clementi made a financial investment in Longman and Broderip and the name of the firm eventually evolved to become Clementi and Co... so it is no surprise to find that a firm that employed this kind of minor decorative painting more than most was Clementi and Co. Through them the tradition lived on.

Clementi's pianos often have elegant casework. In their instruments you will find a brio, an artistic flourish that could not be suppressed, but always with a sense of proportion.

That fine scholar Michael Cole points out that with the Clementi squares "many of them were decorated above the keys with exquisitely painted sprays of flowers by an artist whose identity still remains a mystery".[8]

We get occasional tantalising clues to this world of the nameboard painters when Mr C.F. Colt realised[9] that the fascia of one of his squares by William Rolfe, dated 1805, was painted with flowers in identical fashion to his Clementi upright grand of 1816.

Could it be the same artist employed by two different piano makers? Perhaps a specialist sub-contractor? Or could there be another explanation?

Mr Colt suggests that the floral painting on his Clementi and Rolfe pianos was "a perfect example of the eighteenth and nineteenth century pattern book 'choice' that was available to purchasers, who could add their own name if they so wished—maker, dealer, or even owner....As one would expect, the design has been hand-painted in oils, and the music-loving botanist will quickly spot everlasting sweet peas, rosa centifolia, convolvulus, Turk's cap lilies and blue auriculas in this charming garland."[10]

Mr Colt believed that "Flower paintings incorporated with the name on the nameboard were in vogue from about 1796 to 1807, though some makers had dainty little painted etiquettes till the mid 1820s."[11]

Michael Cole, author of two authoratative books on the early piano, tells me of an experience that raises another possibility.[12]

Clementi, he wrote, supplied "ready made" pianos for two or three other firms, among them John Longman of Cheapside, and "I once had a Clementi and a Longman square in succession through my workshop, made in the same year from the same batch of timber, with the same inlays and identical sprays of flowers painted on the front".

Photo by courtesy of The Royal College of Music, London

The painted decoration of the nameboards of British square pianos from the 1790s to the 1810s became a highly skilled sub-division of piano making...almost a minor art form in its own right. But given the conservative, almost Puritanical, approach to the decoration of British pianos, where did the idea come from?

The only thought I have is that, may be, they were inspired by the superb marquetry on the nameboards of English spinets of the 17th and Early 18th Centuries. This wonderfully appealing example comes from an anonymous spinet of 1708 in the fine Collection of the Royal College of Music. Curiously, I have seen the same motif of the two birds (blackbirds?) facing each other on a number of British samplers of the period and later. And a more formalised version of the "two birds" design is to be found on the back of a 17th Century oak joined armchair at Rufford Hall, Lancashire, dated 1689. I wonder when the design first emerged? Plate No.290.

Photo by courtesy of the Hackett Collection, Photo by David Hackett

Botanical themes were favourites when it came to artist painting of the nameboards of Late 18th Century British square pianos. One of the best exponents was William Rolfe as shown in this c.1805 Rolfe square in the Hackett collection and it is particularly interesting that at least one of his patterns is to be found years later reproduced on a Clementi piano. Did a particular worker change his job? Did both firms choose a design from a pattern book? Or was there some form of collaboration between Rolfe and Clementi? Plate No.291.

◀ A firm that always produced pianos of taste and quality was also bound to decorate their pianos with style and finesse. This elegant name panel, topped with flowers and musical instruments seems to have been a Clementi favourite and was still being used on this square of c.1820 sold by Piano Auctions Ltd. at Conway Hall, London, as Lot 21 on June 30th., 2005. Plate No.292.

Photo by courtesy of Piano Auctions Ltd.

Photo by courtesy of Besbrode Pianos of Leeds

Other makers had their own versions of floral decoration and this one appears on an undated square by Nixon of Dublin in the stock of the large Northern piano dealers, Besbrode of Leeds. Plate No.293.

Photo by courtesy of The Beurmann Collection, Hamburg

This floral decoration is very distinctive on a Longman and Broderip square of 1786. The firm were often described as retailers but undoubtedly had their own "house style". Plate No.294.

A careful study of the detailed research of Dr Clinkscale discloses that a Clementi square piano of 1803[13] had a "floral painted nameboard"; another of 1806[14] "sweet peas on the nameboard"; a third of 1807-10[15] a nameboard with "inscription elaborately lettered and framed with lutes, open book, and floral sprays painted above". As late as 1818[16] a Clementi square still had a nameboard with "painted spray at the ends".

Of course, there comes a point at which even the decoration of the nameboard can transform itself into something more and there is a decidedly exceptional example of this with a Clementi of 1798-1799 in the Chris Maene Collection in Belgium.

This is something of a surprise because, this time, we find the painted nameboard is on a grand piano.

Above the piano keys is the familiar painted foliage and decorative drapes but on either side is to be found an oval which contains a painted allegorical figure, evoking memories of Angelica Kauffmann and Bartlozzi. I have not had an opportunity of studying the instrument at first hand but, in photos, the right hand oval shows a figure with lyre accompanied by a Cupid.

This seems to follow on from an earlier grand piano by Longman and Broderip (Clementi's predecessors) of 1795 in the Cobbe Collection[17] which also had elaborate foliate decoration of the nameboard but without the allegorical figures on the Maene example. Could both have been the unknown Clementi artist at work again?

However, what I have in mind by pictorial painting is something more ambitious: The main body of the case decorated by a fine artist with an actual scene or figure subject.

If we look at the "pre-piano" age the special decoration of early European keyboard instruments reached particular heights in the 16th Century and there are a few of these pictorially painted survivors in British museums.[18]

For example, there is to be found in the Victoria and Albert Museum a claviorganum of 1579 by Lodewijk Theeuwes of London painted with "a scene of Orpheus charming the beasts".[19]

Some twenty-plus early English virginals have survived[20] and among them is one by Gabriel Townsend of 1641, now in a Belgium museum, where the interior lid shows what I take to be a Jacobean version of Orpheus strumming his lute to a lion, a lamb and a varied menagerie, against a stylised landscape. Another elongated picture on the case portrays a coast with sailing boats.[21]

The Victoria and Albert Museum has a virginal of 1642 by Thomas White of London, the lid and drop-front of which bear "rather naïve paintings showing peasants hay-making and gentry promenading".[22]

Another virginal of 1655 by John Loosemore of Exeter opens to reveal decorative paintings "with scenes of a stag-hunt, shipping, Adam and Eve, and various birds, in a country setting".[23]

It is known that Sir James Thornhill designed the lid of a harpsichord for Handel (the design now in the Fitzwilliam Museum) with an allegory in which "Peace introduced Arts & Sciences, who sacrifices to Apollo".[24]

A harpsichord expert, Raymond Russell, pointed out[25] that John Broadwood seems to have sold a harpsichord painted in some degree because, on December 24th., 1774, his records contained the entry: "Miss Skeine bought a octava harpsichord, Blew bordered, No. 710".

But Mr Russell added that "the writer has never seen an original painted English harpsichord, unless the Tisseran at Woollas be so considered".

So any British examples of this time must have been great rarities and pictorial painting of early keyboard instruments was far more a Continental tradition, seen applied to harpsichords like those made by the renowned Ruckers family of Antwerp, whose standing was such they belonged to the Guild of St. Luke, the Painters' Guild.[26] The family firm flourished for at least three generations from 1579.

It was one of the Ruckers harpsichords, painted by Van der Meulen in 1614, that was subsequently to inspire Sir Edward Burne-Jones[27] on the path that led to his "Orpheus" grand, the most outstanding artist-painted case produced by The British Art Piano movement.

Photo by courtesy of The Beurmann Collection, Hamburg

Some makers took pleasure in having their own names presented in decorative fashion. Here an oval, surrounded by a kind of intertwined rope pattern, frames the name of Longman and Broderip on a 1786 square in the Beurmann Collection. Plate No.295.

Photo by courtesy of The Beurmann Collection, Hamburg

A more elaborate oblong with frills was preferred by Christopher Gerock of Cornhill, London on this c.1825 cabinet piano. Plate No.296

A different kind of oval was employed by Nixon of Dublin to frame his name on this square piano of unknown date. Plate No.297.

Photo by courtesy of Besbrode Pianos of Leeds

Rubens and Watteau are both stated[28] to have painted Ruckers harpsichords and one, claimed to be owned by Handel, had not only paintings of flowers and birds but "a monkeys' concert in progress".[29]

In Venice particularly, and in parts of Italy, there was, likewise, a strong tradition of artist painted instruments.

However, according to a prominent pioneer of modern research on piano case design, Michael I. Wilson: "In England....the convention of the painted case (of early keyboard instruments) virtually died out during the eighteenth century, although a few examples in both rococo and neo-classical taste are extant".[30]

Possibly, there might be a logical explanation for this about face: The eternal battle between adherents of British Good Taste and The Extroverts.

The contrast between the unadorned Quaker meeting house and the vivid polychromy of Pugin's Churches; the starkness of Dresser's metalware against the Rococo of the West End silversmiths; black basalt against pottery fairings splashed with colour; Gimson and his pure Cotswold furniture against the Omega Group; the British City gent in his bowler, dark jacket and pin stripes against the King's Road; the concrete of Neo Brutalism against the fripperies of Post Modern: This is an unending struggle reflecting the contradictions of the British character.

Nowhere do we get a more revealing insight into such cultural divides than in the letter written on February 2nd., 1637, by the Secretary of State to King Charles I, Sir Francis Windebank, to an agent in Brussels.[31]

Sir Francis was negotiating the purchase of a harpsichord for the King and nothing but a Ruckers would do. His agent, himself an artist, chose a Ruckers with a painting of Cupid and Psyche by a painter whose name might ring a bell, one Rubens.

The Secretary of State was scornful. He wrote: "If the instrument for sounde and goodnesse be right, I do not much respect the accessories of ornament or paintings, and therefore if you can meete with a very good one plaine and without these curiosities, I should rather make choice of such a one."

This was an argument that was to surface time after time through later centuries: Quality of sound, or beauty of case?

One may pause here to observe that some of the sparse, economical and utilitarian British keyboard instruments that filled this decorative void nevertheless resulted in objects of aesthetic appeal.

Few designs, relying purely on form, have ever come out more instantly eye-catching that the spinets of the Hitchcocks and their competitors in the early 1700s. For my own part I have come across nothing better since in the design of musical instruments. Those who have seen Concorde fly over London for the first time will know the feeling on catching sight of a Hitchcock spinet.[32]

However, this was hardly an encouraging environment for the overt decoration of the piano, when it emerged on this scene as a newly invented instrument and the first British pianos were faithful to British sobriety and reserve.

Nothing could have been simpler than the little square pianos[33] first introduced to London in the 1760s by Johann Christoph Zumpe, an immigrant from Saxony. Should we assume that the austere "casework" of his pianos ("usually unornamented save for a line of inlay"[34]) was a reflection of Germanic ideas, an attempt to cut costs, or the result of prevailing taste and his customers rejection of conspicuous ostentation?

Price, I feel, played the largest part, Zumpe being able to sell his basic model for 16 guineas.[35]

The 18th Century British grand piano employed real cabinet maker's skills but the great majority of those produced still retained the essential reticence of the British approach at this time.

The "British style" of grand piano was a seamless continuation from the harpsichord case style of Tabel, Shudi and Kirkman, the main characteristic being inlaid veneer panels, usually in mahogany, along the sides of the main case. The beauty of the wood itself, with cross banding the sole concession to dramatic effect, was the essential ingredient.

"It is somewhat strange that neither of the Shudis (father and son) attempted any decoration of the cases of their instruments other than that of skilful cabinet work", wrote the expert William Dale.[36]

Against this background of sober restraint some began to develop more ambitious casework, employing fine contrasting woods and veneers. The most startling examples were those involving Robert Adam, Frederick Beck, Robert Stodart and Thomas Sheraton, but these were rare exceptions.

As the 18th Century neared its end the pace of change increased with fashion but, as though semi-apologetically, the most pyrotechnic shows of inlaying skill were reserved to the nameboards of square pianos. Just as minor painted decoration, when it appeared, was very largely to be found on such nameboards.

When then did the British artist painted piano, with work of a definite pictorial character, emerge to reclaim that ancient style of Lodewijk Theeuwes, Thomas White and John Loosemore?

Since the piano was invented in Florence before 1700 by Bartolomeo Cristofori you may imagine that we must search the whole of the 18th Century for this elusive article. But, according to experts, there are only the flimsiest of details of claimed early British pianos and the first known square pianos in Britain date from the mid 1760s[37], the grand piano following. For example John Broadwood, who gave his name to Britain's greatest piano company, is not thought to have built his first grand piano until 1784 and it was sold in January, 1785.[38]

So, effectively, if we were to search through the first 50 years of the British piano for pictorial decorations that would range between c.1766 and c.1816.

I was side-tracked in my initial research by a grand piano owned by Queen Victoria and made by Erard's London factory,[39] simply because it was claimed to incorporate earlier paintings that had belonged to "Anne of Austria", a reference that might have indicated either Queen Anne (1549-1580), wife of Philip II of Spain or their grand-daughter, Queen Anne (1601-1666), wife of Louis XIII of France.

Quite apart from the question mark against the date of these paintings (it has been suggested they are Early 18th Century in style[40]) it did not take me long to realise this could not really be a candidate.

Firstly, if such paintings had come from a harpsichord belonging to either of these Queen Anne's they could not be said to be original to the Erard grand piano, itself not constructed until the Victorian period. And, presumably, these paintings were likely to be Spanish, French or Austrian rather than British.

Other contenders began to present themselves—though seldom with clarity.

A painting I had heard about on the famous Don Godoy "Wedgwood Broadwood" grand of 1796, turned out to be a false lead.

The "Don Godoy", now in the Museum of Fine Arts, Boston,[41] is mainly decorated with ceramics but it also has a verre églomisé painting by Salvador Duchen. A number of experts concur, I discovered, that this is but a replacement for an original miniature of Don Godoy by John Taylor. The whereabouts of this "miniature" are not known but an American expert, Mr John Koster, suggests[42] that, from the original design, it seems to have been an allegory—Godoy depicted as a figure enthroned among clouds, with supporting figures placing a crown on his head.

But can one classify a "miniature" as a pictorial panel?

Only the most tantalising details exist of the earliest British artist painted piano that I have been able to trace.

During the French Revolution, from 1789, the Revolutionaries seized the property of executed or exiled aristocrats.

The "Commission of Arts" took possession during this time of 127 keyboard instruments, of which 64 were pianos. Apart from 20 French instruments, 12 of these by Erard, there were 44 others most of which, surprisingly, were English.[43]

This reflected the considerable popularity of English pianos in France, square pianos being known as "Pianos Anglais" and one Parisian advertiser of the time even offering to swap his Stradivari violin for a Zumpe square.[44]

Very unusually, this early British grand piano, given a date of 1798-1799 and now in the Maene Collection, has elaborate artist painting of the nameboard. Bearing the enamel name plaque of Longman, Clementi & Co. and in mahogany it has the traditional panelled sides but the nameboard has two ovals depicting angel musicians together with elaborate swags and drapes. Plate No.298.

A close-up of the satinwood nameboard of the Longman, Clementi & Co. grand of 1798-1799, with holly and stained fruitwood stringing and mahogany crossbanding, showing its two ovals of angel musicians. Plate No.299.

Photos by courtesy of The Chris Maene Collection, Belgium

I have not personally inspected this artist painted square which was illustrated in "The Connoisseur" in September, 1928, to accompany an article by the expert Philip B. James.

On this Longman and Broderip of c.1790 It appears that the customary floral painting of the nameboard has overflowed to decorate the front and other parts of the case. Mr James described it as "Profusely decorated with paintings of unusual quality". Plate No.300.

Photo by courtesy of Messrs Sotheby's of New Bond Street, London

Some firms seemed to show little or no interest in adding artist painted decoration to the nameboard, preferring to rely on inlay but others adopted it enthusiastically. A firm known to have used artist painting in addition to inlay was that of George Astor and this fine example of c.1805 appeared at Sotheby's as Lot 194 on Nov 22nd 1989. It was stated that the maple nameboard, which had holly and stained fruitwood stringing against mahogany cross-banding, was "painted with flowers and foliage". It reminded me somewhat of floral painting on a Longman & Broderip square of c.1786 in the Beurmann Collection. Plate No.301.

As a popular French song of 1771, titled "The Arrival of the Pianoforte", declaimed:

"What, dear friend! from England dost thou come to me

"Alas, how can I declare war upon thee!"[45]

Among English pianos seized during the Revolution were instruments by Pohlmann, Beck, Beyer and Longman & Broderip.

Pohlmann is often claimed to have undertaken orders for square pianos that his friend Zumpe was too busy to complete but it is said that Pohlmann's instruments had burr veneers over the keyboard.[46]

More than one Pohlmann is reported to have been confiscated in France and just such a piano was known to have been taken from Baron Melchior Grimm. The popularity of the Pohlmann instruments can also be judged from the fact that the firm had previously supplied a piano for Gluck when he appeared at the Paris Opéra in 1772.[47]

But the Pohlmann piano we are concerned with was a square seized from the house of the Marbeuf family during The Terror and, thanks to the meticulous book-keeping of the Revolutionaries, we know this was an artist painted piano.

In his scholarly investigation[48] of the seizure of such pianos and harpsichords, Albert G. Hess found the Revolutionaries had established "The eleventh sub-commission of a 'Commission temporaire des arts' to inventory those of the confiscated ancient and foreign instruments which were 'les plus rares, par leur perfection'."

Two musicians served on this Commission, Antonio Bartolomeo Bruni, a composer of operas and Bernard Sarette, first Director of the Conservatoire National.

Number 224 on the list of confiscated instruments was: "A piano by Johannes Pohlmann, Londini fecit 1776; the paintings on the cover are damaged; estimated 800 francs".

They also seized from the Marbeufs "A harpsichord, painted yellow with gilded stripes", made in 1621.

What the paintings on the Pohlmann piano depicted, or what became of this historical instrument, are questions to which I can supply no answers.

The tragic Marbeuf family had more to worry about than the fate of the first British artist painted piano. The Commission reported, without a trace of emotion, that an Erard piano was seized from another woman "found in the apartment which she occupied with the condemned (women) Marbeuf".

Originally this grand piano was thought to be a Broadwood but Professor Andreas Beurmann never believed this and, when he removed overpainting from the nameboard, his judgement was confirmed...it was a Stodart with a suggested date of c.1785. But Professor Beurmann told me that he had been advised that the exterior decoration was of the 19th Century. Plate No.302.

Photo by courtesy of The Beurmann Collection, Hamburg

Time after time I pursued apparently highly promising leads to these elusive, early, artist painted British pianos, only to find how confusing this area of scholarship can be—and how one must be equipped with a great deal more knowledge than I possess.

So it was when I came across another possible candidate. Michael Cole in his book on Broadwood square pianos mentions a Broadwood piano of 1784, made for a Mr Leonard Cazenove, which had "the front painted, in a plain case". But did it survive? Where is it now?

I had also been told of a grand piano by Robert Stodart of 1784 that was decorated with Neo-Classical figures. Eventually I tracked it down to Heaton Hall, Manchester[49] and it did, indeed, prove to be a unique instrument—but the decoration was in inlay, not painted.

However, this caused me to take a harder look at Robert Stodart and I stumbled across a piano that might have come straight out of Hollywood. Eye-stopping hardly does it justice. It does not, however, appear to be the work of Robert Stodart personally but is inscribed[50] "Matthoeus et Gulielmus Stodart, London, Fecerunt", who are suggested to have been Matthew and William, possibly his nephews, who took over the firm about 1794.

This was a Stodart grand, given a date of c.1785, in the noted Collection of Professor Dr. Andreas Beurmann in Hamburg, Germany, with Chinoiserie decorations. But I had imagined that these might just be a few Oriental motifs at the corners or on the nameboard.

When Professor Beurmann kindly sent me a photograph[51] I was able to see what an intriguing British piano had found its way to the Museum für Kunst und Gewerbe.

The whole case, which had a maple veneer, had been covered with Chinoiserie: full-scale scenes round the side, with the keyboard, the legs of the trestle stand and stretcher all decorated in sympathy.

I was able to understand just what Dr Clinkscale meant by "Chinoiserie decorations—heavily painted on the sides, cheeks, outer lid; square tail".[52]

The question is: What is the date of these paintings? Were they contemporary with the case? And was the case indeed c.1785?

I have not myself had the opportunity of inspecting this Stodart but Professor Beurmann told me that he had himself taken advice and been told that the painting was of the 19th Century.[53]

I also understand that when this grand piano appeared at an auction in 1985 it was believed to be a Broadwood.

Professor Beurmann told me: "I bought it announced as a 'Broadwood grand piano, London, c.1785'....But I knew on the first glance that the instrument is not a Broadwood but a Stodart. And after having carefully removed the overpaint on the nameboard, the Stodart signature appeared as expected."[54]

As to the artist and the person for whom this Stodart was commissioned I can offer no clues. The painting is unsigned.

Where might the inspiration have come from for the Stodart's unusual decoration?

It is well known that there were some "Chinese Chippendale" designs in Chippendale's "The Gentleman and Cabinet-Maker's Director", first published in 1754 but expert opinion is that the British interest in this field started in 1736 with the translation into English of a widely read travel book by the Frenchman Du Halde.[55] During the 1750s, pattern books containing "Chinese" designs were published by W. and J. Halfpenny and Matthew Darly.

One of the Victorian experts on the decoration of old musical instruments, A.J. Hipkins, writing in 1888, said that: "Chinese decoration, which was much in vogue in the early part of last century, was not infrequently applied to clavichords and harpsichords.

"As examples of the latter may be mentioned the instrument that belonged to Queen Sophia Dorothea....and the Ruckers clavecin or harpsichord in the Turin Museum."[56]

Whatever the date of the "Chinoiserie" painting on the case of the Stodart I wondered whether the inspiration for these did not come from old lacquer work or ceramics. Or those Late 18th Century longcase clocks in Chinoiserie.

I showed photographs of the Stodart grand to Ms Rose Kerr, the Chief Curator of the Far Eastern Section of the Victoria and Albert Museum and she told me[57] that "the Chinoiserie decoration on the piano does look as if it derives directly from Chinese sources.

"These could possibly have come from gilt lacquer, or porcelain. The scenes ....seem to come from fragments of different stories, and are too incomplete to allow positive identification. Porcelain often used themes taken from 17th and 18th century woodblock prints."

Another expert in the field, Mary Ginsberg of The British Museum, told me that after discussing photos of the piano with colleagues they had reached a consensus that "the overriding influence is Chinese, not Japanese, exemplified by the Mongolian or Manchu fellow....similar in style to Tang dynasty metal silver appliqués which we have seen before."

However, there did not seem to be a story because one lady, wearing "a very un-Chinese hat, seems to have nothing to do with the Mongolian rider, or the couple standing nearby.

"The paintings differ from lacquer decorated in China in a couple of ways. The decoration is much less crowded than on Chinese export furniture.

"Secondly, the scenes are largely figural. The pagodas are there, and the flowers and rocks; but there are also people in distinct scenes, which is not always true in Chinese wares."[58]

The nearest comparison I can think of to the Stodart grand is "An important George III black lacquer and parcel-gilt piano in the manner of Thomas Chippendale" that appeared at auction at Sotheby's of New York in October, 1999.

This was stated[59] to be of the third quarter of the 18th Century and "decorated all over with Chinoiserie figures at various pursuits, birds and foliage, within floral borders."

A hinged, rectangular top, with bow-fronted ends, opened to reveal the instrument.

A Sotheby's expert stated that: "The vogue for furniture veneered with Chinese lacquer panels taken from screens depicting oriental landscapes and figures was a curious survival in the strict Neo-Classical interiors designed by Robert Adam and his contemporaries.

"Most of the known examples were created for bedrooms and ladies dressing rooms or closets, such as the two commodes supplied to Robert Child for the State Bedroom and Etruscan Dressing Room at Osterley, which are richly decorated with oriental scenes in gold on black ground, and ornamented with burnished gold carved ornament in the Neo-Classical taste."

I discovered another early piano, dated to 1786 and now in the Haags Gemeentemuseum, which had been artist painted but once again my hopes were dashed.

This square piano[60] had been made by Zumpe's sometime partner, Gabriel Buntebart, who had by this time entered into a new partnership with a Mr Sievers.

However, this square was a long way distant from Zumpe's first, severe offerings, this one having a Neo-Classical case perched on four tapered, hexagonal legs.

The case had then, at some time, been decorated with ribbon garlands and an artist has painted the interior lid with a picture of romantic couples flirting on a lawn to the sound of music.

It was described[61] by René Clemencic as being "of typical Classicist exterior. The painting on the lid shows an open-air gathering with loving couples elegantly disporting themselves on a lawn around an antique garden vase.

"The party is being entertained by a gesticulating singer who is accompanied by a lutenist and a violin player. It is Rococo in retreat.

"The instrument's case is of fine veneer, discreetly embellished with cordons. The base and the tapering legs have only a minimum of ornamental relief."

However, I was given the sad news[62] (and saved from disastrous error) by Dr Michael Latcham, The Curator of Musical Instruments at the Haags Gemeentemuseum, that the painting was

◀
Did special sub-contractors carry out the highly skilled artist painting of piano nameboards...or could different workmen all have worked from the same pattern books? This upright grand of 1816 is by one of the most prominent makers, Clementi but Mr C.F. Colt found an extraordinary coincidence when he compared its decorated nameboard with that on a Rolfe square of c.1805. It is identical. Plate No.303.

Photo by courtesy of The Colt Clavier Collection

Photo by courtesy of The Colt Clavier Collection, Bethersden, Kent

How could it be that the painted decoration on the nameboard of this square piano of c.1805 by William Rolfe is identical with that on a Clementi upright grand made years later, in 1816? Plate No.304.

Photo by courtesy of The Royal College of Music

The way the Royal College of Music have painstakingly unravelled the secrets of a luxuriously decorated harpsichord of 1531, through the use of modern science, casts fascinating light on the various treatment such rare treasures received as they survived the centuries. And what might, equally, have happened to early British grand pianos that were decorated.

This investigation of the 16th Century harpsichord, one of the most important instruments in their outstanding Collection, was carried out for the College by the Scientific Department of the National Gallery, using optical microscopy and spectrographic analysis with a laser microprobe.

An item guaranteed to stop you in your tracks, the harpsichord was made by Alessandro Trasuntino of Venice, using cypress and poplar, in the 16th Century, and stands on three turned legs with carved padded lion paws.

But it is the decoration that overwhelms you:

"The front of the nameboard has particularly beautiful decoration with Renaissance motifs in gold, oil and ink", states the College's catalogue and this is matched with ivory beads, painting en grisaille, floral decoration and much else.

The exterior is a dark olive green, painted in grisaille but the interior of the lid Is dramatic—"painted in the style of Paris Bordone of Venice (c.1580), depicting Venus and Cupid".

But just what was the date of this case decoration?

In their official catalogue the College tell us how the science revealed that the lowest paint layer was mauvish grey.

Then came a blue-green layer, applied over gesso but this contained Prussian blue "invented in 1704 and adopted widely soon after its introduction".

Finally came the top layers...but these contain artificial ultramarine, "invented in 1828 and verdigris, which was replaced by more stable green pigments later in the 19th Century".

The Royal College's conclusion: "So it is likely that the present case decoration dates from c.1830-50".

The story of this fine old survivor tells us what might have happened to decorated pianos. Plate No.305.

Photo by courtesy of The Royal College of Music

The decoration of the nameboard of the 1531 Trasuntino harpschord is a thing of beauty - Renaissance motifs in gold, oil and ink against inlay of ebony and boxwood. Plate No.306.

of 20th Century origin and "Underneath it is just a normal mahogany instrument!"

Relying in some measure on the remarkable industry of Martha Novak Clinkscale,[63] a lady who evidently thinks in the same world conquering terms as Professor Pevsner; on an 1885 Exhibition of Historic Musical Instruments,[64] and many other sources, I eventually managed to compile a list of a handful of possible British artist painted pianos for the period 1766 to approximately 1810.

I do not suggest for a moment that this list is comprehensive or that the paintings on such pianos are necessarily contemporary with the case—it is simply the known candidates.

One that seemed to be a certain contender was an upright square of 1798 by the man who patented this type of piano in that very year,[65] the great Dublin maker William Southwell.

What little we know of this piano is connected with its display at the "Loan Collection" of Historic Musical Instruments held at the Albert Hall in 1885, staged as a part of the Inventions Exhibition.

According to the official catalogue[66] Southwell's piano was owned by Mr Walter Gilbey at that time and had "Paintings by Angelica Kauffmann".

That it had paintings in the style of the most famous woman painter of the 18th Century I do not doubt but the chances of the paintings being by the lady Royal Academician herself are, I would suggest, somewhere in the range of implausible to negligible.

But where is this Southwell piano now? I have been unable to trace its history after 1885 and, since I hear no news of a Southwell with "Kauffmann" decoration, do wonder whether it now lies in a modern collection, possibly minus these paintings.

The next piano on my list, ostensibly dating to 1799, is one of the most mysterious since there are obvious stylistic links to the decoration on the Stodart inlaid grand of 1784—you might even think that the artist responsible for this work could only have set about his task after seeing the earlier Stodart grand.

Yet just about everything concerning this piano seems open to question: Its date, its maker and the very decoration itself.

That the piano itself is early there appears little doubt. But how early? That it bears the name of a famous British maker can be readily seen. But did he make it? That it seems at first glance to have early decoration would be the conclusion of many. But just when was the decoration made?

Few pianos could claim more fame by association than this "1799" grand piano since it is now in the Collection of The White House, the home in Washington of the American President. Around it have swirled the great events of history.

On the mystery grand, which is in mahogany veneer with crossbanding, sitting on a four-legged trestle stand, the bentside has been divided into three panels "with painted flower garlands and three goddesses in ovals at the centre of each panel". On the inside lid is a matching painting with "two goddesses and wider (pastoral) scene".[67]

The relationship of the decoration to that on the Stodart grand at Manchester is self evident.

But this is a piano that has already raised questions.

The nameboard bears the inscription: "John Broadwood and Son. Great Pulteney Street Golden Square. London 1799" in an oval.

Martha Novak Clinkscale states baldly: "nameboard not original; decorations added c.1810".[68]

John Koster comments that "because of the apparent fakery with the nameboard, the decoration is suspect".[69]

I am indebted to Mr William G. Allman, The Curator of The White House, for investigating the matter further for me.

Mr Allman told me[70] "there are some serious concerns about the piano donated to The White House in 1962. It bears a 1799 name board of John Broadwood & Son that is probably not original.

"A professional examination in 1983 suggested a c.1806 date for the instrument with the case ornamentation probably later.

Photo by courtesy of the Collection of the Gemeentemuseum Den Haag

This striking square is a Buntebart & Sievers piano of 1786 and on the lid is an artist-painted scene showing an apparently typical Classicist exterior of romantic couples flirting on a lawn to the sound of music. But an expert of The Gemeentemuseum stated that the painting is of 20th Century origin. Plate No.307.

"The Smithsonian Institution, where it was stored as a loan for twenty years after its receipt, felt it dated c.1810.

"It has been in White House storage since 1982, with the instrument deemed to have received too much prior repair and the case to be too badly distorted for proper conservation."

The redoubtable Dr Clinkscale suggests "decorations added c.1810" so, for our purposes, could it be said to be an artist painted piano of 1810?

Judgement on this mystery grand will have to be reserved in the hope that further evidence will come to light.

The next possibility I came across was, again, one of those shown at the Albert Hall in 1885 but dating it is a far from straightforward business.

This was an upright piano "With paintings commemorating the battle of the Nile" and was owned by a remarkable collector, Baron Ferdinand de Rothschild.[71]

The problem is that, according to the official catalogue, this upright had been converted by the fashionable furnishing firm of Wright and Mansfield from a piano originally made in 1799.

Were the paintings part of the original 1799 piano? Aboukir Bay had been fought on August 1st., 1798, when Nelson demonstrated the finer points of attacking in a double line. It seems plausible that the victory scenes could have been done within the year.

Or were they made later when Wright and Mansfield did the conversion? And just when did Wright and Mansfield make that conversion?

A photo showing the whole of the 1801 artist decorated Broadwood square, with a further painting on the front of the lid. Plate No.308.

A close-up view of the smaller painting on the case of the 1801 Broadwood square in the Metropolitan which shows a "reclining Venus with two cupids". Plate No.309.

Photographs by courtesy of The Metropolitan Museum of Art, New York

I do not know the answer to any of these questions.

The next on my list is a Broadwood square of 1801 in the Metropolitan Museum of Art, New York and, once more, this has "painted decorations in the style of Angelica Kauffmann".[72]

Of the pictorial nature of the artist's painting on this Broadwood, constructed in mahogany veneer with light and dark stringing, there is no doubt.

The official Museum Inventory records that this piano has a panel in the centre of the top lid "containing painted scene of Judgement of Paris within a frame painted to simulate carved wood" and there is a smaller panel at the front of the lid with a "painted scene of reclining Venus with two cupids, in grisaille within border of painted beads".

In addition the top, four sides and four tapered legs are painted with "ornamental designs of rinceaux, laurel garlands, scrolls of graduated beads, medallions with figures, heads or trophies, borders of ribbon and flower, anthemion and classical lamp motives, or husks, chiefly in green, brownish red, cream, tan , brown and grey with accents of white, crimson, etc".

On the nameboard there are inlaid, fiddleback panels, possibly of maple. A shaped music shelf connects the legs.

The next candidate I discovered is an upright grand of 1801 by William and Matthew Stodart, once again in the Collection of the Metropolitan Museum of Art.[73]

This is in mahogany veneer and, says the Museum, has "two glass doors lined with velvet panels decorated with painted birds, flowers and musical instruments".

Inside the cabinet, on the left hand, there is also "a parchment panel decorated with a floral design on the reverse parts of 18th Century English legal documents".

The piano sits on four tapered square legs in brass mounts and has a nameboard containing an oval inlaid nameplate with painted festoon of flowers on a light wood ground.

A slightly later artist painted instrument is a Clementi cabinet piano of c.1804 (Dr

Photographs by courtesy of The Metropolitan Museum of Art, New York.

An interior view of the Stodart Upright Grand of c.1801, in the Collection of the Metropolitan Museum of Art, showing the intricate, artist painted floral design. Plate No.311.

◀
What we have here is a typical Upright Grand of c.1801 but with decidedly untypical artist decoration. Made by M. and W. Stodart (the firm that patented the "bookcase" version of the design) the exterior displays two glass doors which, says the official description of the Metropolitan Museum of Art, are "lined with velvet panels decorated with painted birds, flowers and musical instruments". Plate No.310.

Clinkscale suggests[74] "or 1806-07"), now in the "Finchcocks" Collection, which has a mahogany veneer with satinwood banding and light and dark stringing.

The two doors of the upper case have pleated silk panels, satinwood keywell with purplewood banding, stringing and painted flowers. It stands on four tapered legs.

I have not seen it myself but a "classical landscape" is painted on the case top.

Those seeking to unravel the mysteries surrounding these early British artist painted pianos usually find themselves in a room of smoking mirrors, the floor littered with fiendish crossword clues.

Just such a puzzle is provided by the next two pianos on my list and they must be considered jointly. Apparently made by two separate makers, John Preston and the firm of Goulding, D'Almaine, Potter & Co., at different dates, these two artist painted squares yet turn out looking something like brothers.

Each is made in satinwood. Each has six legs. Each has similar painted decoration of three ladies on the front.

The cases appear the same in outline. The delicate, almost emaciated, nature of the tapering legs looks identical. The painted decoration of these seems related.

Photo by courtesy of The Yale University Collection

▲
The Curious Case of the Twin Pianos. This artist painted square piano in the Yale University Collection of Musical Instruments is by Goulding, D'Almaine, Potter & Co. yet you could easily confuse it with a square by John Preston in the Metropolitan Museum of Art. The Goulding square, for which dates from 1800 to 1823 have been put forward, has highly distinctive female portrait heads. Plate No.312.

▶
At first glance you might assume you were looking at the artist painted square by Goulding in the Yale Collection but this is, in fact, a decorated John Preston square, with suggested dates of 1790 to 1805, in the Metropolitan Museum of Art, New York. The decoration, you feel, might have been copied from the same pattern book used for the Goulding piano. Plate No.313.

Photo by courtesy of The Metropolitan Museum of Art, New York

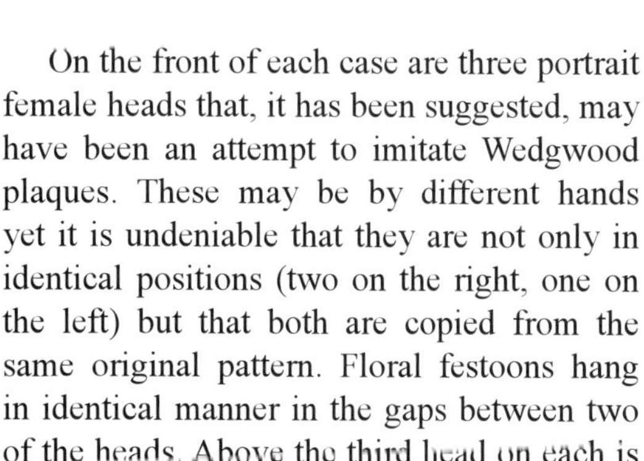

On the front of each case are three portrait female heads that, it has been suggested, may have been an attempt to imitate Wedgwood plaques. These may be by different hands yet it is undeniable that they are not only in identical positions (two on the right, one on the left) but that both are copied from the same original pattern. Floral festoons hang in identical manner in the gaps between two of the heads. Above the third head on each is similar decoration.

It does not seem possible that there is no connection between the design of these two pianos.

The John Preston square, said to be "Hepplewhite style", is now in the Metropolitan Museum of Art, New York and the Museum gives it a wide possible date, 1790 to 1800, although scratched on an inside support are the figures "1787".[75] Dr Clinkscale[76] suggests "c.1790-98". Another expert, Mr John Koster, says[77] it could have been made "as early as about 1795" but, more likely, "about 1800-1805".

Preston himself is believed to have died in 1798 but his son Thomas continued the business, certainly into the mid-1820s. The Prestons held an appointment as "Music Sellers to The Royal Family"[78] and had addresses in London and Dublin.

Whichever of the Prestons made this artist painted square (it carries the name of John Preston but, obviously, the son may have continued to trade under his father's name) it was elegantly constructed in satinwood with narrow rosewood edging and ebony and holly stringing.[79]

The six decorated, square tapered legs on the Preston square have carved Ionic capitals (a seventh leg is said to be missing), the nameboard having cloth-backed scrollwork panels.

According to the Museum's official Inventory this piano has "busts in beaded ovals and (on the lid) two beaded ovals flanking a central rectangular panel surmounted by griffons flanking an urn, the ovals and central panel depicting women and boys playing a variety of classical instruments, all painted somewhat in the style of Angelica Kauffmann".[80]

Dr Clinkscale records[81] that the outer case is "painted with various designs including floral garlands, busts in ovals, women and boys playing instruments".

The square piano by Goulding, D'Almaine, Potter & Co., is now in the Yale University Collection of Musical Instruments and, at first sight, you might easily assume you were looking at the John Preston instrument.

The date of this piano is, once more, subject to academic discussion since the Yale Collection[82] dates it conservatively to c.1815 and Dr Clinkscale[83] suggests "1810-23"—but Mr Koster once more prefers[84] "about 1800-1805".

According to the Yale Inventory description: "The case, in the Hepplewhite style, is of satinwood, with rosewood borders and band inlay of ebony and holly.

"The sides of the case are decorated in oils with festoons of roses and medallions containing busts in classical style.

"The inside of the lid bears a painting in oils of a classically dressed figure seated under a pergola.

"The instrument is supported by six tapering square legs, also inlaid and ornamented with painting."

The nameboard bears an oval cartouche giving the name of the makers and declaring them to be "Music sellers to Their Royal Highnesses the Prince and Princess of Wales".

Dr Clinkscale describes the top and sides of the case as being "painted with cupids playing musical instruments" and the legs having Ionic capitals.[85]

But the Goulding in the Yale Collection has one further surprise for us. One more of the endless piano puzzles fit for the Bletchley cryptographers.

The firm of Goulding, D'Almaine, Potter and Co are known to have had a number of different addresses between 1785 and 1823, most of these in London. But between 1803 and 1816, they also had a Dublin address.[86]

The address that appears on the Yale Goulding square is "20 Soho Square, London & 7, Westmoreland Street, Dublin".[87]

According to John Koster[88] the satinwood veneered square piano by John Preston in the Metropolitan Museum of Art has addresses in London and Dublin and the satinwood square by Goulding in the Yale Collection has "the same London and Dublin addresses".

Mr Koster goes further and draws attention to the "decoration in a similar style" of the Robert Stodart inlaid grand of 1784, the Preston square and the Goulding square.

What is to be made of this? Three different makers with similar decoration over a period between 1784 and, possibly, 1823. A sub-contracting firm who specialised in such decoration? A father and son? All three copying from the same pattern book?

I simply don't know.

And Mr Koster reminds us that there is also the White House's mysterious and doubtful "Broadwood" with decoration that may well have been "inspired" by Robert Stodart's inlaid grand.

A very different article is the mahogany upright grand of evident quality in the private collection of Mr Otto Rindlisbacher of Zurich, Switzerland, which has three artist painted scenes above the keyboard.

This instrument, with a suggested date of c.1806, is by the Royal makers, Jones and Co., who supplied another upright grand to the Prince of Wales.

A cupid appears in each of the flanking scenes on Mr Rindlisbacher's piano but, in the centre, it would appear a musical trio has been conjured up. A central figure sits surrounded by one young lady with a lyre and two others with stringed instruments.

The scroll being held by one of the cupids contains the maker's name.

Photographs by courtesy of Mr Otto Rindlisbacher of Zurich, Switzerland

Three artist paintings in which again, I suspect, some might search for the influence of Angelica Kauffmann or Bartolozzi, appear above the keyboard of this quality upright grand, c.1806, by the Royal makers, Jones and Co. The most important, and central, painting is a delightful vignette showing a figure surrounded by three young maidens, each with a musical instrument. Plate No.314

A Neo-Classical painting above the keys on the Jones upright grand of c.1806 in the Rindlisbacher Collection, Switzerland shows two Cupids playing round a scroll of paper surmounted by a lyre. I am told that this paper has the name of the makers. Plate No.315.

I have seen photos of this piano and Mr Rindlisbacher tells me that the decoration is painted and contemporary.[89]

My own suspicion is that, once again, we should look to the overwhelming popularity of Angelica Kauffmann or Bartolozzi for an influence on these paintings.

The final artist painted piano on my list is a square of 1807 by William and Matthew Stodart, again in the "Finchcocks" Collection, which is in a satinwood veneered case, with maple-veneered keywell, satinwood banding, light and dark stringing, fretwork grills at the ends and standing on four legs with a music shelf.

This is stated to have "women and Cupid painted on top".[90]

I think there are some conclusions that can be drawn from this list.

Self-evidently, these early piano decorators were addicted to Classical themes and a permanent chorus of Cupids, with Goddesses chastely posing as if the Windmill had never closed.

It is intriguing that the Stodart family were responsible for two of these artist painted pianos but, although the firm continued to approximately 1861, I can so far find no mention of any artist painted piano they may have made after 1807. By 1816 the Stodarts had manufactured 4,000 squares alone,[91] so these two can have been but the tiniest percentage of their overall output...always assuming they had anything to do with the decoration in the first place.

Contrast this with Preston and Son: Only one artist painted piano listed for them by Dr Clinkscale[92] between the early 1770s and 1820.

Clementi, a much more prominent and active maker, from 1798 (when he took over Longman and Broderip) to 1832, often used painted embellishments around the nameboard but I could discover but one artist painted example in all this time—that in the "Finchcocks" Collection.

The greatest firm in the industry, then as they were to be throughout the 19th Century, was Broadwood, but all I can find is a solitary artist-painted Broadwood square[93] made in 1801 and mention of another in 1784. It is also my belief that Broadwood seem to

Photo by courtesy of The Metropolitan Museum of Art, New York

Time and again you will find the influence of Angelica Kauffmann cited where paintings appear on British pianos of the Late 18th and 19th Centuries (and on a great deal of painted furniture of the same period).

This anonymous artist painting, showing the "Judgement of Paris", decorates the top of a Broadwood square piano, c.1801, in the Metropolitan Museum of Art, New York and the Museum's official description states "with paintings in the Style of Angelica Kauffmann". Plate No.316.

have been little given to floral decoration on the nameboard, relying virtually always on contrasting veneers, inlay and minor fretwork.

Judged by the considerable output of Broadwood you think that surely they must have produced other artist-painted pianos during this period but we can only go by the evidence available.

What we also gain from this list is unquestionable confirmation of the popularity at this period of the work of the painter Angelica Kauffmann, whose name is cited in connection with no less than three of these pianos.

Mrs Kauffmann was that very rare article a lady member of the Royal Academy but, even more, she could claim to be one of the 36 founding members in 1768.[94]

The Southwell shown at the 1885 Exhibition stated "Paintings by Angelica Kauffman"[95] but the other two, much more wisely, are catalogued as "style of" the lady whose work was so loved by the print makers….and copyists.

Once upon a time hopeful dealers and authors declared pieces of furniture to have been painted by Mrs Kauffmann personally but not a single one of those claims has stood up to modern scholarship.

A pair of side tables in the Victoria and Albert Museum "that in the past would have been attributed to Angelica Kauffmann are now attributed to George Brookshaw"[96] and it is the same elsewhere.

"Much of Angelica Kauffmann's reputation in England rests on her work as a decorative artist", it has been written. "Yet….almost all the decorative compositions attributed to her are reproductive, and were executed after her designs by copyists."[97]

If the Southwell reappears and does indeed prove to have paintings by Mrs Kauffmann herself then it will be one of the wonders of the age for furniture historians.

But what these "style of Kauffmann" pianos do prove is her hold over the Georgian imagination.

According to David Alexander[98] there were "more singly issued stipples engraved in England after the work of Angelica Kauffmann than after any other painter. Between 1774 and 1781—the second half of her stay in England—some 75 stipple engravings were published after her paintings and drawings, and nearly double that number appeared between her departure, in 1781, and 1800".

Her popularity was reinforced by having as one of her printmakers the super-popular Bartolozzi, who signed at least 65 engravings after Kauffmann.[99]

The mythical figures of Greece and Rome who gambolled their way through the Royal Academy in some of her 82 exhibited pictures,[100] continued their career first through prints and then across the furniture and pianos of Britain, thanks to her admiring and profit-seeking copyists.

My provisional list of artist painted pianos cannot, of course, be more than an out-of-focus snapshot, taken some 200 years after the event. How many painted pianos were destroyed as they fell out of fashion? How many are still lodged in private homes and not yet recorded?

The thought of how little I know and how much I must have missed is inhibiting but what it convinces me is that, if this is all I can so far find, a handful of artist painted pianos produced in virtual anonymity to please a few private customers, then this could never have amounted to a British Art Piano movement during the 18th Century or the early 19th Century.

Even in the following period from 1810 to 1850 you will find very few artist painted British pianos such as the Coventry and Hollier upright in Maidstone Museum, c.1840-1844, stated to have a painted panel above the keyboard depicting two musicians.[101]

Such artist decorated pianos as these must have been the exceptions. In the Late 18th Century the British undoubtedly relied, in the main, on Good Taste and restrained cabinet making. And even in the Regency the instruments may have become more showy but you see little call for fine art versions.

Although two of the artist painted pianos were by Stodart the family seem almost invariably to have taken the traditional approach to the piano case. For example, a 1790 grand[102] by the firm had a fascia board "with fruitwood stringing and mahogany crossbanding"; an 1806 cabinet[103] had "nameboard and keyboard sides veneered in satinwood and crossbanded with mahogany"; a square[104] of 1807-10 had "sycamore nameboard with two fretted panels".

Yet, if you look at the production of Astor and Co. you discover a square[105] of c.1784-98 with "flowers painted on nameboard"; a square[106] of c.1790-1800 with "stencilled morning glory swags" on the nameboard; a square[107] of c.1797-1807 with "mahogany nameboard painted with musical motifs"; and a square[108] of c.1810 with "satinwood nameboard with dark blue maker's cartouche, gold letters, green leaves and pink scrolls".

I deduce that such subsidiary painting was, if not the rule, then certainly an accepted practice in the pre-1820 era and that whether you were likely to find it on a square piano was simply a matter of house practice and commercial judgement.

If one believes, as I do, that The British Art Piano only achieved a public identity in the post-1850 period then it is fair to ask: Did the Late Victorians then produce more artist painted pianos?

I think they did but it hardly amounted to an avalanche. The difference was twofold:

Firstly, that the very idea of an "Art Piano" became widespread in the Late Victorian period, primarily through the Trade and Art Press, the most famous examples also being shown to the public by drawings in journals such as "The Graphic", or thrillingly recounted in magazines for women and the social elite. Even the occasional daily paper recorded that such art pianos had been made or gave them serious critical attention at various exhibitions.

Secondly, there was by then public acceptance that an Art Piano could be something more than artist painted.

Photo by courtesy of Christie's Images

The doubts that hang over so many early artist decorated pianos dissolve immediately in the acres of publicity given to Late 19th Century pianos. This is the grand piano called by the Press "the most expensive ever manufactured" when it was made between 1884-1887 for an American millionaire, designed by one Artist Knight, Sir Lawrence AlmaTadema and painted by another Sir Edward Poynter. It was made by Johnstone, Norman and Co. of New Bond Street, London and had a Steinway works. Plate No.317.

You could have no better example of this than Alma-Tadema's "Byzantine" grand which was illustrated in the popular prints, became known throughout the Western world and was accepted as one of the two greatest "Art" pianos produced in Britain (the other being Burne-Jones's painted "Orpheus").

Yet on the "Byzantine" grand itself there was no artist painting—the effect was achieved by luxurious inlays of precious materials and a sculpted silver plaque. Only on the back of the matching piano stool did Alma-Tadema employ his own considerable powers as a painter.

Both the extent of the fashion for artist painted pianos and the natural limits of its clientele are shown by a report[109] that appeared in the "Music Trades Journal" in 1896.

According to this another piano designed by Alma-Tadema in the 1880s for the New York banker Henry Gurdon Marquand but painted by Sir Edward Poynter was, at a reported cost of £15,000, still "the most expensive instrument in America".

The "Journal" said Marquand's grand had "exquisitely painted scenes, representing Greek maidens dancing to the accompaniment of ancient musical instruments…The work is a masterpiece of delicate technic and poetic imagination… However, there were not many people who cared enough about having a fine piano to pay so much for it."

Although "there are not many people who are willing to spend even as much as £5,000 on a piano....Special cases—that is, cases designed to order and with reference to the room in which the piano is to stand—are the rule now, and not the exception, among people of wealth."

They quoted a spokesman for Steinway as saying "Why, there is scarcely a house belonging to New York's four hundred (the group which claimed itself the social elite of America) which does not contain a piano in a specially designed case.

"So great has become the demand for these elaborate and artistic cases that we have engaged our own designers, trained in Europe, in order to do the work here in New York".

The arguments for and against the artist painted piano need no further explanation than this.

Exquisite painting for "people of wealth". Specially designed pianos for "the top 400". Instruments costing £5,000 to £10,000 in the 1890s.

One may regret the passing of patronage and taste that could produce *objets d'art* of such quality but it was a market for the few.

A solution had to be found for the mainstream.

The 19th Century was to see a ferocious battle to dominate the commercial production of pianos but also a matching contest to give the instrument eye appeal. In this the fine artists, decorators and designers all played their part but the true "Art Piano" was always a luxury item for millionaires and the like.

The eventual winners, as they were always bound to be in a mass market, were the Designers, who could offer beauty of form and adornments such as inlaid panels or fretwork which could be produced cheaply in the new steam factories and afforded by the ordinary piano buyer.

Photo by courtesy of The Colonial Williamsburg Foundation, Virginia, U.S.A.

The German-born Johann Christoph Zumpe, who turned himself into an English gentleman, styled himself "the inventor of the Small Piano-Forte" and there are strong arguments put forward on behalf of his claim. Without question he was the founder of the British commercial piano industry.

Of the perhaps 50 or more early Zumpe squares that are estimated to have survived the turmoil of the centuries the earliest known are four from the year 1766.

This very rare example from 1766, in The Colonial Williamsburg Collection in Virginia, U.S.A., is unusual in that it was made in solid walnut but, typically of Zumpe, demonstrates why we should see him as the advance guard of Functionalism. The case enclosed the works in the most simple, economic fashion and the planks from which it was made were left quite plain, the glories of the wood relieved only by small brass hinges. It is much as Zumpe made it—even the rustic beech trestle stand with its square section legs is original. Plate No.318.

Zumpe: Form follows Function

Chapter Eight

To all those musicologists interested in the piano Johann Christoph Zumpe (1726-1790) is in effect the founder of the British piano industry, the man who, in the mid-1760s, introduced the strangely named "English square", a small instrument that was almost invariably oblong in shape.

One could go further and say that the probability is that Zumpe actually invented the square piano itself after coming to London but this would seem to be a matter of continuing academic examination, one of the alternative suggestions being that it emerged in Germany about 1750.[1] Personally, I think the odds are in Zumpe's favour.

Zumpe himself, we should note, in 1780 styled himself as "Mr Zumpe, the inventor of the Small Piano-Forte".[2]

The instrument, as first made by Zumpe, was around 4ft 1in long and approximately 1ft 6in in width, with a depth of just over 6in and made to sit on a separate stand.[3] Tiny and portable compared to the grand piano being developed in London by Americus Backers.

According to Alfred Dolge: "No one holds the title to the name 'father of the commercial piano' so indisputably as (*Zumpe*)".[4] It may be a grey-curled cliché but, for the man who made possible a piano stated to have first sold for 16 guineas[5] and which changed the musical future of the nation, it seems an appropriate compliment.

To appreciate the impact of Zumpe's undercutting you have to remember that, in 1761, Kirkman offered a single-manual harpsichord for 50 guineas and a two-manual for 90 guineas. Shudi's harpsichord prices were somewhat lower, varying between 35 and 80 guineas.[6] This at a time when Shudi's wife could hire her servant, Ann Watson, for £5 a year "and tea".[7]

Zumpe's square was a cheap alternative for the musically inclined and financially able.

As that 18th Century man about music, Dr Charles Burney, explained: Zumpe's pianos "from their low price and the convenience of their form, as well as power of expression, suddenly grew into such favour, that there was scarcely a house in the kingdom where a keyed instrument had ever had admission, but was supplied with one of Zumpe's piano-fortes, for which there was nearly as great a call in France as in England. In short he could not make them fast enough to gratify the craving of the public."[8]

The earliest surviving Zumpe squares all date from the year 1766 and research has shown that the first known public performance featuring a piano took place on May 16th., 1767, when a Miss Brickler sang a song from Handel's "Judith" at her Benefit Concert at Covent Garden, accompanied by the composer-actor Charles Dibdin on "a new instrument call'd the pianoforte".[9] Logic suggests the piano was likely to be by Zumpe, or possibly Backers.

Historians mention a few isolated figures in accounts of the British piano before Zumpe, some now lost in the 18th Century haze, apparently experimenting with the grand piano form but of these episodes there are precious few hard facts and not sight nor sign of a single one of their alleged pianos.

Zumpe it was, proof positive even to a natural doubter like me, who popularised the instrument: The first man to put piano-making on a proper commercial basis and give the square an important economic edge; the first to offer the British a small version of the piano; the man who made his "Pianos Anglaise" so universal that the English Square was copied throughout the Continent and America.[10]

The Zumpe fashion even inspired a Parisian of the 18th Century to advertise that he would swap his Stradivari violin for a Zumpe square [11]

But I see Zumpe, also, as a quite different kind of innovator: The very first Functionalist of the British piano world. Although the words were written by Sullivan over a century later, Zumpe could easily have been the author of Louis Henry Sullivan's maxim: Form follows function.[12]

Not, one presumes, that Zumpe ever thought in these terms. For all I know he may have been a high-minded theorist who read the work of such contemporaries as Marc-Antoine Laugier (1713-1769), who urged us to take as a model of construction a primitive hut.[13] Somehow, I think not.

My guess is that Zumpe was focussed on cost, price and profit. That he was driven by economics to produce the cheapest piano on the market. And none the worse for that, say I, when "In nakedness I behold the majesty of the essential".[14]

What it meant in practical terms was that some of Zumpe's first square pianos were as plain as the planks from which they were made. Nothing extra unless you count the small, ornamental brass strap hinges—beyond this not a hint of added eye appeal.

The trestle stand was so rustic in nature you might think you could knock one up yourself over a weekend (though an assumption which greatly amused the eminent restorer David Hunt).

If beauty was in the eye of the beholder then it had to be in the shape of the article and the glories of the wood itself, almost always a lustrous mahogany.

If you examine the nine instruments listed[15] by Dr Clinkscale for 1766 to 1768, and made solely by Zumpe, you find that all appear to conform to his simple approach to the case and that most are in mahogany. I learned that two of these first nine are in solid walnut but I personally know of no further Zumpe squares in solid walnut.

Photo by courtesy of The Yale Center for British Art, Paul Mellon Collection

Zumpe launched his piano revolution in Britain in approximately 1766 yet, by c.1775, as we see in this remarkable painting, his little square piano was already a desirable ornament to the aristocratic home. This intimate glimpse into the cultural life of the blue bloods is, quite unmistakeably, from the hands of a master, Johann Joseph Zoffany and shows us "The Gore Family with George, 3rd Earl Cowper". Mr John R. Watson, Conservator of Instruments to The Colonial Williamsburg Foundation identifies similarities between their early Zumpe square and the instrument in the painting and In "The Book of the Piano" another expert suggests "The piano is most likely by Zumpe". Plate No.319.

Within the first known year Zumpe must have decided that extra ornamentation was necessary for some customers but this was minimal.

Essentially, Zumpe remained Mr Plain. His idea of decoration amounted to no more than a very thin, restrained line of black inlay on the exterior, running inside the edge of the case (though some, like David Hunt, believe he continued to offer a choice of two models, plain or inlaid).

We can prove that Zumpe was using this inlay by at least 1766 because a famous 1766 Zumpe in mahogany, made for a Dr Crotch and subsequently owned by Sir George Smart and then in The Broadwood Collection, was stated to have "stained fruitwood stringing" when it appeared as Lot 297 at Sotheby's on March 20th., 1980. It is now in the Württembergisches Landesgewerbemuseum, Stuttgart, Germany.

So far as the construction of Zumpe's pianos was concerned there was not a hint of artifice. The oblong case simply enclosed the works in the most economic and practical way. The instrument could then either be played by sitting it on a table (hence the alternative name, "Table Piano") or stood upon its equally plain trestle stand.

Zumpe began making his square pianos around 1766 and, as that careful and eminent piano historian Michael Cole put it so well, "...elaborate veneer work and decoration were never part of Zumpe's scheme. Some of the earliest examples are left entirely plain; there is no inlay even on the nameboard over the keys; the plaque that bears the maker's inscription is cut out and stuck on."[16]

According to Mr Cole, who has probably examined more Zumpes than any other person,

Photo by courtesy of Sotheby's of New Bond Street, London

It is easy to see from this photo just why an alternative name for the English square piano introduced by Zumpe was "the Table Piano". Although it was made to rest on a separate trestle stand it could, just as easily, be placed upon a convenient table for the musician.

This famous Zumpe square from the first known year of production, 1766, was made for a Dr Crotch and was subsequently in The Broadwood Collection, before being auctioned by Sotheby's as Lot 297 on March 20th., 1980.

What can clearly be identified in this illustration is the thin line of black inlay that Zumpe introduced and which became his standard method of decoration, though the well known restorer, David Hunt, told me: "I and others believe there were two models running concurrently throughout his *oevre*" *(one inlaid and one plain)*. Plate No.320.

◀

The Clavichord was described in "The Penny Magazine" in 1842 as "the tinkling grandfather of the pianoforte" and it is evident why so many associated the case design of Zumpe's square with the older instrument. This example of the clavichord, from the 18th Century and thought to be from the land of Zumpe's birth, Germany, was sold as Lot 30 by Sotheby's of New York on October 29th., 1976. Plate No.321.

Photo by courtesy of Sotheby's of New York

◀

Within a year of his first known square pianos, mahogany was to become the wood of choice for Zumpe, as in this well known example of 1767 in the Victoria and Albert Museum. Like all such early squares it was made to sit on a separate, elemental trestle stand and at this time mahogany was such a plentiful wood that Zumpe even made the stand in mahogany.

The case displays all the essential qualities of the Zumpe. In short, it is plain, utilitarian....and Functional.

The only decoration is the standard single black line of inlay (thought on this instrument to be stained boxwood or holly) which follows the outline of the main case. Plate No.322.

Photo by courtesy of the Victoria and Albert Museum

"those made during a ten-year period from 1767 to 1776 show a monotonous uniformity in construction and specification".[17]

One of the rare, entirely plain, survivors of the first known year, 1766, is to be found in the Collection of The Colonial Williamsburg Foundation, Virginia, U.S.A. and still with its original beech trestle stand with square section legs.[18] It is inscribed "Johannes Zumpe Londini Fecit 1766".

A lecturer on Zumpe and expert on early keyboard instruments, Mr John R. Watson, Conservator of Instruments to the Foundation, told me that their Zumpe of 1766 still has its original strings, textiles and baleen. The keyboard has ivory naturals with black stained pear sharps.

"It appears that Zumpe did have an orientation to the clavichord in terms of the shape and overall dimensions of the case", Mr Watson told me. "Ours is plain solid walnut (*mahogany was soon to become Zumpe's norm*) without any veneer...they were sometimes veneered quite nicely, like the 1767 example in the Russell Collection, Edinburgh.

"Interestingly, Zumpe usually blackened the mouldings at the case bottom and the stand. This is unusual for British furniture in general but I've seen it on several Zumpe pianos. The detail is often missed since the ebonizing is usually worn off."

Mr Watson pointed out that in the famous Zoffany painting of "Lord Cowper and the Gore Family"[19] (showing a finely dressed lady playing a square piano in a duet with a cellist), "Although the piano in the picture is not clearly labelled Zumpe, it does show the ebonized mouldings clearly and our 1766 piano has remnants of such ebonizing." Another expert also states: The piano in the painting "is most likely by Zumpe".[20]

Giving further insights into Zumpe's case-making techniques, Mr Watson told me: "In this period, Zumpe used a method to keep the piano from sliding around on the stand that is crude by modern norms. He left a metal pin sticking out of the top of the stand on each leg. The instrument was then jammed down on the stand."

Casters typically included a "swivelling forged wrought iron yoke and a spherical wood caster wheel, often turned of lignum vitae".

Michael Cole makes the interesting observation that when Zumpe did introduce his single black line of inlay (*stained boxwood or holly in the1767 example in the Victoria and Albert Museum*) this was "to give the visual effect of panels". [21] If so, was this an unconscious reflection of the "panel" decoration used on the sides of British grand pianos?

Mr Cole, not only a piano historian but a restorer whose work has enabled him to inspect a great many pre-1800 squares, tells us that the cases of most Zumpes "are made from plain mahogany, a plentiful timber in London at that time...Boards two or three feet wide were commonly available with hardly a blemish. Timber of such quality takes a beautiful polish and has a rich reddish-brown colour. This is nicely set off by the use of fancy-shaped polished brass hinges on the lid, continuing a long tradition on English harpsichords and spinets."[22]

How does it come that both Zumpe and his rivals were able to make such lavish use of what we would now regard as a luxury timber for the cheapest piano on the market? What we have to understand is that this was the Century when it was first being shipped in quantity and so freely available that boards between 24 and 36 inches wide were being advertised.

According to Geoffrey Beard,[23] mahogany begun to be imported regularly into Britain about 1715 and was abundant in Jamaica and the Caribbean, being known, says another authority, as "right Jamaica wood".[24]

Mahogany from the Spanish controlled islands of San Domingo and Cuba, and the Province of Honduras, were other potential sources.

Jamaican mahogany, like that from San Domingo (this latter variety being known as "Spanish mahogany"[25] and, when old, nearly black), was "heavy, strong and close textured. Cuban mahogany was lighter, reddish-brown and used for chairs and carving. Honduras mahogany, which only came in quantity in the second half of the 18th Century, was not only stable but sought by the trade because it could be found in very wide boards, suitable for case furniture."

Michael Cole told me that mahogany from San Domingo was considered very good; the next grade came from Cuba; and that from Honduras was "about half the density, much paler in colour and is so different it could really be a different species".[26]

The mahogany mainly used for British furniture in the 18th Century was "of a peculiarly dark, dense and rich character" but the myth that this was mainly "Cuban" has been bulldozed by the scholarly work of Mr Adam Bowett.[27]

Small quantities of Cuban mahogany were imported in the 1760s and 1770s but he tells us its reputation was not good and "When, in September 1768 the Lancaster furniture makers Gillows ordered timber from one of their Liverpool suppliers, they told him on no account to send Cuban mahogany, because 'it wont do at all'."[28]

It has been shown that, between 1723 and 1763, Jamaica supplied well over 90 per cent of the mahogany imported from the West Indies.[29] Jamaica's importance continued until 1790 but little Jamaican mahogany was shipped commercially after that, a fact regretted by a writer in 1853 because Jamaica had "furnished a great proportion of the largest and most beautiful wood, of which we have seen several specimens in old furniture, marked by a wild irregular figuring and deep colouring, more resembling tortoise-shell than the mahogany in use at the present".[30]

It was not until after the 1850s that Cuban mahogany "began to take a greater share of the British market".[31]

Raymond Russell observed that mahogany had first been used for the lids of harpsichords in the 18th Century "but it soon gained in popularity and was soon applied as veneer, sometimes alone, sometimes as cross banding for walnut panels. Walnut itself quickly lost ground and disappeared in the 1770s, except for special uses such as burr walnut as decoration round the keyboard *(of harpsichords)*."[32]

With such a bountiful supply available, Zumpe was still making some piano cases in solid mahogany more than ten years after he started.[33]

The Zumpe square of 1766 now in the Stuttgart Museum gives Zumpe's address on the nameboard as Princes Street, Hanover Square and this address also appears on the 1767 example in the Victoria and Albert Museum where it is stated to be "written in ink on the nameboard".

Mr Cole tells us that Zumpe's pianos broke with tradition by giving his address on the nameboard. "Not surprisingly, when others saw how prodigiously successful Zumpe had become, the practice was copied by most London piano makers", he says.[34]

Zumpe's desire to reduce everything to essentials evidently extended to that part of the square piano that you could not see, the mechanical action. This was, says another specialist, "of remarkable simplicity".[35]

Here was made evident a creed of starkness, Puritanism, an unclothed truth. With Zumpe form strictly followed function. All relied, for the onlooker, on purity of form.

Or, to quote another famous axiom: Less is more.[36]

The aesthetics may have been the last thing on Zumpe's mind but, as it often is when engineers follow such a path, the results can have a bare-bones beauty. Few objects better illustrate this, for instance, than the early concrete bridges for Britain's Motorways on which one day they will probably slap a satchel of Conservation Orders.

For those of us who admire objects relying purely on form, Zumpe's little squares work splendidly, rustic qualities and all. The proportions, one of the key ingredients, were instinctively judged.

As another expert, Philip James, wrote of the early English square "...though simple it did not lack the fine proportions which are one of the chief characteristics of contemporary English furniture".[37]

Since Zumpe himself had trained as a cabinet maker in Germany one presumes that, in so far as conscious design was involved, he himself must have been the "Designer". But if Zumpe produced working drawings then I have found no trace of these.

It seems logical to suppose that Zumpe's casework followed on naturally from that of the small clavichord, just as Backers and

In 1768, or previously, Zumpe took a partner, Gabriel Gottlieb Buntebart from Strelitz and this square of 1769 demonstrates that the early pianos produced under their joint name were in the familiar, Zumpe Plain style. This one, sold as Lot 58 by Sotheby's on July 19th., 1979, was in the, by now standard, mahogany with fruitwood stringing and inscribed on a boxwood plaque: "Johannes Zumpe et Buntebart Londini fecit 1769, Princes Street, Hanover Square". It also had the shaped brass hinges. Plate No.323.

Photo by courtesy of Sotheby's of New Bond Street, London

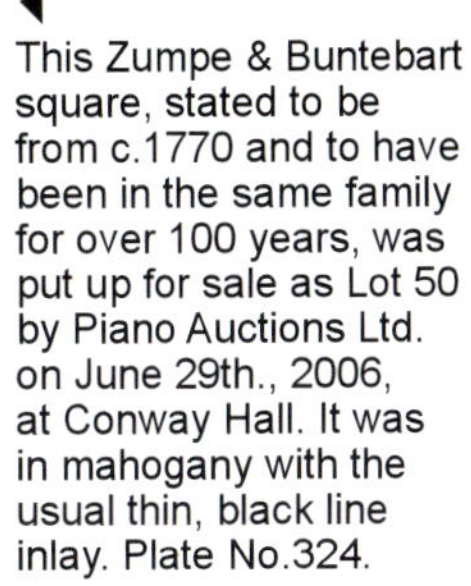

This Zumpe & Buntebart square, stated to be from c.1770 and to have been in the same family for over 100 years, was put up for sale as Lot 50 by Piano Auctions Ltd. on June 29th., 2006, at Conway Hall. It was in mahogany with the usual thin, black line inlay. Plate No.324.

Three photogaphs by courtesy of Piano Auctions Ltd. of Cardington, Bedford and The Conway Hall

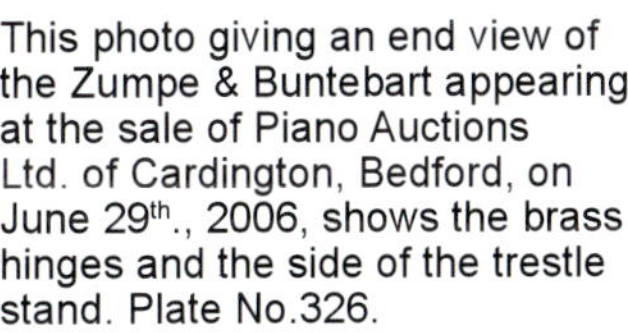

This photo giving an end view of the Zumpe & Buntebart appearing at the sale of Piano Auctions Ltd. of Cardington, Bedford, on June 29th., 2006, shows the brass hinges and the side of the trestle stand. Plate No.326.

A close-up of the name inscription on the Zumpe & Buntebart square, c.1770, put up for sale by Piano Auctions Ltd. at Conway Hall, London, on June 29th., 2006. Plate No.325.

Zumpe & Buntebart were still using solid mahogany for the case and still staying true to Zumpe's plain approach when they produced this square piano in 1775, now to be found at The Museum of Welsh Life. The name inscription is in ink on an applied holly plaque. Plate No.327.

Photo by courtesy of The Museum of Welsh Life, St Fagans, Cardiff

◀

The piano shown in this painting of 1786 is self-evidently in the Zumpe Plain tradition and proves just how early, and how far, the English square travelled to far distant lands. It is said that J.J. Zoffany painted the work, "Col. Blair with his family and an Ayah in an interior" at Cawnpore during his travels in India. Expert opinion is that the piano "is probably by Pohlmann or Zumpe". Plate No.328.

Illustration by courtesy of Sotheby's of New Bond Street, London

▶

When you see this print, "Ars musica", the work of Britain's greatest caricaturist, James Gillray, the four straight section legs of the piano that holds centre stage tell you immediately that it had inherited the Zumpe Plain tradition. But the print dates from 1800 and the apparent broad band of inlay round the back of the case is very unusual. P.S: An expert tells me, "You simply couldn't make a square piano with the keyboard on the right, as he has drawn it". Plate No.329.

Illustration by courtesy of The National Portrait Gallery

Broadwood were to assume the mantle of the harpsichord for their grand pianos.

After he launched his square the demand for Zumpe's instruments was very strong and, from all that we know, continued likewise. So much so, it was suggested by Dr Burney that he had to pass on orders he could not deal with to his countryman Pohlmann.[38] If business was anything like as good as this suggests, why should Zumpe bother to make the slightest change to the casework?

As soon as Zumpe proved the huge potential for the square piano the first competitors rushed in to invade the market he had established. They also copied his simple approach to the case.

I have seen early "plain" examples that, so far as the case is concerned (though I say nothing as to the internal mechanics), I judge to be obviously influenced by Zumpe, and made by Pohlmann, Beyer, Ball and others.

Yet we find that Zumpe becomes an intriguing figure of paradox and ambiguity. In about 1768 he took a partner, Gabriel Gottlieb Buntebart and later we discover the names of the pair on one of the most elaborately inlaid square pianos built in the 18th Century. Could it be that these two unlikely Partners took a lead in key refinements of the casework of the instrument?

If you look at the details of the 22 squares listed by Dr Clinkscale[39] for the ten years of the Zumpe-Buntebart partnership it does not look very likely.

One of the descriptions for a 1777 Zumpe & Buntebart says "Mahogany with stringing; plain stand with four square legs". Other descriptions indicate a similar, simple approach to the case and, even as late as 1778, one is described only as "Mahogany with banding and dark stringing".

It is true that Dr Clinkscale lists a 1768 Zumpe & Buntebart "with four square tapered legs", a second of 1770 with "four tapered square legs…a wide stretcher shelf under the keyboard" and a third of 1770 with "plain French trestle stand with four square tapered legs". But, before we all rush to conclude that the "French frame" was invented in 1768 (some ten years before the earliest date suggested by experts) one ought to reflect that Dr Clinkscale also lists a Zumpe & Buntebart square with "trestle stand (not original)" and another with "stand not original". This is where wise amateurs call in the cavalry (i.e. the professionals).

The wear and tear of the passing centuries, and fashion, have both seen changes (some necessary, some innocent and some with malign intent) to the stands, and other parts, of old musical keyboard instruments. It is a matter for caution.

Yet, there is proof positive of an extraordinary piano that bears the partners' name and is stated to have been made for a Russian Empress and the pair became so fashionable in Britain that Mr Zumpe was able to style himself "Maker to her Majesty and the Royal Family",[40] while Mr Buntebart, in his will, described himself as "large Piano fforte (*sic*) maker to her Majesty"[41] (by which he meant a grand piano but where is it now?).

What kind of pianos can Zumpe and Buntebart have supplied to the British Royal Family, you wonder. As plain and simple as their normal production? Or something very special?

The "her Majesty" involved can only have been a reference to Queen Charlotte (1744-1818), the wife of George III and a passionate devotee of music, who is claimed to have been an early customer of Zumpe's. "Queen Charlotte must have been one of the first to play these instruments", writes Michael Cole[42] and the idea seems wholly convincing, especially when Zumpe claimed Royal patronage.

The German-born Queen had been taught music, singing and dancing and, during a fraught, ten-day voyage at the age of 17, when she crossed the sea from Europe to marry a man she had never seen, she comforted herself by playing the harpsichord, leaving the cabin door open so that others might enjoy her playing. This included her rendition of the British national anthem "God save the King".[43]

The suggestion is also put forward by Mr Cole that when Queen Charlotte travelled to England in 1761 for her marriage "Circumstantial evidence suggests that Gabriel Buntebart was her harpsichord maker".[44] Mr Cole states that Buntebart arrived from Strelitz "at the same time as Queen Charlotte".[45]

After the wedding the Queen established her own private band clothed in uniforms of scarlet and gold and she herself played on a Ruckers harpsichord "in a japanned case", or on a spinet, and also an organ on which she performed the concertos of Handel and above which she placed a magnificent bust of Handel by Roubiliac.[46] A cabinet pianoforte by Broadwood and other pianos were among the items sold[47] at a dispersal of her estate at Christie's in 1819.

There seems little doubt that Zumpe and Buntebart owed much of their Royal patronage to the influence of their friend Johann Christian Bach ("the English Bach") who, after the success of his opera "Orione" in London, was appointed by Queen Charlotte as her Master of Music.

A square piano stated to be a Zumpe and Buntebart of 1777-1778 bearing the personal signature of J.C. Bach, is now in The Cobbe Collection[48] and the two partners are stated to have been "both very closely connected with the court and the immediate coterie of attendants in Queen Charlotte's household".[49]

Royal patronage would undoubtedly have done much to give legitimacy to Zumpe's square piano.

Bach's bank account reveals[50] his financial transactions with Buntebart and also a payment of £50 to Zumpe himself in July, 1768.

Michael Cole, to whom I am indebted for much of the detail on Zumpe, says Bach played an active part in arranging sales of pianos by the partners[51] and the composer is reported to have given one of the earliest public piano concerts in Britain on June 2nd., 1768, probably using a square piano.[52]

◀

That Zumpe's little squares became a fashionable rage, and his customers many, has long been known but did he sub-contract orders he could not fill to his friend Pohlmann? According to Philip James (presumably based on Dr Burney) the demand forced Zumpe to "pass on orders he could not deal with to his countryman Pohlmann". Whether this is so or not, what becomes obvious in the merest scrutiny is that the competitors who rushed in behind Zumpe all produced an approximation of the "Zumpe Plain" case style, as in this Pohlmann of 1769 in the Beurmann Collection with its mahogany exterior, thin stringing and simple trestle stand. You see immediately that a common thread runs through the work of both men. Plate No.330.

Photo by courtesy of The Beurmann Collection, Hamburg

▶

Just how soon Zumpe's piano, and what some may call his anti-Style, spread through the land may be instantly recognized in this square piano of 1774. It is by one of the best known provincial makers, Haxby of York, who is described by Michael Cole as "The first known English maker to embark on the trade". Thomas Haxby, who himself sang in the choir of York Minster had, like so many of them, previously been a maker of spinets and harpsichords but he took enthusiastically to Zumpe's new instrument. This one is in mahogany with stringing, on the usual plain trestle stand and has an inlaid maple plaque stating "Thomas Haxby York 1774". Plate No.331.

Photo by courtesy of The Colt Clavier Collection, Bethersden, Kent

Photo by courtesy of Piano Auctions Ltd. of Cardington, Bedford and The Conway Hall

◀

If the suggested date of "c.1777" (that date appears on the nameboard and an expert assures me it is not in doubt) is anywhere near correct then this mahogany square piano is, as the Piano Auctions Ltd. catalogue states, "very rare indeed", one of the earliest known by a fascinating maker, John Geib. It was auctioned as Lot 30 on Sept 22nd 2005 and the owner had "not encountered another square piano by Geib in his 35 years experience as a collector", we are told. Born in the Rhineland, John Geib (originally Johann Lorenz Geib) came to London and invented a piece of technical kit that enraptures all the pianists before moving to New York in 1797 and founding another successful business in America. But his case style, as you see, is pure Zumpe. Plate No.332.

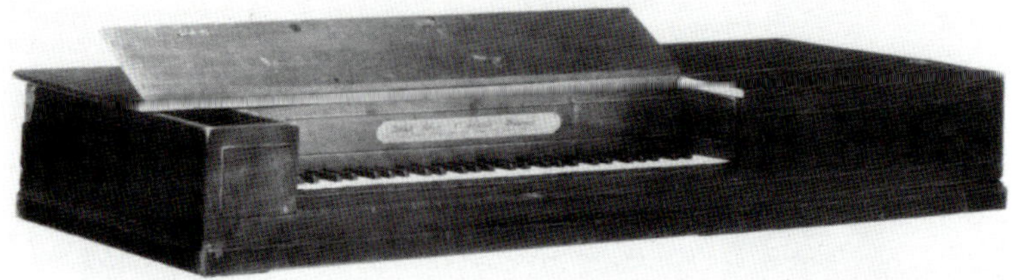

Photo by courtesy of Messrs Sotheby's of New Bond Street, London

Although there are indications that John Broadwood may have commenced making square pianos in 1778 the earliest known surviving squares by him all date from 1780. This example, which appeared as Lot 293 in Sotheby's on March 20th., 1980, was inscribed "Burkat Shudi et Johannes Broadwood Londini fecerunt 1780", a recognition of his father-in-law, who had died in 1773. Although the stand did not survive, the identification with Zumpe's style is unquestionable—from its mahogany case to its ebony and holly stringing. Plate No.333.

In the casework of Adam Beyer, another early Zumpe rival, there is always, it seems to me, a spirit of tasteful, timeless simplicity, though the tradition is wholly that of Zumpe. I have yet to see a vulgar thing from the hand of Adam Beyer and this splendid example of 1780 has found a matching home in the redoubtable Collection of the Haags Gemeentemuseum. Plate No.334.

Photo by courtesy of the Haags Gemeentemuseum, Den Haag

To design enthusiasts Christopher Ganer is best known today for a few superbly decorated pianos yet, to look at this fine little square, a layman might imagine at first glance that he was seeing a Zumpe: the mahogany case has the typical black stringing. What it appears to tell us is that Ganer did not reach his mature style overnight but that his first notions were based on Zumpe. This square was put up for auction as Lot 83 by Sotheby's on March 6th., 1979, when it was said to be "last quarter of the 18th Century". The stand, I was told by an expert, was of later date. Plate No.335.

Illustration by courtesy of Sotheby's of New Bond Street, London

We are always told by the experts that Longman & Broderip were simply retailers, so who might have made this mahogany square of c.1780 I will hazard no guess. But, instead of the more decorative "house" style that became the norm for L. & B. pianos what we have here, unquestionably, is something very much after Zumpe. It was sold by Sotheby's as Lot 378 on May 12th., 1977. Plate No.336.

Illustration by courtesy of Sotheby's of New Bond Street, London

That Zumpe's style was copied by just about everyone who jumped on his bandwagon can be seen in the only surviving instrument known by Thomas Green of Rose Mary Lane, London and now in the Bad Krozingen Collection. This piano is inscribed "Thomas Green Londini Fecit 1785" and is in mahogany with light and dark stringing, while the nameboard has banding and stringing. Unusually for squares, the sound board is painted with roses. Plate No.337.

Photo by courtesy of The Neumeyer-Junghanns-Tracey Collection, Bad Krozingen, Germany

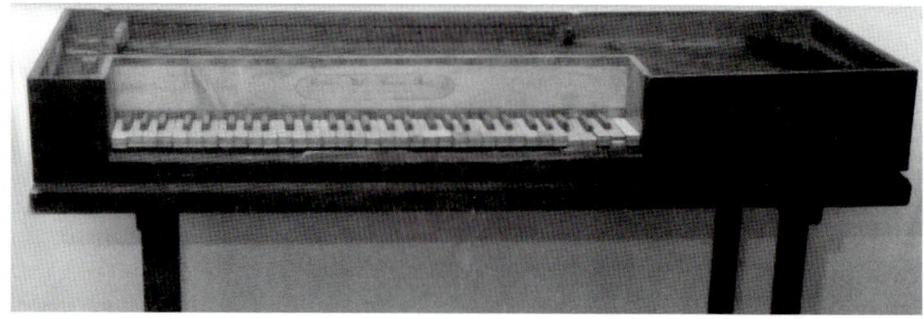

Courtesy of The Hackett Collection, Photo by David Hackett

Another of those who quickly followed Zumpe's lead was James Ball of London and the way in which he, and so many of them, imitated the "Zumpe Plain" style can be seen in this early Ball square. It is in mahogany with a satinwood nameboard and "the usual immaculate black calligraphy in Latin"—the names were often spelt in Latin at this early stage. But I'd be interested to know whether such use of Latin continued after 1795. Plate No.338.

Zumpe made a fortune out of the square piano but John Broadwood made a mass-producing industry. Broadwood might have been a Johnny-come-lately hanging on Zumpe's coat tails but he was an outstanding piano maker and Georgian entrepreneur and this square of 1784 in the Beurmann Collection has the Broadwood qualities: Middle of the road, safe, quality casework. Which did nothing to hide the fact it was in Zumpe's image. Plate No.339.

Photo by courtesy of The Beurmann Collection, Hamburg

Photo by courtesy of The Beurmann Collection, Hamburg

I had not come across a square piano previously bearing the name of J.C.Hancock but this piano, with a suggested date of c.1790, still announces its parentage…born out of the "Zumpe Plain" tradition. But, of course, with both the above Broadwood and this Hancock the proportions are greater. Plate No.340.

All the known facts leave us to assume J.C. Bach must himself have owned a Zumpe square, though I have no direct proof (unless you wish to make your own assumptions about three Zumpe & Buntebart squares that have each been signed on the soundboard by Bach).

Mr Cole says of J.C. Bach that "there can be no doubt" that his keyboard sonatas "were chiefly played by his pupils and admirers on pianos supplied by Zumpe and Buntebart".[53]

It is my belief that these early square pianos by Zumpe anticipated the precepts of Functionalism, of "honest simplification".[54]

And, with our old friend hindsight, we can now follow the subsequent debate that centred round one of the most vital and vitriolic Design issues of the 19th and early 20th Centuries: Ornament versus Form.

A rebel in other ways, John Ruskin argued that: "Ornamentation is the principal part of architecture."[55]

On the other side, were those like Oscar Wilde, who said in 1882: "All machinery may be beautiful, when it is undecorated even. Do not seek to decorate it....all good machinery is graceful, also, the line of the strength and the line of the beauty being one."[56]

The balance swung more and more to those who rejected ornament:

Walter Crane in 1889, "plain materials and surfaces are infinitely preferable to inorganic or inappropriate ornament".[57]

C.F.A. Voysey, "discarding the mass of useless ornaments" would be healthy and desirable.[58]

Louis Sullivan, "....it would be greatly for our aesthetic good, if we should refrain entirely from the use of ornament for a period of years."[59]

Adolf Loos, "The lower the standard of a people, the more lavish are its ornaments. To find beauty in form instead of making it depend on ornament is the goal towards which humanity is aspiring."[60]

It was a path that inevitably led to The Bauhaus and The Modern Movement.

Zumpe, having no idea of these coming theorists, anticipated it all with his first, Functional pianos.

Though one should add that the human desire for ornamentation, which can be seen on the Stone Axe of Montezuma,[61] the decorated canoe paddles of savage tribes, or the tattoos of Oetzi the Ice Man, could not be suppressed by cerebral conviction. You have but to look at the larky fripperies of Post Modernism to see that the pendulum has swung again.

One of the most fascinating facts about Zumpe, a man you might almost have considered anti-style in view of the utilitarian nature of his early casework, was that he is reported to have started his working life as a time-served apprentice to a cabinet maker named Schreiner.

Born on June 14th., 1726, in a modest town called Fürth, near Nuremberg, the son of a master furrier, he is believed to have emigrated to Britain about 1750 (though 1760 has also been suggested[62]) and is known to have worked in London for the harpsichord maker Burkat Shudi for a number of years.[63] Following marriage to an English girl, Elizabeth Beeston, in 1760, Zumpe set up his own business and, as an ex-Shudi employee, you might have expected him to make harpsichords—instead, his sign, according to one of the Mozart family who visited him[64] in 1765, was the "Golden Guittar" and the instrument he made was the cittern, known as the "English Guitar".

Zumpe's workshop was, presumably with an eye to a rich clientele, established at No 7, Princes Street, Hanover Square, London and, says Michael Cole, this house "may be justly claimed as the first building in the world that was devoted to piano manufacture".[65]

The exact date at which Zumpe began to produce his square pianos is unproven but, according to Mr Cole, there are four surviving squares from 1766. In my view Mr Cole has produced the most authoritative research on Zumpe and he suggests that it is the "aberrations and diversity" among these 1766 instruments "that argue strongly that this was his first year of production".[66]

I frankly do not know what to make of a fragment of the "Memoirs of Dr Charles Burney 1726-1769" which appears to raise the possibility that Zumpe might have begun making pianos as early as 1764.

A wonderfully scholarly, annotated version of Burney's "Memoirs", published by three authors[67] through the University of Nebraska

Mystery surrounds the question as to whether, and exactly when, Zumpe might have been in partnership in London with a well known Dutch piano maker, Meinke Meyer. Two square pianos have previously been attributed to the pair and this third example, the nameboard of which is clearly inscribed "Johannes Zumpe et Meyer", with a date of 1778, appeared as Lot 35 at Bonhams of London auction on April 24th., 2006. Plate No.341.

Illustration courtesy of Bonhams of London
Photo by Sarah MacCormack

When Meinke Meyer and his brother Peter returned to Amsterdam from London to become well known piano makers of that city it is fascinating to see how an early, c.1795 example of their work, such as this one in mahogany, appears to have a distinctly English tinge. The brothers' post-1800 squares that I have seen assumed a completely different, Continental character. Plate No.342.

Photo by courtesy of the Haags Gemeentemuseum, Den Haag

Press in 1988, prints various "fragments" of Burney's biography.

One of these, "Fragment 105",[68] is given a tentative date of "Summer 1764?" by the authors, evidently on the basis of various matters mentioned in the text.

This tells how Dr Burney visited an old friend, Samuel Crisp, who lived at Chessington. "I visited him 3 or 4 times in 1764. I sent one of Zumpe's Piano fortes to the old mansion, and every summer all the new Music he wd like to hear".[69]

Are the authors correct with their suggestion of "Summer 1764?" Does this mean that it was in 1764 that Burney sent him the Zumpe piano? Or could this have been at a later date?

I just have no idea.

What caused Zumpe to enter this part of the piano market I know not—perhaps personal interest, or possibly he just spotted a gap for a lower priced keyboard instrument. The suggestion has been made[70] that the square was particularly aimed at women, presumably because it was a more manageable size, or might fit comfortably into a boudoir.

I do not think it would be an exaggeration to say that Zumpe's economical little square became a fashionable rage. He made it possible for the more moneyed classes to own a keyboard instrument when, previously, other keyboard instruments had been the preserve of Royalty and the supra-rich. Whether, in 18th Century terms, we should readily assume this must have been "the middle classes" I am not so sure—Zumpe addressed his customers as "the Nobility & Gentry".[71]

Odd references to Zumpe are found in 18th Century memoirs and letters. Dr Charles Burney, who had bought two Zumpes for himself, wrote to a French correspondent recommending a Zumpe square for the man's daughter[72]; the poet Thomas Gray[73] wrote to another, "You will tell me what to do with your Zumpe which has amused me much"; the author Laurence Sterne wrote to a woman friend, "I have been with Zump (*sic*) and your Piano Forte must be tuned from the brass middle string of your guitar".[74]

I presume that Zumpe must have made hundreds of square pianos for such customers. As Dr Clinkscale records[75] a Zumpe square dated 1782 it appears that he ran his piano-making business directly between approximately 1766 and 1782, a span of some 16 years.

The casualty rate of antique pianos was notoriously high (a combination of changing fashion, mechanical advance and house room) and I would regard this suggestion as being substantially confirmed by Mr Cole's estimate that between 40 and 50 Zumpes (and perhaps more) now survive from the dates 1766 to 1782.

What can be proven is that Zumpe started making pianos by 1766 at the latest and that he was in partnership between 1768 and 1778 with Gabriel Buntebart, this being dissolved by mutual consent on September 24th., 1778.[76]

Whether, as a number of books[77] claim, Zumpe was ever in partnership in London with a well known Dutch piano maker named Meincke Meyer is a mysterious question.

What is known is that in the "Amsterdamsche Courant" of June 10th., 1779, was a report of the recent arrival from London of Meincke Meyer.[78] In this paper Meyer said that he had been a co-worker with Zumpe in London—a "compagnon" to "Mr Zumpi" *(sic)*.[79]

Dr Clinkscale claims that in 1778 Zumpe "worked with Meinke Meyer, whose name appears on many of his pianos".[80]

And she lists two square pianos as being by "Zumpe & Meyer": The first of 1774, in mahogany is, apparently, "location unknown". The second, of 1778, is in Italy and questions have been asked regarding this, particularly the inscription on the nameboard.[81]

However, on April 24th., 2006 a third "Zumpe & Meyer" made its appearance as Lot 35 in a sale by Bonhams of London and was clearly inscribed "Johannes Zumpe et Meyer" with a date of 1778.

An expert told me that its trestle base was, in her view, a replacement as were other parts but that the piano had undoubted Zumpe features.

Regardless of the Zumpe-Meyer question, it is well established that square pianos were later being sold by Frederick Schoene & Co., who styled themselves as "successors to Johannes Zumpe".[82]

Mr Cole states[83] that after Zumpe and Buntebart ended their partnership, the former took a new workshop near Cavendish Square "which in 1782 he relinquished to the brothers Schoene, from his home town Fürth: like him they had previously served an apprenticeship there".

Four surviving pianos are listed by Dr Clinkscale for Schoene & Co between 1785-1795 and, after 1795, a further five under the title of Schoene & Vinsen.[84] But I am told of other "Schoene" pianos.

Regarding two of the Schoene & Co. squares of the 1780s Dr Clinkscale gives some indications of case design.

The first, from 1785, is described as having "Mahogany veneer with walnut and decorative wood inlays in geometric design (stringing) four tapered turned legs".

The second of these, from 1789, is said to have a case of "Mahogany with alternating intarsia bands (stringing) of maple and ebony similar to a fish-bone design (chevron?), original stand, four square tapered legs".

Both of these would seem to indicate an abandonment of Zumpe's plain case and an introduction of Neo Classical ideas.

We are given no clues why Zumpe and Buntebart ended their long association but Buntebart also remained in the piano business, forming a new partnership with Christopher Julius Ludwig Sievers, who died c.1793.

Dr Clinkscale lists one surviving square of 1783 which describes the maker simply as "Gabriel Buntebart and Co." but she records ten further instruments by "Gabriel Buntebart et Sievers", most of them inscribed with the pair's name, between 1784 and 1792. Their pianos are often "a riot of colour" I have been told.

Most case descriptions are sparse but one of 1787 owned by the Period Piano Co. is stated to have a case in "Mahogany and satinwood with mahogany banding and stringing; flower and leaf garland etched or inscribed to right and left of the nameboard label and extending around keywell; stand, wood and stringing match those of the case".

When Gabriel Buntebart himself died in 1794 he left his entire business to his foreman, John Henry Schrader ("for that good Servant and his attention to me in my business") who operated it under the style of Schrader & Hartz.[85]

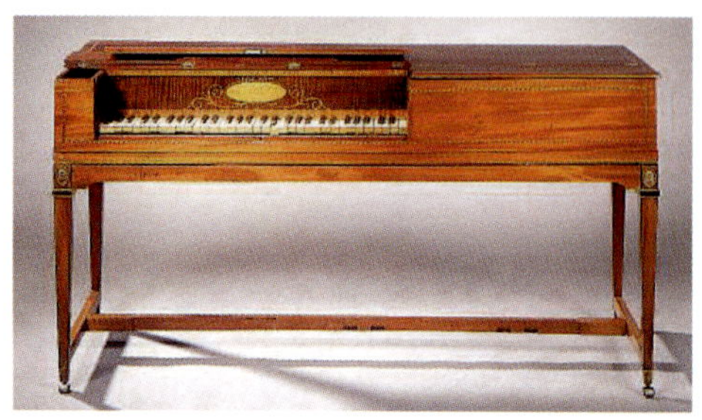

All available evidence sems to suggest that, c.1782, Zumpe handed on his business by some arrangement to Frederick Schoene & Co. who styled themselves "Successors to Johannes Zumpe". I have seen photos of only two Schoene squares and have inspected neither: This one, with a suggested date of 1788, appeared as Lot 1375 at Sotheby's of Amsterdam on December 17th., 2003, when it was described as having a case "finely inlaid with parquetry". Plate No.343.

Photo by courtesy of Sotheby's of Amsterdam

When the Zumpe-Buntebart partnership officially broke up on Sep 24th., 1778, Mr Buntebart took himself a new partner, Christopher Julius Ludwig Sievers and these two were in business until at least 1792, poor Sievers dying c.1793. This square, inscribed "Gabriel Buntebart et Sievers" with a date of 1787 is part of the stock of The Period Piano Co and was stated to be in mahogany and satinwood with mahogany banding and stringing, a floral and leaf garland to left and right on the nameboard. Plate No.344.

Photo by courtesy of The Period Piano Co.

Despite the various exchanges of partners (and the absurd legs) we see from the main case that the Zumpe influence lived on in this Buntebart & Sievers square of 1788, which is in the collection of the Haags Gemeentemuseum. Plate No.345.

Photo by courtesy of the Haags Gemeentemuseum, Den Haag

Gabriel Buntebart and his partner Sievers, may have lived under the shadow of Zumpe but this mahogany square they made in 1792 appears to show them adjusting to the new fashion. Sold by Sotheby's as Lot 178 on November 17th., 1994, this piano has slanting, tapered legs, apron with brackets and nameboard of sycamore with tulipwood crossbanding and decorative stringing. The main case had stringing of boxwood and stained fruitwood. Plate No.346.

Photo by courtesy of Sotheby's of New Bond Street, London

When Gabriel Buntebart died in 1794 he left his business to his foreman ("that good Servant") John Henry Schrader, who presented himself as "Schrader & Hartz". I have seen but one photo of a Schrader and Hartz square and a very interesting little case it has — neat, compact, but conservative in approach. Described only as "late 18th Century" it appeared at Sotheby's as Lot 174 on Nov 20th., 1980, when it was said to be in mahogany "with chequered stringing", the mahogany nameboard having satinwood crossbanding and ebony stringing. Plate No.347.

Photo by courtesy of Sotheby's of New Bond Street, London

Two surviving pianos are listed for Schrader & Hartz by Dr Clinkscale, both "c.1792" and bearing the inscription "Successors to Gabriel Buntebart".[86]

One of these is said to have "Mahogany with chequered stringing; trestle stand with four square tapered legs; mahogany nameboard with satinwood crossbanding and ebony stringing".

Most writers on the piano suggest Zumpe made a fortune through his square piano. Dolge made the claim, in 1911, that it amounted to the stupendous sum of 1,000,000 dollars, so goodness knows what that was supposed to equate to in the 18th Century. Such an estimate seems to me to be stretching good fortune beyond good sense but I think we may take it that Zumpe emerged prosperous and triumphant. At his death Zumpe (who had by then Anglicised his Christian names to "John Christopher") unlike almost all his fellow craftsmen described himself not as a "Piano Forte Maker" but as a "Gentleman". He made bequests to various charities, as well as his widow, and was shown to own leases on six houses besides personal property.

What evidence is there that Zumpe turned away from the honest frugality of his first instruments?

There is one example but which I would treat with the greatest possible caution, that raises the possibility that the Zumpe-Buntebart partnership had a new approach to case design as early as 1770. And we have certain proof that they undertook a commission in 1774 that was quite different in character.

Both these changes would have come, of course after Zumpe had established his partnership with Gabriel Buntebart in 1768 but as to what changes in casework may have been due to the influence of Gabriel Buntebart I can offer no evidence.

It has been argued by Philip James that until about 1780 early squares "varied little and there was no great change in their construction save for a gradual increase in the size of the case and the abolition of the trestle-stand in favour of the 'French frame' with its four taper legs".[87]

This "French frame" (in effect a more sophisticated form of stand) was to completely transform the look of the English square from Zumpe's honest utility to sophisticated artifice, the case itself matching the ambitions of the stand by adopting the inlaid and painted trappings of Neo-Classicism.

Did the name of the French frame indicate a wholly French derivation for the new style?

I failed totally to discover the origin of this description and, indeed, wondered whether it was not just a handy label dreamed up by 19th Century historians but an expert pointed out to me a number of 18th Century references to French frames in The Broadwood Records at The Surrey History Centre.[88]

The earliest of these, for example, reads: "Mr Butler 22nd Feb 1794 A Pianoforte on a French frame with pedal £21".

The expert told me: "It is absolutely clear that the nomination of this piece of kit could not have changed between say 1778 and 1794 and therefore I take this to imply that it was always known in the London trade as a French frame, from which I think we reasonably infer that they thought it originated in Paris, or at least that to them it represented French style."

His view that it was a known 18th Century term was confirmed when I came across research in a book entitled "Music of the Raj" listing pianos imported into India in 1786. This revealed that a Longman and Broderip piano brought in by the merchant ship "Walpole" that year was recorded as having "a French frame".[89]

An early scholar of piano case design, William Dale, argued that the new and distinctive tapering legs of the French frame were an adaptation of the Louis Seize style.[90]

But precisely when was the new style introduced?

Like Philip James, Mr Dale believed it was after 1780.

According to C.F. Colt: "The earliest squares and grands invariably had trestle stands but quite early on more elegant squares would rest on a French stand: Ganer squares as early as 1778 and a Broadwood square by 1787. These 'French' stands consisted of four elegant, tapered legs which could be taken apart for easy transport".[91]

So Mr James and Mr Dale suggest a change from 1780 and Mr Colt from 1778.

Photo by courtesy of Sotheby's of New Bond Street, London

Half the fun with these old pianos is trying to puzzle out the "whys" and "wherefors" but sometimes I simply retire baffled.

This square, catalogued as a Zumpe & Buntebart of 1770, appeared at auction as Lot 100 on November 17th, 1977 but it is a piece that, for me, raises more questions than I have answers.

The main case and nameboard look traditional but what is it doing with four splayed legs when one expert suggests that such an innovation did not come in, at the earliest, until 1778 and, according to others, not until 1780? And why are the legs not tapered in the same way as many others?

How does it come to have feather inlay four times on the front of the case when I cannot think of another British square of that date with such a feature?

This would appear to be a remarkable instance of innovation. Or is there another explanation?

I fear I lack the expertise to proffer an answer. Plate No.348.

However, from a photo I have seen[92] there is a square of 1770 that should perhaps be considered. It has very unusual characteristics that appear to show a pronounced departure from the austerity of Zumpe's early casework but these would need close examination by someone with more expertise than this writer.

The instrument that would seem, from this photo, to indicate a dramatic design change, is a Zumpe and Buntebart square suggested to be 1770 and auctioned by Sotheby's on November 17th., 1977.

The decoration on this piano is apparently more ambitious, the most obvious feature being inlays of feather motifs at the corners, the mahogany case having multiple stringing, shaped brass hinges and a nameboard with ebony stringing and a boxwood name plaque. It also has splayed and tapered legs with brackets at the corners.[93]

How is it possible that this piano could anticipate by nearly ten years the suggested earliest date of 1778 from Mr Colt, or 1780 as suggested by Mr Dale and Mr James?

As I stare at such photos one of the first questions I ask myself is: Are all the features original? The difficulty is that a number of old pianos have, over the centuries, subsequently been "modernised" to keep pace with new fashions or "tarted up by the antique trade"[94] to make them more appealing and, in this particular instance, I have no knowledge either way.

Photo by courtesy of The Smithsonian Institution (N.M.A.H.), Washington, U.S.A.

I thought I might have found another square piano that introduced new features years before others had thought of the idea—it has not only a stand with splayed legs but also a music shelf. However, I am advised that the stand on this square, catalogued by The Smithsonian as a Zumpe & Buntebart of 1770, is not original. So, when built, would it have had the traditional trestle stand? And why does it have butt hinges on the main case? Plate No.349.

My natural caution was reinforced by another noted expert and restorer of the early piano, Mr David Hunt, who told me: "I have recently been researching Ganer and Beck and have discovered at least two pianos which have clearly been 'modernised' in the 1790s with the addition of a frame stand".[95]

Since I have seen only a photo of the 1770 square I am unable to venture any opinion on whether the decoration and stand are contemporary with the instrument.

I thought there might be further evidence to support a suggestion of a change in 1770 with a claimed "Zumpe and Buntebart" square, of the same year, in the Collection of the Smithsonian Institution.

Again, a photo[96] shows a square piano sat on a stand with splayed, tapered legs and, in this instance, with the addition of a music shelf. But I am advised that this stand is of a later date[97] than the piano.

Regardless of either of these two squares, there can be not a doubt of a major change by 1774.

Was this the year in which Zumpe and his partner became involved with one of the most important architectural figures of the 18th Century, Robert Adam? If so, how?

What can be proved is that, in 1774, Robert Adam produced sophisticated, Neo-Classical designs (two alternative ideas) for a square piano for Catherine the Great, Empress of Russia. These are typical Adam confections, dripping with ornament. So far as I can prove these were the first known designs by an architect for a British piano.

And in a Russian Palace is now to be found an extravagantly inlaid square piano by Zumpe and Buntebart, also dated 1774, which one of the foremost piano scholars believes to be the instrument made to the very same Robert Adam design.

The Zumpe and Buntebart discovered[98] in The Palace of Pavlovsk, outside St Petersburg, by Mr Laurence Libin, Research Curator of the Metropolitan Museum of Art, is so foreign to the early Zumpe style that, were it not for the inscription on the piano, you would find it impossible to believe he could have had any part in its making.

The inscription[99] reads "Johannes Zumpe et Buntebart Londini fecerunt 1774 Princes Street Hanover Square" and, regardless of the Adam connection, would appear to prove a change of course.

Photographs by Mr Laurence Libin Courtesy of The Palace of Pavlovsk

Zumpe was Mr Plain personified, the man who created the back-to-basics, simple as can be, square piano. How could he possibly be responsible for this piece of razzamatazz?

Yet, make no mistake about it, the names that appear as the makers as those of Zumpe and his partner Buntebart. And one of the World's leading experts on the early piano, Mr Laurence Libin, believes it is the very piano the pair made for Catherine the Great, Empress of Russia.

What is equally certain is that this square bears the date 1774, the same year in which the architect Robert Adams is proved to have produced two designs for a square piano for the Empress of Russia—the first known piano designs in Britain.

Indeed, Mr Libin believes this Zumpe & Buntebart piano was made to one of those Adam designs.

The piano was discovered by Mr Libin in The Palace of Pavlovsk in Russia and the decoration is every bit as profuse as the photo suggests.

Mr Libin describes the decoration as "stunning", though he adds that features of the casework "indicate that the piano was not finished in Zumpe and Buntebart's workshop but in that of a high-class cabinet maker". Plate No.350.

I know of no other Zumpe & Buntebart even remotely like this. The extravagant decoration shown here is at the top of paired, square tapered legs and is years in advance of the decorative wave that was to sweep over the square piano in the 1790's. Plate No.351.

One of the features of the Zumpe & Buntebart square in The Palace of Pavlovsk is the female profile on the front of the case and Mr Lurence Libin suggests that it is "perhaps intended to represent Catherine", the Empress of Russia. Plate No.352.

However, some features of the case are so different to the normal Zumpe style that Mr Libin suggests that "the piano was not finished in Zumpe and Buntebart's workshop but in that of a high-class cabinet maker".[100]

In a major article in "Early Music" in August, 2001, Mr Libin stated[101] that "the piano's appearance essentially matches", the Adam design drawings.

"Only the shape of the four pairs of square tapered legs differs markedly and the stretcher shown in the drawings has been omitted", he writes.

"Less obvious deviations include the case proportions and minor changes to the decoration; for example, a female profile centred on the front faces left in the drawings and right on the instrument. Whether Adam approved these changes is unknown."

He adds that: "Zumpe's pianos typically have plain, flat mahogany cases, sometimes with narrow stringing and cross-banding, that rest on simple, four-legged trestle stands...

"Catherine's vastly more impressive instrument...stunning decoration includes arcaded natural key fronts of ivory instead of the usual wood fronts...

"The piano's case...displays Adam's architectural approach. Projecting panels on the front, back and side walls give the case a lively three-dimensional rhythm, not unlike the facade of a building....

"As in typical Adam side tables, paired legs separated by an empty central space articulate the form above...

"In architectural terms the frame forms a fluted architrave above which the piano itself forms a frieze...

"Anthemia, in a pattern somewhat altered from the drawings, fill the recessed portions of the front and sides, while the projecting panel...displays as its focal point the...female profile, perhaps intended to represent Catherine. The medallion enclosing this profile covers a bow and quiver crossed by a lyre and supports a festoon.

"Adam's wholly characteristic, detailed design for the top surface of the lid, which centres on a Classical woman seated next to an open music book and playing a seven-string lyre, was closely followed; as elsewhere on the marquetry, many of its details are engraved.

"The lower surface of the lid is decorated in a contrasting, entirely geometric style commonly associated with Thomas Chippendale."

Mr Libin says this treatment "is particularly striking because the lower surfaces of English-style piano lids are rarely decorated" but the design is "not wholly successful" because if the front flaps are folded back "the tops of the large medallions are cut off."

The designs of Adam in 1774 for a square, simply taken as plans and quite regardless of the existence of an actual instrument, tell us, I believe, that the shift of fashion in the approach to the piano took place well before 1780. Utilitarianism had given way to designer cases and the public's demand for "something different".

I should mention one other unusual Zumpe and Buntebart case that I have not seen but found among the diligent listing of Dr Clinkscale.

This is a square of 1773 in the Händel-Haus at Halle, Germany, which is described as "Mahogany, unusual stand with two centre flat legs, low stretcher, legs and flat base making two inverted Ts". Whether this indicates that the stand is of Continental manufacture would be but the wildest form of guesswork.[102] The stand certainly does not conform to any other known Zumpe.

As you might expect and despite the introduction of more sophisticated Neo Classical instruments in the 1780s, British makers of the square piano did not entirely abandon their old, plainer style for some years. There must have been customers who, on either grounds of economy or taste, wanted an instrument made in the old manner. So the two styles, what you might call Zumpe Plain and Neo Classical, co-existed for a while.

Neither was to survive the overpowering onslaught of the Regency.

Main Sources

Although you will find many references to Zumpe in books and articles, all of which recognise Zumpe's important contribution to piano invention, the scholarship of Michael Cole has placed all this in an entirely new perspective and his writings on the subject are a necessary and vital introduction.

I would recommend as an essential scene-setter a lengthy piece "The Twelve Apostles? An Inquiry into the Origins of the English Pianoforte", Pages 9-49, in "The Southeastern and Midwestern Historical Early Keyboard Society Journal", 2000, Vol 18, in which Mr Cole convincingly demolishes the mythology surrounding "The Twelve Apostles", a group said to have included Zumpe as a main figure.

Mr Cole also adds vital new information and conclusions regarding Zumpe in a Chapter "Advent of the Square Piano", Pages 51-63, in his standard work "The Pianoforte in the Classical Era", pub Clarendon Press, 1998.

A biography of Zumpe with background on Buntebart and other associates appear on Mr Cole's internet site www.squarepianos.com

A crucial, pioneering essay on Zumpe was Richard Maunder's "The Earliest English Square Piano?" in "The Galpin Society Journal", 1989.

Martha Novak Clinkscale endeavours to list all known surviving square pianos by Zumpe and his partners in Volume 1, 1700-1820, of her work "Makers of the Piano".

After reading Mr Cole I venture that you will find earlier accounts lacking but if, for scholarly reasons, you wish to consult past works there is a 2-page article "A Square Piano by Zumpe", by Philip B. James, Pages 211-212 of the magazine "Old Furniture", August, 1928 and another piece by Mr James on the same piano in his "Early Keyboard Instruments", Tabard Press reprint 1970 of the 1930 edition, lengthy caption to Plate LVII. See also Page 80 in which Mr James gives a most valuable text: The complete wording of Zumpe's advert in the "General Advertiser", Feb 1st., 1780.

Two square pianos stated to be by Zumpe and Buntebart are among those in The Cobbe Collection and you will find interesting captions to these as Pages 12-13 and 15-16 of the catalogue "Composer Instruments, The Cobbe Collection", pub The Cobbe Collection Trust, 2000.

Endnotes

Chapter One - The Changing Shape of the Piano

[1] "A Descriptive Album of Artistic Pianofortes", pub by John Broadwood & Sons, 1895, Pages 16-17, "The 'Burne-Jones' Grand"; William Dale, "The Artistic Treatment of the Exterior of the Pianoforte", "Journal of the Society of Arts", Feb 15th., 1907, Page 366; See also Michael I. Wilson, "Burne-Jones and Piano Reform", in "Apollo", Nov, 1975, Page 344; "Memorials of Edward Burne-Jones", by Georgiana Burne-Jones, pub Macmillan, 1909, Vol 2, Page 112.

[2] "The Athenaeum", Oct 6th., 1888, Page 454, Col 2.

[3] "A Descriptive Album of Artistic Pianofortes", pub by John Broadwood and Sons, 1895-1896, Page 16.

[4] Catalogue of the 1888 Exhibition of The Arts and Crafts Exhibition Society, Exhibit No 128, Page 121, "Century Guild Cottage Piano".

[5] Robert Palmieri, "Encyclopedia of the Piano", pub Garland, 1996, Pages 66 and 97.

[6] In an E-mail to the author on June 14th, 2006, Dr Eszter Fontana, the Director of the Musum fur Musikinstrumente der Universitat Liepzig, wrote: "There is agreement that the invention of Cristofori was made BEFORE 1700, since an instrument of a new invention was described in 1700". Also Eleanor Selfridge-Field, quoting Sutherland, Page 82, Col 1, on "The Invention of the fortepiano in intellectual history" in "Early Music", Feb, 2005.

[7] Inventory details of the oldest known surviving Cristofori piano in The Metropolitan Museum of Art, New York (Ref: 89.4.1219); Michael Cole, "The Pianoforte in the Classical Era", pub Clarendon, 1998, Pages 3-14; Martha Novak Clinkscale, "Makers of the Piano 1700-1820", pub Oxford University Press, corrected edn 1995, Pages 80-81; Palmieri, 1996, Pages 97-105; David Crombie, "Piano", pub Balafon, 1995, Page 13; David S. Grover, "The Piano", pub Hale, 1976, Page 70; Stewart Pollens, "The Pianos of Bartolomeo Cristofori" in "Journal of the American Musical Instrument Society", 1984, Pages 32-68; Giuliana Montanari, "Bartolomeo Cristofori" in "Early Music", Aug, 1991, Pages 383-396; Eleanor Selfridge-Field, "The invention of the fortepiano in intellectual history", Pages 81-94, "Early Music", February, 2005; "Cristofori's Last Work and his Successors" in "Piano Technicians Journal", Dec, 1985, Pages 15-17. Besides the example of 1720 in the Metropolitan Museum of Art, New York, there is a second Cristofori piano of 1722 in the Museo Nazionale degli Strumenti Musicali, Rome and a third of 1726 in the Collection of the Musiksinstrumenten-Museum der Universität Leipzig.

[8] Selfridge-Field, 2005, "Early Music", Page 81.

[9] Selfridge-Field, 2005, "Early Music", Page 81.

[10] Dr Charles Burney in Abraham Rees' "Cyclopedia" wrote that "The first that was brought to England was made by an English monk at Rome, Father Wood, for an English friend, the late Samuel Crisp, esq. of Chessington, author of Virginia, a Tragedy." But Michael Cole says (Page 19, "The Southeastern and Midwestern Historical Keyboard Society Journal", Vol 18, 2000, article headed "The Twelve Apostles?"): "I have made enquiries through the Catholic Library, Westminster, in an attempt to discover whether he (*Father Wood*) was at any time enrolled at the English College, in Rome. Sadly, there is no record of anyone called Wood in the period 1700-1740." See also David Rowland, "Piano", pub Cambridge University Press, 1998, Pages 15-16.

[11] Rowland, 1998, Pages 15-16; Michael Cole, 1998, Pages 43-44.

[12] Rowland, 1998, Page 16. For a biography of Plenius see Donald H. Boalch, "Makers of the Harpsichord and Clavichord 1440-1840", 3rd edn edited by Charles Mould, Clarendon Press, 1995, Pages 147-148.

[13] Michael Cole, 1998, Page 49.

[14] Michael Cole, "The Twelve Apostles?", Pages 9-49, in Vol 18, 2000, "The Southeastern and Midwestern Historical Society Journal".

[15] C.F. Colt, "The Early Piano", pub Stainer and Bell, 1981, Page 90.

[16] Michael Cole in letter to the author, June 24th., 2004.

[17] Cole, 2000, Page 48 and Cole, 1998, Pages 50-63; "Encyclopaedia Britannica", 1911 edn, Page 566 and 568; Rowland, 1998, Pages 16-17; Alfred Dolge, "Pianos and Their Makers", pub Covina, 1911, Dover reprint 1972, Page 172.

[18] "Encyclopaedia Britannica", 1911 edn, Page 568; Hugh Gough, "The Classical Grand Pianoforte, 1770-1830", in "Proceedings of The Royal Musical Association", 1950-51, Pages 47-48; Dr Reginald S. Clay, "The British Pianoforte Industry" in "Journal of The Royal Society of Arts", Jan 18th., 1918, Page 157, Col 1; Rowland, 1998, Pages 17-18; David Wainwright, "The Piano Makers", Hutchinson, 1975, Page 31.

[19] The historian of Broadwood, David Wainwright, author of "Broadwood by Appointment", pub Quiller, 1982, states (Page 13): "John (*Broadwood*) learnt his craft of joiner and cabinet-maker from his father". A report, undoubtedly emanating from Broadwoods but written 70 years after his death (in "The Pianoforte Dealers' Guide", Oct 25th., 1882, Page 233, Col 1) states that "Probably John Broadwood served his apprenticeship of seven years as cabinet-maker, and it is supposed that he passed this period of his life in Edinburgh". The "Dictionary of National Biography", pub Smith Elder, 1886, Page 364, states "Broadwood is said to have walked from Scotland to London to seek his fortune as a cabinet maker"; Edgar Brinsmead, "The History of the Pianoforte", 1889, Pages 122-123, describes him as "carpenter and joiner"; Crombie, 1995, Page 28, describes Broadwood as "A joiner by trade"; Alfred Dolge, "Pianos and Their Makers", pub California, 1911, reprinted Dover, 1972, Page 244, says he was "A joiner by trade". Virginia Pleasants, "The Early Piano in Britain (c1760-1800)" in "Early Music", Feb, 1985, Page 42, maintains that Broadwood was "already a master joiner and cabinet maker" when he joined Burkat Shudi.

[20] William Dale, "Tschudi, the Harpsichord Maker", pub Constable, 1913; Dr Clay, 1918, Page 155, Col 2; William Leslie Sumner, "The Pianoforte", pub Macdonald, revised 3rd edn 1971, Page 130; David Leigh, "English Square Pianofortes", in "Antique Collector", July, 1988; Pleasants, 1985, Page 42; Wainwright, 1975, Pages 30-31; but see mainly David Wainwright, "Broadwood by Appointment", pub Quiller, 1982.

[21] The Broadwood Archives at Surrey History Centre, Woking, Numbers Book 7, Page 2 of written preface.

[22] In a patent of 1777 for a combined harpsichord-piano, Stodart referred to his newly invented instrument "or grand forte piano"—see Grover, 1976, Page 89.

[23] Leigh, 1988, Pages 31-32.

[24] Michael Cole, "The Pianoforte in the Classical Era", pub Clarendon Press, 1998, Pages 56-57.

[25] James, 1970, Caption to Plate LVII.

[26] "Music Trades Review", Dec 15th., 1890, Page 21, Col 1.

[27] Michael Cole, "The Pianoforte in the Classical Era", pub Clarendon, 1998, Page 63.

[28] Grover, 1976, Page 89.

[29] William Dale in a Paper published in "Proceedings of The Society of Antiquaries", April 28th., 1910, Page 209.

[30] Last Broadwood harpsichord: "The Russell Collection", pub Edinburgh University Press, 1978, Page 65. Last Kirkman harpsichord: "The New Grove Dictionary of Music", 2nd Edn, Page 624, Col 2.

[31] Hermann Muthesius, Page 216 of "The English House", one volume English version of the 3 vol 2nd edn of 1908-1911, republished by Crosby Lockwood Staples, 1979.

[32] Author's research in The Broadwood Archives, Surrey History Centre, particularly Numbers Book No 7, third page; "The New Grove Dictionary of Music and Musicians", Vol 3, Page 324, Col 2; "Exhibition of the Works of Industry of All Nations, 1851, Reports of the Juries", pub Spicer, 1852, Vol II, "Class XA Musical Instruments", Page 716; Grover, 1976, Page 90 and Page 121; Wainwright, 1975, Page 11.
[33] A.J. Hipkins, "Musical Instruments, Historic, Rare and Unique", Plate VI; "English Illustrated Magazine", 1884, Page 227, Col 1; C.F. Colt, "Early Music", Jan, 1973, Page 29, Col 1. I should add that an Upright Harpsichord by Ferdinand Weber of Dublin has been discovered, which is dated 1764: See "Dublin Historical Record", Sep, 1983, "Two Eighteenth-Century Musical Instrument Makers", by The Master Terry de Valera, Page 125.
[34] Sumner, 1971, Page 66; Palmieri, 1996, Page 67, Col 1.
[35] Submission by A.N. Wornum, on behalf of Robert Wornum and Sons, to the Jurors of the Paris Universal Exhibition, 1867. See Page 1 of copy in The Museum of London Archives.
[36] Patent No. 2028, registered Jan 12th., 1795; Grover, 1976, Pages 130-131.
[37] See photo, Page 28, Dominic Gill, "The Book of the Piano", pub Phaidon, 1981.
[38] "Music Trades Review", May 15th., 1887, Page 13, Col 1.
[39] A gentleman who wishes to remain anonymous in private communication to author, April 4th., 2005.
[40] Gill, 1981, Page 28. Rowland, 1998, Page 51. See also Pole, Pages 4-6, quoted by Mactaggart.
[41] Upright grand, in the "bookcase" form, made by R. Jones for The Prince of Wales, 1808: See Philip James, "Early Keyboard Instruments", pub Tabard, 1970, reprint of 1930 edn, Page 144.
[42] "Non-Player Piano Exhibition at Holdenby House", undated, Page 2, "Troup 'Wallclimber' Cabinet Piano".
[43] Patent No. 2264, registered Dec 6th., 1798; Rosamond E. Harding, "The Pianoforte, Its History Traced to the Great Exhibition", pub Cambridge, 1933, Page 220; Grover, 1976, Page 131.
[44] "Encyclopaedia Britannica", 1911, Page 570, Col 1; Edward F. Rimbault, "The Pianoforte", pub Cocks, 1860, Page 151; Harding, 1933, Page 226; Grover, 1976, Page 135; Dolge, 1911, Page 54.
[45] Arthur Loesser, "Men, Women and Pianos", pub Dover, 1990, Pages 248-249.
[46] David Wainwright, "Broadwood by Appointment", pub Quiller, 1982, Page 104.
[47] Submission by A.N. Wornum to the Jurors of the Paris Universal Exhibition, 1867. See page 2 of copy in The Museum of London archives.
[48] "Repository of Arts, Literature, Commerce", Vol VII, No. XXXVIII, February, 1812, Page 111.
[49] "Music Trades Review", May 15th., 1887, Page 13, Col 1.
[50] Rowland, 1998, Page 51.
[51] Catalogue of "Piccolo, Microcordon, Cottage & Cabinet Piano Fortes" manufactured by D'Almaine & Co., in possession of author. It bears the Royal cipher of Queen Victoria.
[52] "An Encyclopaedia of Cottage, Farm and Villa Architecture and Furniture", 1846, Supplement, Pages 1290-91; Grover, 1976, Page 132; Pole, "Musical Instruments in the Great Industrial Exhibition of 1851", Pages 4-6, quoted by Mactaggart; Harding, 1933, Page 226.
[53] Author's research in The Broadwood Archives, Surrey History Centre, Numbers Book 7, fourth page.
[54] David Illion, "The Story of the Early Upright Piano", in "Antique Collector", Feb, 1958, page 11; Crombie, 1995, Page 39-40; Harding, 1933, Plate III(a).
[55] Illion, 1958, Pages 12-14; Crombie, 1995, Page 40; Helen Rice Hollis, "The Piano", pub David and Charles, 1975, Plate 73; Grover, 1976, Plate 32; Harding, 1933, Plates II, III(b) and IV(a); "Encyclopedia of the Piano", 1996, Page 67, Col 1; Emanuel Winternitz, "Keyboard Instruments", pub Metropolitan Museum of Art, 1961, Page 45.
[56] Illion, 1958, page 14; Grover, 1976, Plate 38; Harding, 1933, Plate IV(b) and Plate VIII (a and b).
[57] Raymond Russell, "Catalogue of Musical Instruments", pub Victoria and Albert Museum, Vol 1, Page 64 and Fig. 34; "Magazine of Art", Vol 25, 1901, Page 545; Harding, 1933, Pages 244-45.
[58] Illion, 1958, Page 16, Col 1.
[59] Museum of London "Summary Report" sent to author on May 21st., 2003.
[60] "Magazine of Art", Vol 25, 1901, Page 545, Col 1.
[61] "Official Descriptive and Illustrated Catalogue of the Great Exhibition 1851", Class 10, Philosophical, Musical, Horological, Page 454, No. 490.
[62] "Official Descriptive and Illustrated Catalogue of The Great Exhibition, 1851", Page 453, No 486; Mactaggart, 1986, Page 32, quoting "Newton's London Journal", 1851, Page 34.
[63] "The Queen", Aug 22nd., 1896, Page 372, Cols 1-2.
[64] Patent No. 2446, registered Nov 13th., 1800; Grover, 1976, Page 132.
[65] "The Music Trades", Jan 3rd., 1920, Page 22, Col 1.
[66] Martha Novak Clinkscale, "Makers of the Piano", Vol 1, 1700-1820, Page 30, Col 2,
[67] "Encyclopaedia Britannica", 1911, Page 569-70; Helen R. Hollis, "The Piano", pub David and Charles, 1975, Pages 100-102; Martha Novak Clinkscale, Vol 1, "Makers of the Piano 1700-1820", pub Oxford University Press, 1993, Pages 138-39.
[68] Harding, 1933, Pages 220-224; Crombie, 1995, Page 42.
[69] "The Times", May 7th., 1851, Page 7, Col 1.
[70] Grover, 1976, Page 162.
[71] "The Artist", Oct, 1894, Page 387.
[72] "R. Ackermann's Repository of Arts, Literature, Fashions &c", Oct 1st., 1826, Vol VIII, No. XLVI, Page 245.
[73] See also Wainwright, 1982, Page 219.
[74] Catalogue of "Piccolo, Microcordon, Cottage & Cabinet Piano Fortes" manufactured by D'Almaine & Co., in possession of author. It bears the Royal cipher of Queen Victoria.
[75] Rowland, 1998, Page 50.
[76] Rowland, 1998, Page 50.
[77] Rowland, 1998, Page 50; Caption to Babcock photo, Page 174, Dominic Gill, "The Book of the Piano", Phaidon, 1981.
[78] William Pole, "Musical Instruments in the Great Industrial Exhibition of 1851", Pages 4-6, quoted by P. and A. Mactaggart, "Musical Instruments in the 1851 Exhibition", 1986, Page 15.
[79] "Music Trades Review", July 15th., 1893, Page 19, Col 1.
[80] "The International Exhibition of 1862. The Illustrated Catalogue of the Industrial Department", Page 99, No 5; Grover, 1976, Page 139.
[81] Rowland, 1998, Page 50.
[82] A.N. Wornum, submission to the Jurors, Paris Universal Exhibition, 1867, Page 3.
[83] David Wainwright, "The Piano Makers", Page 113.
[84] Rowland, 1998, Page 50.
[85] Paper entitled "Harry Edward Freund and His Great Square-Piano Bonfire", given by Professor William E. Hettrick, Hofstra University, New York, at the 2003 Conference on Musical Instruments organised by The Galpin Society and The American Musical Instrument Society; a major article on the subject by Professor Hettrick entitled "Harry Edward Freund's Great Square-Piano Bonfire: A Tale Told in the Press", with many bibliographical references, is due to be published in "The Journal of The American Musical Instrument Society", Pages 57-97 and I very much appreciate the author giving me advance sight of this; "On the Beach" in

"The American Musical Instrument Society Newsletter", Vol 29, No 3, Fall, 2000, Pages 4-14 and 20, reproduces articles concerning the event from the trade journal of which Harry Edward Freund was Editor, "The Musical Age"; see also Crombie, 1995, Page 20, Col 3; Gill, 1981, Page 182.

[86] Alan Crawford, "C.R. Ashbee", pub Yale University Press, 1985, Pages 287-292; "The Builder", Jan 17th., 1903, Page 57, Col 3.

[87] Author's observations over some 40 years but a bibliography of faking, forging and the theft of furniture designs might fill an encyclopaedia. For Pianos see, for example, Philip B. James, "The Square Piano and its Origin" in "The Connoisseur", Sep, 1928, Page 9; Correspondence of 1879 in Broadwood scrapbook at Surrey History Centre regarding a man in Kentish Town, London, who was selling "spurious" Broadwood pianos "sold with our name on them"; Cyril Ehrlich, "The Piano: A History", pub Dent, 1976, Pages 43-44; Grover, 1976, Page 158, regarding Broadwood pianos copied as "Bradwood"; "Music Trades Review", July 15th., 1883, Page 27, Cols 1 and 2 on the fine art of "Stencilling".

[88] Franz Josef Hirt, "Stringed Keyboard Instruments, 1440-1880", pub Boston, 1968; William Pole, 1851, Pages 5-6.

[89] A.N. Wornum's submission to the Jury of the Paris Universal Exhibition, 1867, Page 1 of copy in The Museum of London. See also Harding, 1933, Pages 226 and 228.

[90] A.N. Wornum's submission to the Jury of the Paris Universal Exhibition, 1867, Page 2.

[91] Howard Schott, "The New Grove Dictionary of Music and Musicians", 2nd Edn, Page 652, Col 2.

[92] Harding, 1933, Page 381, taken from "The Musical World", Vol 9.

[93] A.N. Wornum's submission to the Jury of the Paris Universal Exhibition, 1867, Page 3. The distinguished expert Philip James very unkindly suggests in his "Early Keyboard Instruments"(1930, 1970 reprint), Page 58, that "In 1811 a lower model about four feet in height, known subsequently as the 'Cottage Piano', was invented by Robert Wornum—a type in which ugliness found its apotheosis in the Victorian age."

[94] Harding, 1933, Page 379, "Appendix F".

[95] "The Academy", June 22nd., 1878, Page 566, Col 3.

[96] Mid-Victorian advert for Boosey & Co. of Holles Street, London, in possession of author.

[97] "The Artist", June 1st., 1884, Page 182.

[98] Pole, 1851, Pages 5-6; Harding, 1933, Page 381.

[99] On the Continent the very small pianos were often called "Pianinos"—see Harding, 1933, Page 232. See also A.N. Wornum, Page 1 of his submission to the Jurors of the Paris Universal Exhibition 1867; and Pole, 1851, Pages 4-6. Broadwood marketed their smallest piano as the "Pianette"—see Wainwright, 1975, Page 112.

[100] A.N. Wornum, submission to the Paris Jury, 1867, Page 1.

[101] "The Penny Magazine", April, 1842, Page 172, Col 1.

[102] Grover, 1976, Page 139.

[103] Quoted by Asa Briggs in "Victorian Things", 1988, Page 248.

[104] Noted by Charles Booth and quoted by Asa Briggs in "Victorian Things", 1988, Page 248.

[105] Rimbault, 1860, Pages 159-160, quoting Professor Thalberg's "remarks drawn up for the Jury of the Exhibition of 1851".

[106] "Punch", 1893 (perhaps from issue of June 17th., 1893), re-quoted in "Music Trades Review", July 15th., 1893, Page 29, Col 2.

[107] The Jury of the 1862 Exhibition in London reported that: "Messrs Broadwood and Sons stand, without controversy, at the head of the pianoforte-makers who exhibit on the present occasion": "Reports of the Juries, Class XVL.—Musical Instruments", Page 4, Col 2. So ubiquitous was the firm that it even earned a line in the verse of Kipling, The Poet of Empire. In "The Song of the Banjo" in 1894 Kipling, who had spent years under Eastern suns, wrote: "You couldn't pack a Broadwood half a mile"—see "Rudyard Kipling's Verse, Inclusive Edition, 1885-1918", pub Hodder and Stoughton, Page 113. See also Grover, 1976, Pages 90 and 121.

[108] Grover, 1976, Pages 90-91.

[109] Grover, 1976, Page 90.

[110] Dolge, 1972, Page 172.

[111] Jury Report of 1851 Exhibition, Vol 1, Page 716; M. Digby Wyatt, "The Industrial Arts of the XIX Century, From the Great Exhibition of 1851", pub Day & Son, 1853, Vol 2, Plate LXXXIII.

[112] Wyatt, 1853, Vol 2, Plate LXXXIII.

[113] Wainwright, 1975, Pages 55-57; Gill, 1981, Page 241; "Music Trades Review", Nov 15th., 1898, Page 17, Cols 2-3; "Music Trades Review", Sep 15th., 1890, Page 26, Col 1.

[114] "Exhibition of the Works of Industry of All Nations, 1851. Reports of the Juries". Vol 1, Page 716.

[115] Palmieri, 1996, Page 68, Col 2.

[116] "The Times", May 7th., 1851, Page 7, Col 1. Rimbault, 1860, Preface, Page V, called it "the 'household orchestra' of the people".

[117] Rimbault, 1860, Page 160, quoting Professor Thalberg's 1851 "remarks drawn up for the Jury".

[118] Rimbault, 1860, Page 160, quoting Professor Thalberg's 1851 remarks.

[119] "Commerce", April 4th., 1894, Page 496, Col 2.

[120] The Rev J.R. Haweis, husband of the authoress who specialised in style advice for the home, quoted by Asa Briggs in "Victorian Things", Penguin, 1988, Page 248.

[121] Wainwright, 1975, Page 85.

[122] Pole, 1851, Pages 16-17.

[123] Grover, 1976, Page 161.

[124] Quoted by Dolge, 1972, Page 173.

[125] Grover, 1976, Fig. 41.

[126] Gough, 1950-51, Page 50; Wainwright, 1975, Pages 96-97.

[127] Sumner, 1971, Page 66.

[128] Kirkman harpsichord of 1781. See C.F. Colt, "The Early Piano", pub Stainer & Bell, 1981, Pages 26-27.

[129] Sumner, 1971, Plate 8b. See also James, 1970 reprint, Page 139 and Plate LIX.

[130] Quoted by Philip James in "Early Keyboard Instruments", reprint by Tabard Press, 1970, Page 54.

[131] B. Kenyon de Pascual, "English Square Pianos in Eighteenth-Century Madrid", in "Music and Letters", 1983, Vol 64, Page 213.

[132] "Pianos", Catalogue of The Chris Maene Collection, pub Gent, Belgium, 2002, Page 68.

[133] "Cabinet Maker", March 14th., 1908, Page 423.

[134] Loudon, 1846, Page 1070.

[135] Harding, 1933, Page 264, 341 and 343; Grover, 1976, Page 120.

[136] Clinkscale, Vol 1, 1700-1820, Page 66, Col 2, No 2.

[137] Patent No. 8959, by T. Doddrell, Registered June 14th., 1884.

[138] Harding, 1933, Page 228.

[139] "Music and Letters", 1966, Vol 47, Page 37.

[140] Lot 168, Page 131, of Sotheby's catalogue of auction on November 8th., 1978.

[141] Clinkscale, Vol 2, 1820-1860, Page 278, Col 1.

[142] Harding, 1933, Page 264 and Page 340.

[143] Harding, 1933, Page 264.

[144] Grover, 1976, Fig 32, Page 139; "The Broadwood Collection of Antique Instruments", pub J. Broadwood & Sons, (1910?), Fig IX, Page 10.

[145] Patent No. 19,248 by S.G.L, Giles, Registered Oct 14th., 1895.

[146] Patent No. 22,340 by C.R.S.J. Hallé. Registered Nov 8th., 1899.

[147] Palmieri, 1996, Page 67, Col 1; Example in Smithsonian Institution, catalogue no. 1992.0192.01. See also G.D.

Garvie and G. Wood's Patent No 5020, Oct 21st., 1882, for an "Automatic musical instrument combined with a sewing-machine".
[148] Harding, 1933, Page 265.
[149] Seen by the author at the Colt Clavier Collection.
[150] Lot 20, "Desk Piano", sold at Sotheby's of New York, April 5th., 1977.
[151] Harding, 1933, Page 243.
[152] Prospectus by Richard Hunt for "The Tavola Pianoforte" shown at the Great Exhibition, 1851.
[153] Harding, 1933, Page 265.
[154] Patent number 1806, registered July 10th., 1866, by Millward after "A communication from abroad by Charles Hess, of Cincinnati, State of Ohio, United States of America"; Harding, 1933, Page 265.
[155] Now in the Musée des Instruments de Musique, 1, Rue Villa-Hermosa, 1000 Bruxelles. See Harding, 1933, Plate XIV.
[156] Grover, 1976, Page 132.
[157] Patent No. 2597, June 28th., 1878, by William Henry Percival, an example of which can be seen at Holdenby House, Northampton, where it is on loan from The Musical Museum, Brentford. See catalogue of "Non-Player Piano Exhibition at Holdenby House", undated, Page 2. Also Grover, 1976, Plate 47.
[158] Patent No 1376, Registered May 9th., 1867.
[159] Patent No 1413, June 5th., 1861, by A. Duguet.
[160] Patent No 315, Feb 4th., 1867, by I. Liebich; See also Patent No. 4508, Nov 1st., 1820, by Peter Hawker; Patent No. 655, March 9th., 1865, by W.T. Hamilton; and Patent No. 3076, Nov 23rd., 1866, by M. Marks.
[161] Patent No 23,662, Dec 22nd., 1892, by J. Fielder and C. Ulrich.
[162] Patent No 6026, March 22nd., 1894, by F.L.Goulvin.
[163] John F. Runciman, "The Pianoforte: Past, Present and Future", "Art Journal" 1894, Pages 142-146.

Chapter Three - Attitudes to Piano Design

[1] Now in The Yale Center for British Art, U.S.A.
[2] "London—World City 1800-1840", Catalogue of Exhibition at Essen, Germany, Edited by Celina Fox, pub Yale University Press, 1992, No 308, Pages 407-408 and reproduced on Page 413.
[3] Hollis, 1975, Plate 82.
[4] William Hardie, "Scottish Painting 1837 1939", Fig. 81.
[5] Waugh, Page 39.
[6] John Ruskin's letter to "The Times" of May 25th., 1854, quoted in full by William Holman Hunt in his book "Pre-Raphaelitism and the Pre-Raphaelite Brotherhood", pub Macmillan, 1905, Vol 1, Pages 418-419.
[7] For an analysis of the picture see quotation of letter by William Holman Hunt, 1905, Vol 1, Pages 418-419; "The Pre-Raphaelites", exhibition catalogue of The Tate Gallery, 1984, No 58, Pages 120-121; "Ruskin, Turner and The Pre-Raphaelites", exhibition catalogue of Tate Britain, 2000, No 193, Page 209.
[8] Letter to the author from Mr Robert Upstone, The Curator of Victorian and Modern British Art, The Tate Gallery, May 2nd., 2002.
[9] Ruskin's letter quoted by Holman Hunt, 1905, Pages 418-419.
[10] Holman Hunt, 1905, Vol 2, Pages 134 and 136.
[11] Bruce J. Talbert, "Gothic Forms Applied to Furniture, Decoration, &c.", pub Birmingham in two parts, 1867-1868, "Introduction", Page 1. This concern lived on even in the 1890s: See "The Artist", Oct, 1894, Page 389, Col 2.
[12] Dr Christopher Dresser, "Principles of Decorative Design", pub Academy, 1973, reprint of 1873 edn., Page 68.
[13] Charles L. Eastlake, "Hints on Household Taste", revised edn 1878, reprinted 1969, Pages 56-57.
[14] Journal of the Society of Arts, Feb 15th., 1907, Page 371, Col 1.
[15] Georgiana Burne-Jones, "Memorials of Edward Burne-Jones", pub Macmillan, 1909 reprint, Vol 2, Page 111.
[16] "Journal of the Society of Arts", February 15th., 1907, Pages 371-372.
[17] Hermann Muthesius, "The English House", English language, one vol abridgement of the 3-vol 2nd edn of 1908-11, re-published in 1979 by Crosby Lockwood Staples, Page 218.
[18] Presented with "The Tickler", Dec 2nd., 1837; copy in The Print Room of The Royal Collection, Windsor.
[19] Wainwright, 1975, Page 85.
[20] 19th Century sales leaflet of Cramer & Co. in possession of author.
[21] J.C. Loudon, "Encyclopaedia of Cottage, Farm, and Villa Architecture", pub Longman, 1836 edn, Page 1069.
[22] Loudon, 1846, Pages 1290-1291.
[23] Henry Whitaker, "Treasury of Designs", pub Fisher, 1847, see Part 3, Caption to "Plate—Grand Piano Forte, for Burttinyoung's Patent Works".
[24] "The Crystal Palace and its Contents", 1851, Page 42, Col 1.
[25] Professor Walter Smith, "The Masterpieces of the Centennial International Exhibition", Vol II, pub Philadelphia, 1876-78, Pages 119-120.
[26] E.W. Godwin, "My Chambers and What I Did to Them", in "The Architect", July 1st., 1876, Page 5, Cols 1 and 2.
[27] "Illustrated London News", Aug 8th., 1885, Page 146, Cols 1-2.
[28] "Furniture and Decoration", March 1st., 1890, Pages 37-39.
[29] John F. Runciman, "The Pianoforte: Past, Present and Future", "Art Journal" 1894, Pages 142-146.
[30] Runciman, 1894, Page 143.
[31] Hermann Muthesius, "The English House", 1979 reprint, Page 218.
[32] "Music Trades Journal", April, 1895, "The Irritating Piano", Pages 62-63, quoting from "The Realm".
[33] Reg Audley in "Cabinet Maker", May, 1900, Pages 290-291.
[34] "The Artist", 1901, Page 185, Col 1.
[35] "Some Pianofortes Designed by Architects", in "Architectural Review", Page 172, 1901.
[36] William Dale, "The Artistic Treatment of the Exterior of the Pianoforte", in "Journal of the Society of Arts", Feb 15th., 1907, Page 364, Col 1,
[37] Mrs J.E. Panton in "From Kitchen to Garret", 1888, quoted by Asa Briggs in "Victorian Things", 1988, Page 248.
[38] "Cabinet Maker", May, 1886, quoted by Gillian Walking, "Antique Bamboo Furniture", pub Bell & Hyman, 1979, Page 67
[39] Eastlake quoted by Geoffrey Wills, in "English Furniture 1760-1900", Guinness Superlatives, 1979, Page 242.
[40] "Ladies Home Journal", Sep, 1894, "Artistic Piano Covers", with drawings of different designs. See also entry of Teubner & Co. at The Great Exhibition of 1851, recorded in "Musical Instruments in the 1851 Exhibition" by P. and A. Mactaggart, 1986, Page 42, Col 2.
[41] "The Studio", Vol 2, No 12, March, 1894, Page 227, Col 2.
[42] Matthew Sweet, "Inventing the Victorians", pub Faber, 2001, Pages XII-XIV, quoting from Frederick Marryat's "A Diary in America", pub Longman, 1839 and other journals; see also Sweet, Page 233.
[43] "The Piano, Organ and Music Trades Journal", March, 1896, Page 224, "Piano Cases", quoting "Musical Age".
[44] R.A. Briggs, A.R.I.B.A. in "Furniture and Decoration", March 1st., 1890, Page 38, Col 1.
[45] "Music Trades Journal", 1896, Page 224. There is also mention of a piano by Pape "covered completely with a veneer of ivory" in "Musical Opinion", June, 1935, Page 813, Col 1; and see Grover, 1976, Page 120.
[46] This was made by a French manufacturer who established a strong London connection, Jean-Henri Pape, c.1851 and I confirmed that it is now at the former Royal residence, Osborne House, on the Isle of Wight: Letter to author from Mr Michael Hunter, The Curator, English Heritage, March 10th., 2004.
[47] "Music Trades Journal", 1896, Page 224.

[48] "Music Trades Journal", 1896, Page 224. See also M.M. Whiting's Patent No 4328, Oct 5th., 1895, for "Plates of phosphor bronze or brass" for ornamenting pianos.
[49] "Official Descriptive and Illustrated Catalogue of The Great Exhibtion 1851", Page 454, No 489, Abraham Dimoline of Bristol.
[50] I. Gregory, E. Farr and W. Tarr's Patent No 2683 of Oct 18th., 1865.
[51] N. Berry's No 6673, N. Berry, June 2nd., 1885.
[52] H. Dixon's Patent No 15,884 of Oct 9th., 1889; see also "Music Trades Review", July 15th., 1896, Page 29, Col 2, "T.W. Harper, Class 3A".
[53] Palmieri, 1996, Page 67.
[54] "Official Descriptive and Illustrated Catalogue of The Great Exhibition 1851", Class 10, Philosophical, Musical, Horological, Page 454, Col 1, No 488.
[55] A.A. Hely's Patent No. 4043 of Oct 5th., 1880. See also W. Wilkinson's invention for decorating pianos with plates of ornamented glass "silvered, stained, or otherwise ornamented", No 1753, July 11th., 1861; and another W. Wilkinson invention for decorating piano legs with coloured rings of glass, Patent No 2344, Oct 7th., 1872.
[56] Crombie, 1995, Page 73. See also photo in "Mail on Sunday", Aug 24th., 2003, Page 12 of section "Property on Sunday".
[57] W. Wilkinson's Patent No 2345, Oct 7th., 1856.
[58] W. Hartfield's Patent No 296, Feb 7th., 1855.
[59] T. Whitburn's Patent No 48 of Jan 4th., 1873.
[60] Patent No 2345, 1856.
[61] Patent No 1753, 1861.
[62] Patent No 1753, 1861.
[63] C. Montagu's Patent No 3558 of Nov 23rd., 1868.
[64] "Commerce", April 4th., 1894, Page 503, Col 1.

Chapter Four: Style, Fashion and the Early Piano

[1] Letter from Halsey Ricardo, "Journal of the Society of Arts", Feb 15th., 1907, Page 370.
[2] Now in The Russell Collection, Edinburgh: See "The Russell Collection", Edinburgh University Press, 1968, No. 24.
[3] Donald H. Boalch, "Makers of the Harpsichord and Clavichord 1440-1840", pub Clarendon Press, Second Edition, 1974, Pages 174-175; and William Dale, "Proceedings of The Society of Antiquities", April 28th., 1910, Page 202.
[4] John Jacob Astor writing from Cheapside on March 14th., 1795 and quoted by William Dale in "Tschudi the Harpsichord Maker", pub Constable, 1913, Page 13.
[5] Geoffrey Beard, "English Furniture", pub by National Trust, 1986, Page 26.
[6] Raymond Russell, "The Harpsichord and Clavichord", pub Faber, 2nd edn, 1973, Pages 91-92.
[7] This gentleman does not wish to be named but wrote to me in June, 2004.
[8] Adam Bowett, "Myths of English Furniture History: Cuban Mahogany", in "Antique Collecting", Feb, 1998, Pages 10-13.
[9] Among them Ms Jenny Nex, the Assistant Curator (Research) of The Royal College of Music; and through Ms Nex another distinguished expert.
[10] Jeremy Montagu, Pages 263-264, "The Galpin Society Journal", March, 1995.
[11] Professor Edward Kottick in E-mail to author, April 29th., 2005.
[12] "Some Notes Made by J.S. Broadwood, 1838, with Observations and Elucidations by H.F. Broadwood, 1862", pub by Broadwoods, 1862, Page 4.
[13] RCM 319, Page 54, Catalogue part II, "Keyboard Instruments", pub Royal College of Music, 2000.
[14] RCM 285, Pages 59-62, Catalogue Part II, "Keyboard Instruments", Royal College of Music Museum of Instruments, 2000.
[15] William Dale, Paper published in "Proceedings of The Society of Antiquaries", April 28th., 1910, Page 209.
[16] William Dale, paper published in "Journal of The Society of Arts", Feb 15th., 1907, Page 366, Col 2.
[17] Rowland, "Piano", 1998, Page 22.
[18] Michael Cole, "The Pianoforte in the Classical Era", pub Clarendon, 1998, Page 133.
[19] C.F. Colt, "The Early Piano", pub Stainer & Bell, 1981, Page 151.
[20] C.F. Colt, "The Early Piano", 1981, Pages 22 and 25.
[21] C.F. Colt, "The Early Piano", 1981, Pages 22-23.
[22] Michael Cole, "The Pianoforte in the Classical Era", Page 255.
[23] Now in the Museum of Fine Arts, Boston. See entry 25, starting Page 161, in "Keyboard Musical Instruments", pub Boston, 1994.
[24] Now in the Albany Institute of History and Art, New York. See David Wainwright, "Broadwood by Appointment", pub Quiller, 1982, Page 86.
[25] Michael Cole, "The Pianoforte in the Classical Era", Page 52.
[26] "Music Trades Review", Dec 15th., 1890, Page 21, Col 1.
[27] Michael Cole, "The Pianoforte in the Classical Era", Pages 55-56.
[28] James, "A Square Piano by Zumpe", "Old Furniture", August, 1928, Page 211.
[29] An expert who wishes to remain anonymous in letter to author April 4th 2005.
[30] Philip B. James, 1928, Page 7, Col 2; Crombie, 1995, Page 20, Col 3.
[31] William Dale, paper in the "Journal of The Society of Arts", Feb 15th., 1907, Page 366, Col 2.
[32] C.F. Colt, 1981, Page 152.
[33] Expert who wishes to remain anonymous in letter to author, June 24th., 2004.
[34] Expert who wishes to remain anonymous in E-Mail to author, June 26th., 2004.
[35] Ian Woodfield, "Music of the Raj", pub Oxford University Press, 2000, Page 22.
[36] William Dale paper published by "Journal of the Society of Arts", Feb 15th., 1907, Page 366, Col 2.
[37] C.F. Colt (who writes here as "M. Colt"), "The Early Piano 1780-1850", in "Antiques International", 1966, Page 248.
[38] C.G. Gilbert, "The Life and Work of Thomas Chippendale", pub Studio Vista, 1978, Page 305.
[39] "List of Instruments" issued as a leaflet by William Stodart & Son of No. 1, Golden Square, London, in 1851 (copy in author's possession).
[40] Clifford Musgrave, "Adam and Hepplewhite and other Neo-Classical Furniture", pub Taplinger, 1966, Pages 69-70.
[41] Sir John Soane's Museum, 13, Lincoln's Inn Fields, London, Museum ref: Adam Vol 25 (13).
[42] Laurence Libin, "Robert Adam's instruments for Catherine the Great", in "Early Music", August, 2001, Pages 355-367.
[43] Michael Cole, "The Pianoforte in the Classical Era", Pages 79-80.
[44] Michael Cole, "The Pianoforte in the Classical Era", Page 286.
[45] Michael Cole, "The Pianoforte in the Classical Era", Page 80.
[46] Ralph Edwards, "The Dictionary of English Furniture", Vol 2, 2nd Revised Edn, 1954, pub Country Life, Page 378, Col 2.
[47] Eileen Harris, "The Furniture of Robert Adam", pub Tiranti, 1963, Page 31.
[48] T.A. Strange, "English Furniture, Woodwork, Decoration", pub by the author, Page 220.
[49] Clifford Musgrave, "Adam and Hepplewhite and other Neo-Classical Furniture", pub Taplinger, 1966, Pages 56 and 68-69.

[50] Eileen Harris, "The Furniture of Robert Adam", Page 32.
[51] Stanley C. Ramsey, Page 2 of his "Introduction" to Interiors, in "Small Georgian Houses", Ramsey and J.D.M. Harvey, pub Architectural Press, 1972.
[52] Philip James, "Early Keyboard Instruments", pub Tabard, 1970, Page 138, Caption to Plate LVIII; Martha Novak Clinkscale, "Makers of the Piano", pub Oxford, Vol 1, 1700-1820, Page 19, Col 2, No. 3; "Lady Leverhulme" exhibition catalogue, "Furniture" section by John Hardy, pub by Royal Academy, 1980, Page 114. For ref to second Beck piano as a square see "The New Grove Dictionary of Music", 2nd edn, Macmillan, 2001, Vol 3, Page 42, Col 1.
[53] Albert G. Hess, "The Transition from Harpsichord to Piano" in "The Galpin Society Journal", 1953, Pages 83-92.
[54] Margaret Cranmer, "The New Grove Dictionary of Music", 2nd edn, pub Macmillan, 2001, Vol 3, Page 42.
[55] John Hardy, "Lord Leverhulme", catalogue of exhibition at Royal Academy, 1980, Page 115, Col 1.
[56] Lucy Wood, "Catalogue of Commodes, The Lady Lever Art Gallery", pub H.M.S.O., 1994, Pages 115-123.
[57] Christie's of New York, Auction of Important English Furniture, Sale No. 9766, Oct 17th., 2001, Lot 345, Pages 332-333.
[58] Alec Cobbe, "Irish Arts Review Yearbook", 1997, Vol 13, Page 75, Col 1.
[59] Alec Cobbe, 1997, Page 75, Col 1.
[60] C.F. Colt, 1981, Page 146.
[61] See photo Plate 5, Cole, 1998.
[62] Albert G. Hess, "The Transition from Harpsichord to Piano" in The Galpin Society Journal, 1953, Page 89, No. 224; and Cole, 1998, Page 72.
[63] Professor Andreas Beurmann in phone call to author, Feb 8th., 2004.
[64] Clinkscale, Vol 1, Page 152, Col 2, No 1.
[65] Michael Cole, "Broadwood Square Pianos", pub Tatchley Books, 2005, Pages 177-178; and Sotheby's catalogue Nov 20th., 1980, Lot 173.
[66] Cole, "Broadwood Square Pianos", Page 177.
[67] Philip James, "Early Keyboard Instruments", pub Tabard, 1970, Page 140 and accompanying illustration. See also James, "The Square Piano and its Origin", in "The Connoisseur", Sep, 1928, illus on Page 7 and accompanying comments.
[68] Inventory details of Broadwood square piano (58.188) supplied to author by The Metropolitan Museum of Art, New York.
[69] Inventory details of William and Matthew Stodart upright grand (89.4.2804) supplied to author by The Metropolitan Museum of Art, New York.
[70] Inventory details of Preston square (1980.217) supplied to author by The Metropolitan Museum of Art, New York.
[71] Communication from Mr Otto Rindlisbacher to the author, Dec 1st., 2003.
[72] Alec Cobbe, 1997, Page 71.
[73] Michael Cole, "The Pianoforte in the Classical Era", Page 110.
[74] "A Catalogue of the Cobbe Collection of Keyboard Instruments with Composer Associations", pub The Cobbe Collection Trust, 2000, Page 18, Col 2, No. 10.
[75] Cobbe, 1997, Page 71, Caption to Plate 1.
[76] Clinkscale, Vol 1, 1700-1820, Page 269, Col 2.
[77] Sotheby's auction catalogue Nov 17th., 1994, Lot 167, Page 45.
[78] Sotheby's catalogue of auction Nov 17th., 1994, Lot 167, Page 45.
[79] Clinkscale, Vol 1, 1700-1820, Page 198, Col 2, No 2.
[80] Philip James, "Early Keyboard Instruments", pub Tabard Press, 1970, reprint of the 1930 edn, Page 143.
[81] Arthur Loesser, "Men, Women and Pianos", pub Dover, 1990, Page 249.
[82] See, for example, the Stodart upright grand in Duke University, illustrated as Fig 5.3, opposite page 129, in Good, 2001; or the upright grand by R. Jones for George IV, now in the Museum of London.
[83] "The Artistic Treatment of the Exterior of the Pianoforte", by William Dale, "Journal of the Society of Arts", Feb 15th., 1907, Page 365, Col 1.

Chapter Five: 1800-1850: Three Major Changes

[1] George Savage, "Dictionary of 19th Century Antiques", pub Barrie & Jenkins, 1978, Page 268.
[2] Simon Houfe, "Regency Taste 1790-1830", in "Antique Collecting", April, 1997, Vol 31, No. 10, Pages 13-16.
[3] Ralph Edwards, "The Dictionary of English Furniture", Vol 2, 2nd Revised Edn, 1954, pub Country Life, Page 378, Col 2.
[4] See for example Lot 58, Page 14, Sotheby's auction catalogue, June 22nd., 1978, where a Broadwood square with "four turned and reeded legs" is stated to be "London, 1805".
[5] Philip B. James, "The Square Piano and its Origin", "The Connoisseur", September, 1928, Pages 4-9 but see Page 9, Col 2.
[6] Harding, 1933, Pages 380-381.
[7] John Koster observes in "Keyboard Musical Instruments in the Museum of Fine Arts, Boston", pub Museum, 1994, Page 199, Col 2, that the Museum's 1804 Broadwood grand "has thicker walls and much heavier framing" than its 1796 Broadwood grand but I believe that my more general observations regarding the continuation of the Tabel style of veneered panels holds good.
[8] C.F. Colt, "The Colt Clavier Collection, Golden Jubilee 1944-1981" catalogue, entry No. 15, G295B, Pages 8 and 11.
[9] C.F. Colt, "The Early Piano", 1981, Page 152.
[10] John Koster, "Keyboard Musical Instruments in the Museum of Fine Arts, Boston", Page 199, Col 2.
[11] William Dale, Page 210 of Paper published in "Proceedings of The Society of Antiquaries", May 26th., 1910.
[12] David S. Grover, "The Piano", pub Hale, 1976, Plate 37.
[13] An interesting comparison can be made with a grand by Muzio Clementi & Co. which is now in the Haags Gemeentemuseum (see "A Checklist of Pianos", No 6). In this Clementi the rectangular "cheek" alongside the keys has been eliminated and replaced by a sweeping curve but late interpretation of the "Tabel" panelled style can be seen along the sides of the main case. Evidently a transitional case. An Astor grand suggested to be "circa 1820", with a curved "cheek" appeared as Lot 20 at Bonhams of London on Oct 2nd., 2006 and there is a similar Astor grand in the Museu du Musica, Lisbon, Portugal.
[14] C.F. Colt, 1981, Page 152.
[15] C.F. Colt, 1981, Pages 116-117.
[16] Sotheby's catalogue, May 3rd., 1979, Page 23, Lot 117. An expert has now told me that this piano must be pre-1840.
[17] C.F. Colt, 1981, Page 116.
[18] Rowland, 1998, Page 50; Caption to Babcock photo, Page 174, Dominic Gill, "The Book of the Piano", Phaidon, 1981.
[19] Rob von Acht, "A Checklist of Pianos", Haags Gemeentemuseum, pub by Museum, 1986, No. 34; and Pascale Vandervellen, "Le Piano de style en Europe à 1850", pub Mardaga,1994, Page 54, Plate 20.
[20] David Leigh, "English Square Pianofortes", in "Antique Collector", July, 1988, Page 31, Col 1.
[21] William Pole, "Musical Instruments in the Great Industrial Exhibition of 1851", Pages 4-6, quoted by P. and A. Mactaggart, "Musical Instruments in the 1851 Exhibition", 1986, Page 15.
[22] For American examples see square by Nunns & Clark of New York, Fig 7.1, in Edwin M. Good, "Giraffes, Black Dragons and other Pianos", pub Stanford University Press, 1982, Page 169; Square by A. Reuss of Cincinnati, Plate 85, Page 99 of Helen Rice Hollis, "The Piano", pub David and Charles 1975; and Square by Steinway of New York, Plate 93, Page 106, Hollis, 1975.

[23] See Collard and Collard's square in "An Illustrated Cyclopaedia of the Great Exhibition of 1851", Page 201.
[24] Rowland, 1998, Page 50.
[25] "Journal of the Society of Arts", Feb 15th., 1907, Page 364, Col 2.
[26] For Henry Fowler Broadwood's attitude see his Obituary, "Music Trades Review", July 15th., 1893, Page 21, Col 1.

Chapter Six - The Emergence of the Designers

[1]An actual hand-coloured print showing plan, elevation and view of a grand pianoforte "in a satinwood case ornamented with marqueterie and with Wedgwood's and Tassie's medallions, manufactured by John Broadwood and Son in 1796 for Don Manuel de Godoy", is to be found in The Broadwood Archives at The Surrey History Centre, Woking (Computer catalogue ref: 2185/JB/82/5). My presumption is that this must be the only known copy of this print, which was reported to be in the possession of the Broadwood company. A photo of this engraving has been reproduced in a book by Philip James and others. A photo I have seen of the engraving by Inigo Barlow, July 1st., 1796, is titled "A Plan Elevation & View of a Grand PIANA *(sic)* FORTE, made for the Prime Minister of SPAIN by M. Broadwood & Son/ Instrument makers to his Majesty" and signed "[T. She]raton del./ J. Barlow sculp./ Publish'd as the Act directs, by I. Barlow July 1, 1796". The first letters of Sheraton's name have been trimmed but I see no reason to doubt the attribution, Barlow having engraved plates for Sheraton's "Drawing-Book" and his trade card. For full background see John Koster, "Keyboard Musical Instruments in the Museum of Fine Arts, Boston", Boston, 1994, Pages 165 and 171, Col 1 and Notes 58 and 59. See also Koster, Fig 8 and Pages 212-228, "The Heritage of Wedgwood", Edited Keith A. McLeod and James R. Boyle, pub from "The Proceedings of the Wedgwood International Seminars", held in the U.S.A. by Wedgwood International Seminars, 1998; Philip James, Page 142 and accompanying Plate LXII, "Early Keyboard Instruments", pub Tabard 1970 reprint; Plate 23, David S. Grover, "The Piano", pub Robert Hale, 1976; Franz Josef Hirt, Page 184, "Stringed Keyboard Instruments", pub Boston, 1986.
[2] John Koster, Boston, 1994, Note 59, Page 178.
[3] Michael I. Wilson, "The Case of the Victorian Piano" in "The Victoria and Albert Museum Yearbook", Vol No 3, 1972, Page 134, Col 2.
[4] James, 1927, Page 263, Col 1.
[5] J.F. Hayward, "A newly discovered commode signed by Christopher Fuhrlohg", in "Burlington Magazine", October, 1972, Page 704; "The Age of Neo-Classicism", Catalogue of 14th Exhibition of Council of Europe, published Arts Council, 1972, Pages 773-774.
[6] R.E.M. Harding, 1933, Plate VII(a); Colt Clavier Collection "Golden Jubilee" catalogue, No. 118, Page 31; and C.F. Colt "The Early Piano", Pages 22-23.
[7] David Crombie, "Piano", Page 28, Col 1.
[8] C.F. Colt, "The Early Piano", pub Stainer and Bell, 1981, Page 25; Martha Novak Clinkscale, "Makers of the Piano", pub Oxford University Press, 1995, Vol 1, 1700-1820, Page 133, Col 2, No 4.
[9] Michael Cole, "The Pianoforte in the Classical Era", pub Clarendon, 1998, Plate 9.
[10] Michael Cole, 1998, Plate 7; Sumner, 1971, Plate 8b. See also James, 1970 reprint, Page 139 and Plate LIX; and Sotheby's catalogue March 20th., 1980, Lot 284 and colour plate.
[11] Clinkscale, Vol 1, 1995, Page 269, Col 1.
[12] "Encyclopaedia Britannica", 1911, Page 570, Col 1; Edward F. Rimbault, "The Pianoforte", pub Cocks, 1860, Page 152; Harding, 1933, Page 226; Grover, 1976, Page 135; Dolge, 1911, Page 54.
[13] Palmieri, 1996, Page 363; Harding, 1933, Page 228; Patent No. 3403, March 4th., 1811.
[14] Professor W.E. Mann's thesis "Piano Making in Philadelphia before 1825", Page 115, in which he quotes Hawkins' advert in the "Aurora" of Philadelphia (May?), 1800.
[15] Clinkscale, Vol 1, 1700-1820, Page 30, Col 2.
[16] Now in The Marlowe A. Sigal Collection, Newton Centre, U.S.A.
[17] "The Broadwood Collection of Antique Instruments", pub London, 1903, Page 10, No IX; David S. Grover, "The Piano", pub Hale, 1976, Page 139; Clinkscale, 1995, Vol 1, Page 35, Col 2, No 46 and Page 36, Col 2, No 51.
[18] Mealy's of Castlecomer auction catalogue, Nov 12th-13th., 2002, Lot 1186, Pages 74-75 and Plate 19.
[19] Professor James Stevens Curl, "A Dictionary of Architecture", Oxford University Press, 2000, Pages 544-545.
[20] "Composer Instruments", 2000, Page 38, No 21.
[21] David Wainwright, "The Piano Makers", Plate 10.
[22] See, for example, Sotheby's auction, Nov 2nd and 10th., 2004, Lots 232 and 234.
[23] See, for example, Georgian sofa table, c.1800, Fig 10, Page 132, "Old Furniture", Nov, 1929; also Regency sofa table sold by Gardiner Houlgate, "Antiques Trade Gazette", Feb 21st., 2004, Page 30.
[24] See, for example, Regency work table sold by Mallams of Oxford, Lot 303, Jan 19th., 2005; Regency games table sold by Mellors & Kirk, "Antiques Trade Gazette", April 10th., 2004, Page 28; Regency table auctioned by Gardiner Houlgate at their Bath Auction Rooms on Feb 26th., 2004; also Page 136, bottom left of "The Pocket Book of Furniture" by Therle Hughes, pub Country Life, 1968.
[25] Edward T. Joy, "English Furniture 1800-1851", pub Sotheby Parke Bernet, 1977, Page 36.
[26] Edward T. Joy, Page 40, Col 2, of "Furniture" in "The Connoisseur Period Guides, Late Georgian 1760-1810", pub The Connoisseur, 1956.
[27] Christopher Gilbert, "The Life and Work of Thomas Chippendale", 2 vols, pub Studio Vista, 1978, Page 121, Vol 1; Photo of Nostell Priory chair, Page 92, Vol 2; Photo of Brockett Hall chair, Page 93, Vol 2.
[28] Clifford Musgrave, "Adam and Hepplewhite Furniture", pub Taplinger, 1966, Pages 38, 192-193 and Illustrations No. 60 and 62.
[29] Thomas Hope, "Household Furniture and Interior Decoration", pub Longman, May 1st., 1807, Plate XXIII.
[30] Rev E. Cobham Brewer, "A Dictionary of Phrase and Fable", pub Odham's, 1952, Page 393.
[31] David Wainwright, "The Piano Makers", pub Hutchinson, 1975, Page 57.
[32] "London—World City 1800-1840", 1992, Page 385, No. 278.
[33] "London—World City 1800-1840", 1992, Page 385, No 278, Col 2.
[34] Philip James, "Early Keyboard Instruments", pub Tabard, 1970, Reprint of 1930 edn, Plate LXIV, Page 144. Mr James also suggests that the "Bookcase" style used for this piano had first been "introduced by William Stodart".
[35] Peter Ward Jones, entry for Wornum, in "The New Grove Dictionary", 2nd edn, Page 571; Clinkscale, 1995, Vol 1, 1700-1820, Pages 326-327; Arthur W.J.G. Ord-Hume, entry for Wornum in "Encyclopedia of the Piano", pub Garland, 1996, Pages 443-444.
[36] Clinkscale, Vol 2, 1820-1860, Page 405, Col 2.
[37] Sidney Newman and Peter Williams, "The Russell Collection of Early Keyboard Instruments", Edinburgh University Press, 1968, Page 57 and illus.
[38] "Repository of Arts, Literature, Commerce", pub R. Ackermann, Vol 7, No XXXVII, Feb, 1812, Page 111 and accompanying Plate.

[39] A.N. Wornum, submission on behalf of Robert Wornum and Sons, to the Jurors of the Paris Universal Exhibition, 1867, Pages 2-3 of copy in the Archives of The Museum of London.
[40] Colt, 1981, pages 116-117; Helen Rice Hollis, "The Piano", pub David & Charles, 1975, Page 82,
[41] Every building by the architect C.F.A. Voysey was "meticulously detailed and in addition Voysey designed the wall-papers and fabrics, the furniture and carpets, the brass or silver lamps and fittings, the spoons and forks, the hinges and handles for doors and drawers….Like Webb and Street, Voysey designed every detail himself and his pupils or assistants had little to do but to make the necessary copies" (John Brandon-Jones, "C.F.A. Voysey" in "Victorian Architecture", pub Cape, 1963, Page 277). For Voysey's theories try "Ideas in Things", in "The Arts Connected with Building", pub Batsford, 1909, Pages 103-137.
[42] Voysey designed a number of pianos. See, for example: Page 218, "The Studio", Vol 7, No. 38, May, 1896.
[43] Angela Partington, "The Oxford Dictionary of Quotations", pub Softback Preview, 4th revised edn, 1996, Page 7, Col 2.
[44] John Nash, "Views of the Royal Pavilion", pub Pavilion, 1991, Page 84 and accompanying illus.
[45] Inventory details (Inventory No RCIN 2591) supplied to author by Mr Matthew Winterbottom, The Royal Collection Trust, July 16th., 2001. See also John Harris Geoffrey de Bellaigue and Oliver Millar, "Buckingham Palace", pub Nelson, 1968, Pages 132-133; H. Clifford Smith, "Buckingham Palace", pub Country Life, 1931, Page 161, Plate 165; Dinkel, 1983, Pages 99-100.
[46] Harris, de Bellaigue and Millar, 1968, Page 133.
[47] Colt, 1981, Page 76.
[48] "Views of the Royal Pavilion", 1991, Pages 60-61; Colt, 1981, Page 78.
[49] Colt, 1981, Page 76.
[50] John Harris, "Regency Furniture Designs 1803-1826", pub Tiranti, 1961: See Plate 20, Pier-Table; Plate 19, Sideboard; Plates 6 and 7, Sofas; all designs from Sheraton's "Encyclopaedia", showing his "twin leg" designs. For G.B.Piranesi see Plate V, after Page 6.
[51] C.F. Colt, "The Early Piano", pub Stainer and Bell, 1981, Page 76 and Illus on Page 79; "The Colt Clavier Collection: Golden Jubilee 1944-1981" catalogue, Page 11, number 16, Code G203B; Colour Plate, after Page 232, of David Wainwright, "Broadwood by Appointment", pub Quiller, 1982; and letter to author March 4th 2004, from Mr W.E. Spiers, Guardian of The Colt Clavier Collection..
[52] John Koster, "Keyboard Musical Instruments in the Museum of Fine Arts, Boston", pub Boston, 1994, Pages 161-180.
[53] "Official Descriptive and Illustrated Catalogue of the Great Exhibition 1851", Class X, Page 455, No 518.
[54] The historian of Broadwood, David Wainwright, author of "Broadwood by Appointment", pub Quiller, 1982, states (Page 13): "John (*Broadwood*) learnt his craft of joiner and cabinet-maker from his father". Most accounts describe Broadwood as a cabinet maker or joiner and sometimes both. The "Dictionary of National Biography", pub Smith Elder, 1886, Vol 6, Page 364 states he "is said to have walked from Scotland to London to seek his fortune as a cabinet-maker".
[55] Michael Cole, "Broadwood Square Pianos", pub Tatchley Books, 2005, Pages 44-45.
[56] Clinkscale, 1995, Vol 1, 1700-1820, Page 30.
[57] Clinkscale, 1995, Vol 1, Page 47, Col 1, No 44.
[58] Sotheby's "Musical Instruments" catalogue, Nov 22nd-23rd., 1989, Lot 193, Page 70.
[59] Hugh Gough, "The Classical Grand Pianoforte, 1770-1830", in "Proceedings of The Royal Musical Association", 1950-1951, Page 43.
[60] "The Crosby Brown Collection of Musical Instruments of All Nations", pub New York, 1903, No 2805, Pages 156-159; Clinkscale, 1995, Vol 1, Page 37, Col 1, No 59. Also Inventory details supplied to author by the Metropolitan, May 9th., 2003.
[61] "Cabinet Maker", March 14th., 1908, Page 422.
[62] Clinkscale, 1995, Vol 1, Page 51, Col 1, No 72.
[63] Martha Novak Clinkscale, "Makers of the Piano", Vol 2, 1820-1860, pub Oxford University Press, 1999, Page 57, Col 2.
[64] Accession notes by Laurence Libin for Accession Number 1972.109, Metropolitan Museum of Art, New York.
[65] Clinkscale, Vol 2, 1820-1860, Page 57, Col 2.
[66] See, for example, Tomkison's Royal grand of 1821 in Colt, 1981, Page 76 and Illus.
[67] See, for example, the Mott grand (Ref: RCIN 2591) normally on display in the Green Drawing Room of Buckingham Palace. An illustration is to be found in "Buckingham Palace" by John Harris, Geoffrey de Bellaigue, Oliver Miller, pub Nelson, 1968
[68] See, for example, the Gothic cabinet for George IV, in Philip James's "Early Keyboard Instruments", pub Tabard 1970 reprint of 1930 edn, Plate LXIV, Page 144.
[69] See, for example, Clementi's brass inlaid square in "The Colt Clavier Collection" catalogue, pub 1981, Page 35.
[70] See, for example, Plate 15 in David Wainwright, "The Piano Makers", pub Hutchison, 1975.
[71] Clive Wainwright, "A.W.N. Pugin's Early Furniture" in "Connoisseur", 1976, Vol CXCI, Page 4.
[72] "The Dictionary of Art", pub Macmillan, 1996, Vol 25, Page 710, Col 1.
[73] Benjamin Ferrey, "Recollections of A. Welby Pugin", pub Scolar Press, 1978 reprint, Pages 1-2. See also Michael Trappes-Lomax, "Pugin, a Mediaeval Victorian", pub Sheed and Ward, 1932, Page 3.
[74] Trappes-Lomax, 1932, Page 3; "Dictionary of National Biography", pub Smith Elder, 1896, Vol 47, Page 5, Col 2.
[75] Ferrey, 1978, Page 40. See also Trappes-Lomax, 1932, Page 2.
[76] "Dictionary of National Biography", Oxford University Press, 1960, Vol XVI, Pages 448-449.
[77] Kenneth Clark, "The Gothic Revival", pub Penguin 1964, reprint of 1928 edn, Page 107.
[78] Wainwright, 1976, Page 4.
[79] Geoffrey de Bellaigue and Pat Kirkham, "George IV and the Furnishing of Windsor Castle", "Furniture History", 1972, Vol VIII, Page 5; Paul Atterbury and Clive Wainwright, "Pugin, A Gothic Passion", pub Yale University Press, 1994, Page 24, Col 2; "Dictionary of Art", Macmillan, 1996, Vol 25, Page 712, Col 1.
[80] Wainwright, 1976, Page 4.
[81] Peter and M.A. Nicholson, "The Practical Cabinet Maker, Upholsterer and Complete Decorator", pub H. Fisher and Son, apparently 1826 but some plates dated 1827, Plate 66.
[82] Sutton Webster in a letter to the author, Feb 25th., 2002.
[83] Nicholson, "The Practical Cabinet Maker", 1826-27, Plate 65,
[84] Simon Jervis, "The Penguin Dictionary of Design and Designers", pub Penguin, 1984.
[85] J.C. Loudon, "Encyclopaedia of Cottage, Farm and Villa Architecture", pub Longman, 1846, Pages 1069-1070.
[86] Design by Robert Mallet in Loudon, 1846, Page 320, No 650.
[87] Loudon, 1846, Page 1069.
[88] Loudon, 1846, Page 1039.
[89] Christopher Gilbert, Introduction to "Loudon's Furniture Designs", pub S.R. Publishers, 1970, Page VII.
[90] Loudon, 1846, Page 1069, No 1961.
[91] Loudon, 1846, Page 1069, No 1962.
[92] Loudon, 1846, Pages 1069-1070.
[93] James, 1930, reprint 1970, Page 58.
[94] Loudon, 1846, Page 1290, No 2334.
[95] Loudon, 1846, Pages 1290-1291.
[96] William Watt's catalogue "Art Furniture", 1877, Plate 12; also Susan Weber Soros, "The Secular Furniture of E.W. Godwin", pub Yale University Press, 1999, Page 243, No 405.
[97] John Gloag, "Mr Loudon's England", pub Oriel Press, 1970, Page 166, Caption to illustration.

[98] Loudon, 1846, Page 1096, No 2021.
[99] Acquired by the Metropolitan Museum of Art, New York, 1959, the gift of Mrs Henry McSweeney (Ref: 59.76).
[100] Clinkscale, Vol 2, 1820-1860, Page 121, Col 1.
[101] Sir John Vanbrugh, "Confederacy", Act 2, I.
[102] Christoph Rueger, "Musical Instruments and Their Decoration", pub David and Charles, 1986, Page 122, Col 1 and Colour Plate 94. For additional colour photos see front cover and Page 61 of "Das Klavier" by Klaus Wolters, pub Schott, 1984.
[103] Rueger, 1986, Page 87 and Plate 40.
[104] Rueger, 1986, Page 64 and Colour Plate 30.
[105] Clinkscale, Vol 2, 1820-1860, Page 121, Col 1.
[106] Inventory details (ref: 59.76) supplied to author by Metropolitan Museum of Art, New York, March 24th., 2003.
[107] Mr Martin P. Levy, Principal of H. Blairman & Sons of 119, Mount St., London W1K 3NL, in letter to author, Sep 18th., 2003.
[108] The Furniture History Society Newsletter, No. 158, May, 2005, Pages 1-3.
[109] Inventory details (ref: 59.76) supplied to author by Metropolitan Museum of Art.
[110] Emanuel Winternitz, "Musical Instruments of the Western World", pub Thames and Hudson, 1966, Page 250.
[111] Quoted by Edward F. Rimbault, "The Pianoforte", pub Robert Cocks and Co., 1860, Pages 160-161.
[112] Charles Newton, "Victorian Designs for the Home", pub V. and A. Publications, 1999, Page 24.
[113] Sutton Webster, letter to author, April 16th, 2002.
[114] Clive Wainwright in "Pugin, A Gothic Passion", Edited Paul Atterbury and Clive Wainwright, pub Victoria and Albert Museum, 1994, Page 131, Col 1.
[115] David Crombie, "Piano", pub Balafon, 1995, Page 31, Col 3.
[116] Jervis, 1984, Page 518, Col 2. See also Whitaker's attack on foreign furniture in "The Builder", June 28th., 1851, Page 408, Col 2.
[117] Henry Whitaker, "Practical Cabinet Maker and Upholsterer's Treasury of Designs", pub 1847, Plate 10.
[118] Whitaker, 1847, Plate 14.
[119] Jervis, 1984, Pages 518-519.
[120] Whitaker, "The Builder", June 28th., 1851, page 408, Col 2.
[121] Clinkscale, Vol 2, 1820-1860, Page 68.

Chapter Seven - Early British Artist Painted Pianos

[1] Professor Edward L. Kottick, "A History of the Harpsichord", pub Indiana University Press, 2003, Page 81.
[2] "The Morning Star", May 29th., 1867, Page 5, Col 1.
[3] See, for example, "roses painted on the soundboard" of the only known surviving square by Thomas Green, dated 1785, in the Bad Krozingen Collection; Martha Novak Clinkscale, "Makers of the Piano", Oxford University Press, 1995, Vol 1, 1700-1820, Page 129.
[4] Alec Cobbe, "Beethoven, Haydn and an Irish Genius: William Southwell of Dublin", in "Irish Arts Review Yearbook", 1997, Vol 13, Page 75, Col 1.
[5] See, for example, the Rolfe square, c.1805, in the Colt Clavier Collection; the Astor square. c.1803. lot 194, Sotheby's, Nov 22nd, 1989; or the Clementi square, c.1815, lot 86, Sotheby's March 6th., 1979.
[6] "A Catalogue of the Cobbe Collection", pub by The Cobbe Collection Trust, 2000, Pages 31 (Col 1) and 35 (Col 1).
[7] Clinkscale, Vol 1, 1700-1820, Pages 184 (No. 13), 185 (No. 22), 187 (No. 35) and others listed.
[8] Michael Cole, "The Pianoforte in the Classical Era", pub Clarendon, 1998, Page 108.
[9] C.F. Colt, "The Colt Clavier Collection, Golden Jubilee 1944-1981", Page 25, No. 70.
[10] C.F. Colt, "The Early Piano", pub Stainer and Bell, 1981, Pages 91-92.
[11] Colt, 1981, Page 146.
[12] Michael Cole in letter to author, June 24th., 2004.
[13] Clinkscale, Vol 1, 1700-1820, Page 68, Col 2, No 9.
[14] Clinkscale, Vol 1,1700-1820, Page 68, Col 2, No 12.
[15] Clinkscale, Vol 1, 1700-1820, Page 69, Col 1, No 16.
[16] Clinkscale, Vol 1, 1700-1820, Page 70, Col 1, No 27.
[17] "A Catalogue of the Cobbe Collection", 2000, Page 35, No. 19.
[18] Philip B. James, "The Decoration of Old Keyboard Musical Instruments", in "Old Furniture", 1927, Pages 256-265; Peter Thornton, "The Decoration of Keyboard Instruments" in "Catalogue of Musical Instruments", Vol 1, Keyboard Instruments, pub Victoria and Albert Museum, 1968, Appendix B, Pages 71-75; A.J. Hipkins and "K.S." "Pianoforte" in "Encyclopaedia Britannica", 1911 edn, Pages 559-574; George Rose, "The Evolution of the Pianoforte" in "The Connoisseur", Vol 13, 1905, Pages 182-195.
[19] Raymond Russell, "Catalogue of Musical Instruments", Vol 1, Keyboard Instruments, pub Victoria and Albert Museum, 1968, Page 48, No 16.
[20] Russell, 1968, Page 5.
[21] Christoph Rueger, "Musical Instruments and Their Decoration", pub David and Charles, 1986, Page 62 and Plates 28/29.
[22] Russell, 1968, Page 50, No 17.
[23] Philip James, "Early Keyboard Instruments", pub Tabard, 1970 reprint of 1930 edn, Page 108, Caption to Plate XXVIII.
[24] The Fitzwilliam Museum "On-line Catalogue", reference No PD.7-1954.
[25] Raymond Russell, "The Harpsichord and Clavichord", pub Faber, 2nd edn, 1973, Page 92.
[26] William Dale, "The Artistic Treatment of the Exterior of the Pianoforte", in "Journal of The Society of Arts", Feb 15th., 1907, Pages 365-366; James, 1970 reprint, Pages 26-27, Plates XXV and XXXVII; William Dale, "Tschudi, the Harpsichord Maker", pub Constable, 1913, Pages 22-23; The Russell Collection catalogue, pub Edinburgh University Press, 1968, Pages 10-15 and 68, No.6.
[27] Dale, 1907, Pages 365-366. See also Illus and Caption to Ruckers harpsichord painted by Van der Meulen, "The Connoisseur", Vol 13, 1905, Page 188.
[28] James, 1927, Page 262, Col 1.
[29] James, 1927, Page 264, Col 1.
[30] Michael I. Wilson, "The Case of the Victorian Piano", in "The Victoria and Albert Museum Yearbook", 1972, Vol No 3, Page 134, Col 1.
[31] Philip James, "Early Keyboard Instruments", pub Tabard, 1970, Pages 35-36; and Raymond Russell, "The Harpsichord and Clavichord", pub Faber, 1973, 2nd edn revised, Pages 161-162.
[32] See for example claimed Handel's spinet, made by John Hitchcock, 1710, "The Connoisseur", 1905, Page 186.
[33] "Catalogue of Musical Instruments", Vol 1, Keyboard Instruments, pub Victoria and Albert Museum, 1968, Page 84, No 29.
[34] James, 1970, Page 52.
[35] Michael Cole, "The Pianoforte in the Classical Era", pub Clarendon, 1998, Page 63.
[36] William Dale, Page 209 of Paper published in "Proceedings of the Society of Antiquaries", April 28th., 1910.
[37] Michael Cole "The Pianoforte in the Classical Era", Clarendon Press, 1998, pages 51-59 and see also Cole's "Broadwood Square Pianos", Tatchley Books, 2005, pages 31-39; Clinkscale, Vol 1, 1700-1820, Page 330, Col 1; David Leigh, "English Square Pianofortes" in "Antique Collector", July, 1988, Page 31; Philip B. James, "The Square Piano and its Origin" in "The Connoisseur", Sep, 1928, Page 5, Col 2.

[38] Information given to author by an expert who has made a detailed study of the records.

[39] In fact these paintings appear to have been TWICE transferred to Erard grand pianos. According to an article "A True Tale of Two Cities", appearing "Ludgate Magazine" in 1894 (details supplied to author by The Royal Collection Trust) the paintings from the Anne of Austria harpsichord were first transferred to "a grand pianoforte of Messrs S. and P. Erard's early manufacture, and thence subsequently to the case of the grand piano now standing in the White Drawing Room". This piano, Erard No. 3985, made it is believed in 1856, is still on display in the White Drawing Room.

[40] Letter to author from Mr Matthew Winterbottom of The Royal Collection Trust, Sep 30th., 2003.

[41] John Koster, "Keyboard Musical Instruments in the Museum of Fine Arts, Boston", pub by Museum, 1994, Pages 161-180.

[42] Koster, 1994, Page 164 (Col 2), Illus, Page 165 and Pages 171-172.

[43] Arthur Loesser, "Men, Women and Pianos", pub Dover, 1990, Page 324; Albert G. Hess, "The Transition from Harpsichord to Piano", in "The Galpin Society Journal", 1953, Pages 75-94.

[44] Philip B. James, "The Connoisseur", Sep, 1928, Page 8.

[45] Quoted by Loesser, 1990, Page 316.

[46] Michael Cole, "The Pianoforte in the Classical Era", pub Clarendon, 1998 Page 70.

[47] Loesser, 1990, Pages 323 and 316.

[48] Hess, 1953, Pages 75-94.

[49] Michael Cole, 1998, Plate 9.

[50] Photograph of nameboard supplied to author by Professor Dr Andreas Beurmann, Sep 30th., 2003. For discussion of relationship of William and Matthew Stodart to Robert Stodart see Clinkscale, Vol 1, 1700-1820, Page 284, Col 1.

[51] Letter to author from Professor Dr. Andreas Beurmann, Sep 30th., 2003.

[52] Clinkscale, Vol 1, 1700-1820, Pages 284-285.

[53] Professor Dr. Andreas Beurmann in telephone conversation with author, Feb 8th., 2004.

[54] Professor Dr. Andreas Beurmann in letter to Author, Oct 18th., 2003.

[55] Edward Joy, "Furniture" pub The Connoisseur, 1972, Page 86, Col 2.

[56] A.J. Hipkins, "Musical Instruments: Historic, Rare and Unique", pub A. & C. Black, 1888, Pages 75-76. See also early 18th Century Italian harpsichord "Painted with simple chinoiserie decoration on a turquoise ground", Lot 159, Sotheby's auction Nov 17th., 1994.

[57] Ms Rose Kerr, the Chief Curator, Far Eastern Section, Asian Department, Victoria and Albert Museum, in letter to the author, Nov 3rd., 2003.

[58] Ms Mary Ginsberg of The British Museum in a letter to the author, Jan 14th., 2004.

[59] Sotheby's of New York, auction Oct 22nd., 1999 (Sale NY 7363), Lot 457.

[60] Rob van Acht, "A Checklist of Pianos: Musical Instrument Collection Haags Gemeentemuseum", pub The Hague, 1986, Page 41, No. 20 and accompanying illus; René Clemencic, "Old Musical Instruments", pub Weidenfeld and Nicolson, 1968, photo and caption, Plate 116, Page 106, text Page 107; Clinkscale, Vol 1, 1700-1820, Page 62, Col 1, No. 4.

[61] Clemencic, 1968, Page 107.

[62] Communication to author from Dr Michael Latcham, Curator of the Musical Instruments Department, Haags Gemeentemuseum, received Nov 14th., 2003.

[63] Martha Novak Clinkscale, "Makers of the Piano", 2 vols, Oxford University Press, 1995 corrected Vol 1 and Vol 2, 1999.

[64] "Guide to the Loan Collection and List of Musical Instruments", International Inventions Exhibition, 1885.

[65] Patent No 2264 by William Southwell, 1798.

[66] "Guide to the Loan Collection and List of Musical Instruments", International Inventions Exhibition, 1885, Page 45.

[67] Clinkscale, Vol 1, 1700-1820, Page 51, Col 1, No 73.

[68] Clinkscale, Vol 1, 1700-1820, Page 51, Col 1, No 73.

[69] Koster, 1994, Page 177, Col 2, No 42.

[70] Letter to author, Feb 11th., 2003.

[71] "Guide to the Loan Collection and List of Musical Instruments", 1885, Page 44.

[72] Inventory details of Broadwood square piano (58.188) supplied to author by The Metropolitan Museum of Art, New York.

[73] Inventory details of William and Matthew Stodart upright grand (89.4.2804) supplied to author by The Metropolitan Museum of Art, New York.

[74] Clinkscale, Vol 1, 1700-1820, Pages 74-75, No 3.

[75] Inventory details of Preston square (1980.217) supplied to author by The Metropolitan Museum of Art, New York.

[76] Martha Novak Clinkscale, "Makers of the Piano", Vol 1, 1700-1820, pub Oxford University Press, 1993, Page 221, Col 2, No 1.

[77] John Koster, "Keyboard Musical Instruments in the Museum of Fine Arts, Boston", pub by Museum, Boston, 1994, Page 177, Col 2, No 42.

[78] Inscription on nameboard of Preston square (1980.217).

[79] Inventory details of Preston square (1980.217).

[80] Inventory details of Preston square (1980.217).

[81] Clinkscale, 1993, Page 221.

[82] Inventory details of Goulding, D'Almaine, Potter and Co. square (4990.1960) supplied to author by The Yale University Collection of Musical Instruments.

[83] Clinkscale, Vol 1, 1700-1820, Page 125, Col 1.

[84] John Koster, 1994, Page 177, Col 2, No 42.

[85] Clinkscale, Vol 1, 1700-1820, Page 125, Col 1.

[86] Clinkscale, Vol 1, 1700-1820, Page 124.

[87] Yale Inventory details (No. 4990.1960).

[88] Koster, 1994, Page 177, Col 2, No 42.

[89] Communication from Mr Otto Rindlisbacher to the author, Dec 1st., 2003.

[90] Clinkscale, Vol 1, 1700-1820, Page 287, No 9; and Illus Crombie, 1995, Page 20.

[91] Margaret Cranmer in "The New Grove Dictionary of Music and Musicians", 2nd Edn, Page 420.

[92] Clinkscale, Vol 1, 1700-1820, Pages 221-222.

[93] The Broadwood square of 1801 now in the Metropolitan Museum of Art, New York (No 58.188); and Michael Cole notes a 1784 Broadwood square "the front painted" page 49, "Broadwood Square Pianos", 2005.

[94] "Bryan's Dictionary of Painters and Engravers", pub Bell, revised edn, 1910, Vol 3, Page 124,

[95] "Guide to the Loan Collection and List of Musical Instruments", International Inventions Exhibition, 1885, Page 45.

[96] Dr James Yorke, Curator of the Department of Furniture, Textiles and Fashion, Victoria and Albert Museum, in letter to the author, Dec 2nd., 2002.

[97] Malise Forbes Adam and Mary Mauchline, "Kauffman's Decorative Work" in "Angelica Kauffman", Edited W.W. Roworth, pub Reaktion, 1992, Page 113.

[98] David Alexander, "Kauffman and the Print Market in Eighteenth-century England", in "Angelica Kauffman", 1992, First page of Chapter.

[99] Alexander, 1992, Page 177.

[100] "Bryan's Dictionary", 1910, Page 124, Col 1.

[101] Inventory details from Maidstone Museum and Bentlif Art Gallery, supplied to author Jan 6th., 2004, by Ms Veronica Tonge, Keeper of Fine & Applied Art. See also Clinkscale, Vol 2, 1820-1860, Pages 92-93.

[102] Clinkscale, Vol 1, 1700-1820, Page 285, No 9.

[103] Clinkscale, Vol 1, 1700-1820, Page 286, Col 2, No 8.

[104] Clinkscale, Vol 1, 1700-1820, Page 287, Col 1, No 11.

[105] Clinkscale, Vol 1, 1700-1820, Page 7, Col 1, No 2.

[106] Clinkscale, Vol 1, 1700-1820, Page 8, Col 1, No 9.

[107] Clinkscale, Vol 1, 1700-1820, Page 7, Col 2, No 6.

[108] Clinkscale, Vol 1, 1700-1820, Page 8, Col 1, No 10.

[109] "Gorgeousness in Pianos", in "Music Trades Journal", Sep, 1896, Page 326 but apparently reprinted from the "New York Courier".

Chapter Eight - Zumpe: Form follows Function

[1] Michael Cole, "The Pianoforte in the Classical Era", pub Clarendon Press, 1998, Pages 56-57, marshals powerful arguments on behalf of Zumpe on the basis of his own detailed and original modern research. Mr Cole's view is supported by Edwin M. Good in "Giraffes, Black Dragons and other Pianos", pub Stanford University Press, 2001, Page 63. Philip James, however, had at a much earlier date, 1930, suggested that the square had emerged in Germany "and there are indications of the manufacture of square pianos....as early as 1750" (see "Early Keyboard Instruments", P. James, 1930, reprint 1970 by Tabard Press, Page 51). He also suggested that German craftsmen had "made their way to England, bringing with them the square piano". James Shudi Broadwood, in my view proven not to be the most reliable of historians, stated in notes written some 70 years after the event and eventually published in 1862, that Zumpe "on his return from Germany, where he had been to visit his relations, brought back with him the first of these instruments seen in England, and about the years 1768 or 1769, began to make them" (see "J.S. Broadwood, 'Some Notes and Observations', London, 1862).

An expert who wishes to remain anonymous and who was able to survey all this evidence retrospectively until June, 2004, told me in a private communication of that month that: "The earliest document that seems to indicate a square pianoforte in Germany dates from 1764 but it is slightly ambiguous and anonymous."

[2] In an advertisement from the "General Advertiser", Feb 1st., 1780, quoted by Philip James in "Early Keyboard Instruments", Tabard reprint, 1970, of the original 1930 edn, Page 80.

[3] James, 1970, Caption to Plate LVII.

[4] Alfred Dolge, "Pianos and their Makers", Dover reprint 1972, Page 172.

[5] Cole, 1998, Page 52. The price seemed to have gone up to 18 guineas in 1771 (see A. Ribeiro, Editor, "The Letters of Dr Charles Burney", 1751-1784, Oxford, 1991, Page 98, footnote 1). This contrasts with Pohlman charging between 16 to 18 guineas in January, 1774 (See Ribeiro, 1991, Pages 163-164).

[6] Donald H. Boalch, "Makers of the Harpsichord and Clavichord 1440-1840", 3rd Edition, 1995 (Charles Mould, Editor), pub Clarendon Press, Page 108, Col 1.

[7] William Dale, "Tschudi the Harpsichord Maker", pub Constable, 1913, Page 60.

[8] Percy A. Scholes, "The Great Dr Burney", Vol 1, pub Oxford University Press, MCMXLVIII, Page 134, quoting from Rees's "Cyclopaedia".

[9] Edwin M. Good, "Giraffes, Black Dragons and other Pianos", pub Stanford University Press, 2001, Page 59.

[10] Cole, 1998, Page 52. See also "Composer Instruments, The Cobbe Collection", catalogue pub The Cobbe Collection Trust, 2000, Page 12 and Page 21 (where it is suggested that Sébastian Erard was one of those who copied Zumpe's square). Michael Cole also states on his Internet site www.squarepianos.com that Zumpe's squares were copied in Switzerland, Spain, Scandinavia and Germany (see "John Zumpe").

[11] Philip B. James, "The Connoisseur", Sep, 1928, Page 8; and "Early Keyboard Instruments", 1970 reprint, Page 53, Note 1.

[12] What Sullivan actually wrote was "form ever follows function" in "The Tall Office Building Artistically Considered", in "Lippincott's Magazine", March, 1896 but I have seen it suggested that Sullivan merely popularised a quotation of Horatio Greenhough.

[13] The frontispiece to the Abbé Marc-Antoine Laugier's "Essai sur l'architecture", 1755, showed a rustic hut made from still-living trees. He argued that a primitive hut had a structural skeleton and was thus the first architectural idea. In doing so, Laugier was developing the ideas of Vitruvius.

[14] Horatio Greenhough in "American Architecture", 1843.

[15] Clinkscale, Vol 1, 1700-1820, Pages 330-331.

[16] Michael Cole, 1998, Page 55.

[17] Michael Cole, 1998, Page 53.

[18] Inventory of The Colonial Williamsburg Foundation and E-mail to the author from Mr John R. Watson, the Foundation's Conservator of Instruments, on July 11th., 2006.

[19] To be found in The Yale Center for British Art.

[20] Dominic Gill (Editor), "The Book of the Piano", pub Phaidon, 1981, Page 239.

[21] Cole, 1998, Page 55; and Philip B. James, "A Square Piano by Zumpe" in "Old Furniture", August, 1928, Pages 211-212.

[22] Michael Cole, "The Pianoforte in the Classical Era", pub Clarendon Press, 1998, Page 55.

[23] Geoffrey Beard, "English Furniture", pub by National Trust, 1986, Page 26.

[24] Adam Bowett "Myths of English Furniture History: Cuban Mahogany" in "Antique Collecting", Feb 1998, Page 13, Cols 2-3.

[25] Beard, 1986, Page 26. Broadwood were still specifying "Spanish mahogany" for an important grand in the Adam style in 1895 but precisely what they meant by "Spanish mahogany" is not spelt out: See "A Descriptive Album of Artistic Pianofortes", pub Broadwood & Sons, 1895, Page 10, Col 2.

[26] Michael Cole in a letter to author of June, 2004.

[27] Adam Bowett "Myths of English Furniture History: Cuban Mahogany" in "Antique Collecting", Feb 1998, Pages 11-13.

[28] Bowett, Feb, 1998, Page 12, Col 1.

[29] Bowett, Feb, 1998, Page 11, Col 2.

[30] Blackie, 1853, quoted by Bowett, Feb, 1998, Page 13, Col 3.

[31] Bowett, Feb, 1998, Page 13, Col 1.

[32] Raymond Russell, "The Harpsichord and Clavichord", pub Faber, 2nd edn, 1973, Pages 91-92.

[33] "Composer Instruments, The Cobbe Collection", 2000, Page 16, Col 2.

[34] Cole, "The Pianoforte in the Classical Era", 1998, Page 61.

[35] James, Tabard, 1970, Page 52.

[36] Mies van der Rohe, New York Herald Tribune, June 28th., 1959.

[37] James, "A Square Piano by Zumpe", "Old Furniture", August, 1928, Page 211.

[38] James, Tabard, 1970, Caption to Plate LVII and Page 52; Edwin M. Good, "Giraffes, Black Dragons and other Pianos", pub Stanford University Press, 2001, Page 59; "Encyclopedia of the Piano", Page 451, Col 2.

[39] Clinkscale, Vol 1, 1700-1820, Pages 331-334.

[40] Quoted by James, 1970, Page 80, from Zumpe's advert in the "General Advertiser", Feb 1st., 1780.

[41] Cole, 1998, Pages 47 and 62.

[42] Cole, 1998, Page 61.

[43] "A Princess of Mecklenburg-Strelitz as Queen of England", Internet site www.people.virginia.edu/.

[44] Michael Cole on his Internet site: www.squarepianos.com See "John Zumpe".

[45] Michael Cole Internet site, "John Zumpe".

[46] H. Clifford Smith, "Buckingham Palace", pub Country Life, 1931, Page 89.

[47] From copy of original catalogue supplied to the author by the Royal Archives.

[48] "Composer Instruments, The Cobbe Collection", catalogue pub The Cobbe Collection Trust, 2000, Pages 15-16.

[49] Cole, 1998, Pages 61-62.

[50] Cole, 1998, Page 62. The actual bank statement showing the payment on July 4th., 1768, is reproduced by Virginia Pleasants in "The Early Piano in Britain (c.1760-1800)", in "Early Music", Feb, 1985, Page 39.

Other Music sources

The Archive of Art and Design, Victoria and Albert Museum branch, Blythe House, 23, Blythe Road, West Kensington, London W14 0QX.
Broadwood Archives at Surrey History Centre, 130, Goldsworth Road, Woking, Surrey GU21 1ND: A vital source for this book.
Cole, Michael, Internet site: www.squarepianos.com
Fitzwilliam Museum "On-line Catalogue".
Music Collection, British Library.
National Art Library, Victoria and Albert Museum.
PianoGen, Internet site of Bill Kibby-Johnson.
Royal Collection Trust.
Royal College of Music.

Caricature

Catalogue of Political and Personal Satires in the British Museum, 11 vols, 1870-1954; Vols 1 to 4 by F.G. Stephens; Vols 5-11 by M. Dorothy George.
Cohn, Albert M., *George Cruikshank, A Catalogue Raisonné*, pub The Bookman's Journal, 1924.
Cruikshank, George, *Four Hundred Humourous Illustrations*, pub Simpkin, 2nd edn., undated.
George, M. Dorothy, *English Political Caricature*, pub Clarendon, 1959.
George, M. Dorothy, *Hogarth to Cruikshank*, publish Penguin, 1967.
George, M. Dorothy, *London Life in the Eighteenth Century*, pub Penguin, 1976.
Hill, Draper, *Fashionable Contrasts: Caricatures by James Gillray*, pub Phaidon, 1966.
Hill, Draper, *Mr Gillray, The Caricaturist*, pub Phaidon, 1965.
Houfe, Simon, *John Leech and the Victorian Scene*, pub Antique Collectors Club, c.1984.
James Gillray, 1756-1815, Arts Council catalogue, 1967.
Jerrold, Blanchard, *The Life of George Cruikshank*, 2 vols, 1882.
Katanka, Michael, *Gillray and Cruikshank*, pub Shire, 1973.
Leech, John, *Four Hundred Humorous Illustrations*, pub Simpkin, 2nd edn., undated.
McLean, Ruari, *George Cruikshank, His Life and Work as a Book Illustrator*, pub Art and Technics, 1948.
Wood, Marcus, *Radical Satire and Print Culture*, pub Clarendon, 1994.
Wynn Jones, Michael, *George Cruikshank, His Life and Work*, pub Macmillan, 1978.

Furniture and related Books and Articles

Adam, Malise Forbes and Mary Mauchline, "Kauffman's Decorative Work" in *Angelica Kauffman*, Edited W.W. Roworth, pub Reaktion, 1992.
Adam: *The Decorative Work of Robert and Thomas Adam*, reproduced from Works in Architecture 1778-1812, pub Batsford, 1901.
Age (The) of Neo-Classicism, Catalogue of 14th Exhibition of Council of Europe, published Arts Council, 1972.
Age of Rossetti, Burne-Jones and Watts, Tate Gallery Exhibition catalogue, 1997.
Agius, Pauline, *Ackermann's Regency Furniture & Interiors*, pub Crowood, 1984.
Agius, Pauline, *British Furniture 1880-1915*, pub Antique Collectors' Club, 1978.
Ames, Winslow, *Prince Albert and Victorian Taste*, pub Chapman and Hall, 1968.
Andrews, John, *The Price Guide to Victorian, Edwardian and 1920s Furniture*, pub Antique Collectors Club, 1973 and 1980 edns.
Anscombe, Isabelle, *Omega and After*, pub Thames and Hudson, 1981.
Anson, Peter F., *Fashions in Church Furnishing 1840-1940*, pub Faith Press, 1960.
Art-Journal Illustrated Catalogue: Official Descriptive and Illustrated Catalogue of The Great Exhibition 1851, pub George Virtue, 1851.
Art Journal, The Exhibition of Art-Industry in Paris, 1855, with *The Artistic, Industrial and Commercial Results of the Universal Exposition of 1855* by George Wallis.
Art Journal Illustrated Catalogue of the International Exhibition, 1862.
Art Journal Illustrated Catalogue of the Universal Exhibition, Paris, 1867.
Art Journal Illustrated Catalogue of London International Exhibition, 1871, by George Wallis.
Art Journal Catalogue of London International Exhibition, 1872, by George Wallis.
Art Journal Illustrated Catalogue of the Paris International Exhibition, 1878.
Art Journal, The Paris Exhibition, 1900, pub 1901, Edit by D. Croal Thomson.
Arts and Crafts Exhibition Society catalogues, 1888 onwards.
Arts (The) Connected with Building, pub Batsford, 1909.
Aslin, Elizabeth, *The Aesthetic Movement*, pub Elek, 1969.
Atterbury, Paul and Clive Wainwright, *Pugin*, pub Yale University Press, 1994.
Atterbury, Paul and Clive Wainwright, *Pugin, A Gothic Passion*, pub Victoria and Albert Museum, 1994.
Auerbach, Jeffrey A., *The Great Exhibition of 1851*, pub Yale University Press, 1999.

Baillie Scott, M.H., *A Book of Furniture*, pub by John P. White, Bedford, 1906.
Bamberger, Louis, *Memories of Sixty Years in the Timber and Pianoforte Trades*, pub Sampson Low, undated.
Banham, Porter and Macdonald, *Victorian Interior Style*, pub Studio Editions, 1995 (first pub 1991 by Cassell as *Victorian Interior Design*).
Beard, Geoffrey, *English Furniture*, pub National Trust, 1986.
Beard, Geoffrey and Christopher Gilbert, *Dictionary of English Furniture Makers 1660-1840*, pub Furniture History Society, 1986.
Bell, Malcolm, *Sir Edward Burne-Jones*, pub Bell, 4th edn reprint, 1899.
Benn, R. Davis, *Style in Furniture*, pub Longmans, 1904.
Binstead, Herbert E., *The Furniture Styles*, pub Pitman, 1929.
Booth, Charles, *Life and Labour of the People in London*, Second Series: *Industry*; pub Macmillan, 1903 in 5 vols (part of Booth's monumental achievement, beginning with *Labour and Life of the People, East London*, Vol 1, first published 1889).
Bowett, Adam, *Myths of English Furniture History: Cuban Mahogany*, in "Antique Collecting", Feb, 1998, Pages 10-13.
Bowett, Adam, *Myths of English Furniture History: Rosewood*, in "Antique Collecting", Feb, 1999, Pages 12-16.
Boyce, Charles, *Dictionary of Furniture*, pub Roundtable, 1985.
Brackett, Oliver, *Thomas Chippendale*, pub Hodder and Stoughton, 1924.
Brandon-Jones, John, "C.F.A. Voysey" in *Victorian Architecture*, pub Cape, 1963.
Brewer, Rev E. Cobham, *A Dictionary of Phrase and Fable*, pub Odhams, undated.
Briggs, Asa, *Victorian Things*, pub Penguin, 1988.
Britain at Work, pub Cassell, undated.
Bryan's Dictionary of Painters and Engravers, pub Bell, revised edn, 1910, 5 vols.
Burne-Jones, Georgiana, *Memorials of Edward Burne-Jones*, pub Macmillan, 1904, 2 vols.

Cabinet-Maker's (The) Assistant, pub in parts, Blackie & Son, 1850-1853.
Callen, Anthea, *Angel in the Studio*, pub Astragal, 1979.
Cassell's Household Guide, pub Cassell, 4 vols, 1869-1871 (revised edn. c.1880; expanded edn in 6 vols, 1911).

Catalogue of the Drawings Collection of the Royal Institute of British Architects, pub Gregg, 1972.
Century Guild: *Catalogue of A.H. Mackmurdo and The Century Guild Collection*, pub The William Morris Gallery, Walthamstow, 1967.
Chippendale, Thomas, *The Gentleman & Cabinet-Maker's Director*, 1st edn 1754 and 3rd edn, 1762.
Clark, Kenneth, *The Gothic Revival*, pub Penguin 1964, reprint of 1928 edn.
Concise Encyclopaedia of Antiques, pub The Connoisseur, 1957.
Cooper, Jeremy, *Victorian and Edwardian Furniture and Interiors*, pub Thames and Hudson, 1987.
Crace, J.D., "Augustus Welby Pugin and Furniture" in *Journal of the Royal Institute of British Architects*, 1894, Pages 517-519.
Crawford, Alan, *C.R. Ashbee*, pub Yale University Press, 1985.
Cromey-Hawke, N., *William Morris and Victorian Painted Furniture*, in "The Connoisseur", January, 1976, Pages 33-43.
Crook, J. Mordaunt, *The Rise of the Nouveaux Riches*, pub Murray, 1999.
Crook, J. Mordaunt (Editor), *The Strange Genius of William Burges*, 1981 catalogue for National Museum of Wales exhibition.
Crystal (The) Palace and its Contents, pub W.M. Clark, 1852.
Cumming, Elizabeth, *Phoebe Anna Traquair (1852-1936) and her Contribution to Arts and Crafts in Edinburgh*, PhD thesis, Edinburgh University, 1985;
Curl, Professor James Stevens, *Oxford Dictionary of Architecture*, Oxford University Press, 2000.

Darby, Michael, *John Pollard Seddon*, pub Victoria and Albert Museum, 1983.
Day, Lewis F., *Some Principles of Every-Day Art*, pub Batsford, 2nd edn revised, 1898.
Day, Lewis F., "Victorian Progress in Applied Design", in *Art Journal*, 1887, Pages 185-202.
de Bellaigue, Geoffrey and Pat Kirkham, "George IV and the Furnishing of Windsor Castle", in *Furniture History*, 1972, Vol VIII, Pages 1-34.
de Voe, Shirley Spaulding, *English Papier Mâché of the Georgian and Victorian Periods*, pub Barrie and Jenkins, 1971.
Dickinson's Comprehensive Pictures of The Great Exhibition of 1851, 2 vols, pub by Royal Commission, 1854.
Dictionary of Art, pub Macmillan, 1996, 34 vols.
Dictionary of National Biography, first published in 66 vols 1885-1901 by Smith Elder; reprinted various times; supplemental vols pub through 20th Century by Oxford University Press, including *Missing Persons*, 1993. New edition of 60 vols as *Oxford Dictionary of National Biography*, 2004.
Dixon, Roger and Stefan Muthesius, *Victorian Architecture*, pub Thames and Hudson, 1991.
Doughty, Oswald, *A Victorian Romantic*, pub Oxford University Press, 2nd edn, 1960.
Dresser, Christopher, *Principles of Decorative Design*, pub Academy Editions, 1973, reprint of 1873 edn by Cassell, Petter and Galpin.

Edwards, Ralph, "The Last Phase of 'Regency' Design", in *Burlington Magazine*, Dec, 1937, Vol 71, No. 417, Pages 267-268 and 270-273.
Edwards, Ralph and Margaret Jourdain, *Georgian Cabinet-Makers c. 1700-1800*, pub Country Life, 3rd Revised Edition, 1955
Elliott, David B., *Charles Fairfax Murray: The Unknown Pre-Raphaelite*, pub The Book Guild, 2000.
Eastlake, Charles L., *Hints on Household Taste*, 1st pub Longmans, 1868, revised edn 1878, reprinted 1969.
Eastlake, Charles L., *A History of the Gothic Revival*, new edn with Introduction by J. Mordaunt Crook, pub Leicester University Press, 1970 and 1978.
Exposition Universelle de 1867 a Paris, Rapports du Jury International, 6 vols, pub Dupont.

Fay, C.R., *Palace of Industry, 1851*, pub Cambridge University Press, 1951.
Ferrey, Benjamin, *Recollections of A. Welby Pugin*, pub Scolar Press, 1978 reprint.
Field, June, *Collecting Georgian and Victorian Crafts*, pub Heinemann, 1973.
Fitzgerald, Penelope, *Edward Burne-Jones*, pub Joseph, 1975.
Fleming, John, Hugh Honour and Nikolaus Pevsner, *The Penguin Dictionary of Architecture*, Penguin, 1975 reprint.
Floud, Peter, "Victorian Furniture", Pages 17-24, plus 8 pages of additional photos, in *The Concise Encyclopaedia of Antiques*, Vol 3, pub The Connoisseur, 1957.
Fox, Celina, *London—World City 1800-1840*, pub Yale University Press, catalogue of 1992 exhibition held in Essen, Germany

Garrett, Rhoda and Agnes, *Suggestions for House Decoration in Painting, Woodwork and Furniture*, pub Macmillan in "Art at Home" series, 1876.
Gilbert, Christopher, Introduction to *Loudon's Furniture Designs*, pub S.R. Publishers, 1970.
Gilbert, Christopher G., *The Life and Work of Thomas Chippendale*, pub Studio Vista, 1978.
Gloag, John, *Mr Loudon's England*, pub Oriel Press, 1970.
Graefe, Richard T., "Marqueterie" in *Wood*, April, 1939, Pages 151-155.
Gray, A. Stuart, *Edwardian Architecture*, pub Wordsworth, 1985.
Graves, Algernon, *The Royal Academy of Arts, Exhibitors 1769-1904*, pub Kingsmead, 1970 reprint of 1905 edn.
Guide to The Lady Lever Art Gallery, pub National Museums and Galleries on Merseyside, 1991.

Hammerton, Sir J.A., Editor, *Concise Universal Biography*, 2 vols, pub Educational Book Co., undated.
Handley-Read, Charles, "England 1830-1901" in *World Furniture*, pub Hamlyn, 1965.
Hardy, John, *Lord Leverhulme*, catalogue of exhibition at Royal Academy, 1980.
Harris, Eileen, *The Furniture of Robert Adam*, pub Tiranti, London 1963.
Harris, Eileen, *The Genius of Robert Adam*, pub Yale University Press, 2001
Harris, John, Geoffrey de Bellaigue and Oliver Millar, *Buckingham Palace*, pub Nelson, 1968.
Harris, John, *Regency Furniture Designs 1803-1826*, pub Tiranti, 1961.
Harrison, Martin and Bill Waters, *Burne-Jones*, pub Barrie and Jenkins, revised edn 1977 and 1990 edn.
Harvey, Charles and Jon Press, *William Morris, Design and enterprise in Victorian Britain*, pub Manchester University Press, 1991.
Harvey, Charles and Jon Press, *Art, Enterprise and Ethics : The Life and Works of William Morris*, pub Frank Cass, 1996.
Haweis, Mrs H.R., *The Art of Decoration*, pub Chatto, 1889.
Hayden, Arthur, *The Furniture Designs of Thomas Sheraton*, arranged by J. Munro Bell, with Intro by Hayden, pub Gibbings, 1910.
Hayward, Helena, "England 1715-1765" in *World Furniture*, pub Hamlyn, 1965.
Henderson, Philip, *The Letters of William Morris to his Family and Friends*, pub Longmans, 1950.
Hollamby, Edward, *Red House*, pub by Architecture, Design and Technology Press, 1991.
Hope, Thomas, *Household Furniture and Interior Decoration*, pub Longman, 1807.
Hope, Thomas, *Costume of the Ancients*, 2 vols, pub William Miller, 1809.
Horner, Frances, *Time Remembered*, pub Heinemann, 1933.
Houfe, Simon, "Regency Taste 1790-1830", in *Antique Collecting*, April, 1997, Vol 31, No. 10, Pages 13-16.
Houghton, Lord, International Exhibition of 1871, *Official Reports on the Various Sections of the Exhibition*, 2 vols, believed 1872.
Hueffer, Ford M., *Ford Madox Brown*, pub Longmans, 1896.

Hughes, Bernard and Therle, *After the Regency*, pub Lutterworth, 1952.
Hughes, Graham, *Renaissance Cassoni*, pub Starcity, 1997.
Hughes, Therle, *The Pocket Book of Furniture*, pub Country Life, 1968.
Hunt, William Holman, *Pre-Raphaelitism and the Pre-Raphaelite Brotherhood*, pub Macmillan, 1905.

International Exhibition of 1862. The Illustrated Catalogue of the Industrial Department, pub Her Majesty's Commissioners, 1862.
International Exhibition, 1862, vol of newspaper cuttings in The Archive of Art and Design, Victoria and Albert Museum.

Jervis, Simon, *The Penguin Dictionary of Design and Designers*, pub Allen Lane, Penguin, 1984.
Jervis, Simon, *Victorian Furniture*, pub Ward Lock, 1968.
Joy, Edward T., *English Furniture 1800-1851*, pub Sotheby, 1977.
Joy, Edward T., "Furniture" in *The Connoisseur Period Guides, Late Georgian 1760-1810*, pub The Connoisseur, 1956.
Joy, Edward T., "Furniture" in *The Regency Period 1810-1830*, pub The Connoisseur, 1962.
Joy, Edward T., *Furniture*, pub The Connoisseur, 1972.
Joy, Edward T. "The Influence of Victorian Exhibitions on Furniture" in *Antique Finder*, April, 1976, Vol 15, Issue 4, Pages 2-5.

Kelly, Alison, *Decorative Wedgwood in Architecture and Furniture*, Country Life, 1965.
Kirkham, Pat, *London Furniture Trade 1700-1870*, pub Furniture History Society, 1988.
Kirkham, Pat, "Inlay, marquetry and buhl workers in England c.1660-1850" in *Burlington Magazine*, June, 1980, Pages 415-419.
Kirkham, Pat, "William Morris's Early Furniture" in *The Journal of the William Morris Society*, Vol IV, No 3, Summer, 1981, Pages 25-28.
Kornwolf, James D., *M.H. Baillie Scott and the Arts and Crafts Movement*, pub John Hopkins Press, 1972.

Lambourne, Lionel, *Utopian Craftsmen*, pub Astragal, 1980.
Late Georgian 1760-1810, The Connoisseur Period Guide, pub The Connoisseur, 1956.
Laugier, the Abbé Marc-Antoine, *Essai sur l'architecture*, pub Paris, 1753.
Lethaby, William R., *Philip Webb and His Work*, 1979 reprint of 1935 edn.
London International Exhibition, 1871: *Official Reports on the Various Sections of the Exhibition* (includes "Furniture and Metalwork" by J.H. Pollen).
Loos, Adolf, *Ins Leere gesprochen, 1897-1900*, Innsbruck, 1932.
Loudon, J.C., *An Encyclopaedia of Cottage, Farm and Villa Architecture and Furniture*, pub Longman, 1836, also 1846 edn.

Macbeth, Lindsay, "The Nuremberg Twist and The Amsterdam Swing: Continental Influence on the Furniture Designs of R.S. Lorimer", in *Scotland and Europe: Architecture & Design 1850-1940*, pub St. Andrews Studies in The History of Scottish Architecture and Design, 1991.
Mackail, J.W., *The Life of William Morris*, pub Dover, 1995 reprint.
MacCarthy, Fiona, *William Morris*, pub Faber, 1994.
Macquoid (Percy) and Edwards (Ralph), *The Dictionary of English Furniture*, 1st Edn 1924-1927; 2nd Enlarged and Revised Edn., by Ralph Edwards, pub Country Life, 1954.
Marks, Henry Stacy, *Pen and Pencil Sketches*, pub Chatto and Windus, 1894.
Marillier, H.C., *Dante Gabriel Rossetti*, 3rd Edn Revised, pub George Bell & Sons, 1904.
Men and Women of the Time, 13th edn., pub Routledge, 1891.
Millais, J.G. *The Life and Letters of John Everett Millais*, 2 vols, pub Methuen, 1899.
Modern Furniture, Consisting of 44 Coloured Engravings from Designs by A. Pugin, J. Stafford of Bath, and Others, pub Nattali, Undated (but 1824?).
Morris and Co., *A Brief Sketch of the Morris Movement*, pub by the Company as a Private Edition, June, 1911.
Morris and Company, Fine Art Society catalogue, 1979.
Morris, May, *William Morris*, pub Blackwell, 2 vols, 1936.
Musgrave, Clifford, *Adam and Hepplewhite and other Neo-Classical Furniture*, pub Taplinger, 1966.
Musgrave, Clifford, *Regency Furniture*, pub Faber, 2nd revised edn., 1970.
Musgrave, Clifford, "England 1765-1800" in *World Furniture*, pub Hamlyn, 1965.
Musgrave, Clifford, "England 1800-1830" in *World Furniture*, pub Hamlyn, 1965.
Muthesius, Hermann, *Das Englische Haus*, pub Berlin, 1904-05; 2nd edn in 3 vols 1908-1911; English language 1 vol abridgement of 2nd edn republished as "The English House", 1979, by Crosby Lockwood Staples.

Nesfield, Wm. Eden, *Specimens of Mediaeval Architecture*, pub Day, 1862.
Newman, Teresa and Ray Watkinson, *Ford Madox Brown and the Pre-Raphaelite Circle*, pub Chatto & Windus, 1991.
Newton, Charles, *Victorian Designs for the Home*, pub V. and A. Publications, 1999.
Nicholson, Peter and M.A., *The Practical Cabinet Maker, Upholsterer and Complete Decorator*, pub H. Fisher and Son, apparently 1826 but some plates dated 1827.

Official Catalogue of the International Health Exhibition, 1884, pub William Clowes.
Official Descriptive and Illustrated Catalogue of The Great Exhibition 1851.
Official Illustrated Catalogue Advertiser, 1851.
Official Illustrated Catalogue Advertiser for International Exhibition of 1862.

Paris Universal Exhibition, 1855, Catalogue of the Works Exhibited in the British Section, pub Chapman and Hall, 1855.
Paris (The) Exhibition, 1855, vol of newspaper cuttings, July, 1853, to Dec, 1855, in The Archive of Art and Design, Victoria and Albert Museum.
Paris Universal Exhibition of 1867, Catalogue of British Section, pub Her Britannic Majesty's Commissioners, 1867.
Paris Universal Exhibition, 1867, English version of official catalogue, pub Imperial Commission, 2nd edn., May, 1867.
Paris Universal Exhibition, 1867, 3 vols of newspaper cuttings in The Archive of Art and Design, Victoria and Albert Museum.
Parris, Leslie, (Editor), *The Pre-Raphaelites*, pub Tate Gallery, 2nd Edn, 1994.
Parry, Linda, (Editor), *William Morris*, pub Victoria and Albert Museum, 1996.
Parry, Linda, *William Morris Textiles*, pub Crescent, 1983.
Pennell, Elizabeth R. and Joseph, *Life of James McNeill Whistler*, 5th revised edn pub Heinemann, 1911 (1st pub 1908).
Pevsner, Professor Nikolaus, *High Victorian Design*, pub Architectural Press, 1951.
Pevsner, Professor Nikolaus, *Pioneers of the Modern Movement*, pub Faber, 1936.
Pevsner, Professor Nikolaus, "Art Furniture of the Eighteen-Seventies" in *Architectural Review*, Jan, 1952, Pages 43-50.
Pollen, John Hungerford, *Ancient and Modern Furniture and Woodwork in the South Kensington Museum* (later the V. and A.), pub by Committee of Council on Education,1874; 2nd rev. edn., pub Victoria and Albert Museum, 1908.
Pollen, John Hungerford, "Furniture and Metalwork" in *Official Reports* of the London International Exhibition, 1971.
Port, Michael H., *The Houses of Parliament*, pub Yale University Press, 1976.
Poulson, Christine, *William Morris on Art & Design*, pub Sheffield Academic Press, 1996.
Pugin, A.W.N., *Fifteenth and Sixteenth Century Ornaments*, in 4 parts, pub Grant, 1904.

Pugin's Gothic Furniture, pub Ackermann, 182- (1827?).
Pugin, A.W. N., *The True Principles of Pointed or Christian Architecture*, pub London, 1841.

Regency, 1810-1830, The Connoisseur Period Guide, pub Connoisseur, 1962.
Reports of Artisans Selected by a Committee of Society of Arts to Visit the Paris Universal Exhibition, 1867, pub Society, 1867.
Reports of the Paris Universal Exhibition, 1855, 3 vols, pub H.M.S.O.
Rimmel, Eugene, *Recollections of the Paris Exhibition of 1867*, pub Chapman, 1868.
Rooke, Thomas, *Burne-Jones Talking*, pub Murray, 1981, Edited by Mary Lago, based on Diaries of Thomas Rooke, 1895-1898.
Rossetti: *Letters of Dante Gabriel Rossetti*, Edited Oswald Doughty and John Robert Wahl, 4 vols covering 1835 to 1882, pub Clarendon, 1965-1967.
Rowarth, Wendy Wassyng, *Angelica Kauffman*, pub The Royal Pavilion, Brighton, 1992.

Saint, Andrew, *Richard Norman Shaw*, pub Yale, 1983 reprint.
Savage, George, *Dictionary of 19th Century Antiques*, pub Barrie & Jenkins, 1978.
Seddon, J.P., *King René's Honeymoon Cabinet*, believed pub 1898.
The Silver Studio Collection, Catalogue of Museum of London Exhibition, 1980.
Sheraton: *The Cabinet-Maker and Upholsterer's Drawing Book* in Four Parts, by Thomas Sheraton, 3rd edn revised, 1802.
Smith, Charles Saumarez, *Eighteenth-century decoration, design and domestic interior in England*, pub Weidenfeld, 1993.
Smith, George, *A Collection of Designs for Household Furniture and Interior Decoration*, pub Taylor, 1808 (facsimile edn pub Praeger, 1970).
Smith, George, *The Cabinet Maker and Upholsterer's Guide*, pub Jones, 1833 (but additional title page bears date 1826).
Smith, J. Moyr, *Ornamental Interiors*, pub Crosby, 1887.
Smith, H. Clifford, *Buckingham Palace*, pub Country Life, 1931.
Smith, Professor Walter, *The Masterpieces of the Centennial International Exhibition*, Vol II, pub Philadelphia, 1876-78.
Soros, Susan Weber, *The Secular Furniture of E.W. Godwin*, pub Yale University Press, 1999.
Speltz, Alexander, *The Styles of Ornament*, pub Batsford, 1910.
Streeter, Colin "Marquetry Furniture by a Brilliant London Master" in *Metropolitan Museum of Art Bulletin*, June, 1971, Pages 418-429.
Surtees, Virginia, *The Diary of Ford Madox Brown*, pub Yale University Press, 1981.
Surtees, Virginia, *The Diaries of George Price Boyce*, pub Real World, 1980.
Survey of London, many volumes, English Heritage.
Symonds, R.W. and Whineray, B.B., *Victorian Furniture*, pub Country Life, 1965 reprint.

Tait, A. Carlyle, "Late Chippendale and Adam Furniture at The Lady Lever Art Gallery", in *Apollo*, Feb, 1948, Pages 36-38.
Talbert, Bruce J., *Gothic Forms, Applied to Furniture Decoration, &c., published in parts*, Birmingham, 1867-1868.
Tallis's History and Description of the Crystal Palace, by John Tallis, 3 vols, 1852.
Tallis's Illustrated London, descriptions by William Gaspey, 2 vols, pub John Tallis and Co., 1851-1852.
Thompson, Paul, *The Work of William Morris*, pub Heinemann, 1967.
Thornton, Peter, *Form and Decoration*, pub Weidenfeld, 1998.
Toller, Jane, *Papier Mâché in Great Britain and America*, pub Bell, 1962.
Trappes-Lomax, Michael, *Pugin, a Mediaeval Victorian*, pub Sheed and Ward, 1932.

Vallance, Aymer, *The Life and Work of William Morris*, pub Bell & Sons, 1897, reprinted by Studio Editions, 1986.
Viollet-Le-Duc, *Dictionaire Raisonné Du Mobilier Francaise*, pub Bance, 1858-1875.

Wainwright, Clive, "A.W.N. Pugin's Early Furniture" in *Connoisseur*, 1976, Pages 3-11.
Walking, Gillian, *Antique Bamboo Furniture*, pub Bell & Hyman, 1979.
Ware, Dora, *A Short Dictionary of British Architects*, pub Allen and Unwin, 1967.
Watkin, Professor David, New Introduction to 1971 reprint of Thomas Hope's *Household Furniture and Interior Decoration* of 1807, pub Dover.
Watkinson, Ray, "Red House Decorated", in *Journal of the William Morris Society*, 1988, Vol 7, Part 4, Pages 10-15.
Watt, William, *Art Furniture from Designs by E.W. Godwin, F.S.A., and Others*, pub Batsford, 1877.
Wedgwood, Alexandra, *A.W.N. Pugin and the Pugin Family*, pub Victoria and Albert Museum, 1985.
Whitaker, Henry, *Practical Cabinet Maker and Upholsterer's Treasury of Designs*, pub in parts by Fisher, Son & Co. and The Caxton Press, 1847.
Wilde, Oscar, *Essays and Lectures*, London, 4th edn, pub Methuen, 1913.
William Morris and the Middle Ages, catalogue of Whitworth Art Gallery, Manchester, exhibition, pub Manchester University Press, 1984.
Wills, Geoffrey, *English Furniture 1760-1900*, pub Guinness, 1979 reprint.
Wood, Lucy, *Catalogue of Commodes, The Lady Lever Art Gallery*, pub H.M.S.O., 1994.
World Furniture, edited Helena Hayward, pub Hamlyn, 1965 (Important essays by Charles Handley-Read, Clifford Musgrave and Helena Hayward).

Yapp, G.W., *Art Industry*, pub Virtue and Co., 1879.

Furniture and related Journals

Ackermann's Repository of Arts, Literature, Fashions &c, 1809-1829.
American Architect and Building News, 1876—.
Antiquaries Journal (journal of Society of Antiquaries of London), 1921 onwards.
Antique Collector, Sep, 1930-April, 1996.
Antique Collecting (journal of The Antique Collectors' Club), 1966—.
Antique Finder, 1962-1975.
Apollo, 1925 onwards.
Architect, Jan, 1869—.
Architectural History (Journal of The Society of Architectural Historians of Great Britain) 1958 onwards.
Architectural Review, 1896—.
Art and Decoration, 1885-1886.
Art Designer, 1884-1888 (Started as *Amateurs' Art Designer*, cntd from March, 1889 as *Home Art Work*).
Art Journal, 1839-1911.
Art Union, 1838-1849.
Art Workman, 1873-1884.
Art Workers Quarterly, 1902-1906.
Artifex, 1968-1971.
Artist, 1880-1902.
Arts and Crafts, 1904-1906.
Athenaeum, 1830-1920.

British Architect, 1874-1919.
Builder, Dec, 1842-Feb, 1966.
Building News, Jan, 1855-March, 1926.
Burlington Magazine, 1903 onwards.

Cabinet Maker, July, 1880 onwards.
Cassell's Illustrated Family Paper, 1853-1867 (followed by *Cassell's Magazine*, 1867-1912).

Cassell's Illustrated Family Paper Exhibitor, 1862, for International Exhibition of 1862.
Century Guild Hobby Horse, 1884-1888.
Charles Rennie Mackintosh Society Newsletter, 1973 onwards.
Commerce, July, 1893-May, 1904.
Connoisseur, 1901-1992.
Country Life, 1897 onwards.
Craftsman, 1901-1916 (cntd. as *Art World*, 1916-1918).

Decoration in painting, sculpture architecture and art manufactures, 1880-1883; cntd as *Decoration and art-trades review*, 1884-1889.
Decorator, 1864.

Ecclesiologist, 1841-1868.
English Illustrated Magazine, 1883-1913.
Enquire Within, Oct, 1890-July, 1923.

Furnisher, Oct, 1899-May,1901.
Furnisher and Decorator, Nov, 1889-Jan, 1892.
Furniture and Decoration, Jan, 1890-Feb, 1894.
Furniture and Decoration and The Furniture Gazette, March, 1894-March 1899.
Furniture Gazette, Oct, 1872-Dec, 1893.
Furniture History (journal of Furniture History Society), 1965 onwards (also Society's *Newsletter*).
Furniture Record, May, 1899-Jan, 1958.
Furniture Record and International Furniture, Feb, 1958-April, 1962.
Gentleman's Magazine, May, 1828-Dec, 1894.
Graphic, Dec, 1869-July, 1932.

Hearth and Home, May, 1891-Jan, 1914.
Home Art-Work, March, 1889 to Jan, 1912.
House, March, 1897-Dec, 1903 (cntd as *House Beautiful*).
House Furnisher and Decorator, 1872-1873.
House & Garden, 1901-1993.
Illustrated Carpenter and Builder, Aug, 1877-June, 1971.
Illustrated London News, 1842 onwards.
Irish Builder, Jan, 1867—.

Journal of Decorative Art, 1881-1937.
Journal of The Decorative Arts Society, 1850 to the Present, 1985 onwards (also *Newsletter* of the Society, 1984 onwards).
Journal of Design, 1849-1852.
Journal of the Edward Barnsley Educational Trust, May, 1995—.
Journal of Pre-Raphaelite Studies, c.1980 onwards.
Journal of The Society of Arts (from 1908 The Royal Society of Arts) 1852 onwards.
Journal of The William Morris Society, 1961 onwards (also separate Journal of American branch, also *Newsletter* of the Society). *Judy*, 1867-1907.

Ladies Home Journal, 1889—.
Lady's Pictorial, March, 1881-Feb, 1921.

Magazine of Art, 1878-1904.
Metropolitan Museum of Art Bulletin, 1905 onwards.

Old Furniture, 1927-1929.
Our Homes and Gardens, 1919-1921.

Pall Mall Gazette, Feb, 1865-1923.
Portfolio, 1873-1893.
Proceedings of the Society of Antiquaries of London, 1843-1920.
Punch, 1841-2002.

Queen, Sep, 1861-Oct, 1970.

Regional Furniture Society Journal, 1987 onwards (also *Newsletter* of Society).
Royal Institute of British Architects Transactions, 1879-1880.

Studio, 1893-1964.
Sylvia's Home Journal, 1878-1891.

Timber, Feb, 1885-Sep, 1973.
Timber Trades Journal, May, 1873—.

Victoria Magazine, 1863-1880.
Victorian Society Annual, 1969—. (Journal of The Victorian Society: Continued as *The Victorian Society Journal* and then *The Victorian*). Also: Society's *Newsletter*.

Woodworker, 1901—.
Workshop, 1868-1872.

Furniture and other Societies

Charles Rennie Mackintosh Society.
Decorative Arts Society, 1850 to the present.
Furniture History Society.
Regional Furniture Society.
Society of Architectural Historians.
Victorian Society.
William Morris Society.

The Author says Thank You

The World of Music

As a would-be author you are in the position of a permanent supplicant. You depend on the kindness of strangers, the desired coin being information. Thus, to the world of music I entered as a beggar and an innocent.

It was amusing, therefore, to discover that not all the prima donnas wore frocks and I came across a few cases of bloody-minded ignorance, some who had risen above the level of their own incompetence and others armoured with such desperate self-promotion and selfishness they would have been naturals for a career in journalism.

Overall, however, I emerged from some years of looking into their orchestra pit with a new respect for the decency, generosity and scholarliness of so many of them. Some of the greatest—men and women with a World reputation within their field—were prepared to give a surprising measure of trust and faith to an amateur they had never met and of whom they knew naught. Music, I found, really doth have charms.

Some of these good people, I fear, I simply wore out with remorseless questions. Faced with my ignorance they had to re-invent the wheel and their patience was heroic. In some cases I exceeded the bounds of good manners and they retired hurt, shell-shocked by the barrage of letters. For that I now apologise.

In all cases I hope they will find in this book some small evidence that I tried to live up to their hopes. None of them, I should explain, are responsible for any error in this book. That responsibility is mine and mine alone. Nevertheless, I could never have reached the Presses without them.

Above all I must thank Mr Michael Cole of Cheltenham, in my opinion the best of today's Piano Historians and a man who, as a specialist restorer to leading Museums and important Private Collections, has had a lifetime of handling many hundreds of these antique pianos. Mr Cole, as I discovered a gentleman of courageous and all too fearless honesty, seeks unwaveringly for the truth and unswervingly for the facts in a way that reminded me of the great reporters, albeit with less artifice than is employed in my trade. I have also found him endlessly generous and kind… unless it means compromising with the truth.

I have learned much from Mr Cole on two fronts: From his acknowledged modern classic "*The Pianoforte in the Classical Era*" and other writings; and in his written answers to those matters I raised. I am a populist and Mr Cole's tone is academic but, nevertheless, he was prepared to save the musicians from some of the gross misrepresentations I might perpetrate, no matter how gauche he may have thought the questions.

Certain areas of piano history you might term Before Cole and others After Cole. The dividing line is Mr Cole's landmark essay "The Twelve Apostles?" published in *The Southeastern and Midwestern Historical Keyboard Society Journal,* Vol 18, 2000. Until this appeared nearly all piano histories subscribed to the myth that a band of 12 instrument makers had escaped the Seven Years War on the Continent to flee to Britain *en masse* and establish the native piano industry. After reading his essay no-one else could promote this romance in the same terms.

I must also thank Mr Cole for letting me see (and thus trusting me with the secrets of his years of toil) advance Chapters of his new book, *Broadwood Square Pianos*, with important revelations about Broadwood and the early piano makers.

I was guided to Mr Cole's key essay by another distinguished specialist in the piano field, Mr Andrew Garrett, a consultant to The National Trust, who drew my attention to important pianos owned by the Trust and dealt with many of my earliest enquiries, thus bearing the brunt of my ignorance. He also paved the way for me in important instances.

I owe a very great deal to a man I never met, the late Mr C.F. Colt, of Bethersden, Kent, who died on July 1st., 1985, aged 74. From Mr Colt's writings I have derived much and, from the extraordinary Collection of Early Keyboards instruments that he gathered together over his lifetime, a great deal more. Ever faithful to his memory, and wishing credit to go only to Mr Colt, is the present Guardian of the Collection, Mr W.E. ("Eddie") Spiers, an ex-Paratrooper and one of the great characters I met on my travels. Mr Spiers has provided much patient help over a period of years and generously given me permission to reproduce photos of the Colt instruments.

Without the help of another leading restorer, Mr David Hunt of Willingham, Cambridgeshire, who is famous for his expertise on early Broadwood grand pianos and travels the World in their cause, I would never have made such progress on the Broadwood "Wedgwood" grands and it is entirely due to his crucial intervention in one case that I received the co-operation I did. I also have to thank Mr Hunt for important contributions to my research on stylistic changes in the grand piano; important observations on Zumpe and Ganer; the still puzzling problem of "Elegant" pianos; and for help with another mystery, Broadwood's "Queen Victoria" grands.

No greater sacrifice could be asked of any piano collector than that which I, totally unreasonably, asked of Mr David Hackett, at a very late stage. "Could you please take one of your square pianos to pieces for me and photograph it?" I requested. Amazingly, he did. Magical photos. A splendid, generous fellow who refused to take a penny to cover even his expenses. Mr Hackett also gave me the benefit of his many years study of early pianos and valuable insight on their construction, saving me from some terrible errors. And finally, when it looked as though I would sink under the weight of work, Mr Hackett agreed to undertake both the "Glossary" and the "Index". So I owe a very great deal to this gentleman.

Since he seems to have spent a lifetime researching piano history before founding and directing his impressive PianoGen web site, you could not have blamed Mr Bill Kibby-Johnson if he had suggested I followed his example rather than try to take a shortcut through his hard-won experience. Quite to the contrary—Bill helped me every time I asked and provided me with numerous photos he has garnered over the years. Without him I would never have learned of two of the most important Broadwood grands.

Just like piano historians, researchers and dealers from all over the World, I have leaned heavily on one of history's more remarkable survivals, The Broadwood Archives. These are housed in the wonderful facilities of the Surrey History Centre at Woking and I have to thank the County Archivist, Mr David Robinson, for much but most of my dealings were with a lady on his staff, Ms Jennifer Waugh, who was a knowledgeable guide and constant help in navigating these Archives. I was then greatly helped by Mr Robert Simonson, especially with research on stylistic changes concerning especially the history of the 1827 grand in the Metropolitan Museum and new designs of the legs of grands c.1809. I must also thank Mr Julian Pooley and the photographer Mr Roy Drysdale of Guildford for various photos he took on my behalf.

A very distinguished man, Mr Laurence Libin, now Research Curator and previously long-time Director of the Department of Musical Instruments at the mighty Metropolitan Museum of Art, New York, from 1973 to 1999, generously supplied me with copies of the photos he took in Russia of a decorated Zumpe and Buntebart square in The Palace of Pavlovsk. I learned much from his important essay on the piano designs of Robert Adam in "Early Music" and he also gave me his thoughts on the "French frame", besides pointing me towards a fascinating Revived Gothic grand.

I have had much kind help from the Met, particularly from Mr Libin's successor as head of the Department. Mr Ken Moore, who provided invaluable information on the Museum's important 1827 grand by Broadwood.

I would never have understood important points about the piano designs of Robert Adam without the guidance of Mr Stephen Astley, Assistant Curator of Drawings, at Sir John Soane's Museum. And am also grateful for the help of Ms Susan Palmer, Archivist, Sir John Soane's Museum.

Another well known authority on the early piano, Mr Kenneth Mobbs of Bristol, founder of the Mobbs Keyboard Collection, kindly wrote to me on a range of issues affecting the piano case.

The most important British 18th Century grand piano, from a design point of view, is the "Don Godoy" grand by Thomas Sheraton and I had valuable help on the Wedgwood pottery decoration from Miss Gaye Blake Roberts, The Curator of The Wedgwood Museum. I was further helped by Mrs June Bonell, the Museum Secretary and Mrs Lynn Miller, the Information Officer.

One of the most remarkable pianos in the British Isles is the "Orpheus" artist-painted grand by Sir Edward Burne-Jones and I must thank the Viscount Asquith for his personal help and The Mells Estate for generous co-operation. The well known London art dealer and historian, Mr Christopher Wood, gave me permission to use his photo of this piano. I also have to thank Mr William Waters, author of a well known book on Burne-Jones, for his thoughts on the artist's pianos.

When I found myself in a research *cul de sac* concerning the designer of another of the most important British 19th Century pianos, the George Henry Blake grand, I was saved from my ignorance by the scholarship of one man, Mr Martin P. Levy, Principal of H. Blairman and Sons of Mount Street, London and one of our leading experts on 19th Century furniture. I was given other important help regarding this instrument by Ms Marian Eines of the Department of Musical Instruments, Metropolitan Museum of Art.

With my research on Holman Hunt and Burne-Jones I had expert guidance from Mr Robert Upstone, The Curator of Victorian and Modern British Art, The Tate Gallery.

William Southwell is quite one of the most fascinating of all piano makers and, in this regard, I have had generous help from Ms Sandra McElroy, Assistant Keeper the National Museum of Ireland; Ms Audrey Whitty, Assistant Keeper the National Museum of Ireland; Mr Adrian Zealand, Dundee Arts Galleries and Museums; and Ms Kim Mawhinney, Curator of Applied Art, Ulster Museum.

I have had continuous assistance both with pianos and illustrations from The Museum of London and owe much to Ms Karen Fielder, Assistant Curator, Social History, Ms Gail Cameron, Assistant Curator and the enthusiastic help of Sarah Williams of their Picture Library and Mr Andrew Batt, the Picture Library Manager.

I could not have been better helped than by a remarkable lady, Ms Stella Beddoe, Keeper of Decorative Art, for Brighton Museum and Art Gallery. Despite her onerous duties Ms Beddoe took special photos for me of their very fine Mott grand and helped on a range of matters.

From the Lady Lever Art Gallery at Port Sunlight Village, which houses the extraordinary Frederick Beck square, I received wonderful help from Ms Anita Byrne, the Administrative Officer and Ms Maeve Halliday, Manager of Information.

A fine museum which gave me the most kindly help concerning a number of pianos in their Collection was The Bowes Museum at Barnard Castle, Co. Durham and I must particularly thank Ms Claire Jones, their Keeper of Furniture.

I had marvellous help from The Museum of Welsh Life at St. Fagans, Cardiff, where they have another stunning Mott grand and other fascinating pianos. Here I have to thank, particularly, Ms Mei Nwen Ruddock and Ms Lowri Jenkins.

Much help concerning the Bevan grand and other pianos in their Collection came over a lengthy period from Mr Adam White, The Curator of Lotherton Hall, near Leeds.

The National Museums of Merseyside have a number of interesting pianos in their Collection and I was much helped by Ms Pauline Rushton, Curator in the Department of Decorative Arts.

With my research on the pianos of Charles Rennie Mackintosh I am particularly indebted to Ms Pamela Robertson, Senior Curator, the Hunterian Museum; Mr Peter Trowles, Curator of The Mackintosh Collection, Glasgow School of Art; and Miss Julie Coleman, Assistant Librarian, Department of Special Collections, University of Glasgow.

I had splendid help on pianos in their Collection from Ms Yvonne Cresswell, Curator of Social History with Manx National Heritage.

The piano historian Mr David Grover kindly wrote to me a number of times amplifying various points in his book.

A gentleman who is better able to describe the constituent parts of a piano design than myself is the expert and Curator, Mr William Dow, who helped me at an early stage of my research.

When I investigated the first "True Upright" pianos of John Isaac Hawkins a crucial obituary of Hawkins was found for me in their archives by Prabha Shah, the Information Librarian at the Science Museum, London and extracts from another important paper were provided by Ms Ruthann Boles McTyre, Head of the Rita Benton Music Library, University of Iowa, U.S.A. I was given other help on Hawkins by Ms Alexandra Alevizatos Kirtley, Assistant Curator of American Decorative Arts at the Philadelphia Museum of Art and by Ms Peggy F. Baird of Huntsville, Alabama. Mr Marlowe A. Sigal, the owner of several Hawkins pianos, kindly gave me information concerning his Collection.

The piano collectors are a wonderful bunch, rich in eccentrics and personalities and I only wish I could have learned more from the evidently suspicious fellow who is reputed to have 120 pianos crammed in his house, including grand pianos tipped sideways in his bedroom. Perhaps he thought I would decamp with a grand tucked under my arm. But on the whole they were amazingly good with their time and help—none more so than Professor Dr Andreas Beurmann of Hamburg, creator of the internationally known Beurmann Collection, who sent me a truly comprehensive set of photos.

An outstanding Collection has also been formed by Mr Chris Maene of Brussels and Ruiselede, Belgium who has generously allowed me to reproduce photos of his pianos.

I owe much to another Continental Collection: The Neumeyer-Junghanns-Tracey Collection at Bad Krozingen and, in particular, to its wonderfully supportive and efficient Artistic Director and Curator, Ms Sally Fortino.

I had marvellous help and photos from Ms Maria Helena Trindade, Director of the Museu da Música, Lisbon, Portugal, which has outstanding British pianos by Wornum, Astor and others.

Mr Otto Rindlisbacher of Zurich generously took special photos for me of the highly unusual Jones & Co. upright grand in his Collection.

I have had much notable help and assistance from Museums around the World.

None more so than from The Ringve Museum in Trondheim and its dedicated Curator, Mr Mats Krouthen (the Ringve is an unexpected home to other non-piano treasures, such as furniture by J.S. Henry and other turn-of-the-century designers).

Awesome is about the only word that seems suitable for the huge and eye-stopping Collection of the Haags Gemeentemuseum, The Netherlands and, there, I was saved from disaster regarding an artist painted square only by the timely advice of Dr Michael Latcham, Curator of Musical Instruments. I was also much helped by Ms Kristina Odenhamn of the Documentation Department.

Another fine Collection is held by the Musée des Instruments de Musique, Brussels and I had particular help from Ms Anne Meurant, Chef de Travaux, who kindly arranged a special photo of a Broadwood upright.

Another gentleman who saved me from terrible error and gave me knowledgeable advice regarding their Collection was Dr Rudolf Hopfner, The Direktor, Kunsthistorisches Museum, Vienna.

Much help on the first Cristofori pianos came from Dr Eszter Fontana, The Director of the Musikinstrumenten-Museum der Universität Leipzig, Germany.

I was given guidance on Shudi and Broadwood by Professor Dr. Otto Biba, of the Gesellschaft der Musikfreunde, Vienna.

Silke Berdux, Curator of Musical Instruments at the Deutsches Museum, Munich, gave me guidance on the British pianos in their Collection.

Mr Robert Holmin of the Stiftelsen musikkulturens främjande, Stockholm, Sweden, kindly arranged for me to have photos of their Clementi upright square.

Mr Bernd Wittenbrink of the Bildarchiv und Fotothek, gave me guidance on pianos in the Collection of the Staatliches Institut fur Musikforschung, Berlin.

I was helped on Beethoven's Broadwood grand of 1817 by Ms Klára Radnóti, Curator of the Musical Instrument Collection, Magyar Nemzeti Muzeum, Budapest, Hungary.

Professor Edward L. Kottick of the University of Iowa, the world renowned harpsichord scholar and a gentleman of keen insight who, with much good humour, found time to give me guidance regarding the claimed 1744 "Battle of Prague" harpsichord by Burkat Shudi for Frederick the Great. Later, he provided information I would not have known how to find on the "faux" panelling of other ancient harpsichords.

I owe much to American experts and particularly to Mr John R. Watson, Conservator of Instruments to the Colonial Williamsburg Foundation of Virginia. Mr Watson was learned indeed on the subject of the Foundation's early Zumpe square and wonderfully knowledgeable on the casework and decoration of their Wornum upright. He also advised me on a Beck square and a Ball grand piano. I was also kindly helped by Ms Marianne C. Martin of the Visual Resources Department of the Foundation.

A gentleman who had spent years researching an horrific but historically important publicity stunt, the Great Bonfire of Pianos in Atlantic City in 1904, did not hesitate to share his hard-won knowledge with me and give endless help. This was no less a person that Professor William E. Hettrick, head of Music at Hofstra University, Hempstead, New York, President of the American Musical Instrument Society 1995-1999, Editor of their "Journal" between 1979-1985 and again later, also Editor of their "Newsletter" from 1999 to 2003.

In a protracted correspondence I must have stretched the patience of Mr Steve Velasquez, Collections Manager of the Division of Cultural History at the National Museum of American History (The Smithsonian) but he was never less than kind and generous with his time, supplying me with crucial help on their piano by Hawkins and others in the Smithsonian Collection.

Another eminent lady who gave me valuable assistance, most particularly with regard to the 1885 Inventions Exhibition and Steinway was Mrs Cynthia Adams Hoover, now retired but then Curator of Musical Instruments at the National Museum of American History. She most generously presented me with a copy of her book "Piano 300".

A very tricky problem concerning a decorated grand piano bearing a suspect Broadwood nameboard was solved for me by Mr William G. Allman, Curator of The White House, Washington.

I had tremendous help on the Cornelius Cox "Wedgwood" grand from Ms Mary Alice Mackay, the Research Curator of the Albany Institute of History & Art, New York and further assistance from Ms Sarah Bennett, Curatorial Administrator of the Institute.

I seem to have turned time after time to Ms Melissa Gold Fournier, the Assistant Museum Registrar of that wonderful institution to which the British owe so much, The Yale Center for British Art. The lady was very patient and never let me down.

I had the most kind help with research into Behning pianos from Ms Bonnie Jo Dopp, Interim Music Librarian, Michelle Smith Performing Arts Library, University of Maryland.

Mr Darcy Kuronen, Curator of Musical Instruments, Museum of Fine Arts, Boston, gave me guidance on the pianos of Chickering and a number of matters.

Mr Nicholas Renouf, Associate Curator, Yale University Collection of Musical Instruments, gave me guidance concerning their Goulding, D'Almaine, Potter & Co. decorated square.

Ms Barbara L. Stark, Assistant to the Director, the National Music Museum, University of South Dakota, gave kind help concerning a Davison & Redpath grand piano.

Mr Steven T. Spiller, Museum & Collections Manager, the Mission Inn Museum, California, gave guidance on a number of British pianos in their Collection.

Mr Chris Hatten, Huntington Museum of Art, West Virginia, gave me much help on their painting known as "The Sisters".

Dr Brenda Neece, Curator of the Department of Music, Duke University, Durham, North Carolina, gave me guidance on their Stodart upright grand.

I had guidance on pianos in their ownership from Dr Jack C. Schuman of Phoenix, Oregon and the Mark Twain Home Foundation, Hannibal, Missouri.

Mr Roger W. Sherman, Executive Director of the Westfield Center, Seattle, went to considerable trouble to find for me an article published many years before on an early English fortepiano.

Often when I was in a jam, rather more times than I care to think about, I asked for the guidance of Ms Amelie Roper, Curator of The Music Collections of The British Library. Never once did she turn me away, never once did she fail to provide the answer. A lady who seems to have a vast store of arcane knowledge. I received other assistance from her colleagues and fellow Curators, Mr Steve Cork and Mr Robert Balchin.

Two other ladies made a great impression on me and gave generously of their knowledge and time:

Ms Jenny Nex, the Curator of the Museum of Instruments, Royal College of Music, who helped me on a number of matters but particularly on Ferdinand Weber and Christopher Ganer.

Dr Hélène La Rue, Curator of The Bate Collection, Oxford, who not only saved me from gross error on the Tisseran harpsichord but then proceeded to take some special photographs for me.

Ms Ruth Shrigley, Principal Curator of Decorative Art at Manchester City Galleries, gave me important background on the remarkable Robert Stodart grand at Heaton Hall.

Ms Margaret Cranmer, Piano Historian and Music Librarian gave me kind guidance on Broadwood grand pianos.

I also have to thank the following:

Mr Martin Hillman, Publications Officer, for much help regarding various instruments in The Russell Collection, Edinburgh.

Professor David Watkin of Cambridge University, the renowned Hope specialist, for guidance on Thomas Hope. And, on another aspect of Hope's life, Ms Di Stiff of the Surrey History Centre.

Mr Martin Ellis, The Curator of Applied Art, Birmingham Museums & Art Gallery, gave me much help on their Burne-Jones' and Broadwood pianos.

Ms Maggie Wood, Keeper of Social History and Ms Alison Clague, Assistant Keeper, Warwickshire Museums for their guidance on the 1721 Tabel harpsichord.

Ms Rosemary Baird, The Curator, The Goodwood Collection, Goodwood House, Chichester for guidance on their Horsburgh piano.

Dr Bradley Strauchen, Deputy Keeper of Musical Instruments, Horniman Museum, London, for guidance on pianos in the Collection.

Ms Sarah Maughan, The Administrator, Holdenby House, Northamptonshire, for guidance on their Collection and particularly their 1851 Exhibition (and may well be Pugin) upright piano. I also had guidance on the 1851 piano from Mr Michael J. Ryder of The Musical Museum.

Ms Laura Houliston, Assistant Curator, Kenwood House, Hampstead, for guidance on pianos in their Collection.

Ms Sue Wyes for guidance on a grand piano now owned by Lord Lloyd-Webber.

Ms Jane Munroe of the Department of Paintings, The Fitzwilliam Museum, Cambridge for guidance on decoration for a harpsichord designed by James Thornhill.

Alex Kidson, Curator of British Art, the Walker Art Gallery, Liverpool, for guidance regarding Sir Joshua Reynolds' painting of a family with their piano.

Mrs Diane P. Naylor of The Devonshire Collection, Chatsworth House, Derbyshire, for guidance on their Shudi harpsichord.

Mr Philip Kennedy, Programme Co-ordinator, The Royal National College for the Blind, for guidance on pianos in their Collection.

Ms Veronica Tonge, The Keeper of Fine & Applied Art, Maidstone Museum, for guidance and photos of pianos in their Collection.

Mrs Jacqueline A. Minchinton, Records Officer, Northampton, for photos and guidance on pianos in their Abington Museum Collection.

Ms Jane Ellis, The Custodian, Fenton House, London, for guidance on their Collection.

Mr Richard Cole of The Musical Museum, Brentford, Middlesex, for guidance on pianos in their ownership.

Ms Jo Eaton, Assistant to the Custodian, Carlyle's House, Cheyne Road, Chelsea, London, for guidance on a Wornum piano and a picture in their Collection.

Ms Christine Milliken, House Steward, Wordsworth House, Cockermouth, Cumbria, for guidance on a grand piano in their Collection.

Dr Frances Palmer, The Curator, The Royal Academy of Music, for guidance on piano research.

Ms Kitty Ross, Curator of Social History, Abbey House Museum, Leeds, for guidance on pianos in their Collection.

Mr Philip Olleson, Reader in Historical Musicology, University of Nottingham, for guidance regarding Dr Charles Burney.

Valérie Malecki of the Centre de Documentation, Du Musee de la Musique, Paris, for guidance on Frederick Beck.

Mr David J. Eveleigh, Curator of Social History, Blaise Castle House Museum, Bristol, for guidance on their Dimoline and other pianos. Also Ms Margaret Raymond of the Museum.

Mr A. Guzanov of The State Pavlovsk Palace Museum, Russia, for guidance on their Zumpe & Buntebart square piano.

Mr John Khouri, the American concert pianist, for guidance on his Broadwood grand.

Mr David Burton, House Manager, Chirk Castle, for guidance on their Shudi harpsichord.

Ms Maggie Gibb, Secretary, The Royal Society of Musicians of Great Britain, for her guidance on the Broadwood grand exhibited at The Great Exhibition of 1851.

The present Earl of Belmore for help regarding his ancestor's "Earl Belmore Wedgwood" grand.

Our life-long friend, the multi-linguist and extraordinarily cultured Marvita Costa, who saved me by interpreting and negotiating with the Russian cultural establishment when all seemed lost.

The Auctioneers

I owe a very great deal to Sotheby's of London for their help over more than 40 years but most particularly to Ms Lydia Cresswell-Jones, Director of 20th Century Decorative Arts and Design, who has never once refused me help, although I must have added to her workload. I am also much indebted to various members of Sotheby's Press Office over these many years; and to members of their Furniture and Musical Instruments Departments (and in the latter particularly Ms Catherine Bowder). Another Sotheby's lady, Ms Elizabeth F. Byrns, Vice-President, Sotheby's of New York, gave me generous assistance with the Chinese Chippendale George III piano.

A specialist auctioneers, Piano Auctions Ltd. of Malting Farmhouse, Cardington, Bedford, who hold their auctions at Conway Hall, Holborn, London, have been a tower of support and encouragement throughout my research, patiently allowing me to take many photos. I have known one of the Directors, Mr Séan McIlroy, since the days when he gave me great help as the then Manager of Phillips of Bayswater's Furniture Hall and another Director, Mr Richard Reason, is their knowledgeable piano expert, forever delving into the mysteries of the instrument.

Since the days when they were both leading Decorative Arts experts with Phillips I owe much to a husband and wife couple who are now independent consultants, Fiona and Keith Baker of Ealing, London (Keith is the fellow you see regularly on television).

I have had generous help with my research over a number of years from Mark Jones, now Branch Manager and Furniture Expert, Bonham's of Knowle, West Midlands, since the days when he was with Phillips.

Ms Sarah Pring, Piano Expert with Phillips and now a Consultant with Bonhams, generously explained to me the numbering system of various piano firms and has given me other kind help with photos.

Ms Lolita Deborah Persaud of Christie's European Furniture Department, New York, gave me kind help regarding an outstanding Beck square.

Mr Leighton Gillibrand, furniture expert at the Bristol Auction Rooms, gave me the most valuable advice regarding the Mickleburgh Collection of pianos.

The Piano Dealers

I have had the most generous help with magnificent photographs from two specialist dealers in antique and decorative pianos:

Mr David Winstone of The Period Piano Co. of Biddenden, Kent; and

Besbrode Pianos of Leeds, Yorkshire.

A noted personality of the music world and dealer in ancient musical instruments, works of art and books, Mr Tony Bingham of Hampstead, magically conjured up for me photos of an instrument I never even knew existed, an upright version of Dr Steward's "Euphonicon".

An international dealer who kindly supplied me with photos is Mr Atanasio Cecchini of Pianosounds of Rimini, Italy.

Cartoons and Illustrations

I owe much to the mystifying ability and great depth of knowledge of Dr Nicholas Hiley, Head of the wonderful Centre for the Study of Cartoons and Caricature at the University of Kent at Canterbury. Every time my research came to a grinding halt in this area Dr Hiley seemed able to name the artist, the date and the very page on which some drawing or print had appeared.

For supplying me with a caricature of "Tom and Jerry" I am much indebted to Mr Robert Ebbutt of Birmingham Arts Library, a Library which has given me the most generous and efficient help over many years. I must also thank Mr Patrick Clarke of the same Library.

The Classics

I must thank J. Lesley Fitton, Curator of Greek and Roman Antiquities at The British Museum, for guidance on Classical influences on 18th Century British design.

Asian Design

I must thank Ms Mary Ginsberg of the Department of Oriental Antiquities, The British Museum, for careful and detailed guidance on the decoration of a grand piano.

For guidance on Chinoiserie decoration on pianos, Ms Rose Kerr, Chief Curator, Far Eastern Section and Mrs Ming Wilson, Senior Curator, Asian Department, Victoria and Albert Museum.

Agriculture

Dr Stephen Bending, Senior Lecturer in English at The University of Southampton, for guidance on Arthur Young.

The World of Furniture and Design

It must be a great many years since I first had the benefit of the advice of Peter Cormack, the Keeper of that fine institution, the William Morris Gallery at Walthamstow, London and he has generously continued to give me guidance whenever I have asked, though I must have added to his workload. I doubt there are many in the land who have a wider knowledge of British design in the second half of the 19th Century and he has been particularly helpful on the subject of the pianos produced by the William Morris circle.

Over a period of years Dr James Yorke, Assistant Curator of Furniture at the Victoria and Albert Museum, has given me generous guidance on a range of issues, even taking me to see furniture by Lewis Day.

I have always had the most generous help from a lady who is a Director of one of the very best art galleries in the country, Ms Annamarie Stapleton of The Fine Art Society of New Bond Street, London. Ms Stapleton is the author of the now standard book on "John Moyr Smith", one of the projects I considered before she beat me to it and did a finer job than I would have managed.

A lady of World reputation on Robert Adam and author of important books on the architect, Ms Eileen Harris, has patiently dealt with my questions in detailed correspondence.

I owe much to Mr Stephen Jackson, Curator of Scottish and European Furniture at the National Museums of Scotland, who has given me guidance over a number of years on many matters.

One of the most eminent writers on 19th Century design, Mr Alan Crawford, author of a monumental biography of Ashbee, kindly gave me guidance on a number of matters.

A fine scholar with a highly impressive range of knowledge, Mr Stuart Evans of Saxmundham, an authority on the Century Guild and much else, generously helped me on a number of questions.

Mr Stephen Wildman, Curator of The Ruskin Library, University of Lancaster and authoritative author on Late 19th Century design, gave me generous guidance.

Quite one of the most impressive Museum experts I met on my travels was Dr Christian Witt-Dörring, Curator of Furniture at the Österreicches Museum für Angewandte Kunst, Vienna, a true European intellectual who gave me a mountain of help, allowing me access to various archives and the furniture collection.

Mrs Linda Parry, President of the William Morris Society, Deputy Keeper at the Victoria and Albert Museum and a renowned expert on textiles and pattern design, has helped me on a number of occasions.

I received kind guidance on Neo-Classicism from Ms Lucy Wood, Senior Curator of the Furniture Department of the Victoria and Albert Museum, a lady who is as good an analyst of furniture as I have come across—doubters should read her Lever Gallery catalogue.

My good friend and boundless enthusiast Gerry Newby, who knows more about the furniture of W.A.S. Benson than anyone else I ever came across and, brave fellow, is even trying to decode the numbering system of William Morris furniture, has helped me over a number of years.

Architecture

Foolishly, very foolishly, I thought years ago that I could study furniture without troubling myself with detailed study of architecture—one of my larger and crasser errors, since the two are bound like Romulus and Remus. As a result I have had to turn to a real scholar, Mr Sutton Webster, every time I have hit a problem over architecture. In a long, patient correspondence he has shown me the way ahead. He is also, it turns out, far better at dissecting a furniture design and I owe him much on this front.

Mr Peter Davey, Editor of The Architectural Review, generously gave me guidance on the terms "Arts and Crafts" and "Free Style".

Professor James Stevens Curl, the distinguished author on architecture, also gave me guidance on "Free Style".

The Dealers

Without the help of one of the best known International dealers in Art Nouveau and the Arts & Crafts, Mr Paul Reeves of 32B, Kensington Church Street, Kensington and Gosditch Street, Cirencester, much of my research might have taken me years longer. With great kindness Mr Reeves supplied me with copies of very rare catalogues in his personal Collection and photos of many pieces of furniture. I am also much indebted to his assistant Mr Richard J.B. Bryers, quite one of the most efficient people I ever came across. Both these gentleman have a mighty range of knowledge.

Known universally in the business as "Patch", Mr Patrick Rogers of the Arts and Crafts Furniture Co., now resident expert to Liberty's, generously allowed me to photograph furniture over some years. I must also thank Liberty's antiques department for similar co-operation and, in particular, Brian Page, who has been such a kind help over so many years.

Another leading dealer in the field where I have always been given a warm welcome and much help, generously allowing me to take photos, is "The Antique Trader" at 85-87, Southgate Road, Islington, London. There I have to thank particularly Mr Jeff Jackson and Mr Brian Thompson.

I have also had generous help from another leading dealer in the period, Art Furniture of 158, Camden Street, London.

I have to thank Mr R.A.B. Kern of Hotspur for guidance on a Chinoiserie square piano.

Royal Collection

I received generous help over a long period from Mr Matthew Winterbottom, Research Assistant (The Queen's Works of Art), The Royal Collection Trust, concerning a number of the Royal pianos.

Marvellous illustrations concerning pianos were found for me in the Print Room of The Royal Library, Windsor Castle, entirely due to the diligence, efficiency and kind advice of Dr Susan Owens, the Assistant Curator.

I was given much help by Mr Michael Hunter, The Chief Curator, Osborne House, Isle of Wight, on Royal pianos in this residence.

I was given detailed and painstaking guidance regarding Queen Charlotte's pianos and other Royal pianos by Miss Samantha McNeilly, Assistant Registrar, The Royal Archives, Windsor Castle.

I was much helped on photos of Royal pianos by Mrs Siân Cooksey, Picture Library Assistant, Royal Collection Enterprises and also by Miss Jane Sharland.

Librarians, Archivists and others

For many, many years we have inflicted ourselves on our two local libraries, who have sustained us throughout our research with amazingly good humour. We have to thank particularly:

Geoff Brown, Library Manager and all our other friends at Twickenham Library; and

Roy Kelly, our poet Librarian and all good friends at Richmond Reference Library.

My good friends, and fine photographers, Simon Suckling and Ken Wormald, each came to my rescue when I badly needed photographs and could not take them myself.

I must also thank: Mr Martin Durrant of the Victoria and Albert Museum Picture Library; Mrs Diana Kay, Picture Library Manager at the auctioneers Phillips; Ms Julie Coleman, Assistant Librarian, Department of Special Collections, Glasgow University Library; Ms Carol Futers, Archives Assistant, Hertfordshire County Council; Ms Eileen Sullivan, Ms Julie Zeftel, Ms Rebecca Akan, Ms Jeri Wagner and Mr Oleg Kreymer of The Metropolitan Museum of Art, New York; Ms Lyn Morgan, Archivist, Glasgow City Council; Ms Jill Tovey, Archivist to The Croome Estate Trust; Miss Anna Smart, College Librarian, the Royal Northern College of Music; Ms Hester Swift, Librarian, The Law Society Library; Mr David L. Jones, Librarian, House of Lords; Mr Nicholas Hough, House of Lords Information Office; Mr Peter Ross, Guildhall Library, London and his colleague Ms Ruth Barriskill; Ms Helen Trompeteler, Picture Librarian, National Portrait Gallery; Mr Matthew Bailey, Assistant Picture Library Manager, National Portrait Gallery; Ms Liz Stacey, Picture Researcher, National Trust Photo Library; Ms Angela Minshull of Christie's Images; Ms Tracey Walker, Picture Library, Manchester City Art Galleries; Ms Danielle Catera and Ms Lizabeth Dion of the Department of Rights, Museum of Fine Arts, Boston; Ms Margrit Prussat of the Deutsches Museum, Munich; Mr Rhys Griffith, Principal Archivist, London Metropolitan Archives; Mr Iain J. Harrison, Picture Library, Birmingham Museums; Ms Laura Robertson, Senior Archivist, Buckinghamshire County Council; Ms Eleanor Nannestad, Community Librarian, Lincolnshire Archives; Mrs A. Harbour, Mount Edgcumbe House; Mr Alex Edouard, The Bridgeman Library; Ms Sheila Simmons, Librarian, Malvern Library; Mr A.J. Mealey, Local Studies Librarian, Coventry.

Booksellers

The Emperor of Ephemera, Neil Garland, 60, Cowlersley Lane, Huddersfield HD4 5UB (just about the best in his business) has found me remarkable illustrations and lost treasures.

My old friend Brian Mills of Glossop, expert dealer in art and design books who, for most of a lifetime, has been finding me rare gems. Brian's catalogues, with anarchic humour and sharp appreciation, have always been a good start to any day.

I owe much to two of the great book dealers who have departed for the Reference Library in the sky:

The great Seligman who, from his den in Cecil Court, ruled the art book world, reviving interest in lost genius, starting new fashions in collecting and playing off we mad bibliomaniacs as we fiercely competed for his treasures. If I remember rightly, Mr Seligman is depicted in a painting by R.B. Kitaj, "Cecil Court, London", entering with a bunch of flowers.

The gnome-like Andrew Block from whom I finally, grudgingly, obtained the ultimate accolade...entry into his basement where he kept the real gems. Although I only knew him post-war he must, I think, have been the same Mr Block who, in 1933, published "A Short History of the Principal London Antiquarian Booksellers".

My Part Authors

I have endeavoured to avoid pills, potions and the little green bottle all my time but at last have found myself at the mercy of the medical profession. That being so, I hoped that Finley Dunne had it right ("A patient in th' hands iv a doctor is like a hero in th' hands iv a story writer: He's goin' to suffer a good dale but he's goin' to come out all right in th' end") rather than Heraclitus or Anthony Burgess.

Since I am still around I am a walking advertisement for my Doctors and the N.H.S. and, to all concerned, I must express my gratitude for buying me the time to finish, at least, this volume.

So far, I must report, it has been an education and quite good fun. I have always been resolutely unclubable since the days I rejected the Boy Scouts and the Youth Club but now, like it or lump it, find myself a member of an exclusive club.

By their actions my Doctors and others in the N.H.S. have made themselves my Part Authors and, if they have read this far, will have to consider whether they did the World any favours. They are:

My eminent surgeon Mr David Hrouda, F.R.C.S., U.R.O.L., of Charing Cross Hospital, the Peter Pan of the Senior Consultants since, like the Policemen, he looks impossibly young to be doing the job. I was delighted when I discovered he used a surgical, and no doubt artistic, technique known as "the Da Vinci method". I have no doubt he is heading onwards and upwards.

My very wonderful Specialist, Dr Alison Falconer, M.B., B.Chir. Camb., M.R.C.P., F.R.C.R., Research Fellow ("the human face of the N.H.S.", I was told by one of the Charing Cross Hospital staff). Professionally impressive, warm, caring and dedicated...but, no doubt having something to do with the fact that she is a Cambridge Honours graduate with an M.A., leaving you with the uncomfortable feeling that she is several brains brighter than yourself.

My Consultant at West Middlesex Hospital, Mr Emeke Uwechue, a gentleman with that most valuable of medical gifts, a sixth sense when it comes to diagnosis.

Our family doctor, Dr Branko Momic, as good a G.P. as you might wish for, decent, concerned and giving his all. The man who first spotted trouble on the way.

A lady of practical kindness and specialist knowledge, Urology Nurse Practitioner Jessie Ahluwalia and her staff at West Middlesex hospital.

Our African Princess, the statuesque and formidable "Sister K" (Sister Donatienne Kabamba) and the nurses of Ward 7 North, Charing Cross Hospital.

And our saviours, the dedicated, cheerful team of "Miss L.A. 3"

And finally....

This book would never have been possible without my Book Designer, Dan England, a rare article indeed: A man who does what he says he will do. Always professional, always "Mr Reliable" and always there for me despite what turned out to be an eccentric project with, for both of us, unexpected difficulties.

My Master Printer, Sav Focas, who picks up the printing faults even I didn't see.

And my oldest friend in journalism, the photographer Harold Chapman, maker of many books, who gave me encouragement and advice over many years.

Index
by David Hackett

References to illustrations give the page number, and are in **bold type.** Where there is relevant text on the same page, this is not indexed separately.